Philosophy
Before Socrates

Philosophy Before Socrates

An Introduction with Texts and Commentary

Richard D. McKirahan, Jr.

Hackett Publishing Company, Inc.
Indianapolis/Cambridge

Copyright © 1994 by Hackett Publishing Company, Inc.
All rights reserved
Printed in the United States of America

00 99   3   4   5   6   7

For further information, please address
  Hackett Publishing Company, Inc.
  P.O. Box 44937
  Indianapolis, Indiana 46244-0937

Design by Dan Kirklin

Library of Congress Cataloging-in-Publication Data

McKirahan, Richard D.
    Philosophy before Socrates : an introduction with texts and
commentary / Richard D. McKirahan.
        p.   cm.
    Includes bibliographical reference and indexes.
    ISBN 0-87220-176-7.—ISBN0-87220-175-9 (pbk.)
    1. Pre-Socratic philosophers.   2. Philosophy. Ancient.
3. Science, Ancient.   I. Title.
B187.5.M35   1994
182—dc20   93-46837
                                                          CIP

The paper used in this publication meets the minimum requirements of
American National Standard for Information Sciences—Permanence of
Paper for Printed Library Materials, ANSI Z39.48–1984.
                              ∞

for Voula

Contents

Preface

Greek philosophy had been flourishing for over a century when Socrates was born (469 B.C.). Socrates' thought, as well as that of all later Greek philosophers, was strongly influenced by the work of the early pioneers in the field, both the philosopher-scientists known as "Presocratics" and the fifth-century Sophists. The theories, arguments, and concepts of the early Greek philosophers are also important and interesting in their own right. And yet this seminal period of philosophical and scientific activity is much less familiar than the work of Socrates, Plato, and Aristotle.

This state of affairs is partly, perhaps principally, due to the nature of the evidence about thinkers before the time of Plato and Aristotle. In contrast with these two great philosophers, many of whose works survive in entirety, not a single work of any of the "Presocratic" philosophers has been preserved from antiquity to the present, and we have only a few short writings of the Sophists. We are confronted instead with a variety of quotations and paraphrases of their words, summaries of their theories, biographical information (much of it fabricated), in some cases adaptations and extensions of their views, and also parodies and criticisms. These materials come from a wide range of authors who write with different purposes and biases, and whose reliability and philosophical and historical acumen vary enormously.

These circumstances have led some scholars to despair of the possibility of reaching the truth about the early philosophers. The present book, however, is founded on the belief that it is possible to sift through the information and develop interpretations which, though incomplete and not demonstrably correct, have a high degree of internal coherence, mutually reinforce one another, have some historical plausibility, and may be approximations to the original ideas and intentions of the thinkers in question.

Four features of this book deserve comment and explanation. First, since much of the fascination in dealing with early Greek philosophy comes from working out one's own interpretations of the evidence, I have made it a principle to present most, and in many cases all, of the fragments of the philosophers discussed, as well as other important evidence on their thought. Except in the few cases that are noted, the translations are my own. I have aimed to provide translations that are as literal as possible, given the differences between Greek and English. Readers are thus in a position to formulate their own understanding of the early philosophers and to form their own judgments of the interpretations I have put forward.

Second, since our knowledge of these philosophers is largely based on source materials other than their own writings, and since these materials are of unequal value, I have made a point of identifying the source of each passage and (in chapter 1) of discussing the principal sources and commenting on their strengths and weaknesses. In this way readers can assess the value of the evidence and decide for themselves how to weigh it and how confidently to base an interpretation on it.

Third, during the period covered in this book, knowledge had not yet been divided into the separate categories of philosophy, science, and their subfields. Most of the Presocratic "philosophers" treated topics which we find more scientific than philosophical, and none of them drew clear lines between his philosophical and his scientific oeuvre. In fact, the earliest Presocratics focused mainly on issues that we assign to the fields of cosmology, meteorology, biology and matter theory. Thus, in order to be faithful to the thought of the sixth- and fifth-century philosophers, "philosophy before Socrates" must include scientific issues as well; to omit topics *we* consider unphilosophical would be to amputate vital portions of their thought without which the remainder would make little sense. Accordingly, I have devoted rather more space to scientific topics than is usual in books of this sort, though in many cases much of the interest the scientific ideas have for us lies in the level of philosophical sophistication on which they are founded.

Fourth, the thinkers treated in this book lived in, and to some extent were the products of, particular times and places. Where possible and appropriate I have said something about their lives and their cultural environment; for these circumstances had important effects on the early Greek philosophers, just as the ideas of these men had important effects on Greek civilization.

Acknowledgments

My interest in early Greek philosophy and science began with graduate seminars on the Presocratics given at Harvard by the late G. E. L. Owen, and my work owes a deep debt to his inspiring teaching and writings, even though I have come to disagree with some of his interpretations. John Murdoch's courses on ancient and medieval science which I attended at the same time were models of clear exposition and of history of science at its best. A National Endowment for the Humanities Seminar on The Exact Sciences in Antiquity taught at Yale by Asger Aaboe opened my eyes to pre-Greek mathematics and astronomy and gave me a wider scientific context in which to situate Greek science. My education in the interpretation of texts in ancient philosophy has been advanced by attending for the past twenty years the meetings of the West Coast Aristotelian Society led by Julius Moravcsik and, for almost as long, the meetings of the Southern California Readers of Ancient Philosophy. I have benefited greatly from the revolutionary work on Greek science done by G. E. R. Lloyd, who has set for me an example of what is possible in this field. I should like to thank him for his friendship and support, which have meant a great deal to me.

I offer my thanks to Professors A. A. Long, John Malcolm, Henry Mendell, Michael Wedin, and Mary Whitlock Blundell for their helpful comments on drafts of the book and for their encouragement. In addition, I am grateful to the students in my courses at Pomona College for their willingness to use the manuscript in lieu of a textbook and for their many valuable suggestions. Finally, I am deeply indebted to Paul Coppock for his generous editorial assistance and to Patricia Curd, who commented on more than one version of the manuscript as I was revising it for publication, and whose suggestions in many cases prompted significant alterations and, I believe, improvements.

Claremont, California
December 1993

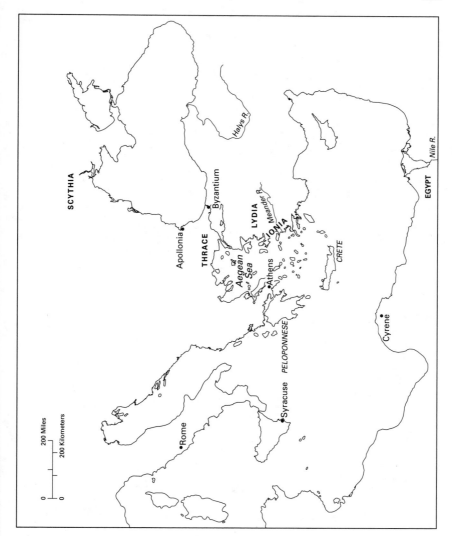

The Eastern
Mediterranean

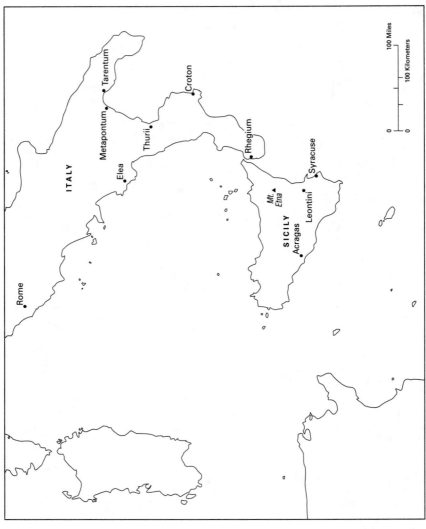

Sicily and
Southern Italy

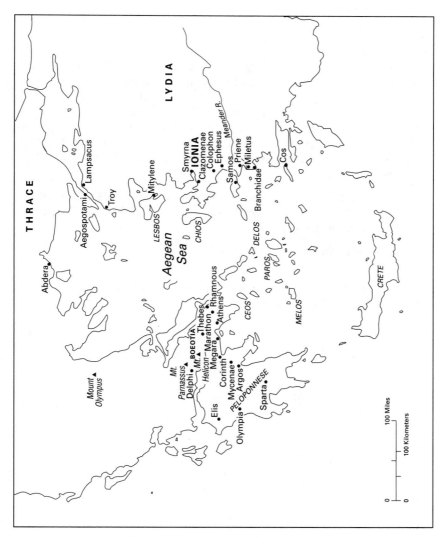

Greece and
Western Asia Minor

Abbreviations

DK   H. Diels and W. Kranz, *Die Fragmente der Vorsokratiker*, 6th ed., Berlin, 1951 and later editions. The standard edition of the Presocratic Philosophers. Each Presocratic is assigned a number. The fragments of each Presocratic are also assigned numbers preceded by the letter "B." Thus, the number for Heraclitus is 22, and Heraclitus' fragment 101 is referred to as DK 22B101. Testimonia are likewise identified by numbers preceded by the letter "A." The DK references are used very widely in books and articles on the Presocratics.

HGP W. K. C. Guthrie, *A History of Greek Philosophy*, 6 vols., Cambridge, 1962–1981. The first three volumes are relevant to the period treated in the present work.

KR   G. S. Kirk and J. E. Raven, *The Presocratic Philosophers*, Cambridge, 1957.

KRS G. S. Kirk, J. E. Raven and M. Schofield, *The Presocratic Philosophers*, 2nd ed., Cambridge, 1983.

1

The Sources of Early Greek Philosophy

When we read a work by a modern author, we usually have no trouble about getting an accurate, complete text. Reliable editions can normally be found. It may be useful to read what others say about the work, but we are in a position to judge its merits and accept or reject the opinions of others according as they square with our own. It is very different with ancient authors.

Before the invention of printing in the fifteenth century A.D., the prototype of a work was a document handwritten by the author or dictated to a scribe. "Publication" consisted in having copies made (again, by hand) and distributing them to interested people.

No ancient prototypes survive, so ancient works come to us only through copies, or rather, copies of copies an unknown number of removes from the original. The earliest complete surviving text of Plato, for example, was written in the late ninth century, some 1250 years after Plato's death, and, in fact, closer in time to us than to him. In the best cases, then, we have one or more complete manuscripts of the text, from which scholars known as textual critics attempt to determine what the author actually wrote.

Each time a text was copied by hand, the scribe might introduce errors, especially as the Greek language changed over the centuries. As a result, the manuscripts of a work disagree at those points where different errors were introduced. A modern printed text of an ancient work is based on the determination of its editor as to which of the different manuscript readings and suggestions made by scholars is most likely to be correct at each point. The uncertainty of the text is a factor constantly to keep in mind.

The situation of the philosophers covered in this book is far worse than the case described above, since, except for two short writings by Gorgias, not only the prototypes but all the copies of their works have perished. We know these thinkers first through quotations or close paraphrases of what they wrote contained in works that survive (whose authors either had the lost writings or relied on other authors who did have access to them), and second through information about them preserved in other authors. These surviving works too underwent the process of copying described above, with its attendant possibility for introducing errors. We must also know the nature (including the interests, prejudices, approaches, and purposes) of the authors and texts containing information on the early Greek philosophers in order to decide how far we can trust them and how they may have distorted the original. The problematic nature of the evidence entails that there is ample room to disagree with any selection and interpretation of

1

ancient evidence on early Greek philosophy, including the present one, and further that a book of this length and nature must presuppose solutions to issues still under debate.

Only rarely can we be certain that an interpretation is correct. In fact, beliefs about particular views and about the overall importance of a thinker's contributions can vary widely, depending on which sources are accepted and which are preferred over others. For each early philosopher the information is like a jigsaw puzzle with many pieces missing and to which some of the pieces at hand do not really belong. The project is to put the pieces together as best we can, throwing away the ones that do not fit, and on the basis of the partial picture that results, to sketch in the missing area of the puzzle. Among the most fascinating features of studying early Greek philosophy are the possibilities of assigning different weights to different pieces and putting the pieces together in different ways. In this field there is no unanimity among experts, and those who disagree with this book's interpretation of a text, or who find another arrangement of the evidence more satisfying, are encouraged to see how well their ideas agree with information not included in this book and with other interpretations that have been proposed. The list of books for further reading at the end of this book can be used as a starting point for such research.

There are two types of sources for the presocratics: fragments—quotations containing the philosopher's actual words—and testimonia—passages providing information about the thinker without quoting his words.

FRAGMENTS. Quotations vary in length from a single word to an extract of over fifty lines of Parmenides. In some cases a considerable number of fragments are preserved: there are some three hundred fragments of Democritus, for example. Some fragments are found in works as early as the writings of Plato, who lived only a generation or two after the original works were written, while others come from works as late as the tenth century A.D.

In dealing with purported fragments, one of our first concerns is how accurately they quote the original words.[1] Earliness of the source does not guarantee accuracy of the quotation. Many comparatively early writers[2] tend to quote from memory, so that a purported quotation may actually be a paraphrase. Another problem is that fragments are frequently taken out of their original contexts, most obviously in the anthologies of quotations that became widespread from the last three centuries B.C. As a result, we may

---

1. A related problem is where a quotation begins and ends, since the ancients did not use quotation marks, and it can be uncertain what is fragment and what is context. Fragments of poetry have been set in larger type than fragments of prose.

2. These include Plato, Aristotle, and Plutarch.

know that a thinker held a view, but not know his reasons—a serious obstacle to understanding. Further, the people who quote the Presocratics do not always understand them and frequently embed the fragments in alien contexts. Finally, there are inauthentic fragments: misquotations or quotations incorrectly attributed, imitations, and forgeries.

TESTIMONIA. Much material on the early Greek philosophers—their lives, writings, and theories—varying from the reliable to the fictitious, comes from sources that range from the near contemporary (including some of the presocratics themselves) to authors closer in time to us than to the philosophers they discuss.

I shall now briefly survey the authors and writings that contribute most to our knowledge of early Greek philosophy, setting out the purposes, the sources, and where relevant, the biases of each.[3] Since the purpose is to discuss our information about early Greek philosophy, and fragments tend to be found in the same sources as testimonia, the distinction between them is not important for now.

PLATO (427–347 B.C.), who probably knew personally some of the thinkers treated here, must be used with caution since his interests in quoting and discussing the views of other philosophers are not historical but philosophical, and he frequently treats them with humor or irony. His purposes do not require a fair reconstruction of views in their original context. He was downright hostile to the Sophists, so that what he tells us about them appears in an unfriendly light. Because of the powerful influence of Plato and his student, Aristotle, who shared this hostility, the Sophists were largely ignored by later sources interested in preserving early thought.

ARISTOTLE (384–322), however, had a serious interest in the history of philosophy, and it is ultimately to him that we owe practically all of our knowledge of the presocratics. Aristotle's standard practice is to survey the evidence relevant to his topic, including the opinions of earlier thinkers, then to explore the difficulties they present and attempt to find out what truth there may be in these opinions.[4] Again, Aristotle's motives are not what we would call historical. He does not aim to give complete expositions of the theories of others, but selects and surveys views he finds useful for his purposes. He can fail to mention some of the writers who treated the topics under discussion, and he does not systematically survey as many topics as we might wish. In spite of his limitations as a historian and source,

3. See pp. 80–81 and 355–56 for discussion of the source materials on Pythagoras and the Pythagoreans, and on the Sophists.

4. Aristotle describes his method in *Nicomachean Ethics* 7.1.

the accounts he gives of his predecessors[5] have irreplaceable value. To some extent—and this for better or for worse—Aristotle invented the concept of "presocratic" philosophy as we still think of it (although he did not use that term).

Following Aristotle's approach, three of his immediate followers in the Peripatetic school, which he founded, produced important historical surveys. EUDEMUS compiled a history of mathematics, astronomy, and theology; MENO, a history of medicine; and most important for us, THEOPHRASTUS wrote extensively on earlier philosophers from Thales to Plato (i.e., those earlier than Aristotle). If all of Theophrastus' material had survived, our knowledge of early Greek philosophy would be much improved. As it is, we have a good deal of only a single book, *On Sensation*, which does, however, enable us to form an opinion of his methods and value as a historian. He was influenced by Aristotle's choice of topics, and judged the views he reports from an Aristotelian perspective. He does not treat theories in chronological order, but groups them under different heads (e.g., theories that declare that like is perceived by like). Although his own writings are almost completely lost to us, they were summarized in later times and practically all our extant post-Aristotelian information on the presocratics comes either from Theophrastus himself or from these summaries. Hence his great importance to the "doxographic tradition" (the name given to the ancient works recording the opinions of philosophers).

In the sixth century A.D., SIMPLICIUS, a Neoplatonist philosopher and the author of extensive commentaries on Aristotle's works, quoted earlier philosophers in discussing Aristotle's remarks on them, and added other material whose ultimate source is Theophrastus. Simplicius is of special interest to us because he wished to understand the early thinkers as well as Aristotle. He occasionally gives long and apparently accurate extracts from works that had become rare.

Two other important surviving texts deserve mention. One is the *Placita*[6] *Philosophorum*, or *Opinions of the Philosophers*, attributed to Plutarch (c. 50–120 A.D.) but probably written after his death, in the second century A.D. (hence its author is called pseudo-Plutarch). It is a summary of earlier views on each of over one hundred philosophical topics. The second text is the *Eclogae Physicae*, or *Selections on Natural Philosophy*, of John of Stobi, otherwise known as Stobaeus, who wrote in the fifth century A.D. This is a collection of quotations and summaries of over five hundred poets and prose writers. The content of these two works is very similar because they were based on a common source, now lost, which was composed around

5. Especially in *Metaphysics* 1 and *Physics* 1.
6. "Placita" is the title given to ancient doxographic collections.

100 A.D. by an otherwise unknown author named AETIUS. This work, which has been partially reconstructed mainly from the materials in pseudo-Plutarch and Stobaeus,[7] is an updated version of earlier collections of *Placita* going back to Theophrastus and Meno.[8]

CICERO, the Roman orator and statesman of the mid-first century B.C., wrote important accounts of post-Aristotelian Greek philosophy that contain historical surveys of philosophical views going back to the presocratics.

HIPPOLYTUS, a bishop of Rome in the late second or early third century, wrote a work (in ten books) entitled *Refutation of all Heresies*, which argues that Christian heresies coincide with views of Greek philosophers.[9] Book 1 contains doxographical accounts of fourteen presocratics whom Hippolytus describes as "natural philosophers." Moreover, the comparisons of the heresies with pagan philosophers in the later books are an important source of fragments, since Hippolytus frequently quotes the presocratics to help make his points.[10]

DIOGENES LAERTIUS' (third century A.D.) work, *Lives of the Philosophers*, is an ambitious but undiscriminating collection of a wide variety of materials on philosophers from Thales on down to centuries after the end of our period. Among the over two hundred sources he used, three sorts of materials need to be mentioned: first, biographies of the philosophers that began to be written in the third century B.C., frequently with unreliable or even fabricated information; second, philosophical "successions" of a kind that began to appear in the second century B.C., which identify one philosopher as the student, associate, or follower of another; third, chronological writings, especially the *Chronica* of Apollodorus (second century B.C.). In

---

7. The detective work on the origin of these materials and the reconstruction of Aetius' text is due to H. Diels in his fundamental work (in Latin) *Doxographi Graeci* (Berlin, 1879). Diels identified Aetius as the author of the common source of pseudo-Plutarch and Stobaeus on the basis of Theodoret, a fifth-century bishop, who both quotes and names Aetius.

8. Again, Diels' *Doxographi Graeci* is the primary work on the doxographical tradition from Theophrastus to Aetius, but a reevaluation of his conclusions is currently under way, and the resulting picture is likely to be more complex and nuanced than that of Diels.

9. Exactly how this strategy makes for a refutation is disputed. It is usually thought to be a smear campaign: pagan views are false, or at least unchristian, so the evidence that Hippolytus presents establishes that the heresies are false or unchristian too.

10. Hippolytus' value as a doxographic source is considered by most to be low despite Osborne's attempt (*Rethinking Early Greek Philosophy* [London, 1987]) to raise his stock.

this verse work Apollodorus attempted to record the dates of significant events and people from the fall of Troy to his own times. His dating was extremely influential in ancient times, but his methods involved shaky assumptions,[11] and his research must have been based on rather sparse materials.

The nature of our sources might lead a reasonable person to despair. Indeed some scholars have held that even Aristotle and Theophrastus are unreliable[12]—and if these two cannot be used, we are in truly desperate straits. Nevertheless, in some cases we have enough fragments to form a fair judgment of a philosopher's views on at least some topics. And in many cases the evidence of testimonia can be used, once allowance is made for the authors' methods, sources, interests, and prejudices. It is reasonable to suppose that, in some cases at least, we can attain an approximation to what the philosopher actually thought.

11. For example, he assumes that a philosopher is forty years old at the time of his most important work, and that a pupil is forty years younger than his teacher.

12. Notable sceptics are H. F. Cherniss, *Aristotle's Criticism of Presocratic Philosophy* (Baltimore, 1935); and J. B. McDiarmid, "Theophrastus on the Presocratic Causes," *Harvard Studies in Classical Philology* 61 (1953): 85–156, reprinted (in shortened form) in Furley and Allen, *Studies in Presocratic Philosophy*, vol. 1 (1970).

2

Hesiod and the Beginnings of
Greek Philosophy and Science

Since antiquity the beginning of Greek philosophy has been placed in Miletus in the early sixth century B.C. The first philosophers, Thales, Anaximander, and Anaximenes, the story goes, invented and made rapid developments in a new way of looking at and thinking about the world. This claim is largely true, but it is not the whole truth. These men gave a new direction to ways of thought found much earlier in Greece, and proposed new kinds of answers to questions that had been asked and answered long before. A look at Thales' precursors will enable us to see better why the early philosophers were interested in the particular issues they took up and to form a more accurate appreciation of their achievement.

The present chapter will concentrate on Hesiod, who lived in the late eighth or early seventh century, a century before Thales. Though he presents himself as a poor farmer from rustic Ascra in Boeotia, Hesiod was a widely recognized poet whose chief works, *Theogony* ("Birth of the Gods") and *Works and Days*, permit us to grasp some important points of difference and similarity between prephilosophical and presocratic Greek thought.

A principal difference between them is that traditional Greek mythology, focussing on the Olympian gods, is omnipresent in Hesiod yet absent from the presocratics. For Hesiod, the world is an assemblage of deities (Heaven, Earth, Hills, etc.) and is governed by gods conceived as large-scale, immortal, anthropomorphic beings who combine superhuman powers with human feelings, emotions, desires, motivation, and reasoning, as well as such human qualities as favoritism, ambition, and inconsistency. Some gods, especially the earliest born, are less anthropomorphic, and some verge on allegory (such as Blame, Distress, Quarrels, Famine, Work, and Lies[1]), but the chief figures have incipient personalities (motherly Gaia, crafty Kronos, wise Zeus, wily Prometheus) and are doers of deeds. These anthropomorphic gods control the events in the world that fall into their various departments. Since the gods are competitive and jealous of their prerogatives, and their departments are not wholly separate, the world does not have perfect order. The gods can be capricious, and phenomena occur through their arbitrary will. Further, gods can help and harm humans, so individuals and states must try to keep them favorably disposed by prayers, gifts, etc.,

[handwritten marginal note: having human form or characteristics]

---

1. Cf. *Theogony*, lines 226–32.

although even pious behavior does not guarantee the assistance of these notoriously fickle deities.

Hesiod's view of the gods and their relation to the world stemmed from tradition, which commanded belief. *Theogony* does not claim to contain new ideas, or Hesiod's own ideas. Here too he differs from the presocratics, whose accounts of the world were their own inventions and so were not isolated from criticism as well-entrenched traditional material can be.[2]

At the same time, Hesiod is not just a teller of familiar myths. Even *Theogony* endeavors to shape the traditional material on which it is based according to discernible principles of order. Hesiod's belief that the world is ordered intelligibly to humans, in other words that it is a KOSMOS (world order, ordered world), is a fundamental article of faith for the presocratics, as is his operating principle that it can be correctly described and communicated to others in language.[3] Another common feature is the importance of the divine in the world, although the presocratics' notion of divinity is no longer anthropomorphic, arbitrary, or competitive. Finally, Hesiod and the presocratics share an interest in certain features of the world, both physical (notably in its history and composition, as well as in astronomical and meteorological phenomena) and moral (above all, in justice).

Theogony presents its main theme, the ascendancy of Zeus to secure and lasting power, in a definite chronological sequence:

1. Origin of early divinities down to and including the Titans, children of Gaia (Earth) and Ouranos (Heaven); as soon as they are born Ouranos conceals them in a hiding place within Gaia.
2. Kronos, the chief Titan, assisted by Gaia, castrates Ouranos and assumes command.
3. Origin of the Olympian gods, children of Titans Kronos and Rhea; Kronos eats them as soon as they are born, except Zeus, who escapes through the help of Gaia and Rhea.

2. Hesiod's assertion that he received his song directly from the Muses (*Theogony*, lines 22–34) is matched by Parmenides' attribution of his poem to an unnamed goddess, (**11.1**, especially lines 24–32). Empedocles (**14.61, 14.64** and **14.80**) and Heraclitus (cf. **10.30, 10.44, 10.47**, and **10.1**) also claim divine warrant for their philosophy. But here, too, Hesiod has a stronger claim on his audience's belief: the non-Olympian deities of the presocratics will not have carried the same degree of conviction.

3. The completeness and consistency of the accounts of the world offered by Hesiod and the presocratics are open to question, though, as the discussion of their views will make plain.

4. The Olympians, led by Zeus, defeat the Titans in battle; Zeus assumes command.
5. Zeus alone defeats Typhoeus, child of Gaia and Tartaros (Underworld).
6. The Olympians proclaim Zeus their ruler; he gives out rank and privileges to each.
7. Zeus swallows his consort Metis (Counsel, Wisdom) to prevent her having a child who would usurp his place as king of the gods; thus Zeus's rule will last forever.

The central element of this sequence is the story of divine rulership, held in turn by Ouranos, Kronos, and Zeus. Hesiod gives a distinctive version of this myth, which existed in various forms throughout the eastern Mediterranean and Near East, notably in the Babylonian succession myth *Enuma Elish*, which probably goes back a thousand years before Hesiod.

But the succession myth makes up only about one-fourth of *Theogony*. About one-third of the poem consists of material that fits the title—the births of gods from the beginning down to the children and grandchildren of the Olympian gods—and displays an interest in issues the presocratic philosophers would take up. Hesiod's account of the earliest gods bears this out.

2.1 First of all Chaos came into being. Next came   116
    broad-breasted Gaia (Earth), the secure dwelling place
      forever of all
    the immortals who hold the peak of snowy Olympus.
    And murky Tartaros (Underworld) in a recess of the
      broad-roaded Earth,
    and Eros (Love), who is the most beautiful among the
      immortal gods,   120
    who loosens the limbs and overpowers the intentions and
      sensible plans
    of all the gods and all humans too.
    From Chaos there came into being Erebos (Darkness) and
      black Night.
    From Night, Aither (bright upper air) and Hemera (Day)
      came into being,
    which she conceived and bore after uniting in love with
      Erebos.   125
    Gaia first brought forth starry Ouranos (Heaven)
    equal to herself, to cover her all about
    in order to be a secure dwelling place forever for the
      blessed gods.

She brought forth long mountains, beautiful shelters of divine
Nymphs who live in wooded mountains,   130
and also gave birth without delightful love to the barren sea,
Pontos, raging with its swelling waves. Then,
bedded by Ouranos, she gave birth to deep-swirling Oceanos
and Koios and Kreios and Hyperion and Iapetos
and Theia and Rhea and Themis and Mnemosyne   135
and Phoebe with a golden wreath and lovely Tethys.
After them, last of all, was born crafty-minded Kronos,
the most terrible of the children, and he hated his mighty father.
(Hesiod, *Theogony*, lines 116–38)

This passage begins the theogonic myths and ends with an ominous note
that foretells the first struggle for mastery of the world. Several features
need comment. First, Chaos. Although in later antiquity the word meant
what it means for us, it has been argued convincingly[4] that here it refers to
the gap between earth and sky. The first stage in the development of the
present world was the separation of heaven and earth, the differentiation of
an already existing thing. The world did not arise out of nothing, and there
was no creator. Hesiod explains neither how the sum total of existence
came into being nor how it came to be divided.

Second, Hesiod's theogony is also a cosmogony ("birth of the ordered
world"). Many of the primordial gods have the names of regions of the
physical world, and are conceived as identical with those regions. The
births of Gaia, Tartaros, and Ouranos, for example, are the origins simultaneously of three divine figures and the three largest areas of the universe:
Earth, Underworld, and Heaven. *Theogony* thus gives us a picture of the
structure of the physical world as Hesiod understood it. The world is a
divine place, literally full of, made up of, gods, although many of Hesiod's
divinities had no myths or worship, and anthropomorphism is so slight or
altogether lacking that it is difficult to know even whether to capitalize the
names. As to the physical structure of the universe, Hesiod shows an
interest in large-scale geographical features of the earth, the large-scale
cosmic features, and in astronomical and meteorological phenomena, all of
which he treats as divine. But his interest here does not go beyond naming
them, identifying their parentage, and asserting their existence.

Third, Hesiod accounts for the origin of most of the gods with a process
found in the realm of humans and animals. Eros (Love) appears early on
the scene and afterwards parenting occurs through sexual reproduction,
though there is inconsistency even here; some gods are born of only one

4. KRS, pp. 36–41.

parent and the earliest few, including Eros, come into being without parents at all. Hesiod offers no explanations of these exceptional cases.

Fourth, in Hesiod's hands parentage becomes a device for ordering the diverse world, making it a KOSMOS. In the beginning all is dark, and from dark Chaos emerge Night and Erebos (Darkness). Dark Night produces Hemera (Day) and bright Aither. Earth and Heaven produce geographical entities. These genealogies and others manifest organizing principles or patterns of order: like produces like, opposite produces opposite.

Finally, an inconsistency. If "Chaos came into being" means that Earth and Heaven separated, it hardly does to have Earth (by herself) giving birth to Heaven a few lines later. This is one piece of evidence among others that *Theogony* combines different versions of stories, though not always seamlessly. This shows that Hesiod is no prisoner of tradition. He does not simply retell old stories, but puts them together in new ways, subordinating them to a larger purpose.

The following lines give us a rough picture of the KOSMOS.

2.2   . . . as far beneath Earth as Heaven is from Earth.   720
    For that is the distance from Earth to murky Tartaros.
    For a bronze anvil falling nine days and nights
    from Heaven would reach Earth on the tenth.
    And a bronze anvil falling nine days and nights
    from Earth would reach Tartaros on the tenth.   725
    Around Tartaros a fence of bronze has been built. Night is
      poured round
    its throat in three layers. Above it
    grow the roots of Earth and of the barren Sea.
    There the Titans are hidden away beneath the murky
    darkness through the plans of cloud-gathering Zeus,   730
    in a dark place at the ends of the huge Earth.
    They have no way out, since Poseidon has set bronze
    doors upon it and a wall runs in both directions.

            . . .

    There are the sources and limits   736
    of dark Earth and murky Tartaros,
    and the barren Sea and starry Heaven, one after the next,
    unpleasant and dank, and the gods loathe them.
    It is a huge chasm, and not within an entire complete year   740
    would a person reach its floor if he first came to be within
      its gates,
    but gust after hard gust would bring him this way and that. . . .

And the dread house of dark Night
stands covered in black clouds.   745
In front of these things [Atlas] the son of Iapetos stands
    and holds
the broad heaven on his head and tireless arms
without moving, where Night and Day draw near
and greet each other as they cross the great threshold
of bronze. The one will descend while the other   750
goes out, and the chamber never contains both at once,
but one is always outside,
wandering over the earth, while the other is within
and waits for the time of her own journey to arrive.
The one holds far-seeing light for those who live on
    the earth,   755
while deadly Night holds in her hands Sleep,
brother of Death, and is covered in murky cloud.
There the children of black Night have their homes—
Sleep and Death, dreadful gods, nor does
shining Helios [Sun] ever look upon them with his rays   760
as he ascends the Heaven or as he descends from Heaven.
                    (Hesiod, *Theogony*, lines 720–33, 736–61)

These verses do not present a coherent description from which we could
draw a map. For example it is hard to see how Atlas, who stands in the
Underworld, can hold up the Heavens. But the KOSMOS is given a definite
size and a roughly symmetric structure:

1. Heaven at the top;
2. The gap between Heaven and Earth which is bright by day and dark
   by night;
3. Earth surrounded by the river Ocean, which flows back into itself;[5]
4. A similar gap between Earth and Tartaros,[6] which is always dark,
   gloomy and stormy;
5. Tartaros at the bottom.

A crude sketch of Hesiod's cosmos might look like this, where the sides of
Heaven bend down at the edges to touch the Ocean and something sym-
metrical happens below. Gates to the underworld allow the passage of Day
and Night. On the other hand, since the Sun never sees the Underworld, it

5. *Theogony*, l. 776.
6. This gap is also called Chaos (l. 814).

is in Heaven during the day and at night is carried round Ocean from west to east, to rise again the next day.

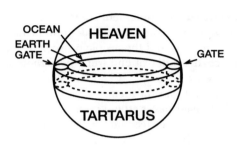

In the more familiar myths of the succession stories, by contrast, anthropomorphism prevails. Gods have the same bodily parts that humans do, the same motivations and feelings (e.g., hate, pain, fear, revenge, sexual desire, desire for power), and they and their actions are evaluated in terms which apply to humans (wicked, clever, shameful, just, etc.). Ouranos, Kronos, and Zeus, up to the overthrow of Kronos, derive their supremacy from strength and violence, but the rule of Zeus introduces a different kind of administration of the world.

> **2.3** But when the blessed gods had completed their labor 881
> and decided by force the dispute about the Titans' powers and
>   privileges,
> then by the advice of Gaia they urged
> wide-seeing Olympian Zeus to be king and to rule
> the immortals. And he distributed well the powers and privileges
>   among them.
>
> (Hesiod, *Theogony*, lines 881–85)

When the Olympians defeat the Titans, they follow the advice of their grandmother Gaia and urge Zeus to rule. His supreme strength and his mighty weapon the thunderbolt make him an obvious choice. But he does not simply seize power; his rule is legitimated by a kind of election by acclamation. Moreover, he delegates some of his power, assigning duties and privileges to the other Gods, so that Demeter, for example, becomes goddess of agriculture.

Further, Zeus' rule is wise and good. By swallowing his consort Metis (Counsel, Wisdom), he receives her attributes. His second consort is

Themis (Order, Right). His offspring include Eunomia (Good Order), Dike (Justice), Eirene (Peace).

In *Works and Days*, Hesiod stresses Zeus' justice.

2.4 Those who give straight judgments to foreigners   225
         and citizens and do not step at all aside from justice
         have a flourishing city and the people prosper in it.
         There is Peace, the nurse of children, throughout the land,
             and wide-seeing Zeus
         never ordains harsh war for them.
         Famine and Disaster never attend men of straight judgment, 230
         but with good cheer they feed on the fruits of their labors.
         For these the Earth bears the means of life in abundance.
             In the mountains the oak tree
         bears acorns at the top and bees in the middle.
         Their woolly sheep are heavy with fleece.
         Women give birth to children who are like their fathers.   235
         They flourish continuously with good things and do not go
         on boats, but their fertile fields bear fruit.
         But for those who have thoughts of evil violence and
             cruel deeds,
         wide-seeing Zeus son of Kronos has ordained justice.
         Often indeed the entire city of an evil man suffers,   240
         when he sins and plans wicked deeds.
         The son of Kronos brings a great disaster on them
             from heaven,
         Famine and Disease together, and the people perish.
         Women do not give birth, but houses are diminished
         through the cunning of Olympian Zeus. Again, on another
             occasion   245
         the son of Kronos either destroys their broad army or their
             city wall
         or takes vengeance on their ships at sea.
                                        (Hesiod, *Works and Days*, lines 225–47)

The just Zeus rewards justice in humans and punishes their injustice, and so stands as the guarantor of a moral order in the KOSMOS as a whole, and specifically in the human sphere.

Theogony surprisingly says little about humans. (It would be less surprising if it said either much or nothing at all.) The Pandora myth recounts the origin of woman (fashioned out of earth by Hephaistos), but already "mortal men" existed and had dealings with the gods. *Works and Days* has another version of Pandora[7] and, without any attempt to make it fit with the Pandora story, the myth of five generations of humans.

   2.5 First of all, the immortals who dwell on Olympus   109
          created a golden race of humans endowed with speech.   110
          They lived under Kronos when he reigned in heaven.
          They lived like gods with carefree hearts
          far from toil and grief. Wretched old age
          did not afflict them, but unchanged in legs and arms
          they delighted in feasting apart from all evils.   115
          They died as if overcome by sleep. They had all
          good things. Of its own accord the fertile land
          bore fruit bounteous and in plenty. They lived off their
             fields
          as they pleased, in peace, with many good things . . . [8]
          But since the earth covered this race,   121
          through the counsels of Zeus they are noble
          spirits dwelling on earth, protectors of mortal humans . . .
          givers of wealth; indeed they got this royal privilege.   126
          Afterwards, those who dwell on Olympus created
          a second race, of silver, one much worse,
          and resembling the golden race in neither body nor thought.
          A child was brought up by its dear mother for a hundred
             years,   130
          a complete baby, playing in its house.
          But when they grew up and reached the measure of their age,
          they lived for only a brief time, suffering pains
          through their folly. For they could not keep from treating
             each other
          with violence and outrage and were unwilling to worship   135
          the immortals or to perform sacrifices at the holy altars of the
             blessed ones,
          which local custom declares right for humans to do. Then Zeus,
          the son of Kronos, put them away in anger because they would
             not pay
          honors to the blessed gods who dwell on Olympus.
          But when the earth had covered this race too,   140

---

7. The two versions of Pandora occur at *Works and Days*, lines 54–105, and *Theogony*, lines 570–601.

  8. I omit lines 120, 124–25, whose authenticity is doubtful.

the second one, they are called blessed mortals beneath the earth
and honor attends these too nevertheless.
Father Zeus created out of ash trees yet a third,
bronze, race of humans endowed with speech, wholly different
    from the silver race,
terrible and mighty. They devoted themselves   145
to the grievous works of Ares and to violence. They did
    not eat
grain, but had a powerful spirit of adamant;
crude people. Their might was great and invincible arms
grew from their shoulders on their stout limbs.
Their armor was bronze, their houses were bronze,   150
and they worked with bronze tools. There was no dark iron.
And overcome by their own hands,
nameless, they went to the dank house of cold Hades.
Black death took them even though they were
terrible, and they left the shining light of the sun.   155
But when earth had covered this race too,
Zeus, the son of Kronos, created yet a fourth one
upon the fertile earth, one more just and good,
the divine race of heroic men who are called
demigods, the race before the present one upon the boundless
    earth.   160
Evil war and dread battle destroyed
some of them fighting for the flocks of Oedipus
at seven-gated Thebes, the land of Cadmus.
Others it killed after bringing them in ships over the great gulf
of the sea to Troy for the sake of fair-haired Helen.   165
There the end of death covered some,
while father Zeus, the son of Kronos, established others
at the ends of the earth and bestowed on them life and a place
    to live apart from humans.
And they dwell with carefree hearts   170
in the Islands of the Blest near deep-swirling Ocean,
blessed heroes, for whom the fertile land
bears honey-sweet fruit flourishing three times a year,
far from the immortals, and Kronos rules over them. . . .
Then Zeus made another race of humans endowed with speech,
    who now are upon the earth.
I wish I were not among the men of the fifth generation,
but either had died earlier or were born afterwards.   175
For now it is a race of iron. Never will they
cease being worn down by distress and sorrow

day and night. The gods will give them harsh troubles.
But even so, these too will have good things mixed with their evils.
(Hesiod, Works and Days, lines 109–79)

In this picture of overall decline, the race of heroes between those of bronze and iron is exceptional. This anomaly suggests that the account is based on different traditions about human history. Hesiod adapts the myth of the metallic races to accommodate the tradition of the godlike heroes of Troy and Thebes, too important to omit. Faced by a problem comparable to a theory which fails to fit obvious facts, he refuses to settle for a simple, uniform pattern conflicting with important data.

In Hesiod's account the races are all created by the gods, but their ends come about variously. The Golden Race just died out. The Bronze Race destroyed itself in war. The fate of the Heroic Race was as the mythological tradition required. Zeus destroyed the Silver Race for refusing to worship the gods, and he will destroy the Iron Race because of its moral degeneracy.

2.6 Zeus will destroy this race too of humans endowed with
    speech,   180
when they come to have gray hair at birth.
A father will not be like his children nor will they be at all
    like him,
nor will a guest be friendly to his host
or comrade with comrade or brother with brother as before.
They will quickly come to dishonor their parents as they grow
    old,   185
and will find fault with them, speaking with bitter words,
abominable people and ignorant of the gods' vengeance . . .
There will be no thanks for one who keeps his oath or is just   190
or good, but men will rather praise the evildoers
and violence. Justice and reverence will be based
in strength. The evil person will harm the better man,
addressing him with crooked words, and he will swear an oath
    upon them.
Ugly-mouthed envy, with a hateful look, delighting in evil,   195
will accompany all miserable men.
Then Aidos (Reverence) and Nemesis (Righteous Indignation),
    their fair skin
covered in white robes, will abandon humanity
and go to Olympus from the broad-roaded earth, to be
among the tribe of immortals. Bitter greed will be left   200
for mortal humans, and there will be no defense from evil.
(Hesiod, Works and Days, lines 180–201)

Viewed broadly, Hesiod's poems present a historical picture of the world from its origins to the present, and forecast its future. The present world order is governed by the Olympian gods under Zeus, the most powerful and potentially ruthless. As the champion of order and justice, he firmly enforces a system of values in the universe, however far the ideal of a justice which punishes an entire city for the transgressions of a single individual may be from our own notion of justice.

The traditional mythological picture did not encourage speculation about nature without reference to the gods. Many events are due to the gods—not only episodes of myth, but ordinary everyday occurrences. Rain is the doing of Zeus the sky-god. When crops grow or fail to grow, Demeter is responsible. In a sense, this account of events posits unvarying relations between them and their divine causes, but the gods' willfulness and inconstancy tend to undermine attempts to understand or control events that affect us. Interest will focus more on individual events and the gods responsible for them than on general regularities, relationships, and laws.

This attitude underlies even the parts of *Works and Days* in which Hesiod gives practical advice. He advocates work as the key to success,[9] but is keenly aware of obstacles to the generalization that hard work ensures success. First, injustice (one's own or that of one's fellow citizens) may be punished by famine and plague, regardless of how hard one works (2.4). Second, the gods' inconsistency means that sometimes the sluggish will be as successful as the hard worker.[10] Not hard work but Demeter fills one's barn with food.[11] Even when work brings wealth it is because the gods favor those who work, and when idleness brings poverty it is because the gods are angry at the idle.[12] The favoritism of the Olympians is present here even where we would look for regularities and explanations of a mundane sort.

Hesiod's world ruled by the Olympians has limited potential as a well-ordered KOSMOS governed by intelligible principles. Even if the possibilities of chaotic disorder are tempered by Zeus' overall commitment to rule and justice, Hesiod is far from achieving a complete and consistent account of how chaos is avoided. On the other hand, his view of the world as a KOSMOS

---

9. Hesiod's chief concern is the farmer's life, where success is measured mainly by the extent and quality of one's fields and flocks, the bounty of the harvest, and the possession of the qualities in oneself and one's family that help attain these material goals.

10. *Works and Days*, lines 479–90.

11. *Works and Days*, lines 298–301.

12. *Works and Days*, lines 302–9.

would remain an essential part of Greek philosophical thought along with his goal of producing a coherent unified understanding of the structure, origins, and operations of the KOSMOS. His practice of employing different sources of information and using one to correct or supplement another was also important in later philosophical and scientific method. There is even a kind of critical stance towards sources in the Muses' address to Hesiod:

2.7 We know enough to make up lies which are convincing,   27
     but we also have the skill, when we've a mind, to speak the truth.
                                        (Hesiod, *Theogony*, lines 27–28)

The philosophers of sixth-century Miletus managed to take the decisive steps of abandoning mythological ways of thought and rejecting traditional ways of looking at the world. To them we will turn, after a short discussion of the conditions in Miletus in the early sixth century which could have contributed to this decisive revolution in thought.

3

Miletus in the Sixth Century:
The Cultural Setting for the
Beginnings of Philosophy

Western philosophy and science trace their beginnings to the Ionian Greek city of Miletus, on the Aegean coast of Asia Minor, in the early years of the sixth century B.C. Thales of Miletus, whom Aristotle calls the founder of this type of philosophy, reputedly predicted the eclipse of the sun which occurred May 28, 585, and his fellow countrymen Anaximander and Anaximenes maintained an apparently unbroken tradition until the late sixth or early fifth century. The distinctive Milesian approach was also pursued in the sixth and fifth centuries by philosophers who, although not from Miletus, tended to have Ionian origins (notably Anaxagoras and Democritus). The questions these men posed and their answers are more the matter of science than of philosophy, as we think of those fields, but their speculation prompted others to raise what we recognize as philosophical issues, and their intellectual attitudes and methods were adopted by the thinkers who pursued those issues philosophically.

Miletus and numerous other Greek cities in the Aegean islands and the west coast of Asia Minor were established around 1000 B.C. after the collapse of the bronze-age culture of the Greek mainland known as Mycenaean civilization. From the eighth century the Greeks both from the homeland and from these newer settlements came into contact with other peoples, and founded colonies, either to establish permanent trading posts or to shed excess population. These colonies were established round the coast of the Black Sea, in Southern Italy and Sicily, and elsewhere on the Mediterranean seaboard. The founder of many colonies, Miletus developed into a prominent and wealthy community active in shipping, trade, and industry, and enjoying commercial relations with other Greek cities from the Black Sea to Sicily and with non-Greek civilizations, notably Egypt, Mesopotamia, and the Lydian people of inland Asia Minor.

Miletus was a POLIS (plural, POLEIS), a city-state, not a country or nation in any modern sense. Greece existed neither as a political entity nor even as a concept until after our period. The Milesians shared with other Greeks the Greek language, a social structure, and a cultural heritage that can loosely be called Homeric, in the sense that they accepted the oral epics which we know as the *Iliad* and *Odyssey* as their own tradition and recognized the Olympian gods. Much of the cultural life and all of the political life of a POLIS was under its own control.

The society of Miletus was aristocratic and secular. Unlike the older and more culturally prestigious civilizations of Egypt and Mesopotamia, the Greeks tended to keep their religious institutions separate from administrative and military matters. There were state religious cults and practices, but much religious activity took place at the level of the family or other social groups within or transcending the POLIS. Moreover, unlike the older civilizations, the Greeks did not have sacred texts or an official class of hereditary, professional priests, much less an Egyptian-style divine monarch. Religious practices varied from place to place and from individual to individual. Even if the Homeric epics were the common property of all Greeks, the stories they told of the gods did not amount to dogma in which everyone was expected or compelled to believe. To this extent the claim that Homer was the Bible of the Greeks is wrong. In fact, possibly in Homer himself and certainly in Hesiod, Homer's approximate contemporary, we find a speculative attitude towards the gods which tends in the opposite direction from dogma.

The spread of political authority to an aristocratic class required a measure of cooperation and discussion. Written law codes, too, introduced in this period, called for reasoned argument. Cases at law would in principle be won or lost according as the facts of the case were established and shown by argument to conform or conflict with the laws. In principle, decisions would not be made on arbitrary or personal grounds, but according to rational criteria. How far these principles were carried out in practice is another question. Still, the existence of the principles as principles will have exerted some pressure in actual cases and made available an ideal or standard which could be applied elsewhere.

Contact with Egypt and Mesopotamia had powerful effects seen clearly in the "orientalizing" art of the eighth and seventh centuries and in some of the ideas and discoveries attributed to the Milesian philosophers. Some early Greek philosophers are reported to have learned from sages of the East—evidence that the Greeks of the period were open to ideas from foreigners, although they never simply copied, but adapted foreign elements and made them their own. This adaptive borrowing may even have played a decisive role in the rise of Greek science and philosophy.

Why philosophy started in early sixth-century Miletus is likely to remain without a definitive answer. Several factors were doubtless relevant: the relative freedom of thought (including speculative thought) and expression possible in the absence of a monolithic centralized religion and political administration; a sufficient accumulation of wealth to provide to some the leisure for speculative thought; the fact that literacy was not restricted to a certain caste of the population and to bureaucratic purposes; the beginnings of the practice of reaching decisions through public debate conducted according to rational principles; contact with several other cultures and openness to foreign ideas.

Since these social, economic, and political circumstances were found equally in other Greek cities, they are insufficient by themselves to account for the origin of philosophy and science in Miletus. Nor does Aristotle's opinion, that people are in a position to study philosophy only when their practical needs are taken care of and they have leisure time available for speculation,[1] point to Miletus alone among Greek cities as the starting place of theoretical thought. In the present case, the decisive reason for the beginning of philosophy and science is that individuals with the intellectual interests and vigor of Thales, Anaximander, and Anaximenes were born and nurtured in Miletus under conditions that allowed their genius to be expressed in certain ways.

1. Aristotle, *Metaphysics* 1.1 981b13–25.

4

Thales of Miletus

Thales of Miletus, the reputed originator of the Greek philosophical and scientific tradition, lived in the first part of the sixth century, as is shown by his alleged prediction of the solar eclipse of 585 B.C. Thales' all-round wisdom became legendary. ("The man's a Thales!" exclaims a character in one of Aristophanes' comedies[1] written almost two centuries after Thales lived.) In an oft-told but historically improbable story,[2] King Croesus of Lydia asked Thales for help in transporting his army across the river Halys, and Thales divided the river, making it passable by diverting its course upstream from the army's position, so that some or all the water flowed behind the camp, rejoining the original river bed downstream. He advised the Ionian cities of Asia Minor to form a political union with a centrally located common governing council,[3] advice which if taken might have made the Ionian cities better able to resist Persian expansion. He is the only presocratic named among the Seven Sages. And as the earliest subject of both an "absent-minded professor" story and a defense of philosophy against charges of uselessness, he is emblematic of the different responses philosophy provoked in its cultural setting.

4.1 Once while Thales was gazing upwards while doing astronomy, he fell into a well. A clever and delightful Thracian serving-girl is said to have made fun of him, since he was eager to know the things in the heavens but failed to notice what was in front of him and right next to his feet.
(Plato, *Theaetetus* 174a = DK 11A9)

4.2 The story goes that when they found fault with him for his poverty, supposing that philosophy is useless, he learned from his astronomy that there would be a large crop of olives. Then, while it was still winter, he obtained a little money and made deposits on all the olive presses both in Miletus and in Chios. Since no one bid against him, he rented them cheaply. When the right time came, suddenly many tried to get the presses all at once, and he rented them out on whatever terms he wished, and so

1. Aristophanes, *Birds* l. 1009 (not in DK).
2. Herodotus, *Histories* 1.75 (= DK 11A6).
3. Herodotus, *Histories* 1.170 (= DK 11A4).

made a great deal of money. In this way he proved that philosophers can easily be wealthy if they desire, but this is not what they are interested in.

(Aristotle, *Politics* 1.11 1259a9–18 = DK 11A10)

Astronomy

Both these no doubt fictitious stories portray Thales as an astronomer, which chimes with his prediction of the eclipse. But here we run across the two central problems in understanding Thales. Did he really found Western science and philosophy, or did he simply parrot the theories and discoveries of others? On what did he base his theories? His prediction of the eclipse could not have resembled modern ones, which specify not only the day but also the path of the eclipse and the time of partial and total eclipse at different places along its path. Modern predictions require much precise knowledge which was not available until much later (e.g., the elliptical orbits of earth and moon were determined in the seventeenth century), and although some needed facts, such as the sphericity of the earth, were known in later antiquity, there is no reason to suppose that Thales knew them.[4]

Still, the prediction is well attested. The best evidence is that of the fifth-century historian Herodotus. In recounting a war between the Medes and the Lydians he says:

> 4.3 As they were having equal success in the war, it happened that in the sixth year, when a battle was being fought, the day suddenly became night. Thales of Miletus had foretold to the Ionians that this loss of daylight would occur, setting as a limit the very year in which the change occurred.
>
> (Herodotus, *Histories* 1.74 = DK 11A5)

Two things should be noticed in Herodotus' account. Thales predicted the year of the eclipse, not the date or time of day, and he is not said to have predicted that the eclipse would be visible at any specific place. Now both of these features accord with contemporary Babylonian methods of predicting eclipses. If solar eclipses are recorded over a sufficiently long time, patterns of their occurrences emerge which can be used to make rough predictions even without modern astronomical knowledge. The Babylonians, keenly interested in eclipses and other astronomical phenomena for astrological

---

4. The evidence for this assertion is the astronomy of Thales' immediate successors, which does not recognize a spherical earth and which was in other ways grossly unsuited to making accurate predictions of celestial phenomena.

and religious purposes, kept meticulous records from the mid-eighth century and so had a data base sufficient for such limited predictions.

Adequate records for such predictions cannot be amassed in one person's lifetime, but Thales could well have come into contact with Babylonian astronomy. He probably travelled to Egypt, and given Miletus' international connections, he may have visited Babylon too. Further, people versed in Babylonian astronomy may have visited Miletus. In these circumstances, Thales may have learned to make predictions himself, or may merely have reported a Babylonian prediction. In any case, unless he simply made a lucky guess (in which case his prediction is on the same level as Anaxagoras' prediction of the fall of a meteorite), at most the prediction shows interest in a different style of astronomy from that found in Hesiod and a familiarity with Babylonian methods; it cannot be seen as a major discovery due to Thales himself which inaugurated new realms or new methods of knowledge.

Mathematics

In his *History of Geometry*, Aristotle's follower Eudemus reports that Thales introduced geometry to Greece from Egypt, made discoveries of his own, and transmitted to posterity the principles of many theorems, "attacking some more generally and others more perceptually."[5] Among other achievements he is credited with the theorem that triangles with one side and the two adjacent angles equal are congruent, for "he must have used this theorem to show the distance of ships at sea in the way he did."[6] This statement gives a clue to how later historians of geometry approached their subject, and also leads us once more to question Thales' originality.

Greek geometry, as canonized in Euclid's *Elements* (c. 300 B.C.), proceeds by proofs based on definitions and other unproved principles. It deals more with general theorems than with specific problems, and is not primarily devoted to calculations. In these respects it differs from earlier mathematics, including Egyptian geometry. Ancient historians of mathematics from Eudemus on assumed that Greek geometry had this distinctive character from the start and that it developed cumulatively, with successive mathematicians contributing proofs of new theorems or organizing existing knowledge into a comprehensive system of proofs. Accordingly, they said that Thales, the founder of Greek mathematics, passed on the principles of

---

5. Eudemus, cited in Proclus, *Commentary on the first book of Euclid's Elements* 65.7–11 (= DK 11A11).

6. Ibid., 352.14–18 (= DK 11A20).

many theorems to posterity, and they sought to attribute particular theorems to him. However, recent historians of Greek mathematics reject this
approach. The notion of proving results is unlikely to have sprung full-
grown from the head of the first Greek geometer like Athene from the head
of Zeus, but more probably developed over an extended period of time,
perhaps influenced by the use of proofs in philosophy, which are not found
before Parmenides.

The mention of Thales' use of the angle-side-angle congruence theorem to show the distance of ships at sea indicates the following method.
From two points on the shore (*A*, *B*) determine the angles between shore
and ship (*a*, *b*). Construct equal angles on the shoreward side of those
points and continue the lines until they intersect (*C*). The distance from *C*
to the shoreline will be equal to the distance from ship to shore.

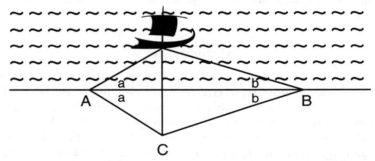

This application of geometry does presuppose knowing certain properties
of triangles, but contrary to Eudemus' inferences, it implies nothing about
Thales' inventing a proof of the angle-side-angle theorem or even of his
having a concept of proof.

Eudemus' vague assertion that Thales attacked some theorems "more
generally and others more perceptually" may give insight into the nature of
Thales' "proofs." His proof that a circle is bisected by its diameter[7] perhaps involved folding or cutting a drawn circle and showing that the two
pieces match. Such an argument might be called perceptual. Nowadays this
kind of procedure would not count as a legitimate proof, and even by
Euclid's day it had fallen out of favor. But it does contain the germ of the
idea of mathematical proof (showing one fact to follow from others) and
constitutes a decisive step away from the practical and empirical mathematics of the Egyptians.

7. Ibid., 157.10–11 (= DK 11A20).

So far Thales is an ambiguous figure. He may have made original scientific discoveries (inventing the notion of proof would make him one of the most important figures in the entire history of human thought), and yet he may only have imported the scientific knowledge of other peoples. His speculations about water, however, belong to quite a different area of thought.

Water

Aristotle's survey of some of the opinions of his philosophical forebears contains the most important testimonium about Thales.

> **4.4** Causes are spoken of in four ways, of which . . . one is matter. . . . Let us take as associates in our task our predecessors who considered the things that are and philosophised about the truth. For it is clear that they too speak of certain principles and causes. Therefore it will be useful to our present inquiry to survey them, for either we will find some other kind of cause or we will be more confident in the ones now being discussed.
>
> (Aristotle, *Metaphysics* 1.3 983a26–b6, not in DK)

Aristotle's purposes are clear. He does not aim to discuss the complete theories of former philosophers sympathetically and in context; he wants only to see if they contain anything relevant to his own philosophical task of identifying different types of causes. His starting points are his own notion of "cause" and his view that there are precisely four kinds of causes, and despite his assertion in the final sentence, he proves reluctant to acknowledge additional kinds, let alone to admit any radically different approach to the subject of causes. He continues with a strongly Aristotelian account of what a "material cause" is.

> **4.5** Of those who first pursued philosophy, the majority believed that the only principles of all things are principles in the form of matter. For that of which all existing things are composed and that out of which they originally come into being and that into which they finally perish, the substance persisting but changing in its attributes, this they state is the element and principle of things that are. . . . For there must be one or more than one nature out of which the rest come to be, while it is preserved.
>
> (Aristotle, *Metaphysics* 1.3 983b6–18 = DK 11A2)

This notion of underlying matter was Aristotle's invention. Even though earlier thinkers regarded one or more types of substance as somehow primary, Aristotle is anachronistic in assuming that their notions of primacy coincided with his, or even that their theories addressed the problems that engaged him. He goes on to mention Thales.

> **4.6** However, not all agree about the number and form of such a principle, but Thales, the founder of this kind of philosophy, declares it to be water. (This is why he indicated that the earth rests on water.) Maybe he got this idea from seeing that the nourishment of all things is moist, and that the hot itself comes to be from this and lives on this (the principle of all things is that from which they come to be)—getting this idea from this consideration and also because the seeds of all things have a moist nature; and water is the principle of the nature of moist things.
>
> (Aristotle, *Metaphysics* 1.3 983b18–27 = DK 11A12)

This passage tells us three things. (a) Thales says the earth floats on water, (b) Aristotle interprets Thales as declaring that water is the "material cause" as defined above, and (c) Aristotle has to guess Thales' reasons for giving primacy to water. If Aristotle infers (b) from (a), we must question Thales' originality again. For in discussing another passage which attributes (a) to Thales, Simplicius remarks:

> **4.7** Aristotle speaks quite strongly against this view, which was prevalent perhaps because the Egyptians recounted it in mythological form and Thales perhaps imported the doctrine from there.
>
> (Simplicius, *Commentary on Aristotle's On the Heaven*
> 522.16–18 = DK 11A14)

Again, we may have borrowing from Egypt, this time borrowing not of science but of myth. Aristotle himself mentions the possibility that Thales simply continued earlier mythical ways of thought, though he rejects the idea.

> **4.8** Some believe that very ancient people, long before the present generation, who first speculated about the gods, also made this supposition about nature. For they made Ocean and Tethys parents of coming to be and said that the oath of the gods was water, which they called Styx. For the most ancient is the most honored, and the most honored thing is what is used to swear by.
>
> (Aristotle, *Metaphysics* 1.3 983b27–33 = DK 11A12)
> (continuation of 4.6)

On the other hand, whatever its source, Thales' claim that the earth rests on water may have been intended to explain natural phenomena. One source tells us that Thales held that the motion of this subterranean water was the cause of earthquakes.[8] In this case Thales has made a decisive break with traditional explanations of earthquakes as due to Poseidon. Moreover, in hypothesizing an unobserved natural state of affairs (no one had seen the earth resting on water) to explain an observed phenomenon, Thales was making an intellectual move which has remained a principal part of scientific thinking to this day.

It is unlikely that Thales wrote down his views on water as a cosmological principle. If Aristotle had had any such book he would not have been so vague and so quickly driven to guesswork. Still, he regards Thales as the founder of his own philosophical and scientific tradition, not just an importer of foreign ideas or a teller of myths like Homer and Hesiod (who are behind the reference to Ocean and Tethys in **4.8**). Even if Thales' ideas stem from mythology, at the very least he demythologizes them, and this is a crucial move for philosophy and science. How, then, did he present the demythologized ideas? There are two main lines of interpretation.

First, the traditional view, which follows Aristotle, is that for Thales in some way all things are water; they are made or composed of water. Thus, Thales' main question is "What are all things made of?" and as far as we know he is the first to ask this question, and his answer is of the same type as those given by later presocratics and by physicists up to the present day.

This idea is open to a number of objections, which not only seem obvious to us, but which Thales' immediate successors avoid in their theories—objections such as, "If everything is composed of water, how can there be different kinds of substances in the world, some of them, such as fire, seemingly opposed to water?" and "Even if (as Aristotle indicates) water is necessary for the origin and maintenance of other things, why should we think that water is their only constituent?" It is unclear what if any response Thales would make to these criticisms. But in this period it is not surprising if theories are open to obvious and devastating objections, and the mere fact that there are decisive reasons to reject a theory is no reason at all to think it was not actually held.

On the second interpretation,[9] towards which I incline, Thales' principal question is, "What is the source of all things?"[10] In identifying water as the source he harks back to Greek and Near Eastern mythological accounts of the origin of the earth, with which his assertion that the earth floats on water fits nicely. On this view, Thales' interests are different from his successors'. Again, he looks backward rather than forward, with the result that his successors not only gave different answers but also changed the

8. Seneca, *Natural Questions* 3.14 (= DK 11A15).

9. KRS, pp. 92–94.

10. The key word, ARCHE, can mean "origin," "beginning" as well as "principle."

nature of the question, so that the main thrust was no longer historical (focusing on what the original state was and how the present conditions of the world arose) but in a broad sense physical (focusing the basic forms of matter and how different substances are composed of them). On this reading Aristotle is wrong to place Thales alongside those concerned with these "physical" issues, and Thales is the only Greek philosopher to accept certain Near Eastern views.

Souls and Gods

Aristotle reports that Thales believed magnets possess soul because they move iron, and infers that he judged the soul to be a thing that causes motion.[11] Thales also held that amber (which has magnetic properties when rubbed or heated) possesses soul.[12]

It is hard to know what to make of these statements. The idea that the soul is the principle of life was widespread in Greek thought. The presence of soul makes a thing alive; when a living thing dies, it no longer has a soul. Thus, Aristotle held that plants and animals possess souls. He held further that motion is characteristic of life, especially in his broad sense of "motion" which includes growth and changes in quality—"motions" that even plants possess. Thus, the presence of soul, and therefore of life, implies motion.

Thales attributes soul to things not normally thought to be alive. Is he proposing a version of hylomorphism, the view that matter has life, so that life is found in all things whatever? Also, since magnets and amber cause other things to move, is Thales' point that the notion of soul should be extended to include things that cause motion in other things? Or instead of moving in these exciting new directions does he just want to reinforce (in a nonmythological context) a prephilosophical animistic conception that many parts of what we regard as inanimate nature are actually alive?

The following passage may help resolve these questions.

> 4.9 Some declare that it [the soul] is mixed in the whole [universe], and perhaps this is why Thales thought all things are full of gods.
>
> (Aristotle, *On the Soul* 1.5 411a7–8 = DK 11A22)

Here Aristotle says that Thales believes all things are full of gods and suggests, without asserting confidently, that he believes soul pervades the whole world and that these two ideas are related. If the link between souls

11. Aristotle, *On the Soul* 1.2 405a19 (= DK 11A22).
12. Diogenes Laertius, *Lives of the Philosophers* 1.24 (= DK 11A1).

and gods is valid (an assumption which is possible, though not certain), Thales' most important surviving doctrines can be connected as follows, though the interpretation is speculative and the elements of Thales' thought it pulls together may have been separate.

Water is primary since it is prominent in the physical makeup of the world (occurring on the earth, above it in the form of rain, and below it as the water on which the earth floats) and is needed for the generation and maintenance of living things and of some apparently nonliving things. Thales conceives of water not as a chemically pure substance, but as the moist element quite generally—in the sea, in rain, in sperm. Water's unceasing mobility, seen especially in the continuous movement of the sea, rivers, and rain, reveals it to be a living substance. If everything is made of water or ultimately arises from water, the life force of water pervades the whole world, showing up in some things more than others (just as some things are wetter than others). Moreover, as a living thing with no beginning in time (everything else owes its beginning to *it*), and apparently no end in time either, water is divine (since for the Greeks the primary characteristics of the divine are immortality and power independent of human will). Hence all things, being composed of or arising from water, are full of the divine.

Thales is a threshold figure, standing at the beginning of the Western scientific and philosophical tradition, but strongly influenced by the past. Of the little we know about him, much fits both the picture of Thales as the brilliant innovator and of Thales as the importer of others' ideas. Both versions are partly true. His prediction of the eclipse is at best Babylonian, not Greek, yet his demythologized understanding of the world, whatever its details, is new. Although Thales remains a Janus-faced figure, the same cannot be said of Anaximander, the second Milesian philosopher, whose originality and imagination are beyond doubt.

5

Anaximander of Miletus

If Anaximander was sixty-four in 546, as our best source[1] says, he was twenty-five at the time of Thales' eclipse, which agrees with the tradition that he was Thales' successor in investigating nature. His picture of KOS-MOS and his ways of thought can be gleaned from the surviving information (including one fragment) on his physical speculations.

Astronomy

5.1 He was the first to discover the gnomon and set one up on the sundials at Sparta . . . indicating the solstices and equinoxes, and he constructed hour-markers.
(Diogenes Laertius, *Lives of the Philosophers* 2.1 = DK 12A1)

A gnomon (originally "carpenter's square") is the raised piece whose shadow indicates the sun's position. Most ancient sundials indicated not only the time of day by the direction of the shadow but also the season of the year as a function of the sun's height in the sky (higher in summer, lower in winter) marked by the length of the shadow. At the summer and winter solstices the shadow is respectively shortest and longest; on the equinoxes, the sun rises and sets due east and west, and the path of the shadow during the course of the day is a straight line. (On other days it traces a curved arc of a hyperbola.) With appropriate markings a sundial will show both time of day and distance from the solstices and equinoxes.

5.1 attributes all this to Anaximander, but the information must be treated with caution. Since Herodotus says that the Greeks learned the use of the gnomon and the twelve parts of the day from the Babylonians,[2] Anaximander may have introduced sundials to Greece (without inventing them), though some sources[3] credit Thales with determining solstices, which may point to his knowing about the gnomon.

Anaximander is also said to have been the first to construct a sphere,[4] i.e., a celestial globe or map of the heavens, but it is doubtful whether he did so.

1. Diogenes Laertius, *Lives of the Philosophers* 2.2 (= DK 12A1).
2. Herodotus, *Histories* 2.109 (= DK 12A4).
3. Diogenes Laertius, *Lives of the Philosophers* 1.23 (= DK 11A1) and Der-cyllides, cited in Theon of Smyrna, p. 198,14 (Hiller) (= DK 12A26).
4. Diogenes Laertius, *Lives of the Philosophers* 2.2 (= DK 12A1).

Map

Anaximander was the first Greek mapmaker. He "was the first to draw the inhabited world on a tablet"[5]—an achievement that, though doubtless crude, will have drawn on knowledge gained from his own travels (we have already seen him in Sparta; he also led an expedition to found a colony on the Black Sea), and also from consultations with merchants and other travelers. Although his map was improved by a fellow Milesian, Hecataeus, who was active around 500, in the mid-fifth century their work was ridiculed by Herodotus, who gives us an idea of the design of such early maps.

> 5.2 I laugh when I consider that before now many have drawn maps of the world, but no one has set it out in a reasonable way. They draw Okeanos [the river Ocean] flowing round the earth, which is round as if made by a compass, and they make Asia equal to Europe.
>
> (Herodotus, *Histories* 4.36, not in DK)

Earthquake

Cicero tells of Anaximander warning the Spartans of an impending earthquake and advising them to abandon the city and sleep in the fields.[6] It is debated whether Anaximander knew some lore, such as the behavior of animals, on which to base a prediction, or whether the story was fabricated to enhance his reputation.

Physical Theories

The APEIRON as ARCHE

Anaximander's views on the ARCHE (starting point, basic principle, originating source) are preserved in three sources, each derived from Theophrastus.[7] I combine them as follows.

> 5.3 Of those who declared that the ARCHE is one, moving and APEIRON, Anaximander . . . said that the APEIRON was the ARCHE and element of things that are, and he was the first to introduce this name for the ARCHE [i.e., he

---

5. Agathemerus 1.1 (= DK 12A6).

6. Cicero, *On Divination* 1.50.112 (= DK 12A5a).

7. Simplicius, *Commentary on Aristotle's Physics* 24.13–18 (= DK12A9); Hippolytus, *Refutation* 1.6.1–2 (= DK 12A11); pseudo-Plutarch, *Stromata* 2 (= DK 12A10).

was the first to call the ARCHE APEIRON].[8] (In addition he said that motion is eternal, in which it occurs that the heavens come to be.[9]) He says that the ARCHE is neither water nor any other of the things called elements, but some other nature which is APEIRON, out of which come to be all the heavens and the worlds in them. This is eternal and ageless and surrounds all the worlds.

According to this account, for Anaximander the APEIRON is the stuff of which all things are composed. On this influential view, Anaximander's APEIRON replaces Thales' water as the Aristotelian "material cause" of all things. I have already called this interpretation of Thales into question; as we will see, for Anaximander it cannot stand. Theophrastus says Anaximander was the first to use the word APEIRON in this context, and that the APEIRON differs from water, fire, and other familiar materials identified by others as the basic stuff, but he does not describe it except to say that it is eternal, ageless, and in motion, and that a plurality of heavens and worlds arise or are born out of it and are surrounded by it.

The word APEIRON is a compound of the prefix A-, meaning "not," and either the noun PEIRAR or PEIRAS, "limit, boundary," so that it means "unlimited, boundless, indefinite," or the root PER-, "through, beyond, forward," so that it means "unable to be got through," "what cannot be traversed from end to end." Although in Aristotle it can mean "infinite," in dealing with the presocratic period it is misleading to understand the word in this relatively technical sense.[10]

5.3 contains three hints about what APEIRON means for Anaximander. Since it surrounds the heavens and worlds, it is (1) indefinitely (though not necessarily infinitely) large, spatially unlimited. Since it is eternal and ageless, (2) it is temporally unlimited. Since it is no definite substance like water, it is (3) an indefinite kind of material. All three interpretations have ancient authority. The first two correspond to reasons Aristotle cites for believing that something exists which is APEIRON,[11] while the third results from an argument for making the original substance APEIRON that Aristotle cites and later writers attribute to Anaximander:

8. This phrase is also translated "he was the first to introduce this very term of ARCHE," i.e., the first to use the term "ARCHE" itself. Simplicius makes this point at *Commentary on Aristotle's Physics* 150.22–25 (not in DK), and he may have meant to make it in the current passage (ibid., 24.13–18) too, but the translation given in the text best suits the Greek of the current passage.

9. This obscure sentence probably means that the heavens come to be in the APEIRON by means of its eternal movement.

10. In this book, I usually translate APEIRON as "unlimited," except for passages from Aristotle and later sources (such as 5.4) in which "infinite" seems appropriate.

11. Aristotle, *Physics* 3.4 203b23–26, b16–17.

5.4 The infinite [APEIRON] body cannot be one and simple . . . if it is conceived, as some say, as that which is aside from the elements, and from which they generate the elements. . . . For some make the infinite this [i.e., something aside from the elements], rather than air or water, to keep the others from being destroyed by the one of them that is infinite. For they contain oppositions with regard to one another, for example, air is cold, water wet, fire hot. If any one of them were infinite, the rest would already have been destroyed. But as it is, they declare that the thing from which all come into being is different.

(Aristotle, *Physics* 3.3 204b22–29 = DK 12A16)

If the Aristotelian ideas (especially the concept of elements and the identification of air, etc., as elements and the use of APEIRON in the sense of "infinite") are discounted, **5.4** may record Anaximander's own proof that the originative material differs from any definite substance. Water and other familiar materials possess definite properties, yet there are things that lack any given property and some with opposite properties. But if everything is made of or arose from water, everything must have the properties of water. Further, since, as Anaximander thinks, opposites conflict with one another, an unlimited amount of a material with definite characteristics would long since have destroyed things with opposite characteristics (even supposing that they existed in the first place), swamping them by the vastly larger quantity of their opposites. Thus Thales is refuted, whether he held that all things are composed of water or that all things have their ultimate origin in water.

This is a powerful argument for an originative substance with no definite characteristics. The APEIRON, then, is neither water nor fire, neither hot nor cold, nor heavy nor light, nor wet nor dry, nor light nor dark. As the ultimate source of all the things and all the characteristics in the world, it can be none of those things, can have none of those characteristics. It is thus difficult to describe. (Ancient complaints that he failed to specify what kind of material the APEIRON is are off the mark, as is Aristotle's belief that it is a substance of a definite kind, intermediate between fire and air, or between air and water.) When Anaximander says it is eternal, ageless, in motion, and that it surrounds and is the source of everything else, he may be describing it as fully as his language and concepts permitted.

Since it is eternal and in motion, the APEIRON possesses characteristics which, as we saw in discussing Thales, qualify it as divine.

5.5 This does not have an ARCHE, but this seems to be the ARCHE of the rest, and to contain all things and steer all things,[12] as all declare who do not

---

12. It is tempting to add "governing" or "steering" all things to the list of the APEIRON's attributes given above, but it is not certain from **5.5** that Aristotle has

fashion other causes aside from the infinite . . . and this is divine. For it is
deathless and indestructible, as Anaximander says and most of the natural
philosophers.

(Aristotle, *Physics* 3.4 203b10–15 = DK 12A15)

Being divine, immortal, and in motion, it is alive, like Thales' water, and
thus capable of generating a (living) world. What kind of motion does it
have? Three answers given by modern scholars are that it has a vortex
motion like a whirlpool, in which the heavier parts move to the center and
the lighter to the edge, that it has a circular motion, and that its motion is
"shaking and sifting as in a sieve."[13] None of these interpretations has
substantial support, and it is best not to press the question. If the APEIRON
had a definite type of motion, an analogous argument to the one above
would apply: how could all the different kinds of motion we observe have
arisen out of a primordial substance endowed with only one specific kind of
movement? It is best to suppose that Anaximander thought the APEIRON was
in motion because otherwise no change could occur and the world could
never have originated, but that he said nothing definite about the nature of
the motion.

Cosmogony: The Origin of the World

For Anaximander the existence and the interaction of opposites stand in
need of explanation. This outlook is intelligible as a reaction to Thales'
problem of accounting for the existence of fire given the priority of water.
Anaximander believes that the opposites hot and cold are equally important
in the structure and operation of the world and accordingly gives them a
prominent position in his cosmogony.

5.6 He declares that what arose from the eternal and is productive of [or,
capable of giving birth to] hot and cold was separated off at the coming to
be of this KOSMOS, and a kind of sphere of flame from this grew around
the dark mist[14] about the earth like bark about a tree. When it was broken
off and enclosed in certain circles, the sun, moon and stars came to be.

(pseudo-Plutarch, *Stromata* 2 = DK 12A10) (continuation of 5.11)

Since the APEIRON is neither hot nor cold, it does not favor either opposite
over the other, but how can something neither hot nor cold generate both

---

Anaximander in mind when he uses this word, which he may have taken from other
early philosophers, such as Heraclitus (10.44), Parmenides (11.12 l.3), Diogenes of
Apollonia (17.5 sec. 1).

13. J. Burnet, *Early Greek Philosophy*, 4th ed. (London, 1930), p. 61.

14. AER, the Greek word translated here as "dark mist," is discussed below, p. 49–50.

opposites? Anaximander's solution is to declare that hot and cold arose from something capable of giving birth to hot and cold, and this thing is "separated off" from the APEIRON. Neither hot nor cold will overwhelm the other since they are created at the same time and with equal power.

Other problems arise regarding the thing that generates hot and cold. It arises from the undifferentiated, uniform mass of the APEIRON through "separating off," a process found elsewhere in Anaximander's system, in which apparently part of an existing thing is isolated so as to take on an identity separate from the original thing, and as such behave differently from the thing from which it arose. But (perhaps because Anaximander said little about these crucial issues) we have no clues about how "separating off" takes place, what the thing is that produces hot and cold, or how it produces them.[15]

5.6 identifies several stages in the formation of the world. First there is the APEIRON, referred to here as "the eternal." From the APEIRON, through the process of "separating off," arises something capable of giving birth to hot and cold. The hot and cold which arise from this are described concretely as flame and dark mist. The flame is a spherical shell that tightly encloses the mist "as the bark encloses a tree" (a simile possibly due to Anaximander himself). Since at this stage there are only two things, fire and mist, corresponding to hot and cold, the mention of earth refers to a later stage of differentiation which may occur simultaneously with the breakup of the sphere of flame into circles to make the sun, moon, and stars (cf. **5.8**).

Anaximander's approach to his fundamental problem, which can be rephrased as "How does the determinate diversity of the world come out of the indeterminate uniformity of the APEIRON?" is already clear. The APEIRON appears only at the beginning of the process; afterwards things take their own course. The world's diversity is due not to the intervention of Olympian gods but to a small number of processes such as differentiation of one thing into many and "separation off" of one thing from another. The dark mist is differentiated into the air we breathe and the earth we stand on, which was originally moist. Its currently dry state is due to a further process of differentiation.

> **5.7** They claim that at first all the region about the earth is wet. When it is
> dried by the sun, that which evaporated causes winds and turnings of the

15. The alternate translation in **5.6**, "capable of giving birth," has led some to think that hot and cold were produced through some sort of biological process; but biological processes are inexplicable at this primitive stage of the world. At any rate, the word (which in any case was not Anaximander's) can mean "productive" without any biological overtones.

sun and moon, and the remainder is sea. For this reason they believe that
it is being dried and becoming smaller and finally it will some day be dry.
(Aristotle, *Meteorologica* 2.1 353b6–11 = DK 12A27)

"Separating off" is invoked again to account for the breakup of the sphere
of flame to form the heavenly bodies (**5.8**).

Despite Anaximander's unclarity on some important points, his overall
picture is impressive, as is his understanding of the logical requirements of
generating a complex world out of a simple originative material.

Cosmology: The Articulation of the World

5.8 The stars come to be as a circle of fire separated off from the fire in the
KOSMOS and enclosed by dark mist. There are vents, certain tube-like
passages at which the stars appear. For this reason, eclipses occur when
the vents are blocked. The moon appears sometimes waxing sometimes
waning as the passages are blocked or opened. The circle of the sun is
twenty-seven times <that of the earth> and that of the moon <18
times>, and the sun is highest, and the circles of the fixed stars are
lowest.
(Hippolytus, *Refutation* 1.6.4–5 = DK 12A11) (continuation of **5.12**)

5.9 Anaximander says that the sun is equal to the earth, and the circle where
it has its vent and on which it is carried is twenty-seven times the size of
the earth.   (Aetius 2.21.1 = DK 12A21)

5.10 Anaximander says that the stars are borne by the circles and spheres on
which each one goes.   (Aetius 2.16.5 = DK 12A18)

5.11 He says that the earth is cylindrical in shape, and its depth is one-third
its breadth.   (pseudo-Plutarch, *Stromata* 2 = DK 12A10)

5.12 The earth's shape is curved, round, like a stone column. We walk on one
of the surfaces and the other one is set opposite.
(Hippolytus, *Refutation* 1.6.3 = DK 12A11)

There are many interesting points here. First, there is no appearance of
mythology or mention of the traditional divinities. Second, the heavenly
bodies are made of fire, a substance familiar from human experience.
Third, Anaximander boldly measures the size of the universe and adopts a
terrestrial standard to measure it. Fourth, he assumes that the sizes and
distances of the earth and heavenly bodies are related by simple proportions, with emphasis on the number three. Fifth, he assumes that the
KOSMOS has a simple geometrical structure. Sixth, different phenomena
(eclipses, phases of the moon) are due to a single mechanism.

Anaximander's universe has a simple symmetric structure. At the center is the earth, a cylinder one-third as high as it is broad. We live on one of the flat surfaces. Around the cylinder are rings of fire surrounded by mist which makes them invisible except where a hole in the mist lets the fire shine through. The stars are closest to the earth, the sun is farthest, with the moon in between. (Anaximander may have reasoned that since fire rises upwards, the purest fire must be furthest from the earth; the sun's brightness and heat are greatest, so the sun is made of the purest fire and thus is furthest from the earth. By similar reasoning the feeble light of the stars places them closest.) The sun is the same size as the earth. (Quite possibly he held that the moon has this size too; sun and moon appear roughly the same size in the sky.) Approximately once a day each star is carried round its circular path: either the mist together with the hole moves round the ring of fire, or the mist, hole, and fire all rotate together. The diameter of the moon's circle is eighteen times the size of the earth, that of the sun's is twenty-seven times.[16] These figures make it likely that the distance of the stars from the earth was put at nine times the earth's size. Anaximander declares that wind is the cause of the sun's and moon's oblique paths relative to the stars, which shows that he knew of the obliquity of the ecliptic. As the sun and moon are different distances from the earth, their orbits can be oblique without colliding with each other or with the stars. The circles of the stars do not intersect, so there is no possibility of collision.[17] The essential features of this system can be represented in a simple diagram, and perhaps the "sphere" he is said to have constructed was a model of his astronomical ideas.

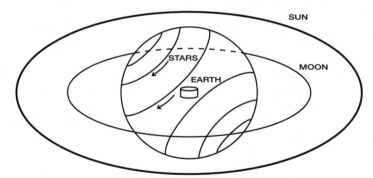

16. In fact the value of eighteen times for the moon is not attested. Aetius gives the value of twenty-eight times for the sun (2.20.1 = DK 12A21) and nineteen times for the moon (2.25.1 = DK 12A22), figures which may be due to an attempt to refine the system to take into account the thickness of the sun and moon.

17. Whether Anaximander had anything to say about the motions of the planets (which were well known to the Babylonians) is unknown. Planetary motions could have raised problems for his simple model.

Anaximander might have explained how the sun and moon can be seen through the mist which surrounds the stars by pointing out that mist can render some things invisible and yet not others. It can hide a nearby object from view while permitting a bright light much farther away to be seen clearly.

Anaximander holds that the earth is immobile at the center of the universe, a view shared by most of his successors[18] until Copernicus. Unusual is the sophisticated argument on which he bases this belief.

> 5.13 Some, like Anaximander . . . declare that the earth is at rest on account of its similarity. For it is no more fitting for what is established at the center and equally related to the extremes to move up rather than down or sideways. And it is impossible for it to make a move simultaneously in opposite directions. Therefore, it is at rest of necessity.
> (Aristotle, *On the Heaven* 2.13 295b11–16 = DK 12A26)

This too is to be understood as a criticism of Thales, who had the earth resting on water (**4.6**). What, then, did the water rest on? As long as one thing needs to be supported by another, there is no end. Anaximander cuts off this infinite regress at the start with the first known application of the Principle of Sufficient Reason, according to which, in Leibniz' formulation, "no fact can be real or existent . . . unless it has a sufficient reason why it should be thus and not otherwise."[19] In the present case, Anaximander reasons that the earth is at rest since its "equal relation to the extremes" implies that there is no sufficient reason for it to move in one direction rather than any other.

Further, the presuppositions underlying this argument have great methodological interest. On the basis of the senses we believe that all things move downwards and also that the earth, on which we stand, is at rest. Anaximander accepts the latter of these conflicting judgments and rejects the former as applying to the earth, and does so on the basis of symmetry and geometrical structure. On this account of his reasoning, Anaximander is intolerant of contradiction, adopts a critical stance towards sensory information, is ready to reject some sense-based judgments in favor of

18. Notable exceptions for our purposes are some Pythagoreans and the Atomists.
19. Leibniz, *Monadology*, sec. 32. Aristotle criticizes Anaximander's argument from the standpoint of Aristotelian physics at *On the Heaven* 2.13 295b16–296a22 (not in DK), comparing it to "a hair, which, it is said, however great the tension, will not break under it, if it is evenly distributed, or the man who, being extremely hungry and thirsty, and both equally, is equidistant from food and drink, and therefore bound to stay where he is" (b30–33).

others, and appeals to mathematical and logical considerations in constructing his theory.

Anaximander is interested in meteorological as well as astronomical phenomena and sees no distinction between the two, but accounts for both by the same processes:

> **5.14** Winds occur when the finest vapors of dark mist are separated off and, while in motion, are gathered together. Rain occurs from the vapor arising from the things beneath the sun. Lightning occurs whenever wind escapes and parts the clouds.
>
> (Hippolytus, *Refutation* 1.6.7 = DK 12A11)

> **5.15** [Concerning thunder, lightning, thunderbolts, waterspouts and hurricanes] Anaximander says that all these result from wind. For whenever it [wind] is enclosed in a thick cloud and forcibly escapes by its fineness and lightness, then the breaking creates the noise and the splitting creates the flash, in contrast with the blackness of the cloud.
>
> (Aetius 3.3.1 = DK 12A23)

Once again "separating off" is responsible for generation. The finest vapors become wind, leaving the thicker remains to become cloud. This time "separating off" originates change not only in what is separated off but also in the remainder. The resemblance between this process and that which generates the sea and winds at the beginning of the world (5.7) makes it likely that that process, too, occurs through "separating off."

Anaximander's belief that thunder and lightning result from wind being enclosed in cloud and then breaking out is reminiscent of his account of the origin of the heavenly bodies. (If, as seems likely, lightning is fire bursting out from the cloud, it resembles the celestial bodies, which are fire surrounded by dark mist.)

The passages above make it clear that for Anaximander the world arose from the same processes that maintain it. He therefore deserves the title of the first uniformitarian, as the eighteenth- and nineteenth-century geologists were called who held that processes found today, such as erosion and volcanic activity, are responsible for the geological features of the earth.

Anaximander used his understanding of present-day phenomena to project future events (5.7). His belief that the earth is drying up could well have been based on the silting up of the harbor of Miletus.[20]

---

20. This process, which is due to alluvial deposits of the river Meander at whose mouth the city was situated, has continued to the present, advancing the shoreline so far that the Aegean cannot now be seen from the site of ancient Miletus.

Anaximander also has an account of the origin of living creatures, including humans.

> **5.16** Anaximander says that the first animals were produced in moisture, enclosed in thorny barks. When their age increased they came out onto the drier part, their bark broke off, and they lived a different mode of life for a short time.   (Aetius 5.19.4 = DK 12A30)

> **5.17** He also declares that in the beginning humans were born from other kinds of animals, since other animals quickly manage on their own, and humans alone require lengthy nursing. For this reason, in the beginning they would not have been preserved if they had been like this.
> (pseudo-Plutarch, *Stromata* 2 = DK 12A10)
> (continuation of **5.6**)

> **5.18** Anaximander . . . believed that there arose from heated water and earth either fish or animals very like fish. In these humans grew and were kept inside as embryos up to puberty. Then finally they burst and men and women came forth already able to nourish themselves.
> (Censorinus, *On the Day of Birth* 4.7 = DK 12A30)

The origin of animals is explained similarly to the origin of the universe and meteorological events: more complex things arise out of simpler things, and new things come into existence after being enclosed tightly in something else and breaking out of the container.

The distinction we feel between living animals and inanimate matter (such as heated water) is inappropriately applied to Anaximander, whose originative material is in some sense alive (see p. 36), so that all its products, including earth and water, inherit its vital force. Animals and humans, with a greater concentration of vitality, differ in degree, not in kind, from the rest of the KOSMOS.

Particularly striking is Anaximander's recognition and solution of a problem arising from the helplessness of human infants. If the first humans came into this world as babies, they could not have lasted long enough to propagate the race. How, then, did they come into being? This "first generation problem" can be answered by positing a god who creates adult humans or by asserting that the world and the human race have always been in existence. However, both these solutions conflict with basic features of Anaximander's system. Accordingly, he takes an original and ingenious approach, having the first humans nurtured in other animals until self-sustaining.

For his claims that animals arose in the sea before they emerged to live on dry land and that humans developed from fish, and for recognizing the need for a different original form for humans and the difficulties of adapting to different habitats (perhaps implicit in the short lives of the animals who first moved onto dry land), Anaximander is sometimes called the father of evolution. This interpretation is wrong, however, since he says nothing about the evolution of species. His problem of how to account for the first generation of each kind of animal, to get each kind of animal established once and for all, is different from Darwin's. Moreover, he makes no mention of such Darwinian mechanisms as natural selection.

Anaximander's Fragment

How the World Works

Aside from a few words in the testimonia that have an early ring, all that survives of Anaximander's writings is one fragment which seems to have been quoted out of its correct context.

> **5.19** The things that are perish into the things out of which they come to be, according to necessity, for they pay penalty and retribution to each other for their injustice in accordance with the ordering of time, as he says in rather poetical language.
>
> (Simplicius, *Commentary on Aristotle's Physics* 24.18–21 = DK 12B1 + A9)

The last words of **5.19** show that some of the preceding is in Anaximander's own words, but the extent of the fragment is uncertain.[21] I find it likely that the words from "according to necessity" to the end are Anaximander's and that the preceding words paraphrase his thought. We have a picture of a world full of change—things coming to be and in turn being destroyed. These changes are ordered in two ways: (1) when a thing (*A*) is destroyed *A* turns into something definite—the same sort of thing that perished when *A* came to be; (2) each thing has a determinate time span. In addition, comings-to-be and destructions are acts of injustice that one thing (*A*) commits against another (*B*) and for which *A* is compelled to make restitution to *B*.

The process here described seems to have nothing to do with the APEIRON but can easily apply to the opposites hot and cold, which we have seen are important in the beginning of the world and which are also

21. For discussion, see C. Kahn, *Anaximander and the Origins of Greek Cosmology* (New York, 1960), pp. 168–178, 193–96; and KRS, p. 118, which summarizes G. Kirk, "Some Problems in Anaximander," *Classical Quarterly* 5 (1955):22–38; reprinted in *Studies in Presocratic Philosophy*, vol. 1, ed. D. Furley and R. Allen (London, 1960), pp. 323–49.

important in the present state of things. The alternation of the seasons is an obvious case in point. In the region of Miletus it is reasonable to say that hot prevails in summer, cold prevails in winter, and spring and fall mark an even balance between hot and cold. When summer comes, hot commits injustice by driving out cold and occupying some of its territory. In due time hot must pay a penalty in which cold is recompensed for this injustice first by a return to an even balance (in the fall) and then by a period in which cold drives out hot (winter). But now cold has committed injustice against hot, and so must make recompense in turn. Hence there occurs an endless cycle of regular alternation between states where first one and then the other opposite dominates.

Deployment of other pairs of opposites such as wet and dry, light and dark, rare and dense, either singly or in combination, can account for many features of the world. The change of the seasons is also marked by orderly alternation between wet and dry, and between light and dark (reflecting the longer period of daylight in summer). Day and night can be analyzed in terms of light and dark; a more detailed account will also bring in hot and cold. The alternation of rare and dense can perhaps be seen in successive periods of wind ("the finest vapors") and cloudy or stormy weather ("thick cloud"). There is also a broad contrast between the sun as hot, dry, light, rare, and at the edge of the universe, and the earth (together with the sea) which is cold, wet, dark, dense, and at the center. Moreover weather can be seen as the interplay of these two groups of opposites.

If the argument in 5.7 that the world is drying up implies that when it is completely dry it will stay that way forever or cease to exist, it cannot agree with the fragment. Anaximander should hold instead that corresponding to the present period of increasing dryness there have been and will again be periods of becoming wetter,[22] and he could have found mythological evidence that the world is inundated from time to time.[23]

This account of the fragment focuses on the opposites, which have special importance for Anaximander, but the fragment may be meant to describe other "things that are" as well, for example, animals and humans (along the general lines of "ashes to ashes and dust to dust"). However, Anaximander recognized that there are difficulties in extending it to some entities (see p. 42).

The fragment occupies an important place in the history of philosophy and science. It contains a general account that applies to a wide variety of

22. Xenophanes held a similar belief. See 7.17.

23. The myth of Deucalion's flood (in ways comparable to Noah's flood), which Aristotle accepted as based on fact (*Meteorologica* 1.14 352a32–35), is the most obvious source.

phenomena. It contains the germs of the ideas of the conservation of matter and of a dynamic equilibrium in which opposed principles alternately preponderate over one another in such regularly repeated cycles as we find, for example, in a swinging pendulum and in a spring with a weight attached to it moving indefinitely up and down. Although the prevalence of hot over cold or of cold over hot changes from time to time, the system has an overall stability that continues without external interference. The fragment also contains the beginning of the idea of a law of nature which holds inevitably ("according to necessity") and operates uniformly and impersonally.

A notable feature of the fragment is its legal language: "pay penalty and retribution," "injustice," and "the ordering of time" (as if time plays the role of a judge assessing penalties in criminal trials). The legal language may strike us as no more than a colorful metaphor, but that response reveals our distance from Anaximander. To assume that it is a metaphor presupposes a radical difference between the world of nature (where injustice and the like are not really found) and the world of humans (where they are): humankind is somehow distinct from nature, and the two realms operate according to different principles. This interpretation, though congenial to those who hold that social, moral, and evaluative language applies only in the human sphere, is inappropriate for Anaximander and other presocratics, who place humans squarely in the natural world. The injustice which hot commits on cold is the same kind as that which a robber commits on a victim—taking something which is by right not its own—and the penalty assessed by a judge according to the law is of the same sort as that assessed by time according to necessity—restoration of what was taken and payment of an additional amount as a fine. In Greek, DIKE ("justice") and its opposite have descriptive as well as evaluative force. Descriptively, injustice is taking something not one's own; evaluatively it is bad. This evaluation applies to all acts that, descriptively, are unjust, regardless of the nature of the agent. Further, the idea that justice or retribution comes inevitably accords with a view of justice expressed by other authors of the Archaic period,[24] and the notion that the cosmic principle of justice is fair to the rival contenders is doubtless due to the ideal of justice on which the legal system known to Anaximander was based.

All Greek philosophers assume that the world we perceive is a world of change and motion. Anaximander expresses this idea in describing the world as the scene of opposites in a continuous conflict, which is governed by necessity and justice. Although hot and cold are the only opposites the

24. For example, Hesiod, *Works and Days*, lines 213–73, 280–85, 320–34; Solon, frs. 1, 3; Theognis, lines 197–208.

sources mention, the fragment equally well accounts for the interaction of others. As other pairs of opposites are prominent in Pythagoras and Heraclitus,[25] it would be excessively cautious to hold that Anaximander had only the one pair in mind.

We tend to think of opposites like hot and cold as qualities which belong to substances. There is something that is hot or cold—food, for example. Since "hot" sounds odd as a grammatical subject or object, let alone as an agent, we feel that the assertion "hot commits injustice against cold" requires explanation. In thinking this way, we are unconsciously following Aristotle, who was the first to distinguish clearly between qualities and substances and to say that (except in special contexts) substances are the only proper subjects of discourse. As he points out,[26] one quality can be opposite to another quality, but substances do not have opposites. Hot is the opposite of cold, but fire is not the opposite of water. Calling them opposites is just shorthand for saying that they have opposite qualities. Again, to apply this analysis to Anaximander would distort his thought. Before Aristotle, hot food might have been conceived in various ways. For example, the hot might have been thought a part of the food, or something in the food.[27] Since fire is preeminently hot, it might have been thought to have a special relation to the hot. Anaximander may simply have identified fire as the hot and (in the early stage of his cosmogony) identified dark mist as the cold, or he may not have spoken of the hot and the cold at all, only of their concrete embodiments fire and mist. Similarly, he may have conceived of the war between opposites not primarily in terms of qualities, but in terms of their manifestations: summer and winter, day and night, drought and flood, etc.

Finally, the fragment apparently describes the world around us as a stable, ongoing system that maintains itself without any limit in time. Summer and winter, it suggests, will alternate forever. The APEIRON may have acted only once, at the beginning of the world; once generated, the world went on without further dependence on it. Alternatively, the APEIRON may play an ongoing role in the world, if the governing or "steering" function 5.5 refers to is correctly assigned to it. In that case, there will be some link between the APEIRON and the necessity mentioned in the fragment. In any case, Anaximander focuses on the world around him. He describes its

25. See **9.35** and **10.48, 10.49, 10.53–10.73**.

26. Aristotle, *Categories* 5 3b24–25, 8 10b12–15.

27. Plato develops these ideas in connection with his theory of Ideas (*Phaedo* 96–107). They form an important part of the background of his treatment of the differences between statements like "the food is hot" and those like "the food is [identical with the] hot" (*Sophist* 250–57).

origin (perhaps because Thales had given such an account, or because Hesiod had done so, or because of a more widespread Greek concern with origins and parentage) but not its destruction. Rather, on the present interpretation, the fragment suggests that the world will never be destroyed.

This interpretation of the fragment leaves some problems. A created but indestructible KOSMOS requires a sharp distinction between the one-time cosmogonic process and the ever-repeating processes of the developed world, a distinction which sits uneasily with the uniformities Anaximander posits between these two stages of the history of the universe. It thus requires a conspicuous exception to the symmetry which is so prominent in his accounts of cosmic phenomena. It also requires that the fragment's account of "things that are" fail to apply to such notable things as the earth, sun, and other members of the KOSMOS that form the setting in which the regular changes take place.

Some of these problems can be solved by interpreting the fragment to cover the origin and destruction of the world as well as of things in the world, but at the price of abandoning the long-term stability the fragment favors and of leaving it unclear why the world will be destroyed. This dissatisfying situation may be due to gaps in the source material or to Anaximander himself, who probably did not ask the same questions modern interpreters do and whose demands for coherence and standards of what counts as a satisfactory account were surely different from ours.

6

Anaximenes of Miletus

Anaximenes was called Anaximander's pupil and associate. That and the fact that he was from Miletus are practically all that we know about his life. Even his date is uncertain, though he was probably somewhat younger than Anaximander. Aristotle and the doxographical tradition speak of his theory that air is the basic substance and provide some details of his cosmology, but that is about all. Anaximenes was perhaps less bold a thinker than his teacher, but it was to his theory rather than Anaximander's that later presocratics looked back for the details of their views on astronomy and meteorology.

Air, the Material Principle

6.1 Anaximenes . . . like Anaximander, declares that the underlying nature is one and APEIRON, but not indeterminate as Anaximander held, but definite, saying that it is air. It differs in rarity and density according to the substances <it becomes>. Becoming finer it comes to be fire; being condensed it comes to be wind, then cloud, and when still further condensed it becomes water, then earth, then stones, and the rest come to be out of these. He too makes motion eternal and says that change also comes to be through it.

(Theophrastus, quoted by Simplicius,
Commentary on Aristotle's Physics 24.26–25.1 = DK 13A5)

6.2 Anaximenes . . . said that the principle is unlimited [APEIRON] air, out of which come to be things that are coming to be, things that have come to be, and things that will be, and gods and divine things. The rest come to be out of the products of this. The form of air is the following: when it is most even, it is invisible, but it is revealed by the cold and the hot and the wet, and movement. It is always moving, for all the things that undergo change would not change unless it was moving. For when it becomes condensed and finer, it appears different. For when it is dissolved into what is finer, it comes to be fire, and on the other hand air comes to be winds when it becomes condensed. Cloud results from air through felting,[1] and water when this happens to a greater degree. When condensed

---

1. Felting is "the production of nonwoven fabric by the application of heat, moisture and mechanical action, causing the interlocking or matting of fibres" (*Encyclopaedia Britannica*, 15th ed., s.v. felting). The term here is extended to describe another process in which the product is denser than, and so has different properties from, the ingredients.

still more it becomes earth and when it reaches the absolutely densest
stage it becomes stones.   (Hippolytus, *Refutation* 1.7.1–3 = DK 13A7)

By making the originative material a definite kind of substance, Anaximenes seems at first sight to take a step backward. Anaximander accounted
for opposites by positing a neutral principle with no definite properties of
its own. If this was Anaximander's response to the objection to Thales'
theory, "if all things are (or originated from) water, why isn't everything
wet?," Anaximenes' theory seems open to a similar objection: if everything
is made of air, why doesn't everything have the specific characteristics of
air? How can he account for the diversity in the world on the basis of a
single originative principle of a definite kind?

Anaximenes could reply by pointing out weaknesses in Anaximander's
theory. Theories, he might say, should be based on principles that are
familiar, understandable, known to exist, and found in the world around us,
but there is no evidence that the APEIRON exists, only Anaximander's reasoning. It is unfamiliar and alien to our experience, barely describable or
comprehensible; it is not found in our KOSMOS. Air is a better principle
than the APEIRON in these respects. In fact, there can be no objection to
theories based on a single principle of a definite kind as long as they
generate the wide variety of things found in the KOSMOS in an acceptable
way. Further, Anaximander's account of the generation of the KOSMOS is
itself crucially flawed in precisely this way, since it depends on something
whose origin from the APEIRON is left obscure.[2]

Whether or not Anaximenes actually criticized Anaximander this way, he
accounts for the origin of this world's diversity out of a single substance,
air. Air can take on different appearances, and when conditions are right it
even becomes different types of substances. When suitably rarefied it becomes fire and when suitably condensed it becomes wind, earth, etc. This
idea may have come from reflection on the freezing of water and the
melting of ice, events in which apparently different materials are seen to be
forms of the same thing. In this way the question "Why doesn't everything
have the properties of air?" receives a straightforward answer: everything
does have the properties of air; its properties include being fire (in certain
conditions), being water (in other conditions), etc. Also, the processes by
which air takes on these properties are comprehensible. Rarefaction and
condensation simply mean that there is more or less air in a given region—
notions more familiar than Anaximander's obscure processes.

Several details of Anaximenes' theory require closer examination. "Air"
translates the Greek word AER, which in earlier writers, including Anaxi-

---

2. See p. 37, on "that which is productive of hot and cold."

mander,[3] means dark mist. The bright, clear part of the atmosphere, as distinct from the misty lower part, was called AITHER. **6.2** shows that for Anaximenes AER is much closer to our notion of air, close enough to justify translating it by its English derivative. In its most "even" state, air lacks any perceptible properties. Since we cannot perceive it, we must infer its existence, but the inference is not difficult. Anaximenes associates breath and air, and he knows that our breath (which is like a feeble wind) can be hot or cold, properties that "reveal" air. If what we breathe out is the same as what we breathe in, what we inhale is air even if it is imperceptible, as on a dry, windless day of the appropriate temperature.

Like Anaximander's APEIRON, Anaximenes' air is (or can be) imperceptible. But the fact that air has an imperceptible state is not crucial. From one point of view, there is so far no reason for making air the principle. Ice is a form of water, but equally water is a form of ice; water is condensed air, and air is rarefied water. From this point of view any (or all) of the "phases" of air can serve as the basic substance. Anaximenes had other reasons for making air primary.

Anaximenes accounts for Anaximander's principal opposites, hot and cold, in terms of the most important pair of opposites in his own system, rare and dense.

> **6.3** Or as Anaximenes of old believed, let us leave neither the cold nor the hot in the category of substance, but <hold them to be> common attributes of matter which come as the results of its changes. For he declares that matter which is contracted and condensed is cold, whereas what is fine and "loose" (calling it this way with this very word) is hot. As a result he claimed that it is not said unreasonably that a person releases both hot and cold from his mouth. For the breath becomes cold when compressed and condensed by the lips, and when the mouth is relaxed, the escaping breath becomes warm through the rareness.
>
> (Plutarch, *The Principle of Cold* 7 947F = DK 13B1)

This passage is important in many ways. First, it shows how Anaximenes related two pairs of opposites that appear unrelated. Because breath is rare, it is warm; because it is dense, it is cold. Thus, hot and cold depend on, in some sense are functions of, can be explained in terms of, or reduced to rare and dense. In this way Anaximenes advances our understanding of the world by reducing the range of independent phenomena through increasing the number of intelligibly connected features. The world becomes more intelligible as the range of related phenomena is increased.

---

3. The word occurs in **5.8**, **5.11**, and **5.17**, where it is translated "dark mist."

Second, rarity and density are quantitative notions: more or less of the same stuff in the same place. Hot and cold, qualitative notions, are accounted for in terms of quantitative notions. Anaximenes thus frequently receives credit for being the ancestor of a basic attitude of science, the desire to express concepts quantitatively.[4] However, there is no reason to think that he conceived of analyzing rarity and density in numerical terms (e.g., that a cubic meter of air if condensed to half a cubic meter becomes water, and if condensed to one-tenth a cubic meter becomes stone), much less that he had a notion of mass that would enable him to "weigh" fire, wind, and cloud, and so compare the amount of air in them to the amount in water or stone. Moreover, though "more" and "less" are quantitative concepts, it is not clear that Anaximenes understood rare and dense in that way. For us, rarity and density depend on how much of something there is in a given volume, but the idea of "a given volume" is rather sophisticated, and dense and rare themselves can be thought of as qualities just as well as hot and cold can. Anaximenes had the idea of analyzing one feature in terms of another, but it is anachronistic to see him as the originator of the belief that science is essentially quantitative.

Third, **6.3** reports the first piece of reasoning preserved from Greek philosophy and enables us to form an impression of Anaximenes' way of thinking. The account of the relation between hot and rare and between cold and dense is based on familiar phenomena easily observable by anyone who follows Anaximenes' directions. Anaximenes derives his theory from the evidence by describing the observed phenomena and generalizing on the basis of that description. He notes that the breath feels cold when blown through pursed lips, describes the situation as air feeling cold when condensed, and states the general claim that matter which is condensed is cold and, apparently, that condensation makes it cold, not vice versa.

It is going too far to say that Anaximenes conducted a scientific experiment, but he did base the account on repeatable observational evidence. On the other hand, the observation admits of other explanations, as the following criticism points out.

> **6.4** A person who blows out air does not move the air all at once, but blows through a narrow opening of the lips, and so he breathes out just a little air but moves much of the air outside his body, in which the warmth from his body is not apparent because of its small amount.
>
> (pseudo-Aristotle, *Problems* 34.7 964a13–16, not in DK)

---

4. See pp. 92, 115 for further discussion of this point with reference to the Pythagoreans.

Nor does Anaximenes explain how to deal with obvious counterexamples to his theory. Wind, which, as slightly condensed air, should be cool, can be hot. Mist can be cool or hot (fog or steam). Rocks, which should be the coldest things, can be hot. (This is not to say that such cases would defeat him. For example, he might say that rocks are very cold when they are being formed, though afterwards they can become warm.) It is noteworthy too that Anaximenes' conclusion is exactly wrong, although a theory's mere rightness or wrongness is no appropriate gauge of whether it is reached scientifically. In general, putting a substance under pressure makes it hotter, not colder, as Boyle's law asserts for gases and as also happens for most liquids and solids.

Other substances are products of the rarefaction and condensation of air. What status do rarefaction and condensation have? Are they causal principles of motion and change, so that Anaximenes' system in fact has three principles? Apparently not. Aristotle, who was interested in this question, asserts that Empedocles was the first to distinguish principles of change,[5] and that Anaximenes had only a material principle.[6] Condensation and rarefaction, then, describe what happens to air: fire is air in a state of rarefaction, water is condensed air.[7]

The following passage, which describes some of air's properties, suggests how air becomes rarefied and condensed.

> **6.5** Anaximenes determined that air is a god and that it comes to be and is without measure, infinite and always in motion.
> (Cicero, *On the Nature of the Gods* 1.10.26 = DK 13A10)

This passage is written in Latin, but "without measure" perhaps and "infinite" certainly represent APEIRON, which **6.1** and **6.2** use to describe air. The assertion that "it comes to be" may mean that Anaximenes explicitly said that gods come to be out of air, or simply that air comes to be—say, when water is rarefied. Here the key attribute of air is its unceasing motion. This need mean only that as a whole or in general air is characterized by motion, not that every bit of air is always in motion. When air moves enough to be noticed, it is a breeze, which is already a condensed form of

5. Aristotle, *Metaphysics* 1.4 985a29–31 (= DK 31A37).

6. Aristotle, *Metaphysics* 1.3 984a5–6 (= DK 13A4), cf. 983b6–8 (= DK 11A12).

7. Evidence against this interpretation can be found at Aristotle, *Physics* 1.6 189b12–14, (not in DK), which may identify Anaximenes' "dense" and "rare" as active principles that affect passive air. I give this passage little weight since it ignores air's own active nature in Anaximenes.

air. Thus, it seems that air by its own mobile nature is condensed in some places and rarefied in others, and so other substances come into being.

What are these substances? The sources agree that air becomes fire when rarefied, and when condensed more and more it becomes in turn wind, cloud, water, earth, and stones. Although this list includes fire, air, water, and earth, the appearance of other substances shows that these four were not yet canonical.[8] After giving this list, **6.1** notes briefly "the rest come to be from these." This statement corresponds to **6.2**'s assertion "the rest come to be out of the products of this." Anaximenes must have said something about the origin of other substances than the ones so far mentioned. How detailed a treatment did he provide?

At one extreme, he could have given an extended treatment of how different substances arise from the sorts of matter identified. At the other extreme, he may have said no more than the sources. Either reading supports two significantly different theories: (a) a two-tier system, with fire, air, etc., serving equally as ingredients of other substances, and (b) a three-tier system, with fire, wind, etc., being formed out of air, and other things being formed of these (fire, wind, etc.) but not of air. In (b) air corresponds roughly to protons, neutrons, and electrons in classical chemistry; fire, water, etc., correspond to elements such as hydrogen and oxygen; and other substances like wood correspond to compounds such as water and carbon dioxide. On interpretation (a), air is an "element" alongside fire, etc., and nothing corresponds to the subatomic level.

Can we decide between the possibilities? **6.2** more clearly points to the three-tier system than **6.1** does, but **6.1**, which is neutral between the two interpretations, probably stays closer to the original Theophrastean account. Thus, as far as the sources go, either interpretation is possible. However, the following considerations tip the balance in favor of the two-tier view. Not only are fire, etc., formed of air, but air can come to be out of the others, as is implied in **6.5**'s statement that air comes to be. But the process of air coming to be out of water, as when, for example, mist rises from the sea and eventually becomes so thinned out as to be invisible air, seems more like a phase-change (water to ice) than like a dissolution of something into its constituent parts (water being broken up into hydrogen and oxygen). Also, air seems to be a constituent of the world on the same level as fire, wind, etc., and equally able to join in forming compounds.

The question remains whether Anaximenes offered a detailed account of how compounds are formed. The absence of information on the matter

---

8. Empedocles was the first to make these four his elements; they are prominent also in Plato and Aristotle.

favors a negative reply. If he had gone much further than the vague statements preserved in **6.1** and **6.2**, Aristotle and Theophrastus, who had
interests in these issues, would surely have said so.

The only surviving sentence of Anaximenes' works[9] describes another
role of air.

> **6.6** Just as our soul, being air, holds us together and controls[10] us, so do
> breath and air surround the whole KOSMOS.   (Anaximenes, DK 13B2)

6.6 identifies the soul with air, following a well-attested prephilosophical
view that the air we breathe is our soul or vital principle, that which
distinguishes the living from the nonliving and from the dead. When we
stop breathing not only do we die, but also our body decomposes. Thus, the
air which is our soul maintains us in existence, it "holds us together." It
also "controls us," though just what it controls and how it exercises control
are unclear.

Anaximenes continues Anaximander's tendency to see humans as part of
the KOSMOS, subject to the same principles as the rest of nature. In comparing humans and the universe, **6.6** contains the first explicit use of the
microcosm-macrocosm analogy, the view that humans and the universe are
constructed or function similarly,[11] which would be developed further by
later presocratics. The exact point of the comparison is unclear, since
"surrounding" is different from "holding together" and "controlling," but
it asserts that in some sense air functions similarly in the universe as it does
in humans. It follows that we can use what we know about humans to
understand the universe and vice versa. The function of air in the universe
is, then, to hold it together, surrounding it, pervading it, and keeping
everything in its right place. To take the simile further, air controls the
KOSMOS, presumably by regulating astronomical and meteorological events
and perhaps other events too, through its controlling motions. Moreover,
because air plays the same role in the universe as it does in humans, and it
makes humans alive, it seems to follow that the universe is alive. This
interpretation finds support in the Milesian tendency already found in
Thales and Anaximander to imbue all things with life force. Air gives life to
its offspring, including the entire KOSMOS. In any case, since the animating

---

9. The authenticity of this fragment is disputed, but even if some of the words it
contains were not in the original, it is at least a close paraphrase.

10. I follow KRS (p. 159 n.) in translating SUNKRATEIN as "hold together and
control." If this is an overtranslation and the Greek means only "hold together,"
then my following remarks must be weakened accordingly.

11. "Microcosm" derives from the Greek MIKROS, "small" + KOSMOS.

substance is now the primary material substance, Anaximenes incorporates the "breath soul" into the scientific tradition while using this traditional belief as a prop for his own theory and perhaps as a reason for choosing air as the basic type of matter.

The Gods

Although **6.5** may imply only that air has divine attributes, **6.2** reports that gods come into being from air[12]—which may reflect an attempt to link physical theory with Olympian religion. Air is the substance out of which all other things are ultimately made, therefore gods arise out of air. Not only do the gods have a beginning, they are subordinate to Anaximenes' physical theory. This view accords with evidence that he held that the rainbow (traditionally the Olympian goddess Iris) is caused by the sun's rays striking a dense, black cloud.[13] It becomes explicit that Anaximenes believes the gods and goddesses of myth have nothing to do with the origin or maintenance of the universe. Air does that. Any divinities there are aside from divine air must have a vastly diminished role.

Cosmogony and Cosmology

6.7 When the air is felted the earth is the first thing to come into being, and it is very flat. This is why it rides on the air, as is reasonable.
(pseudo-Plutarch, *Stromata* 3 = DK 13A6)

6.8 Anaximenes, Anaxagoras and Democritus say that its flatness is the cause of its staying at rest. For it does not cut the air below, but covers it like a lid, as bodies with flatness apparently do, since these are difficult for winds to move because of their resistance. They say that the earth does this same thing with respect to the air beneath. And the air, lacking sufficient room to move aside, stays at rest in a mass because of the air beneath. (Aristotle, *On the Heaven* 2.13 294b13–20 = DK 13A20)

6.9 Likewise the sun and moon and all other heavenly bodies, which are fiery, are carried upon the air on account of their flatness.
(Hippolytus, *Refutation* 1.7.4 = DK 13A7)

Like Anaximander, Anaximenes tackles the problems of the origin of the earth and the reasons for its stability. The earth resulted from "felting"[14]

12. St. Augustine attributes this view to Anaximenes as well (*City of God* 8.2 = DK 13A10).
13. Aetius 3.5.10 and Scholia on Aratus p. 515,27 M (both = DK 13A18).
14. See p. 48, n. 1.

(the word is likely to be Anaximenes' own), an appropriate term to use in describing the thickening of air into earth. Again we find cosmic events explained in terms of familiar processes (this time a technological process) with no reference to the supernatural.

Anaximenes agrees with Anaximander that the earth is flat, but does not follow his predecessor's hypothesis that it stays motionless without support. The earth and the celestial bodies are supported by and "carried on" the air, an account evidently meant to explain why they do not fall, not why the one is at rest while the others move. The air's constant motion accounts for the movements of the celestial bodies; what needs explanation is the non-movement of the earth. Anaximenes proposes that the earth somehow sits atop the air beneath it and keeps it from moving out of the way to let the earth fall. It is difficult to make sense of this theory, since air surrounds the earth on all sides. Anaximenes may have been thinking of leaves, which fall more slowly than more compact objects because of their wind resistance—but they do fall, just because the air beneath them moves round them out of their way. He may also have had boats in mind, though the sources do not say so.

> **6.10** The stars came into being from the earth through moisture rising up out of it. When the moisture is rarefied fire comes to be and the stars are composed of fire that has risen aloft. There are also earthen bodies in the region of the stars carried around together with them.
>
> (Hippolytus, *Refutation* 1.7.5 = DK 13A7)
> (continuation of **6.9**)

The fiery stars did not come to be from the original air, but resulted from exhalation of moisture from the earth, perhaps as it was originally being condensed out of air. How earthen bodies could reach the starry vicinity is left unclear. The moist exhalation may have played a role. These bodies were presumably posited to account for meteorites, possibly also for eclipses.

> **6.11** He says that the stars do not move under the earth as others have supposed, but around it, as a felt cap turns round our head. The sun is hidden not because it is under the earth but because it is covered by the higher parts of the earth and on account of the greater distance it comes to be from us. Because of their distance the stars do not give heat.
>
> (Hippolytus, *Refutation* 1.7.6 = DK 13A7)
> (continuation of **6.10**)

> **6.12** Many of the ancient speculators on the heavens believed that the sun is not borne under the earth, but around the earth and in this region, and that it disappears and causes night because the earth is high towards the north [or, towards the pole star].
>
> (Aristotle, *Meteorologica* 2.1 354a28–33 = DK 13A14)

If Anaximenes envisaged the earth as supported on a sea of air, he might have thought that the heavenly bodies, especially the sun, could not pass under the earth without disturbing its serene poise. The felt cap analogy neatly solves this problem. To serve as a model for the region of sky from the north celestial pole to the sun's path through the stars, the felt cap will be a segment of a spherical shell whose diameter is large enough not to intersect the sea of air beneath the earth. The shell rotates on an axis extending from the north celestial pole through the earth. The sun does not move under the earth, but around it. The fixed stars move in circles round the celestial pole, all at the same speed, maintaining the same positions relative to one another. The cap is a handy model, because as it turns, the various points on its surface maintain constant relative positions. The north part of the earth is tilted towards the celestial pole, or rather the celestial pole is tilted towards the north part of the earth, and this is why the sun, moon, and some of the stars go beneath the horizon as they revolve about the pole. This tilt could be the source of calling the northern parts of the earth "higher."[15]

The KOSMOS will look something like the following diagram.[16]

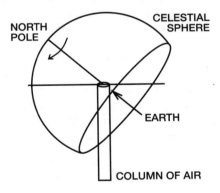

15. This model cannot account for all the visible stars, unless the spherical segment cuts through the column of air beneath the earth.

16. Miletus' latitude is 38° north; the sun's positions at the summer and winter solstices are 23½° north and south of the celestial equator, respectively.

The view that the stars give no warmth because of their great distance
(**6.11**) contradicts Anaximander's theory that the stars are closer to the
earth than the moon and sun are. It is also true.

Anaximenes held that the seasons are due to the sun,[17] and that the
moon is illuminated by the sun, and he gave the correct account of lunar
eclipses.[18] One source credits him instead of Anaximander for discovering
the use of the gnomon and placing the hour markers at Sparta.[19]

Anaximenes' accounts of meteorological phenomena emphasize the role
of air.

> **6.13** Anaximenes stated that clouds occur when the air is further thickened.
> When it is condensed still more, rain is squeezed out. Hail occurs when
> the falling water freezes, and snow when some wind is caught up in the
> moisture.   (Aetius 3.4.1 = DK 13A17)

He explains earthquakes differently from Thales.

> **6.14** Anaximenes declares that when the earth is being drenched and dried
> out it is broken, and earthquakes result from these hills breaking and
> collapsing. This is why earthquakes occur in droughts and also in heavy
> rains. For in the droughts, as was said, the earth is broken while being
> dried out, and when it becomes excessively wet from the waters, it falls
> apart.   (Aristotle, *Meteorologica* 2.7 365b6–12 = DK 13A21)

Though Anaximenes' cosmology differs from Anaximander's in important
details, the two men have much in common—an interest in natural phenomena and the goal of accounting for these phenomena in terms of the
intelligible behavior of natural substances. These features of their systems
are their legacy to the Greek philosophical and scientific tradition, and
were followed by the later Presocratics.

---

17. Aetius 2.19.1.2 (= DK 13A14).
18. Theon of Smyrna p. 198,14 (Hill) (= DK 13A16).
19. Pliny, *Natural History* 2.187 (= DK 13A14), cf. **5.1**.

7

Xenophanes of Colophon

Born in Colophon, not far from Miletus, Xenophanes was acquainted with Milesian thought to which he gave a distinctive expression. A poet with wide-ranging interests, he may not have written a systematic account of the universe like Anaximander and Anaximenes. Although he is younger than Pythagoras, his intellectual connections with Miletus make it best to treat him out of chronological order.

He says he was still composing verse at the age of ninety-two.

7.1 Already there are sixty-seven years
tossing my thought throughout the land of Greece.
From my birth there were twenty-five in addition to these,
if I know how to speak truly about these matters.
(Xenophanes, DK 21B8)

"Tossing about" may indicate that for all those years he had no fixed residence, possibly a result of the Persian conquest of Colophon, c. 546. This interpretation places his birth c. 570 and his death not before 478.[1]

The literary tradition[2] remembers him more for poetry which ridicules poets and philosophers (e.g., **9.1**) than for philosophy. Some forty fragments survive, over a hundred lines, though much of this material is not on philosophical subjects. There are special problems connected with the doxography of Xenophanes,[3] but despite these difficulties we can form some opinion of his ideas through his surviving verses.

1. These dates are compatible with other evidence—principally Xenophanes' references to others (Thales, Pythagoras, and Epimenides), a reference to him in Heraclitus, and later (not necessarily correct) reports that he was Anaximander's pupil and Parmenides' teacher, and that he composed an epic on the foundation of Elea (540 B.C.).

2. I refer to such nondoxographic sources as Strabo (DK 21A20), Apuleius (DK 21A21), Proclus' *Commentary on Hesiod* (DK 21A22), Scholia on Homer's *Iliad* (DK 21A23), and Athenaeus (DK 21A27).

3. Plato (*Sophist* 242d = DK 21A29) and Aristotle (*Metaphysics* 1.5 986b21–23 = DK 21A30) call Xenophanes an Eleatic and the teacher of Parmenides because Xenophanes' description of god superficially resembles the Eleatic account of what is. As Theophrastus (in Simplicius, *Commentary on Aristotle's Physics* 22.26–30 = DK 21A31), following Aristotle (*On the Heaven* 3.1 298b14–20 = DK 28A25), regards Xenophanes' doctrines as irrelevant to the study of nature and consequently says little about him, the normal doxographic sources are poor on

Attacks on Traditional Religion

The Milesians were unanimous in recognizing the divine nature of their primary substances, but accounted for the world in terms of natural processes. This approach to the universe has devastating implications for the Olympian religion. There is no room left for anthropomorphic gods governing natural phenomena and human destiny or for stories of strife among the gods that imply that the divine realm is itself not well ordered and so is incapable of regulating our world in an ordered, comprehensible manner. These conclusions are implicit in Milesian natural speculation, but were first drawn by Xenophanes, who lashes the Olympians with vigor and points the way to a rational theology. He mounts his attack on the traditional religion on five fronts.

First, the Olympian gods are immoral. They live a disorderly existence on a lower moral level even than humans.

7.2 Give us no fights with Titans, no, nor Giants
      nor Centaurs—the forgeries of our fathers—
      nor civil brawls, in which no advantage is.
      But always to be mindful of the gods is good.
              (Xenophanes, DK 21B1, lines 21–24)

7.3 Homer and Hesiod have ascribed to the gods all deeds
      which among men are a reproach and a disgrace:
      thieving, adultery, and deceiving one another.
                          (Xenophanes, DK 21B11)

Second, beliefs that gods physically resemble humans are questionable.

7.4 Mortals believe that the gods are born
      and have human clothing, voice and form.
              (Xenophanes, DK 21B14)

7.5 Ethiopians say that their gods are flat-nosed and dark,
      Thracians that theirs are blue-eyed and red-haired.
                          (Xenophanes, DK 21B16)

Xenophanes. *On Melissus, Xenophanes and Gorgias* offers a fabricated and erroneous account of Xenophanes' doctrines (chs. 3–4 = DK 21A28). Though written a few centuries after Aristotle, this treatise somehow found its way into the corpus of Aristotle's writings and, in turn, confused other sources, which use it to supplement the meager information in Theophrastus.

7.6 If oxen and horses and lions had hands
and were able to draw with their hands and do the same things
as men,
horses would draw the shapes of gods to look like horses
and oxen to look like oxen, and each would make the
gods' bodies have the same shape as they themselves had.

(Xenophanes, DK 21B15)

7.5, which may represent extremes among human conceptions of the gods (Thrace being the northernmost region well known to the Greeks and Ethiopia the southernmost), is an early instance of Greek curiosity about other peoples, which is a delightful part of Herodotus' *Histories* and an important ingredient of the fifth-century NOMOS-PHYSIS debate.[4] More relevant to our purposes is the argument that **7.5** implies: we Greeks think the gods have the appearance of Greeks, yet all other peoples portray the gods as having the distinctive characteristics of themselves;[5] but a god cannot simultaneously have the characteristics of all human peoples, and there is no reason to prefer one anthropomorphic account to another. More radically, by like reasoning **7.6** challenges the very conception of anthropomorphic gods. In this case too, the belief stems from humans projecting their own nature onto the divine.

Xenophanes rejects religious tradition in favor of rational considerations. Greek, "barbarian," and hypothetical bovine views of the gods are put on an even footing and cancel each other out, leaving no grounds to prefer one over the others. This brings them all equally into question.

Third, gods are not born and do not die. This criticism, implicit in **7.4**, is made explicit in the following passage.

7.7 Xenophanes used to say that those who say that the gods are born are just as impious as those who say that they die, since in both ways it follows that there is a time when the gods do not exist.

(Aristotle, *Rhetoric* 2.23 1399b6–9 = DK 21A12)

It was impious to deny the Olympians' immortality (although some pre-Olympian survivals, such as the cult of Zeus' grave in Crete, did so). Xenophanes maintains that the divine is eternal, not just immortal, and so declares accounts of the births of the gods, including Hesiod's *Theogony*, equally impious.

Fourth, there is no divine hierarchy.

4. See chap. 19.

5. This claim overlooks the God of the Hebrews and also the theriomorphic gods of the Egyptians, who were known to the Greeks of Xenophanes' time.

7.8 It is unholy for any of the gods to have a master.
                                        (pseudo-Plutarch, *Stromata* 4 = DK 21A32.)

Zeus' preeminent rank among the gods here falls under attack. Though elsewhere Zeus' rule is a basis of order among the potentially unruly Olympians and in the world, Xenophanes finds it intolerable for anything divine to be constrained. Fifth, the gods do not meddle in human affairs.

7.9 He always remains in the same place, moving not at all,
        nor is it fitting for him to go to different places at different times.
                                        (Xenophanes, DK 21B26)

7.9 contrasts strongly with Homer's gods, who move from Olympus to their sanctuaries to the battlefield of Troy, their minds often on human events in which they actively participate.

Positive Theology

Like the Milesians, Xenophanes does not question the presence of the divine in the universe, only the way it was conceived. His attacks imply that god is not immoral or responsible for evil, is not anthropomorphic, is eternal, self-sufficient, independent and master of everything, and unmoving.
    God is described in a number of fragments as well as **7.9**.

7.10 God is one, greatest among gods and men,
         not at all like mortals in body or thought.
                                        (Xenophanes, DK 21B23)

7.11 All of him sees, all of him thinks, all of him hears.
                                        (Xenophanes, DK 21B24)

7.12 But without effort he shakes all things by the thought of his mind
         [or, by the active will proceeding from his insight[6]].
                                        (Xenophanes, DK 21B25)

Abandoning religious tradition as a source of truth about god, Xenophanes turns to reason, appealing to the rational criterion of "what is fitting" to determine god's nature and attitudes. In keeping with the Milesian conception of the divine, god is deanthropomorphized and impersonal, but not isolated from the universe, of which he[7] is fully aware (though not through

6. This interpretive translation is due to K. von Fritz, "NOUS, NOEIN and their derivatives in Presocratic Philosophy," *Classical Philology* 40 (1945):233–42, and given in KRS, p. 170. "Thought" and "active will" translate PHREN. The PHREN is an internal body part, perhaps the diaphragm, which was sometimes considered the location of the thinking processes.

7. In describing god, Xenophanes uses masculine forms of adjectives.

human sense organs) and over which he exercises control ("shakes all things"), though not by physical might, but effortlessly and through his thought, without having to move from place to place. God is eternal. Most important, and contrary to earlier Greek views, Xenophanes is a monotheist, as **7.10** emphatically proclaims.[8]

It is natural for us to think that Xenophanes' god must be immaterial, but the fragments do not say so much. "Not at all like mortals in body or thought" (**7.10**) does not imply that he has no body any more than it implies that he does not think—and he does think (**7.11**). He has no limbs or special sense organs, but this, too, does not prove that he has no body. As we shall see, the fifth-century atomists were the first presocratics clearly to conceive of an immaterial, noncorporeal existing thing, and this idea came only with difficulty.

Like Anaximenes' air, Xenophanes' god controls the world; is he identical with the whole universe, then, or with one of its major components, as is the case for the divine entities of the Milesians? An argument against these views would go like this. The world is full of motion, but Xenophanes' god does not move (**7.9**); therefore, he is not part of the world. A counterargument would go as follows. Xenophanes' god always remains in the same place (**7.9**); therefore, he occupies some place, so that he has a location in the world. Moreover, if without moving he causes all things to move, he must be present everywhere. The conclusions of these arguments need not contradict one another. They point to a conception of god as a divinity that permeates the world and causes change in it but is distinct from the things it affects. This picture requires a distinction between god and the world such that the former is an active principle and the latter is passive, and it calls for an account of how the one can act on the other and how the other can be affected by it. That Xenophanes failed to address these questions is suggested by the silence of the sources and confirmed by the remark (**7.13**) that he "made nothing clear," which Aristotle makes with this sort of issue in mind.[9]

8. In **7.10** the phrase "among gods and men" is a "polar" expression, which emphasizes a point by mentioning extreme cases, "polar opposites." Since "among gods" contradicts Xenophanes' monotheistic message, either the expression had wholly lost its original associations (cf. "navy blue") or else Xenophanes mischievously employs it to describe his unique god. It follows from Xenophanes' fourth objection to the traditional religion that no god is greater than others.

9. There are other interpretations of Xenophanes' theology, notably that of Guthrie (*HGP*, vol. 1, pp. 376–83), who believes Xenophanes' god is spherical and identical with the KOSMOS. Guthrie relies heavily on **7.13**, the dramatic concluding words of which, however, could equally well have come from a person whom the sight of the heaven inspired to believe not that the heaven is divine, but that it is

Though there are gaps, Xenophanes' view of the relation between god and the world amounts to the following. The world for all its diversity and change possesses an underlying unity. All its movements are controlled by the unitary divinity that pervades it. Moreover, god controls things through thought, more precisely "through the active will proceeding from his insight": his complete awareness of the world (implied in 7.11) gives him insight or complete understanding, and on the basis of this understanding he wills things to happen. More explicitly than in the Milesians, intelligence, not the whims of the Olympians, governs the world. This is perhaps the most important feature of Xenophanes' theology.

Physical Ideas

Unlike his predecessors, Xenophanes did not have a cosmogony. Aristotle implies that he held that the world is ungenerated and therefore eternal.[10]

> 7.13 Some declared the universe to be a single substance . . . not supposing that what is is one, like some of the natural philosophers, and generating <the universe> out of the one as out of matter, but speaking differently. For the others add change, since they generate the universe, but these people say it is unchangeable. . . . Xenophanes, who was the first of these to preach monism . . . made nothing clear . . . but looking off to the whole heaven he declares that the one is god.
> (Aristotle, *Metaphysics* 1.5 986b10–25, part in DK 21A30)

Positing an eternal KOSMOS brings advantages. Xenophanes needs to account for only how the world functions, not how it arose, and does not need to distinguish and account for differences between the cosmogonic process and the processes that maintain the world order. His task in describing the world is reduced to discussing its present composition and operation.

---

moved by god. Also, it is a difficulty for this view that Xenophanes' god causes motion in the world (7.12). First, if god is motionless (7.9), he cannot be identical with a world containing motion. (Even if the world as a whole does not move, still, parts of it do, and there are obvious problems in holding that parts of god move.) Second, since Xenophanes holds that there is motion in the world, Aristotle is wrong to associate him with the Eleatics who deny that motion exists. I therefore dismiss 7.13, along with other testimonia Guthrie cites, on the grounds that they incorrectly represent Xenophanes as a proto-Eleatic.

10. The principle is widespread in early Greek philosophy that things not subject to generation are not subject to destruction either.

Xenophanes was interested in the same issues as the Milesians: the basic materials, astronomical and meteorological phenomena, and the origin of life. His conscious demythologizing is evident in his accounts of several natural phenomena, among them the rainbow:

7.14 She whom they call Iris, this thing too is cloud,
purple and red and yellow to behold.
(Xenophanes, DK 21B32)

7.15 Xenophanes says that the things on boats which shine like stars,
which some call the Dioscuri,[11]
are little clouds which shine as a result of the motion.
(Aetius 2.18.1 = DK 21A39)

The basic substances are two in number.

7.16 All things that come into being and grow are earth and water
(Xenophanes, DK 21B29)

The following fragment demotes Anaximenes' air (in the form of wind) from its primary place.

7.17 Sea is the source of water and the source of wind.
For not without the great ocean would there come to be
in clouds the force of wind blowing out from within,
nor the streams of rivers nor the rain water of the upper sky,
but great ocean is the sire of clouds and winds and rivers.
(Xenophanes, DK 21B30)

The main opposition is not between hot and cold as in Anaximander or dense and rare as in Anaximenes, but between wet and dry, in the form of water and earth.

7.18 Xenophanes declared that the sea is salty because many mixtures flow together in it. . . . He believes that earth is being mixed into the sea and over time it is being dissolved by the moisture, saying that he has the following kinds of proofs, that sea shells are found in the middle of the earth and in mountains, and the impression of a fish and seals have been found at Syracuse in the quarries, and the impression of a laurel leaf in the depth of the stone in Paros, and on Malta flat shapes of all marine

11. Literally, "sons of Zeus," the term was used to refer to Castor and Polydeuces (Pollux).

life. He says that these things occurred when all things were covered with mud long ago and the impressions were dried in the mud. All humans are destroyed when the earth is carried down into the sea and becomes mud, and then there is another beginning of coming to be, and this change occurs in all the world orders.

(Hippolytus, *Refutation* 1.14.5–6 = DK 21A33)

The importance of this passage lies more in its reasoning and use of evidence than in the doctrine it records. Particularly impressive is Xenophanes' marshalling of facts to support his thesis, which indicates a belief that the best way to prove a theory is to provide the greatest amount and widest variety of evidence possible. Thus, Xenophanes does not simply say that the world used to be drier; he assembles evidence that it was once even wetter than now. From this evidence for a period of increasing dryness followed by one of increasing wetness, he concludes not that the history of the world consists of only one swing from wet to dry and back to wet, but apparently that there is periodic alternation between states of extreme dry and extreme wet, with human life being extinguished in each period of extreme wet and then regenerated as the world dries out.[12] This implies that he believes in a principle of causation according to which, in some sense, similar conditions lead to similar results. Moreover, he may have had the rudiments of a cyclical view of history in which similar events are periodically repeated.[13]

Human Knowledge

As the first presocratic to reflect on the frailty of our ability to gain knowledge, Xenophanes is the father of epistemology. He was also hailed in antiquity as the father of scepticism for the following fragment.

7.19 No man has seen nor will anyone know
the truth about the gods and all the things I speak of.

12. That Anaximander believed in alternating periods of extreme wet and extreme dry (p. 44) is an inference from his statement that the earth is drying up and his general belief in alternating periods of the dominance of opposite qualities. Some interpreters have held that Anaximander thinks the world is drying up once and for all, and when it becomes completely dry it will be reabsorbed into the APEIRON. If they are correct, then Xenophanes was the first to say that there is alternation between the extreme states. In fact, he does not say this much, but it is highly likely that he believed it.
13. This notion would be developed more fully by Empedocles.

> For even if a person should in fact say what is absolutely
>   the case,
> nevertheless he himself does not know, but belief is fashioned
>   over all things [or, in the case of all persons].
>   (Xenophanes, DK 21B34)

Xenophanes assumes that only what is true or is the case can be known, but he claims that truth does not guarantee knowledge. Far from it. He contrasts knowledge and belief, or opinion, and maintains that true opinion falls short of knowledge. Simply saying something true (and presumably believing it) is no guarantee that you know it. Thus, he distinguishes between (1) *P* is true, (2) *A* truly believes that *P*, and (3) *A* knows that *P*.

According to **7.19**, beliefs can be had on all subjects (or can be had by all people, or can be manufactured by each person for him- or herself), but on some subjects humans cannot attain knowledge. Perhaps (in view of his own use of evidence[14]) the point is that on these subjects we cannot amass enough evidence to guarantee us knowledge as opposed to mere belief.

7.19 does not present Xenophanes as a thoroughgoing sceptic, but it places his confident assertions and clever reasoning in a different light. If knowledge is unattainable on subjects Xenophanes studies, he cannot claim to have proved his own views, only to have shown them to be likely. This interpretation accords with a short fragment which has been taken to be the conclusion of his philosophical book.

7.20 Let these things be believed as resembling the truth.
                                     (Xenophanes, DK 21B35)

Further, although his theory about god and Olympian religion counts as opinion, not knowledge, still there is a reason why his theory, which is the product of rational inquiry, is superior to the traditional view which is accepted without reflection.

7.21 By no means did the gods reveal all things to mortals from
  the beginning,
    but in time, by searching, they discover better.
                                     (Xenophanes, DK 21B18)

7.21 unsurprisingly rejects divine revelation as a source of knowledge. That is not the sort of thing Xenophanes' god (note the plural in the fragment[15])

---

14. See p. 65–66.
15. The point of **7.21** l. 1 is that knowledge does not come from divine revelation, not that there are gods that reveal things to mortals.

does. Diligent research as pursued by Xenophanes and the Milesians leads to better discoveries. The best—that is, full knowledge—has been ruled out by **7.19**, so in the context, "discover better" means doing a better job than belief in divine revelation can, and, in fact, the best job possible under our limited circumstances.

Finally, a fragment, perhaps related to Xenophanes' views on the frailty of human knowledge, introduces the notion of the relative nature of judgments which Heraclitus would take up.[16]

> **7.22** If god had not created yellow honey,
>   they would say that figs are far sweeter.
>   (Xenophanes, DK 21B38)

Conclusion

Xenophanes' interests are wider than those of his Milesian predecessors. His physical speculations place him in the Milesian tradition. His views on the divine and his remarks relating to the nature and limitations of human knowledge and how to attain it contain important ideas which grew to maturity in the following generations. Together with his contemporary, Heraclitus, Xenophanes introduces concerns about method and the theoretical limits of human knowledge, which altered the course of presocratic thought from speculating about nature to theorizing about the basis for such speculation. In this change of direction we have, in an important sense, the birth of Western philosophy.

16. See p. 135–36.

8

The Early Ionian Achievement

We are now in a position to assess the difference between the thought of the early Ionians (I shall use this label for Thales, Anaximander, Anaximenes, and Xenophanes) and what went before, and to identify some features of the new way of thought.[1]

In the opening chapters of the *Metaphysics*, Aristotle says,

> 8.1 That it [wisdom] is not concerned with making things is . . . clear from the examples of the earliest philosophers. People both now start and in the beginning started to do philosophy because of wonder. At first they wondered about the obvious difficulties and then they gradually progressed to puzzle about the greater ones, for example, the behavior of the moon and sun and stars and the coming to be of the universe. Whoever is puzzled and in a state of wonder believes he is ignorant (this is why the lover of myths is also in a way a philosopher, since myths are made up of wonders). And so, if indeed they pursued philosophy to escape ignorance, they were obviously pursuing scientific knowledge in order to know and not for the sake of any practical need.
>
> (Aristotle, *Metaphysics* 1.2 982b12–21, not in DK)

Aristotle stresses philosophy's impractical nature and hints at the difference between philosophy and myth. A little later he identifies Thales as the founder of the philosophical tradition and marks him off from those like Homer who were "terribly ancient, long before our own times . . . [the] first to speculate about the gods."[2]

In considering Hesiod we saw that even that early "speculator about the

---

1. Several treatments of this and related topics are collected in *Studies in Presocratic Philosophy*, vol. 1, ed. D. Furley and R. Allen (London, 1970). Especially noteworthy are H. Cherniss, "The Characteristics and Effects of Presocratic Philosophy," pp. 1–28 (reprinted from *Journal of the History of Ideas* 12 [1951]: 319–45); F. Cornford, "Was the Ionian Philosophy Scientific?" pp. 29–41 (reprinted from *Journal of Hellenic Studies* 62 [1942]: 1–7); G. Vlastos, "Review of F. M. Cornford: *Principium Sapientiae*," pp. 42–55 (reprinted from *Gnomon* 27 [1955]: 65–76); K. Popper, "Back to the Presocratics," pp. 130–53 (reprinted from K. Popper, *Conjectures and Refutations* [London, 1963]); and G. Kirk, "Popper on Science and the Presocratics," pp. 154–77 (reprinted from *Mind* 69 [1968]: 318–39). More recently, G. Lloyd has written extensively on these issues, most notably in *Magic, Reason and Experience* (Cambridge, 1979), and *The Revolutions of Wisdom: Studies in the Claims and Practice of Ancient Greek Science* (Berkeley, 1987).

2. Aristotle, *Metaphysics* 1.3 983b27–29 (= DK 1B10).

gods" did not simply retell familiar tales. His two principal works, broadly speaking, present overviews of the external world and the human world, with some effort to provide an integrated picture. The world is ordered to some extent on a rationally comprehensible basis. The *Theogony* puts traditional myths together into a unified story of the development of the world up to the rule of Zeus, which still prevails and will continue forever. The chief physical parts of the differentiated world (sky, earth, underworld, mountains, rivers, etc.) and such other prominent features of existence as love, day, and night are generated in a way familiar from human and animal life, birth, which for most of Hesiod's divine figures is the result of the union of a male and a female parent. Hesiod accounts for the present world by telling its history—how it developed from a simpler, earlier situation into its present complex state. The world is characterized by order, with the inferior divinities performing the functions assigned to them by Zeus. In fact, it is a moral order, since Zeus is closely associated with Justice, Peace, etc., and (in *Works and Days*) is the guarantor of justice through a system of rewards and punishments.

The early Ionians took over much from Hesiod. Most important is the concept of an ordered world comprehensible to human intelligence. But their manner of expression and reasoning was dramatically different, as was their conception of order. It is certainly wrong to say that these were the first Greeks who asked all the questions they did, and to regard Hesiod as a primitive mythologist, but it is also incorrect to deny all value to Aristotle's distinction between philosophy and mythology, even mythology of Hesiod's sophisticated kind.

Xenophanes' theological fragments show most strikingly the departure from earlier ways of thinking. Xenophanes criticizes mythological stories for attributing to the gods shameful actions like theft, adultery, and deceit, which are frequent events in the Homeric epics and the *Theogony* (7.3). Such behavior is inappropriate to the divine and so is wrongly ascribed to the gods. Xenophanes rejects tradition as a source of knowledge about the divine and substitutes human reason, in the rational criterion "what is fitting" (7.9). Humans can determine the nature of god as Xenophanes does, first finding reasons to question traditional ideas (7.2–7.6) and then constructing an acceptable view of the divine. In developing his theology along rational lines, Xenophanes does not simply bowdlerize Homer; he discards the Olympians altogether. There is only one god, who governs the world by the thought of his mind (7.12)—a far cry from the boisterous polytheism of Mount Olympus where jealous gods frequently come into conflict and rule the world according to their whims and ambitions, through physical might and intimidation.

Do away with gods governed by human passions, emotions, and caprices, and the world takes on a different face. No longer is the thunderbolt the weapon Zeus hurls at objects of his wrath. No longer can puzzling events be shrugged off as due to the will of the gods. There is a rational order in the world and knowledge of it can be attained, for just as we can understand the single god who rules the world, so, since god rules it rationally, as rational beings we can hope to understand how it works. Early Ionian philosophy sought after this understanding.

The early Ionians share with Homer and Hesiod a belief in the divine governance of the world as has already been shown for Xenophanes. In addition, Thales roundly declares that all things are full of gods (**4.9**), and Anaximander and Anaximenes claim for their originative substances the attributes of being eternal and eternally in motion, in effect making them divine (**5.5, 6.5**).

The early Ionians and Hesiod have the common aim of understanding the history of the world, its present constitution, and the principles on which it functions. Anaximander, whose interest in origins is most evident, begins his account with the eternal APEIRON, from which the world took its start. He describes the origin largely in terms of entities and processes still found in the developed KOSMOS and which are prominent in his treatment of its present state, although it is unclear how his principle of cosmic justice, in which opposites in turn commit injustice upon and make reparation to one another (**5.19**), is related to the APEIRON or to the way the world came to be. Nevertheless, this principle can explain many diverse phenomena, including the regular succession of day and night, of winter and summer, of flood and drought. It plays the role of a general scientific law, like Newton's Law of Universal Gravitation, which is applied to a wide variety of events; we explain those events by showing that they fall under the law. Further, this principle not only accounts for much of the order observed in the world around us, but also guarantees that it will last.

Xenophanes takes a different approach, declaring the world's eternity (**7.13**), so that it has always been and always will be. Since the KOSMOS is eternal, Xenophanes need not account for its origin, only for its present composition and operation, though he too shows an interest in its history (**7.18**).

The world presents itself as a chaotic diversity of things and events. In order to comprehend it we need to locate order in the chaos, unity in the multiplicity, limit in the unlimited. The traditional world view found its principle of order, unity, and limit in the gods. Lightning might strike here or there, now or then, but it is always caused by a single thing: the will of Zeus. There are limits on the amount of order the Olympians could bring, and there is something unsatisfactory about explaining the apparently random behavior of lightning by reference to a capricious being. Laws of nature do not explain events in such terms. Anaximander's law makes reference to "the ordering of time" (**5.19**), and some translators capitalize "Time" as if he intended some measure of personification. Even if they are correct, there is no suggestion that Time acts capriciously in establishing order or in dealing out penalties for injustice.

Explaining events through universal laws is one way to order the universe. Another is to show that things are more closely related than their bewildering variety suggests. Hesiod's genealogical account is one way of relating entities to one another. The early Ionians adopted another strategy, identifying a small number of basic principles and claiming that other things can be explained in terms of these. Thales and Anaximenes each posited a single principle, water and air respectively (**4.6, 6.1, 6.2**). Anaximenes thought that all things are composed of air in its various phases (which include fire, wind, water, etc.). Thales may have held that all things are made of water, but may instead have offered a cosmogony in which the present-day world developed out of (rather than is composed of) water as a single original substance. Anaximander proposed a cosmogony beginning with a single substance of indefinite nature, the APEIRON (**5.6**). Xenophanes identified earth and water as the basic substances (**7.16**).

The types of explanation the early Ionians used mark a further break from their predecessors. Homer's epics portray individual humans in particular sets of circumstances, with their own individual goals and individual deeds, and much of Hesiod's *Theogony* treats the (unique) history of Zeus' rise to power and the particular events which preceded and attended it. Cosmological matters receive attention largely because of this interest in individual events. It is quite otherwise with the early Ionians, whose interests center on the KOSMOS rather than on particular people, and for whom the individual is to a large extent seen as an instance of a universal. The principal questions now are "How did the whole world come into being?" "How did animal life arise?" "What are all things made of?" "Why do eclipses occur?" "What is lightning?" rather than "Why was that tree struck by lightning?" "What is the significance of that eclipse?" or "What is my (or Achilles') ancestry?" The universality of the answers implicit in the theories of the early Ionians is another consequence of abandoning modes of explanation in terms of personified deities. Thunder is due to a natural principle which operates uniformly and impersonally. Every thunderclap is caused by a certain specifiable set of natural circumstances, and whenever those circumstances occur, thunder results. The focus on the universal and impersonal, rather than the particular and personal, forms an important feature of the philosophical and scientific tradition which the early Ionians began. Aristotle says explicitly that philosophy and science deal primarily with universals,[3] and modern science still has as one of its main tasks the description and explanation of particular events through universal laws.

Another point of difference between the early Ionians and Homer and Hesiod is their attitude toward tradition. Put very crudely, where Homer and Hesiod worked within traditional frameworks,[4] the early Ionians rejected tradition as a source of knowledge and set rational criteria in its place. It is hard to underrate either the intellectual courage it took to make this step or the profound and continuing effects it has had on human civilization. In doing away with the Olympians and accounting for the world in other ways, the early Ionians forfeited the only means of justifying their beliefs that had previously been available. (This assertion should not be misunderstood. No doubt rational considerations and argument had frequently been used in the past, in Greece and elsewhere. What is new is the application of intellectual tools to cosmology and theology, and the belief that these tools are sufficient for the task.) They rejected Homer's and Hesiod's authority and challenged a way of looking at the world that was universal both among the Greeks and among all the foreign peoples known to the Greeks at the time. Xenophanes discarded Homeric theology because "it is not fitting," and his authority for doing so was his own reasoning. It is hard to think of a bolder move.

Moreover, once tradition is rejected as an authoritative source of knowledge, theories must stand or fall on their own merits. This approach has been followed by philosophy and science to this very day, and in assessing the early Ionian theories we have been employing the method they invented. But what are appropriate grounds for judging theories? The early Ionians show increasing sophistication in this area too.

Some of the methods used by Hesiod and the early Ionians have already been mentioned. I shall now describe another aspect of Ionian rationality, which I call rational criticism, and which is possibly the most important feature of Ionian speculation. The theories of Anaximander and Anaximenes were developed in reaction to their predecessors. Anaximander and Anaximenes reflected on earlier theories, identified objections, and

---

3. Aristotle, *Metaphysics* 1.1, cf. *Posterior Analytics* 1.31, 2.19.

4. This is not to say that they followed tradition blindly. In chap. 2, I suggested that Hesiod put traditional myths together in new ways for his own purposes. Homer, too, may well have innovated. The absence of earlier and contemporaneous evidence makes certainty impossible, but in general the Greeks tolerated variations and innovations in their myths more than we might expect; tradition was flexible up to a point. My claim is that Homer and Hesiod remained within the Olympian tradition, whereas the early Ionians abandoned it.

produced new theories immune to those objections. They rejected theories because they failed to fit observed facts or to satisfy rational criteria. This way of criticizing old theories and proposing new ones is public in a certain sense. Theories are not accepted or rejected through mysterious processes controlled by a few privileged individuals. This was much truer in the Greek world than in ours. During the period covered by this book, when science and philosophy were not the specialized disciplines they later became, theories were accessible to all intelligent people, and philosophical and scientific debates at least sometimes took place in public settings. The evidence for or against a theory and the criteria by which theories were judged were capable of being stated publicly. Others were then in a position to evaluate the theory and criteria for themselves, to decide whether the criteria were cogent, how far a theory satisfied those criteria, and how well it fit the empirical facts. Moreover, the same sort of examination could be applied to new theories. So it happened that the process of rational criticism led to successive theories, each improving on its predecessors. The level of sophistication and the plausibility of the theories advanced rapidly. Traditional accounts of the world were driven from the scene, for mythology is hard put to withstand critical scrutiny or mount a rational defense.

We can also hazard an account of why this method began in sixth-century Ionia. The Greeks of the archaic period were open to new ideas. In art they borrowed and assimilated motifs from a variety of foreign cultures; the same was not possible in philosophy or religion. Faced with rival systems of gods and religious traditions going back so far into antiquity as to make incredible Homer's stories of gods walking on earth only a few centuries previously, the Greeks could not simply keep their own gods and also accept others. But they were not in the position of nineteenth-century South Sea islanders confronted by just one prestigious civilization with its ancient and well-established religion. They faced two such civilizations, the Egyptian and the Mesopotamian, each with its own pantheon, mythology, and views on the origin of the world. In this unusual if not historically unique situation, it is understandable that a few highly intelligent and reflective people should have come to question their own religious tradition and the others as well, inventing and developing ways of examining beliefs for their plausibility and intelligibility. It is also understandable that this examination should have led to dissatisfaction with all known religions, mythologies, and world systems, and to a desire to replace them with more satisfactory accounts, and that it should have been applied to the new theories in their turn.

Another feature of early Ionian speculation is its propensity towards bold generalizations based on little evidence. Such readiness to generalize beyond carefully controlled limits is nowadays unacceptable in science and philosophy, but in the presocratic era, on the contrary, speculation needed this degree of recklessness for progress to be made at all. As there was no agreement on a general theory of how the world works, it is not surprising that attention was paid mainly to finding the outline of an acceptable overall theory and not to working out details within a single theory. It is premature to proceed to details until such an overall theory is adopted; in fact, detailed explanations make no sense except in the context of a general theory.[5] And since all the theories of the early Ionians had obvious shortcomings, it was too soon to begin the careful, controlled work we associate with science and philosophy. Further, the notion of working out details was as yet hardly known to the intellectual tradition the Milesians began.

The word that best suits the theorizing of the early Ionians is HISTORIE, "inquiry," a general term which is different from "science" and "philosophy" as we understand them in that it does not prescribe a specific subject matter or method. (The historian Herodotus used this word to describe his own work; hence it came to have the meaning "history.") Indeed, the early Ionians offered accounts of an astonishing range of topics—from the origin and constitution of the KOSMOS to the nature of change, to the origin of life, to questions of astronomy, meteorology, geology, and theology. They did not recognize any disciplinary boundaries and had no conception of specialization. They are justifiably said to have invented "the conception of nature as an all-inclusive system ordered by immanent law,"[6] although they had no single word for "nature."[7]

The experimental method, characteristic of science since the Renaissance, was unknown in the sixth century. In fact, very few experiments are recorded for the thousand-year history of Greek science. Further, many of the theories of the early Ionians and of the presocratics in general are not subject to empirical testing. It is difficult or impossible to think of evidence that could be observed with techniques or technology available in sixth-century Greece that would conclusively prove the theories right or wrong. And there is no reason to think that the theories were stated with any notion that they might be or should be subject to such verification or falsification. Still, that is not to deny altogether that they are based on observation of the world. In some sense they must have been, since their aim was to account for the observed world and to do so in terms of

5. These remarks are made with the early Ionians' treatments of cosmogony and the material principle mainly in mind. In areas such as meteorology, where there was more agreement, more attention was paid to details.

6. H. Cherniss, op. cit. (n. 1), p. 10.

7. PHYSIS came to be used in this sense no earlier than the late fifth century.

processes and substances that are either familiar from observation or somehow analogous to or extrapolated from observed phenomena.[8]

Another methodological approach largely missing in the thought of the early Ionians is that of deductive proof. As far as we can tell, they tended not to argue for their views, but to proclaim them.[9] To a very large extent, accounts of the history of early Greek thought, including the present one, involve attempts to reconstruct reasoning that could have led to the theories which the testimonia assert that individual thinkers proposed; the reasoning they actually employed is lost—perhaps it was never recorded, perhaps they did not think it an important thing to record.

The Ionian scientist-philosophers, then, did not use the sorts of evidence and argument we associate above all with science (experimental evidence) or philosophy (deduction). Their approach is not well described as either a priori or empirical. Rather, the style of thought characteristic of the early Ionians is frequently called "speculation," and this word, or rather what it represents in their thought, requires some comment. To speculate means, primarily, to think up ideas, especially new ideas. The word does not suggest any specific procedure of thinking, as perhaps do words such as "investigate" and "prove," though it does tend to exclude irrational fancies. It was suggested above that the early Ionians employed a characteristic rational-critical approach in handling others' theories and supporting their own, but this approach is hardly a clear method. Different theories conflicted with different empirical facts, and different theories fared better or worse according to which rational criteria might be adopted. The standard for accepting a theory seems to be the vague criterion of what is plausible. Each of the early Ionians had a story to tell of the nature and history of the universe, and their goal was to tell the most plausible story, as measured by an incompletely specified set of rational criteria.

The Milesians developed an increasingly sophisticated set of rational criteria along with their increasingly sophisticated theories, and progress in both areas went hand in hand. Before long some thinkers began to take a conscious interest in method. Xenophanes raised questions in this area, which became more central for the Pythagoreans, Heraclitus, and the Eleatics. The heightened interest in philosophical issues that we find in the first half of the fifth century stems in part from these reflections on the nature of knowledge, its limitations, and how it can be attained.

---

8. Xenophanes' use of fossil evidence (**7.18**) is the best known case of empiricism among the early Ionians.

9. Here there is need for great caution in view of the almost complete absence of original texts for the early Ionians and our consequent dependence on the doxographical tradition. The doxographers tended to be interested in what was believed, not why it was believed or with what reservations.

The final question I shall take up is whether there was a Milesian school of philosophy. There is a long-standing tradition of referring to Thales, Anaximander, and Anaximenes as the Milesian school. The sources link Anaximander with Thales as his "pupil and successor," "hearer" (i.e., student), and "associate," and Anaximenes is said to be related in all these ways to Anaximander. They have much in common. Not only were they all from Miletus, but they also shared an attitude of mind and an intellectual approach. They worked on many of the same problems and were in close agreement on methods and theories, although they differed significantly in details. Each of them learned from his predecessors and continued their work. This much can be stated with reasonable confidence, but is it enough to constitute them as a school?

A recent book on the post-Aristotelian period of Greek philosophy describes a philosophical school as "not, in general, a formally established institution, but a group of like-minded philosophers with an agreed leader and a regular meeting place, sometimes on private premises, but normally in public. School loyalty meant loyalty to the *founder* of the sect . . . and it is in that light that the degree of intellectual independence within each school must be viewed. It was generally thought more proper to present new ideas as interpretations or developments of the founder's views than as criticisms of him. . . . The virtually unquestioned authority of the founder within each of the schools gave its adherents an identity as members of a 'sect.'"[10]

Some elements of this account, which was written to describe the Stoic, Epicurean, and other Hellenistic philosophical schools, can be adapted to the Milesians. The independence and critical stance we have seen in Anaximander and Anaximenes do not count against the existence of a Milesian school, nor does the absence of evidence that there was a formally established institution or a regular meeting place. We may be inclined to question whether the later Milesians felt any particular loyalty to Thales or thought of themselves as being under his authority and merely interpreting or developing his views, but it would be risky to base a decision on this doubt, since we know nothing about Anaximander's or Anaximenes' attitudes and motives.

The Milesian school is sometimes compared to the Pythagorean school or society, which existed by the end of the sixth century. But there are important features the Pythagoreans share with the Stoics and other later philosophical schools that the Milesians lacked, and their absence is a strong reason to deny that there was a Milesian school of philosophy. Throughout the entire course of the sixth century we hear of only three

10. A. Long and D. Sedley, *The Hellenistic Philosophers*, vol. 1 (Cambridge, 1987), p. 5 f.

active figures in Miletus. They have a succession of teacher-student relations, but we know of only one student for each teacher. With the Pythagoreans, by contrast, there was kind of religious society, and even for the early
years we have several names of people associated with Pythagoras and his
sect. The Milesian "school" seems to be an invention of the doxographers
who wrote at a time when philosophy was largely associated with "schools"
and who assumed that the association which evidently took place between
Thales and Anaximander and between Anaximander and Anaximenes must
have taken place in a school.

9

Pythagoras of Samos and the Pythagoreans

Pythagoras' Life and the Pythagorean Movement

Although details of Pythagoras' life and work are unclear, even mysterious, the following brief account is widely accepted. Born on the island of Samos c. 570, he left c. 530 on account of disagreement with the policies of the tyrant[1] Polycrates. At this time or before, he visited Egypt and Babylonia. He settled in Croton, a Greek city in southern Italy, where political life was based on associations or clubs. A Pythagorean association soon came to prominence, bringing Croton to increased military and economic importance. This association was characterized by certain religious and philosophical views, and is frequently called a school or brotherhood. Pythagoras and his followers are said to have governed the state so well that it was truly an aristocracy ("government of the best").[2] Similar associations were formed in other Greek cities in south Italy. Pythagorean power in Croton lasted unbroken for twenty years, but c. 500 many leading Pythagoreans were murdered in a revolution. Pythagoras himself escaped to Metapontum, where he died.

Pythagoras was far more than a politician. A religious and moral reformer, he inaugurated a way of life that made the Pythagorean associations distinctive and exclusive. His followers were devoted to his sayings, which they collected, memorized, and passed down. He was a charismatic figure who became the subject of legends: he killed a poisonous snake by biting it; a river hailed him by name; he made predictions; he appeared simultaneously in two different places; he had a golden thigh. The people of Croton addressed him as Hyperborean[3] Apollo.[4] Pythagoreans identified three types of rational beings: gods, humans, and beings like Pythagoras.[5]

The Pythagorean movement did not end with the Founder's death. The revolution in Croton and Pythagoras' death were only temporary setbacks, and the Pythagorean associations' political importance in southern Italy increased in the first half of the fifth century. However, mid-century saw anti-Pythagorean uprisings throughout the area. At Croton, a house where

---

1. For this term, see p. 361.

2. Diogenes Laertius, *Lives of the Philosophers* 8.3 (not in DK).

3. Literally, "beyond the North Wind." Several myths associate Apollo with this distant place.

4. Aristotle fr. 191 (Rose), Aelian *Varia Historia* 2.26 (both = DK 14,7).

5. Aristotle, fr. 192 (Rose) (= DK 14,7).

the Pythagoreans were gathered was set on fire and all but two were burned alive. Their meeting houses elsewhere were destroyed too, their leaders killed, and the whole region was severely affected. Afterwards the character of the movement changed. Some fled to mainland Greece. Those who stayed were centered in Rhegium, but some time later, perhaps about 400 B.C., almost all left Italy, with the notable exception of Archytas, who became an able monarch at Tarentum, where Plato visited him in the early fourth century. The Pythagorean movement effectively died out in the fourth century, as the scattered remnants of this persecution were unable or unwilling to organize and establish active Pythagorean centers again.

Even so, the influence of Pythagoras continued throughout antiquity. Philosophically its most important legacy is the strong stamp it left on Plato's thought, as found notably in the myths of the afterlife at the end of *Gorgias, Phaedo,* and *Republic,* in the cosmology of the *Timaeus* (see pp. 101–102 and n. 40), in Plato's belief in the importance of mathematics, and possibly in some fundamental aspects of his theory of Ideas.

Later on, "Neopythagoreans" from the mid-first century B.C. to the third century A.D. emphasized the religious, superstitious, and numerological aspects of Pythagoreanism, and followed some of Plato's successors, from three-hundred years before, in combining Pythagorean ideas with elements of Plato's thought. These Neopythagoreans followed the common ancient practice of ascribing their own doctrines to the Founder in order to gain authority for their views, which they regarded as implicit in or extensions of his teachings. Neopythagorean beliefs were absorbed from the third century A.D. by the Neoplatonists, and it is to Neoplatonist writings based largely on Neopythagorean works that most of our information about Pythagoras is due.

Sources

Information about Pythagoras and Pythagorean philosophy in our period presents special difficulties. There are few contemporary or near-contemporary references. The Pythagorean influence present in many of Plato's dialogues is of some help, but cannot be the basis of a detailed historical treatment because of the difficulties in distinguishing Pythagorean ideas from Platonic developments of them. Aristotle gives valuable information about Pythagorean doctrines, but rarely mentions Pythagoras, more frequently speaking of "those who are called Pythagoreans" or "the Italians," as though unwilling to attribute the doctrines he reports to Pythagoras himself. Moreover, Aristotle's information is hard to interpret since he is out of sympathy, even impatient, with Pythagorean doctrines, which do not fit well into his own system. Although Neopythagorean and Neoplatonic writings provide abundant materials on Pythagoras' life and teachings, they are mostly unhistorical and worthless for reconstructing the thought of Pythagoras and his followers in the fifth century.

We are no better off as regards original writings. Pythagoras wrote nothing and neither did his early followers. There are many references to Pythagorean secrecy, an unsurprising feature of a religious brotherhood, and reports of the evil end that befell one early follower for revealing a secret, a discovery in geometry.[6] The earliest Pythagoreans for whom there are authentic fragments are Philolaus (who lived in the second half of the fifth century and perhaps as late as 380) and Archytas (early fourth century).

The following account of the early Pythagorean school, which is based mainly on Aristotle's discussions and on works on Pythagorean philosophy by two of Aristotle's pupils,[7] stresses the philosophical and scientific elements of Pythagoreanism rather than the religious and political, but the many facets of Pythagorean thought are closely linked, and it is important to bear in mind the fundamental religious strand that pervades them all. (Those who wish to omit the religious aspect of Pythagoreanism should skip ahead to p. 91.)

Early Source Material

Most of the contemporary and near-contemporary evidence on Pythagoras and fifth-century Pythagoreanism is found in the following passages.

Xenophanes mocks Pythagoras' belief in the transmigration of souls.

9.1 Once he passed by as a puppy was being beaten,
 the story goes, and in pity said these words:
 "Stop, don't beat him, since it is the soul of a man, a friend
 of mine,
 which I recognized when I heard it crying."
 (Xenophanes, DK 21B7)

Heraclitus, whose life overlapped Pythagoras', comments sarcastically about Pythagoras and others.

9.2 Much learning ["polymathy"] does not teach insight. Otherwise it would have taught Hesiod and Pythagoras and moreover Xenophanes and Hecataeus. (Heraclitus, DK 22B40)

---

6. See p. 99.

7. These pupils are Dicaearchus and Aristoxenus of Tarentum, a friend of the group known as the last generation of Pythagoreans, who are identified as pupils of Philolaus. Their works are excerpted in Neoplatonic works.

9.3 Pythagoras the son of Mnesarchus practiced inquiry (HISTORIE) more than all other men, and making a selection of these writings constructed his own wisdom, polymathy, evil trickery.   (Heraclitus, DK 22B129)

Ion of Chios (born c. 490), in describing Pherecydes, a sixth-century mythographer and author of a *Theogony*, says:

9.4 Thus he excelled in both manhood and reverence
    and even in death has a delightful life for his soul,
    if indeed Pythagoras was truly wise about all things,
    he who truly knew and had learned thoroughly the opinions
       of men.

                                                    (Ion, DK 36B4)

Herodotus (485/4–c. 430) reports the story that Greeks in the region of the Black Sea told of Pythagoras' Thracian slave Zalmoxis. I paraphrase.

9.5 After being set free, he [Zalmoxis] returned to Thrace. He decided to civilize his compatriots, who were primitive and stupid, since through his contact with Greeks and especially with Pythagoras, who was "not the weakest sophist [wise man] of the Greeks," he had become acquainted with the Ionian way of life and with more profound sorts of people than could be found among the Thracians. "He built a hall in which he received and feasted leading Thracians, and taught them the better view, that neither he nor his guests nor any of their descendants would die, but would come to a place where they would live forever and have all good things." To convince them of his teaching, Zalmoxis disappeared for three years, living in a secret underground chamber, while everyone thought him dead. In the fourth year he reappeared above ground, and since then the Thracians believe in immortality.
                              (Herodotus, *Histories* 4.95 = DK 14,2
                       [the quoted words are an adaptation of Godley's translation])

Empedocles, who adopted some Pythagorean beliefs, describes Pythagoras[8] in this way.

9.6 There was a certain man among them who knew very holy matters
    who possessed the greatest wealth of mind,
    mastering all sorts of wise deeds.

---

8. Most interpreters believe that these verses praise Pythagoras, but there was doubt even in antiquity. According to Diogenes Laertius, *Lives of the Philosophers* 8.54 (= DK 31A1), some held that they describe Parmenides.

> For when he reached out with all his mind
> easily he would survey every one of the things that are,
> yea, within ten and even twenty generations of humans.
>
> (Empedocles, DK 31B129)

Plato says of Pythagoras:

> **9.7** Is Homer said to have been during his life a guide in education for people who delighted in associating with him and passed down to their followers a Homeric way of life? Pythagoras himself was greatly admired for this, and his followers even nowadays name a way of life Pythagorean and are conspicuous among others.   (Plato, *Republic* 10 600a–b = DK 14,10)

Herodotus says Egyptian religious customs forbid people to wear wool into temples and to be buried in woolen clothing, and he links those practices with the Pythagoreans.

> **9.8** The Egyptians agree in this with those called Orphics . . . and with the Pythagoreans; for it is likewise unholy for anyone who takes part in these rites to be buried in woolen garments.
>
> (Herodotus, *Histories* 2.81 = DK 14,1)

Plato, while outlining the mathematically based curriculum of his philosopher kings, says that the Pythagoreans assert that astronomy and harmony are sister sciences, and that they

> **9.9** . . . measure audible concords against one another and look for numbers, but do not ascend to the level of considering problems generally and asking which numbers are concordant, which are not, and why.
>
> (Plato, *Republic* 7 530d–31c, not in DK)

Interestingly, the contemporary references (**9.1–9.3**) are ambivalent at best. Heraclitus' references to Pythagoras' wide-ranging knowledge and his intellectual curiosity (HISTORIE [9]) are evidence that Pythagoras engaged in the kind of inquiry pursued by the Milesians.[10] (Samos is only a few miles from Miletus.) As Heraclitus criticizes many of his predecessors but not the

---

9. See p. 75.

10. Some believe that **9.2** pairs Pythagoras with Hesiod *as opposed to* Xenophanes and Hecataeus, the former as religious thinkers, the latter as representing the new ways of thought, and that the writings **9.3** refers to are writings of the Orphic sects who believed in an afterlife and the immortality of the soul. This is the interpretation of W. Burkert, *Lore and Science in Ancient Pythagoreanism* (Cambridge, Mass., 1972; first German ed., 1962).

Milesian philosophers,[11] the charges in **9.2** and **9.3** may be addressed to aspects of Pythagoras' thought that differ from Milesian-style investigations. The charge of lacking insight may mean only that he did not see eye to eye with Heraclitus, but there may be something specific in the claims that his wide knowledge is plagiarized or based on the ideas of others and is "evil trickery."[12] Heraclitus may be expressing his contempt for Pythagoras' mystical, religious views or possibly for some physical doctrines which he found seriously wrong.

9.1, **9.4**, **9.5**, and **9.6** associate Pythagoras with a belief in an afterlife. The soul upon death might enter the body of a lower animal or a human. **9.4** suggests that one's fate after death is a reward or punishment for one's character in the previous life, and perhaps refers to the later attested view that the reward for an outstandingly good life is eternal happiness untouched by the need for rebirth. **9.5** is a patent attempt by some Greeks[13] to claim a Greek origin for a native Thracian belief (Zalmoxis was a Thracian god, not a human). The portrait of Zalmoxis as an imposter may be meant to reflect negatively on Pythagoras himself. The remark in **9.7** on Pythagoras' disciples and way of life illustrates the special nature of the Pythagorean "brotherhood," whose principal beliefs, many of them bound closely to the belief in reincarnation, were traced back to the Founder. Moreover, the strong Pythagorean interest in mathematics and in a mathematical approach to harmonics and astronomy (attested to by Plato in **9.9** and by Aristotle in **9.19**), which goes back at least to the mid-fifth century, may have originated with Pythagoras himself.

Immortality and Reincarnation

The religious message of Pythagoras is based on the doctrine of the immortality of the individual soul, which is recounted in the following passage along with other related beliefs.

> **9.10** First he declares that the soul is immortal; then that it changes into other kinds of animals; in addition that things that happen recur at certain intervals, and nothing is absolutely new; and that all things that come to be alive must be thought akin. Pythagoras seems to have been the first to introduce these opinions into Greece.
>
>   (Porphyry, *Life of Pythagoras* 19 = DK 14,8a)

11. See **10.5**, **10.16**, **10.71** and discussion on p. 131.

12. The word is also rendered "worthless artifice" (Guthrie, *HGP*, vol. 1, p. 157), "artful knavery" (KRS, p. 217), and "imposture" (Burnet, *Early Greek Philosophy*, p. 134).

13. Not including Herodotus himself, who is sceptical about the whole tale.

The final statement in **9.10** is disputed,[14] but the views mentioned are certainly Pythagorean. In declaring the soul immortal, Pythagoras obliterated the barrier the Olympian religion placed between humans and gods. "Immortal" is, for the Greeks, tantamount to "divine."

The doctrine is a development of ideas of the Milesian philosophers, who made their originative substances immortal and divine, and held that divinity was widespread in the KOSMOS. According to Anaximenes (**6.6**), the human soul is composed of the divine originative substance, air. It is no great leap to infer that the soul is immortal. The Pythagoreans gave special importance to breath in their cosmogony (**9.27**, **9.28**), and some Pythagoreans identified the soul with air.

> **9.11** Some of them [the Pythagoreans] declared that the soul is the motes in the air, and others that it is what makes the motes move.
> (Aristotle, *On the Soul* 1.2 404a17 = DK 58B40)

Another Pythagorean view of the soul mentioned by Aristotle (though not identified by him as Pythagorean) is that it is a HARMONIA. This theory also appears in Plato's *Phaedo*, where it is presented by a pupil of the Pythagorean Philolaus and endorsed by another Pythagorean, Echecrates. However, in the *Phaedo* it is used to disprove the soul's immortality: if the soul is a HARMONIA of the parts of the body, when the body becomes seriously ill the HARMONIA, and therefore the soul, is destroyed.[15] But if the HARMONIA theory of the soul implies that the soul is not immortal, how can it be reconciled with Pythagorean philosophy? One solution is to suppose that the original Pythagorean idea was that the soul, like the whole universe, is a HARMONIA of numbers (cf. **9.36**).[16] As such it does not suffer the decay and alteration that affect the body, but is the same in kind as the divine KOSMOS. Insofar as it is polluted or tainted by its association with the body, it contains an element of discord which the Pythagorean way of life aims to remove, thus restoring it to a state of perfect order (KOSMOS).

Pythagoras represents a new and radical challenge to the Olympian tradition. To promote each human, or *part* of each human, to the level of the gods simultaneously devalues the gods and their worship and raises the importance of our care for ourselves, or more precisely for our *selves*, where

---

14. Many give priority to Orphism. (See n. 83, n. 10.)

15. Plato, *Phaedo* 85e–86d.

16. Guthrie, *HGP*, vol. 1, pp. 306–19. Guthrie discounts the idea that the soul is a HARMONIA of bodily parts as an intrusion from fifth-century medical writers like Alcmaeon who believed that health is a balance, or HARMONIA, of the elements or parts of the body.

the self is the soul as opposed, say, to the body. Moreover, this doctrine is not anthropocentric. Not only human souls are at stake; all living things possess souls. Only thus can transmigration of souls take place. Our concern is for all ensouled things, with whom we are in a literal sense related.

The doctrines of the immortality and transmigration of souls imply a major restructuring of values. Our interests, even our egoistic interests, now extend beyond our selves and beyond this lifetime. Further, if what we do and how we live in this life affect our soul's next incarnation, as **9.4** suggests, then we have strong prudential reasons to choose certain actions and ways of life over others. The Pythagorean way of life (**9.7**) aimed to improve the soul and to attain for it the best possible destiny, which consists either in attaining the best of reincarnations or in complete freedom from the necessity of continued rebirth through reunion with the divine universal soul.[17]

The following passages say more about this doctrine.

9.12 The Egyptians were the first to declare this doctrine too, that the human soul is immortal, and each time the body perishes it enters into another animal as it is born. When it has made a circuit of all terrestrial, marine, and winged animals, it once again enters a human body as it is born. Its circuit takes three-thousand years. Some Greeks have adopted this doctrine, some earlier and some later, as if it were peculiar to them. I know their names, but do not write them.

(Herodotus, *Histories* 2.123 = DK 14,1)

9.13 Heraclides of Pontus says that Pythagoras said the following about himself. Once he had been born Aethalides and was believed to be the son of Hermes. When Hermes told him to choose whatever he wanted except immortality, he asked to retain both alive and dead the memory of what happened to him. . . . Afterwards he entered into Euphorbus and was wounded by Menelaus. Euphorbus said that once he had been born as Aethalides and received the gift from Hermes, and told of the migration of his soul and what plants and animals it had belonged to and all it had experienced in Hades. When Euphorbus died his soul entered Hermotimus, who, wishing to provide evidence, went to Branchidae, entered the sanctuary of Apollo, and showed the shield Menelaus had dedicated. (He said that when Menelaus was sailing away from Troy he dedicated the shield to Apollo.) The shield had already rotted away and only the ivory facing was preserved. When Hermotimus died, it [the soul] became Pyrrhus the Delian fisherman, and again remembered everything. . . .

17. A case for the latter view is made on the basis of little evidence by Guthrie, *HGP*, vol. 1, p. 203.

> When Pyrrhus died it became Pythagoras and remembered all that has
> been said.
> (Diogenes Laertius, *Lives of the Philosophers* 8.4–5 = DK 14,8)

The Greeks Herodotus infuriatingly refuses to name in **9.12** are thought to
include the Pythagoreans. **9.13**, which is attributed to a good source,[18]
differs from **9.12** in important points. According to **9.13** but not **9.12**, the
soul spends time in Hades as well as in living things. In **9.13** but not **9.12**,
the soul sometimes animates plants in addition to animals and humans. In
9.12 but not in **9.13** the soul occupies all animals in between human
incarnations, as if all souls have the same fate. Finally, the 3000-year span
between successive human incarnations in **9.12** is incompatible with the
three human incarnations of Pythagoras' soul which **9.13** places after the
Trojan War.[19] Some of the discrepancies may stem from the fact that **9.12**
claims to be giving an account not of Pythagorean beliefs but of Egyptian
ones (although the Egyptians, who had an elaborate doctrine of the afterlife, did not believe in transmigration). The Greeks referred to allegedly
borrowed beliefs from the Egyptians, but there is no guarantee that they did
not alter them. In any case, neither passage proves that the Pythagorean
belief in reincarnation involved rewards and punishments for previous lives.
Still, the likelihood is great that it did. First, there is the evidence of **9.4**.
Also, Empedocles, who was influenced by Pythagoreanism, held that the
best sort of animal for a soul[20] to occupy is a lion, and the best sort of plant
a laurel (**14.131**), and that the best souls become outstanding men and even
blessed gods (**14.132**, **14.133**). Poems from the early fifth century, which
may have been written for people with Pythagorean beliefs, refer to judgment after death leading to rewards in subsequent lives for outstanding
success in this one[21] and to everlasting happiness in the Isles of the Blest as
the reward of "all those who have had the courage to keep their soul
completely away from unjust deeds for three stays in each place [on earth
and in the underworld]."[22] Moreover, later Pythagoreans held these beliefs.

This evidence makes it plausible that early Pythagoreans believed not

---

18. Heraclides of Pontus was a pupil of Plato and a contemporary of Aristotle, and
had a special interest in the Pythagorean movement.

19. The date of the Trojan War was disputed in antiquity, but it was usually put at
about 1200 B.C.

20. Empedocles speaks of the DAIMON instead of the soul. For the equivalence of
the two notions in Empedocles, see p. 286.

21. Pindar, fr. 133 (not in DK) = KRS passage 410, p. 317.

22. Pindar, *Olympians* 2.56–77 (not in DK) = KRS passage 284, p. 286.

only that the soul is immortal and passes into one living being after another (directly or after a time in Hades), but also that some incarnations are preferable to others and the next kind of being a soul will inhabit is determined by a postmortem judgment of its previous life. These beliefs formed the basis of the Pythagorean religion and way of life.

Prohibition on Killing; Dietary Restrictions

Many features of the Pythagorean life can be understood from this perspective. The aim of life is to ensure a good future for the soul. Vegetarianism, prominent in the Pythagorean life, results from the belief in transmigration and the kinship of all living things. Bluntly put,[23] what you kill and eat for dinner may have the soul of your dear departed mother or father. More generally, since all living beings are related, it is an equal offense to kill anything, without reference to the possibility that its soul might once have ensouled a human. If it is alive, it is at least a distant relative. Any killing is tantamount to murder; eating animals amounts to cannibalism. Empedocles developed this idea in much greater detail[24] than can be attributed to the Pythagoreans from early sources, but there is no reasonable doubt that violating this prohibition was the premier form of injustice which merited punishment after death.

There are difficulties about this doctrine, which amounts to a rationalization of the instinctive prephilosophical Greek horror of incurring pollution by bloodshed. First, if all living things are related, killing and eating plant life (possibly including fruits and vegetables, which can, loosely speaking, grow into plants) should be prohibited too, so that Pythagoreans could eat only a very few things, such as milk and honey; yet there was no general ban on vegetable foods. Quite likely only some plants, such as laurels,[25] were thought to have souls. Second, there is conflicting evidence about the prohibition on eating meat, some sources declaring that all meat was prohibited, others that only certain kinds were, still others denying that any such prohibition existed. A sensible approach to this contradictory information is to see in it traces of variations in Pythagoreanism, whose initial ban on all meat ceased to be observed rigorously in the fifth-century diaspora, when there were only scattered remnants of the Pythagoreans and hence the likelihood of local deviations from the original norm.

Another notorious practice of the Pythagoreans was their refusal to eat beans. The amount of ancient speculation about this dietary aberration

23. See Empedocles, **14.137**.
24. See p. 286.
25. See p. 87.

proves that the custom was found odd and that there was no obvious reason for it. We are told that beans were banned because their flatulent tendency disturbs our sleep and our mental tranquillity, because they resemble testicles, or the gates of Hades, or the shape of the universe, or because they are used in allotting political offices (a reference to antidemocratic Pythagorean politics), or because if buried in manure they take on a human shape, or because their stems are hollow so that they are connected directly to the underworld, and so on.[26] On a plausible recent interpretation,[27] Pythagoras introduced this prohibition because eating beans can be bad for health: some people grow ill upon eating the fava beans which are common in south Italy, so the ban on beans might be a practical expedient, not a ritual abstention.

AKOUSMATIKOI and MATHEMATIKOI

9.14 There are two kinds of the Italian philosophy called Pythagorean since two types of people practiced it, the AKOUSMATIKOI and the MATHEMATIKOI. Of these, the AKOUSMATIKOI were admitted to be Pythagoreans by the others, but they did not recognize the MATHEMATIKOI, but claimed that their pursuits were not those of Pythagoras, but of Hippasus. . . . The philosophy of the AKOUSMATIKOI consists of unproved and unargued AKOUSMATA to the effect that one must act in appropriate ways, and they also try to preserve all the other sayings of Pythagoras as divine dogma. These people claim to say nothing of their own invention, and say that to make innovations would be wrong. But they suppose that the wisest of their number are those who have got the most AKOUSMATA.
(Iamblichus, *Life of Pythagoras* 81, 82 = DK 18,2, 58C4)

The AKOUSMATIKOI (the word derives from AKOUSMA, "thing heard") learned and accepted Pythagoras' sayings simply on the strength of Pythagoras' having said them, but refused to recognize continued mathematical and scientific research as part of the Founder's intentions. In contrast, the MATHEMATIKOI (from MATHEMA, "learning" or "studying," not specifically mathematical learning and studying, although the study these Pythagoreans pursued was largely mathematical) promoted the scientific studies Pythagoras allegedly began, while acknowledging the religious side of Pythagoreanism. This split, between the religious, conservative, dogmatic

26. These and other explanations are discussed by Guthrie, *HGP*, vol. 1, pp. 184–85.
27. R. Brumbaugh and J. Schwartz, "Pythagoras and Beans. A Medical Explanation," *Classical World* 73 (1980): 421–22.

AKOUSMATIKOI and the scientific, progressive, intellectually active MATHE-
MATIKOI, resembles the sectarianism often found in the early history of
religious movements.

The AKOUSMATA

Some Pythagorean practices are called AKOUSMATA. Their role is described thus.

> **9.15** All the AKOUSMATA referred to in this way fall under three headings.
> (a) Some indicate what something is, (b) others indicate what is some-
> thing in the greatest degree, and (c) others what must or must not be
> done. (a) The following indicate what something is. What are the Isles of
> the Blest? Sun and Moon. What is the oracle at Delphi? The tetractys,
> which is the harmony in which the Sirens sing. (b) Others indicate what
> is something in the greatest degree. What is most just? To sacrifice. What
> is the wisest? Number, and second wisest is the person who assigned
> names to things. What is the wisest thing in our power? Medicine. What
> is most beautiful? Harmony.
>
> > (Iamblichus, *Life of Pythagoras* 82 = DK 58C4)
> > (continuation of **9.14**)

Examples of the third type of AKOUSMATA are found in the following
passages.

> **9.16** <Pythagoras ordered his followers> not to pick up <food> which had
> fallen, to accustom them not to eat self-indulgently or because it fell on
> the occasion of someone's death . . . not to touch a white rooster, be-
> cause it is sacred to the Month and is a suppliant. It is a good thing, and
> is sacred to the Month because it indicates the hours, and white is of the
> nature of good, while black is of the nature of evil . . . not to break
> bread, because friends long ago used to meet over a single loaf just as
> foreigners still do, and not to divide what brings them together. Others
> <explain this practice> with reference to the judgment in Hades, others
> say that it brings cowardice in war, and still others that the whole uni-
> verse begins from this.
>
> > (Aristotle, fr. 195 [Rose], quoted in Diogenes Laertius,
> > *Lives of the Philosophers* 8.34 ff. = DK 58C3)

> **9.17** Do not stir the fire with a knife.
> Rub out the mark of a pot in the ashes.
> Do not wear a ring.
> Do not have swallows in the house.
> Spit on your nail parings and hair trimmings.

Roll up your bedclothes on rising and smooth out the imprint
of the body.
Do not urinate facing the sun.
>   (a selection from Iamblichus, *Protrepticus*
>   21 = DK 58C6, tr. Guthrie)

Some of the justifications in **9.16** are moral precepts (behave with moderation, respect the gods), but others reek of prephilosophical ways of thought.
Still others point to an aspect of Pythagoreanism that remains to be discussed, the study of the KOSMOS with the aid of mathematics.

So far, Pythagoreanism hardly deserves space in a treatment of early
Greek philosophy. The religious side is in many ways the antithesis of the
rational approach to nature. Not only does it contain superstitions and
other taboos, it makes no attempt to justify or systematize them. The
AKOUSMATIKOI followed Pythagoras differently from the way Anaximenes
followed Thales and Anaximander. They aimed to preserve his ideas, not to
criticize or enlarge them. Their acceptance of the AKOUSMATA unproved
and unargued (**9.14**) is unphilosophical and unscientific.

The MATHEMATIKOI

The situation is different with the MATHEMATIKOI, whose ideas deserve a
place in any study of Greek thought. Still, their work was carried out
against the religious backdrop sketched above, and after looking at some of
their main ideas I shall suggest some points of contact between the two
faces of Pythagoreanism.

The scientific side of Pythagoreanism marks a new approach to understanding the world. Number takes precedence over matter, mathematical
accounts of phenomena are preferred to descriptions in terms of physical
constituents, and perhaps definitions and proofs begin to take the place of
the Ionians' "likely stories" in explaining the relations among things.

The Concordant Intervals

The starting point for these developments was the Pythagorean discovery
that concordant musical intervals can be expressed mathematically. The
musical intervals of the octave (C–C'), fifth (C–G), and fourth (C–F) were
basic to Greek music. In the seven-stringed lyre, four of the strings were
tuned to pitches separated by these intervals (e.g., C, F, G, C') and the
other three were put at different pitches depending on the "mode" desired.
In a lyre the strings all have the same length: it is clear that the higher notes
come from the tauter strings, but there is no obvious numerical relation

between pitch and tension. In a monochord, a single-stringed instrument with a movable bridge, changing the position of the bridge changes the pitch produced by plucking or bowing the string, which remains under the same tension. There are a limitless number of possible positions the bridge can have, and so an unlimited number of possible pitches. When the bridge is placed exactly halfway between the fixed ends of the string, the note produced is an octave higher than that produced by the entire length of the string. This is the case no matter how long the string is, what the string is made of, or how taut it is (as long as it is taut enough to produce a tone). The essence of the octave is the numerical ratio 2:1, not the actual length or material involved in making the sound. Since the intervals of the fifth and fourth are also expressible in terms of the ratios of small whole numbers (3:2 and 4:3, respectively) music appears to result from the imposition, by means of number, of order and limit on the unlimited continuum of possible tones.

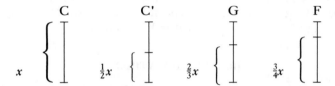

It is difficult to imagine how wonderful and surprising it must have been to learn that fundamental features of music could be expressed numerically. After all, we are used to expressing qualitative notions in quantitative, numerical terms. We measure and count color, sound, weight, and speed in wavelengths, grams, and feet per second. In fact, we regard quantitative treatment as one of the hallmarks of science. This discovery, which was possibly made by Pythagoras himself, was the first time any quality was reduced to a quantity, and so it stands at the beginning of this aspect of our scientific tradition. Also, within Pythagorean thought, the discovery had important effects on mathematics, cosmology, and the doctrine of the soul.[28]

Before taking these topics up, however, I shall introduce two concepts that are central to them: KOSMOS and HARMONIA. KOSMOS, a word that it is said Pythagoras was first to apply to the universe, has two basic meanings: orderly arrangement and ornament. It combines the notions of regularity, tidiness, and arrangement on the one hand with beauty, perfection, and positive moral value. The Ionians had already treated the world as a KOSMOS, but the Pythagoreans enlarged and deepened this idea to apply to

---

28. For the soul as HARMONIA, see p. 85.

the mathematical structure and religious significance which they found in the world around them. HARMONIA, from which our word "harmony" comes, originally meant a fitting together, connection, or joint. Later it meant the string of a lyre, and then a way of stringing the lyre, i.e., a tuning or scale. The essence of the order in the world, the Pythagoreans believed, is located in the connections of its parts, i.e., KOSMOS depends on HARMONIA, especially on HARMONIA based on number. This doctrine was first applied to musical HARMONIA, but was later extended more widely.

The following diagram, which the Pythagoreans called "the tetractys of the decad" and by which they swore their most solemn oaths, represents the numbers involved in the analysis of the three principal harmonic intervals.

•

•　•

•　•　•

•　•　•　•

The tetractys was called "the harmony in which the Sirens sing" and was mystically identified with the oracle at Delphi (see **9.15**). The following passage mentions some of its other associations.

> **9.18** The tetractys is a certain number, which being composed of the four first numbers produces the most perfect number, ten. For one and two and three and four come to be ten. This number is the first tetractys, and is called the source of ever flowing nature since according to them the entire KOSMOS is organized according to HARMONIA, and HARMONIA is a system of three concords—the fourth, the fifth, and the octave—and the proportions of these three concords are found in the aforementioned four numbers.
>
> (Sextus Empiricus, *Against the Mathematicians* 7.94–95, not in DK)

We will come back to the statement that the KOSMOS is arranged according to HARMONIA in discussing Pythagorean cosmology, but the general nature of Pythagorean thought can be gathered from this passage. The concordant musical intervals are accounted for in terms of the numbers one, two, three, and four. These are assumed to explain the structure of the universe, and a particular way of exhibiting them takes on a sacred character, as does their sum. The kind of thought found here works by association rather than logical analysis. It moves too fast and too far for our taste, although no faster or farther than earlier presocratic philosophers had done.

Pythagorean Number Theory

The Greek word for number is ARITHMOS, and ARITHMETIKE, the study of numbers, corresponds to what mathematicians now call number theory rather than to arithmetic, the method of calculating with numbers. Perhaps because of their discovery of the numerical basis of music, the Pythagoreans pursued—and may have initiated—the study of numbers, their different kinds and properties, and their principles. The following sketch of Pythagorean number theory includes some developments which probably come from a later period than ours (the Neopythagorean period), but which are in the spirit of early Pythagoreanism.

An important step in understanding a subject is to classify and to define the subject as a whole (in this case, number) and its subdivisions (the types of numbers). The Pythagoreans were first to distinguish and define odd and even numbers, prime and composite numbers, square numbers, and cube numbers. They also made some classifications no longer used, such as triangular and oblong numbers. These numbers, as well as squares and cubes, are called after the shapes into which an appropriate number of units, or pebbles, can be arranged. In thinking of 9 as a square number because 9 dots can be arranged in a certain pattern, the

Pythagoreans have in mind a spatial representation no longer present when we write $9 = 3^2$ and think of "squaring" as the algebraic operation of multiplying something by itself. They also defined a number N as triangular, pentagonal, etc., if N dots can be arranged to form an equilateral triangle, pentagon, etc. The tetractys of the decad represents the fourth triangular number, 10. Similarly they defined a number N as oblong if N dots can be arranged to form a rectangular figure with sides differing by one, i.e., if there is a number M such that $N = M(M + 1)$. The smallest oblong number is 2 (= 1×2), the next is 6, then 12, etc.

This manner of representing numbers spatially makes it possible to see and to prove certain numerical relations. Consider square numbers. Beginning from 1, which for some purposes was not considered a number, we form the first square number by placing three dots around it in the form of a "gnomon" (literally, "carpenter's square"). The next square number is formed by wrapping another gnomon around the previous one.

This time the gnomon has five dots. In this way it is evident that each square number results from adding successive odd numbers, and that we reach the next square number by adding the next odd number to the last square number reached. If $N = 1 + 3 + \ldots + M$, then N is a square number, and the next square number $= N + (M + 2)$. Another result is represented by the formula $(N + 1)^2 = N^2 + 2N + 1$. Consider the gnomon used in moving from 3^2 to 4^2.

$4^2 = 3^2$ plus the gnomon, and the gnomon can be divided into three parts, of which two have 3 units each, and the other is a single unit, i.e. $4^2 = 3^2 + (2 \times 3) + 1$, and this relation holds for any pair of successive square numbers.

This style of proof is ingenious, but has limitations. Most obviously it is restricted to whole numbers. In addition, it is not a general proof, but a series of particular cases, though the general principle is correct, and the proof can be made respectable if put into the form known as mathematical induction.

By extending the notion of a gnomon the Pythagoreans spoke of wrapping gnomons around triangular, pentagonal, oblong, etc., numbers and so could prove other results. One important result is that just as the sequence of square numbers is generated by adding successive odd numbers, so the sequence of oblong numbers is generated by adding successive even numbers. The following diagram shows the relation between square and oblong numbers. Since omitting the left column yields square numbers, the sequence of oblong numbers differs from the sequence of square numbers by a unit at each stage.

The numbers forming the "sides" of square numbers always have the same ratio. We would write $2^2 = 2 \times 2$, $3^2 = 3 \times 3$, $\ldots N^2 = N \times N$, and $2:2 = 3:3 = \ldots = N:N$. On the other hand, the numbers forming the "sides" of successive oblong numbers have a different ratios: $2:1$, $3:2$, $4:3$, $\ldots$ This fact leads to the doctrine of the principles of number.

Principles of Number

A prominent feature of Ionian thought is the desire to identify a small number of principles from which the world is constructed or out of which it has grown: the world depends on a small number of principles and can be accounted for in terms of them. The Pythagoreans believed that number is fundamental to the world, that somehow the world can be accounted for in terms of number. But there is no end to the number of numbers. They therefore needed to account for numbers in terms of a small number of principles, so that these principles ultimately serve as the principles for all things.

Several Aristotelian testimonia are relevant here.

9.19 At the same time as these [Leucippus and Democritus] and before them, those called Pythagoreans took hold of mathematics and were the first to advance that study, and being brought up in it, they believed that its principles are the principles of all things that are. Since numbers are naturally first among these, and in numbers they thought they observed many likenesses to things that are and that come to be . . . and since they saw the attributes and ratios of musical scales in numbers, and other things seemed to be made in the likeness of numbers in their entire nature, and numbers seemed to be primary in all nature, they supposed the elements of numbers to be the elements of all things that are.   (Aristotle, *Metaphysics* 1.5 985b23–986a2 = DK 58B4)

9.20 The elements of number are the even and the odd, and of these the latter is limited and the former unlimited. The One is composed of both of these (for it is both even and odd) and number springs from the One; and numbers, as I have said, constitute the whole universe.
                                        (Aristotle, *Metaphysics* 1.5 986a17–21 = DK 58B5)

9.21 The Pythagoreans similarly posited two principles, but added something peculiar to themselves, not that the limited and the unlimited are distinct natures like fire or earth or something similar, but that the unlimited itself and the One itself are the substance of what they are predicated of. This is why they call number the substance of all things.
                                        (Aristotle, *Metaphysics* 1.5 987a13–19 = DK 58B8)

9.22 They say that the unlimited is the even. For when this is surrounded and limited by the odd it provides things with the quality of unlimitedness. Evidence of this is what happens with numbers. For when gnomons are placed around the one, and apart, in the one case the shape is always different, and in the other it is always one.
                                        (Aristotle, *Physics* 3.4 203a10–15 = DK 58B28)

9.22 refers to the gnomon-wrapping described above and shows how even is linked with unlimited, and odd with one. The successive figures formed by wrapping gnomons with odd numbers of dots "around the one" are all square and so have the same shape, whereas in the sequence of oblong figures formed by wrapping gnomons with even numbers of dots around the two,[29] no two shapes are the same (since the ratios of their sides are different).

9.19 says that the Pythagoreans thought the elements of numbers are the elements of all things, and **9.20** identifies the elements of number as the even and the odd, which compose the One, from which springs number, of which the universe is composed. The generation implied by **9.20** is:

$$\text{even and odd} \rightarrow \text{the One} \rightarrow \text{number} \rightarrow \text{the universe}$$

On the other hand, **9.21** does not mention even and odd, but makes it clear that the limited and the unlimited are the two principles, and associates unity with the limited, whereas **9.20** makes the One composed of both odd and even. Here the generation seems to be:

$$\text{unlimited and limited} \ (= \text{ the One}) \rightarrow \text{number} \rightarrow \text{all things}$$

These passages leave much unclear, and their inconsistencies are particularly puzzling since Aristotle is likely to have been well informed and the passages occur in the same book, a mere page away from one another. As we shall see, Aristotle is quite out of sympathy with the Pythagoreans and cannot make sense of their view that number is the principle of the KOSMOS. Still, **9.22** establishes a connection between even and unlimited and between odd, one, and limited or limit, and we can understand in a general way the desire to find a way of generating numbers out of a small number of principles, though it is unclear whether this generation takes place in time (so that there is a time when even and odd exist, but not yet the numbers) or represents not a temporal priority but one of another kind.

Geometry

We have already seen that Thales had an interest in geometry, though his contribution is unclear. The claim in **9.19** that the Pythagoreans were "first to advance" the study of mathematics is frequently understood to refer to

---

29. The text says merely "and apart." Perhaps this refers to a diagram Aristotle drew as he gave the lectures for which the *Physics* is the notes. What is "apart" is the extra row of dots, which when added to the square numbers makes oblong numbers.

their contributions to geometry, although their interest in number theory and their belief that numbers are the key to the KOSMOS would be enough to justify the statement even if they had done nothing to advance geometry. The Pythagorean theorem is one of the most famous geometrical propositions, and ancient sources attribute its discovery to Pythagoras himself.[30] But Pythagoras did not discover Euclid's proof (which could not have been worked out before the late fifth century), and if all he did was to state the theorem, he may have learned it when he visited Babylon, where it was known, though not proved.

In evaluating the Pythagoreans' contributions to geometry, three pieces of evidence are crucial: first and earliest, Aristotle's statement in **9.19**; second, the history of mathematics composed by Aristotle's pupil Eudemus, of which an important extract is preserved in Proclus' *Commentary on the First Book of Euclid's Elements*; and third, attributions of particular geometrical results to the Pythagoreans. The difficulty here is that Aristotle is positive but vague, Eudemus gives no prominence to Pythagoras or anyone known to be a Pythagorean, and the specific attributions, while showing that Eudemus and others did acknowledge a Pythagorean contribution to geometry, do not provide enough evidence to understand the nature and extent of Pythagorean geometry.

Two questions in particular remain open. Did the Pythagoreans discover the incommensurability of the side and diagonal of the square, and did they invent the notions of mathematical proof and the arrangement of theorems into a deductive system?

The first question, which many have thought important both for Pythagoreanism and for the history of mathematics, asks whether the Pythagoreans discovered that if a square has sides of length A and diagonals of length B, then there are no whole numbers M, N such that $A:B = M:N$. We would express this fact by saying that the ratio $A:B$ is irrational, or equivalently that $\sqrt{2}$ is irrational. This discovery preceded the work of Theodorus of Cyrene,[31] who extended it in the late fifth century, proving in effect which square roots are irrational as far as $\sqrt{17}$.[32] Euclid presents two different theories of proportion, one of which works only for "rational magnitudes" (those that can be represented as the ratio of whole numbers) and one of which works for "irrational magnitudes" (those that

30. Diogenes Laertius, *Lives of the Philosophers* 8.12 (not in DK); Porphyry, *Life of Pythagoras* 36 (not in DK); Athenaeus, *Table Talk* 10.13 (not in DK). But it is far from certain that Pythagoras actually made the discovery. See T. L. Heath, *History of Greek Mathematics*, vol. 1 (Oxford, 1921), pp. 144–49.

31. Iamblichus, *Life of Pythagoras* 36 (not in DK), asserts that Theodorus was a Pythagorean.

32. Plato, *Theaetetus* 147d (= DK 43,4).

cannot be so represented) as well. The obvious inference is that the former theory was worked out before the discovery of the irrational, and the latter, which is due to the fourth-century mathematical genius Eudoxus, was developed afterwards. Some attribute the earlier theory to the Pythagoreans (recall their interest in the ratios of whole numbers in connection with the musical intervals), and hold in addition that the discovery of the irrational caused a crisis for the Pythagoreans since it showed that the world could not be entirely accounted for through whole numbers. Some declared that Hippasus, an early Pythagorean, perished at sea through divine retribution for revealing this discovery, as if divulging the existence of the irrational and making public the shortcomings of the Pythagorean numerical conception of the world was a great scandal.

The second question is equally important for the history of mathematics and philosophy. What distinguishes Greek from Babylonian and Egyptian mathematics is the notion and prominence of proofs. The earlier cultures developed methods of doing arithmetic and calculating areas, and the Babylonians had some interest in the relations of numbers that was not entirely practical, but it was the Greeks who discovered and developed the idea of showing how one fact follows from others, and arranging facts into a logically ordered system. This is the practice of Euclid's *Elements* (c. 300 B.C.), parts of which are familiar to anyone who has studied geometry. Euclid was by no means the first person to prove theorems. Eudemus names several writers of "Elements" before Euclid, beginning with the fifth-century mathematician Hipparchus, and the practice of proving theorems must have been well established before Hipparchus, who will have arranged and systematized existing theorems and proofs. To whom, then, do we owe the discovery of proofs? Did the idea of proof come from mathematics, or did it start elsewhere? And why did it arise at all?

One suggestion[33] is that rigorous proofs are more likely to have arisen in connection with negative than with positive results. With positive results, say that the sum of the angles of a triangle is equal to two right angles, you can "see" that they hold by inspecting a few cases, perhaps with the help of cutting or folding the figure. This sort of procedure makes no pretense to rigor, but it does establish the result (at least for reasonably obvious facts in arithmetic and geometry). With negative results it is quite different. If you want to show that if A, B are the side and diagonal of a square, then there are no whole numbers M, N such that $A:B = M:N$, you cannot examine all possible pairs of whole numbers and show that none of them has the property in question. If your only way of showing that a proposition is true is to examine specific cases, you can never prove this result, only that none

---

33. A. Szabó, *The Beginnings of Greek Mathematics* (Dordrecht and Boston, 1978), pp. 185–216.

of the pairs so far considered has the property. Establishing a negative result in arithmetic or geometry therefore requires a proof, and in fact such problems, perhaps even the one involving the side and diagonal of the square, may have given rise to the idea of proving theorems.

It is further claimed that the idea of rigorous proof was first developed in philosophy and then applied to mathematics.[34] On this view, the sophisticated arguments of the Eleatic philosophers Parmenides and Zeno,[35] who proved negative results (e.g., that there is no motion), came first and mathematical proofs came second. However, our evidence does not allow us to say for certain whether the priority goes to mathematics or to philosophy. It is safe to say that deductive arguments were first used in both fields in the first half of the fifth century, and it is likely that they originated in south Italy, where both the city of Elea and the Pythagorean movement were located. Thus, a Pythagorean connection is possible, but cannot be proved.[36]

It is nevertheless certain that the Pythagoreans were interested in geometry. Their interest in reducing things to numbers naturally led them to do the same for geometry. The relations between the two fields are seen in the definitions of the basic entity in each field, the unit and the point. (A unit is a point lacking position, and a point is a unit having position.[37]) Numbers are pluralities of units, and lines, planes, and solids are determined by pluralities of points. One way in which one-, two-, and three-dimensional space depends on points is indicated in the following fragment of *Pythagorean Numbers*, a work by Plato's nephew Speusippus.

> **9.23** <The number 10 contains> formulas for lines, surfaces, and solids; for one is a point, two a line, three a triangle, and four a pyramid, and all these are primary and the starting points for the other figures of each kind.   (Speusippus, fr. 4 [Lang] = DK 44A13)

Here we are to think of the number ten as represented in the tetractys of the decad and so composed of the numbers one, two, three, and four in that

---

34. *Ibid.*, pp. 216–20.

35. See chaps. 11, 12.

36. It cannot be excluded that the inspiration for deductive proofs came from the Ionian geometrical tradition that originated with Thales and which made important contributions well into the fourth century, even though this method of argument was not characteristic of early Ionian philosophy. See Guthrie, *HGP*, vol. 1, pp. 218–19 for a statement of the pro-Ionian, anti-Pythagorean view. B. L. vander Waerden advocates the view that Thales invented the notion of mathematical proof (*Science Awakening* [Groningen, 1954], pp. 87–90).

37. Aristotle, *Metaphysics* 13.9 1084b26–27 (not in DK) and *On the Soul* 1.5 409a6 (not in DK).

order. Two points determine a straight line, three points not in a straight line mark the corners of a triangle, and four points not in the same plane the vertices of a pyramid. These are the simplest one-, two-, and three-dimensional figures.

Again we see how Pythagorean reductionism works. In each situation we treat the minimal case and that is supposed to take care of the more complicated cases. How it does so is vague; there is no reason to suppose that, for example, all plane figures (including ones with curved sides) are triangles or can be formed out of or approximated by triangles.[38] Moreover, we see again the "associative" nature of Pythagorean thought,[39] for geometrical points are different from arithmetical units, and straight lines are determined by two points in a different way from that in which the number two is composed of two units.

Generation of the Physical World

Having in some way generated geometrical figures out of numbers, the Pythagoreans' next task was to generate the physical world.

> 9.24 From the unit and the indefinite dyad spring numbers; from numbers, points; from points, lines; from lines, plane figures; from plane figures, solid figures; from solid figures, sensible bodies, the elements of which are four: fire, water, earth, and air; these elements interchange and turn into one another completely, and combine to produce a universe [KOSMOS] animate, intelligent, spherical, with the earth at its center, the earth itself being spherical, and inhabited round about.
> (Alexander Polyhistor, *Pythagorean Notebooks*, quoted in Diogenes Laertius, *Lives of the Philosophers* 8.25 = DK 58B1a, tr. after Hicks)

The reference to the four elements may make this theory later than Empedocles, who seems to have been the first to base a physical theory on them, but even so, it is likely to describe a genuinely Pythagorean theory. Another passage says more about the geometrical structure of the four elements.

38. This last result and the fact that all plane figures with straight sides can be broken up into triangles were known to Euclid, and so may have been known to the Pythagoreans, but they do not seem to be the inspiration for this generation of lines, planes, and solids out of points.
39. See p. 93.

9.25 There being five solid figures called the mathematical solids, Pythagoras says that earth is made from the cube, fire from the pyramid, air from the octahedron, water from the icosahedron, and from the dodecahedron is made the sphere of the whole.   (Aetius 2.6.5 = DK 44A15)

The shapes mentioned are the five regular solids, the only geometrical solids in which all edges are equal, all faces are congruent and equilateral, and all vertices form equal solid angles.

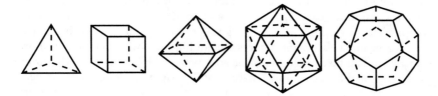

The cube has six faces that are square; the pyramid, octahedron, and icosahedron have for faces four, eight, and twenty equilateral triangles respectively; and the dodecahedron has twelve regular pentagons. Clearly the dodecahedron is not a sphere, although it and all the others can be inscribed in a sphere (all their vertices touch the surface of the smallest sphere that encloses them). **9.25** may allude to making balls by cutting twelve pieces of leather into pentagons, sewing them together and then stuffing them so that they fill out to a spherical shape (like soccer balls), but the details of the theory remain obscure.[40] Nevertheless, the attempt to account for the physical nature of the universe in terms of basic kinds of matter and to analyze these in terms of the small, definite, finite number of simple geometrical bodies is thoroughly Pythagorean in nature.

Alongside this "mathematical reductionist" approach we find traces of a cosmogony which makes the origin of the KOSMOS analogous to the generation of numbers.

9.26 When the unit had been constructed—whether from planes or surfaces or seed or from something they are at a loss to specify—the nearest parts of the unlimited at once began to be drawn in and limited by the limit.
                    (Aristotle, *Metaphysics* 14.3 1091a15–18 = DK 58B26)

40. This view of the four elements and the shape of the KOSMOS is also found in Plato (Plato, *Timaeus* 53c–57c, not in DK), and it is disputed whether Plato owed these ideas to the Pythagoreans or whether later writers wrongly ascribed to the Pythagoreans Plato's theory.

9.27 The Pythagoreans also said that void exists, and enters the universe from the unlimited breath, the universe being supposed in fact to inhale the void, which distinguishes things. For void is that which separates and distinguishes things that are next to each other. This happens first in numbers; the void divides their nature.

(Aristotle, *Physics* 4.6 213b22–27 = DK 58B30)

9.28 The universe is unique, and from the unlimited it draws in time, breath, and void, which distinguishes the places of separate things.

(Aristotle, fr. 201 [Rose] = DK 58B30)

This account has both early and late elements. The idea that unlimited breath surrounds the KOSMOS recalls Anaximenes (6.2), and the picture of the KOSMOS growing by inhaling this breath is at home among early Ionian ideas, while the conception of this breath as void cannot antedate Parmenides and may show influence of the fifth-century Atomists. The overall picture is that the universe is formed by the imposition of limit on the unlimited. Limit, determinacy, definiteness, and number are associated with order and intelligibility. As the musical scale is formed by imposing determinate numerical relations on the indefinite and continuous spectrum of sound, and numbers are generated when the determinate unit (representing limit) imposes order on the "indefinite dyad" (representing the unlimited [9.24]), the KOSMOS too is formed when the unit (representing limit) operates on the unlimited. Order begins in the center of the universe and expands by assimilating unordered, unlimited stuff into the ordered universe.

The KOSMOS, being ordered and limited, is finite in extent, and hence must have a physical boundary and a geometrical shape. Thus the Pythagoreans could put to use the dodecahedron, which was left out when shapes were assigned to the elements. An important feature of the order in the KOSMOS is that its parts are separate, distinct from one another. The void keeps things apart and performs an analogous function in the ordered realm of discrete, whole numbers, separating each from the rest and guaranteeing to each its identity and uniqueness. 9.28 adds that time was also drawn in from the unlimited. The idea here is that the unlimited has a temporal as well as a spatial aspect, and the KOSMOS has both spatial and temporal order which are imposed in analogous ways by the limiting principle.

The Pythagorean cosmogony is different from the Ionian ones—so different, in fact, that it is hard to believe that the KOSMOS that results is the world around us. At the least it seems that the account fails to address a number of crucial issues. As the following passage shows, Aristotle, who wrote a (no longer extant) treatise on the Pythagoreans, and so must have had access to relevant materials, shares these feelings.

9.29 Those called Pythagoreans use stranger principles and elements than the natural philosophers do. The reason is that they did not take their principles from perceptible things . . . yet everything they discuss and treat has to do with nature; for they generate the heaven and observe what happens regarding its parts, its attributes and the events in it, and use up the principles and causes on these, as if they agreed with the others, the natural philosophers, that what exists is precisely all that is perceptible and contained by what they call the heaven. . . . However, they say nothing about how there can be motion if limit and unlimited and odd and even are the only things assumed, or how without motion and change there can be generation and destruction, or the behavior of the bodies that move through the heavens.

(Aristotle, *Metaphysics* 1.8 989b29–990a12 = DK 58B22)

It is possible, then, that what the Pythagoreans said really was unclearly or incompletely stated, so perhaps the broad sketch given above of how they founded their KOSMOS on numbers and on the principle of imposing limit on the unlimited is as far as it is reasonable to go.

Pythagorean Cosmology

The Pythagorean account of the KOSMOS contains three noteworthy features: its rejection of the geocentric picture, the role of the number ten, and the harmony of the spheres.

9.30 Although most say that the earth is situated at the center <of the universe> . . . those in Italy called Pythagoreans assert the contrary opinion. For they declare that fire is at the center and the earth is one of the stars and by being carried in a circle round the center it causes night and day. Further, opposite to this one they construct another earth which they name "counter-earth." In this they are not inquiring for theories and causes with a view to the phenomena, but are forcing the phenomena to fit certain theories and opinions of their own, and trying to bring them into line. Many others agree that the earth should not be put at the center, finding reliability on the basis not of the phenomena but rather of their theories. For they believe that the most honorable thing deserves to have the most honorable region, and that fire is more honorable than earth, and that the limit is more honorable than what is intermediate, and the extremity and the center are limits. So, reasoning from these premises they think that not it but fire is situated at the center of the sphere. Moreover, the Pythagoreans call the fire occupying this region Zeus' guardhouse because the most important part of the universe should be the best guarded, and the center is most important, as if "center" had a single meaning and the center of the spatial extension and of the thing itself were also the natural center. But just as in animals

the center of the animal is not the same as the center of its body, we must suppose the same to hold concerning the whole heaven.
(Aristotle, *On the Heaven* 2.13 293a18–b8 = DK 58B36)

9.31 Philolaus says that there is fire in the middle around the center, which he calls the hearth of the universe and the house of Zeus and the mother of the gods, and the altar, bond, and measure of nature. Moreover, he says that what surrounds the universe at the furthest extreme is another fire. The center is by nature first. Around it ten divine bodies dance—after the sphere of the fixed stars, the five planets; after them, the sun; beneath it, the moon; beneath it, the earth; beneath it, the counter-earth; after them all, the fire of the hearth keeping its position around the center. (Aetius 2.7.7. = DK 44A16)

9.32 They supposed . . . the entire heaven to be a HARMONIA and a number. And all the characteristics of numbers and HARMONIAI (plural of HARMONIA) they found corresponding to the attributes and parts of the heaven and to the entire ordering, they collected and made them fit. If anything was missing anywhere they eagerly filled in the gaps to make their entire system coherent. For example, since they think the number ten is something perfect and encompasses the entire nature of numbers, they declare that the bodies that move in the heaven are also ten. But since only nine are visible, they invent the counter-earth as the tenth.
(Aristotle, *Metaphysics* 1.5 986a2–12 = DK 58B4)
(continuation of **9.19**)

The KOSMOS consists of a fiery center orbited by the counter-earth, earth, moon, sun, Mercury, Venus, Mars, Jupiter, Saturn, and the fixed stars.[41] **9.32** objects to the Pythagoreans' reason for positing the counter-earth, though modern physicists, who are used to positing the existence of entities on the basis of theory, might be somewhat sympathetic. Some ancient sources, including perhaps Aristotle himself, say that the Pythagoreans used the counter-earth to account for lunar eclipses.[42]

The Pythagoreans were the first to remove the earth from the center of the KOSMOS, and their reasons as reported in **9.30** and **9.31** are not astronomical, but religious ("house of Zeus") and metaphysical ("the center is the most important"). It is not surprising that this idea was not adopted even by all Pythagoreans (**9.24** shows that some Pythagoreans placed the earth at the center of the universe) or by most other ancient astronomers,

41. The outer planets are invisible to the naked eye and were only discovered in 1781 (Uranus), 1846 (Neptune), and 1930 (Pluto).
42. Aristotle, *On the Heaven* 2.13 293b21–25 (not in DK), Aetius 2.29.4 (= DK 58B36).

who retained the traditional geocentric view.[43] However, the proponents of this theory defended it against the astronomical objection that the circular appearing orbits of the heavenly bodies imply that the earth is in the center of the KOSMOS.

> **9.33** Since the earth's surface is not in fact the center, but is distant from the center by its whole hemisphere [i.e., radius], the Pythagoreans feel no difficulty in supposing that although we do not occupy the center the phenomena are the same as if the earth were at the center. For they hold that even on the current view [that the earth is at the center] there is nothing to show that we are distant from the center by half the earth's diameter.   (Aristotle, *On the Heaven* 2.13 293b25–30, not in DK)

Nevertheless, the claim that some have maintained, that the Pythagoreans discovered that the earth is a planet, overstates the case, seeing that they held the false view that the earth (as well as the sun, moon, etc.) all go round a central fire, rather than round the sun. Nevertheless, the fact that they could conceive of the earth's not being at the center is an important advance, and from this perspective "the identification of the central fire with the sun is a detail in comparison."[44]

The Pythagorean doctrine of the music of the spheres was based on several basic features of Pythagoreanism—harmonics, cosmology, and mathematics—and caught the fancy of literary authors in later antiquity and the Renaissance. The clearest and most sober account is given by Aristotle.[45]

> **9.34** Although the assertion that a harmony arises from the motion of the heavenly bodies since the sounds that are produced are concordant, is expressed cleverly and remarkably by its proponents, it does not contain the truth. For some think a sound must be produced when bodies of such great size are in motion, since it happens with bodies on earth too which do not have so great a bulk and do not move with so great speed. And when the sun and moon and the stars which are so great in number and size move so quickly, there must be a noise overwhelming in loudness. Assuming these things and that the speeds, which depend on the

43. An important ancient exception to this view was the theory of Aristarchus of Samos (first half of the third century) who hypothesized that "the fixed stars and the sun remain unmoved and that the earth revolves about the sun on the circumference of a circle, the sun lying in the middle of the orbit" (Archimedes, *The Sand-Reckoner* 4–5, not in DK).

44. Burnet, *Early Greek Philosophy*, p. 299.

45. This doctrine first appears in Plato (Plato, *Republic* 10 616b–617d, not in DK).

distances, have the ratios of the concords, they declare that the sound of the stars in circular motion is harmonious. But since it appeared illogical that we do not hear this sound, they declare that the reason is that the sound is present to us from birth, and so is not evident in contrast to the opposing silence, for noise and silence are recognized by contrast to one another. And so the same thing happens to humans as to bronzesmiths: as a result of habituation there seems to be no difference.

(Aristotle, *On the Heaven* 2.9 290b12–29 = DK 58B35)

This gives some meaning to the statement that "they supposed the whole heaven to be an attunement and a number" (**9.32**). The pitches of the various notes correspond to their speeds, which depend on their distances (from the central fire). Indeed the Pythagoreans are said to have been "first to discover the order of the positions of the planets."[46]

Opposites

The importance of the notion of opposition, already present in Anaximander and Anaximenes, continues in later philosophers, including the Pythagoreans, some of whom developed it in a distinctive way.

9.35 Others of this same school declare that there are ten principles arranged in parallel columns:

limit	unlimited
odd	even
one	plurality
right	left
male	female
at rest	moving
straight	bent
light	darkness
good	evil
square	oblong

This is how Alcmaeon of Croton too seems to have understood things, and either he took this theory from them or they from him. . . . He says that most human matters are pairs, identifying as the oppositions not definite ones like the Pythagoreans . . . but the Pythagoreans described how many and what the oppositions are.

(Aristotle, *Metaphysics* 1.5 986a22–b2 = DK 58B5)

(continuation of **9.20**)

46. Eudemus, quoted in Simplicius, *Commentary on Aristotle's On the Heaven* 471.5–6 (= DK 12A19); Guthrie, *HGP*, vol. 1, p. 298.

The table of opposites contains twenty opposites but ten principles, each pair counting as one principle. The table manifests interest in a wide range of aspects of the world, including moral values, which accords with the Pythagoreans' use of numbers to account for features of the physical universe and also for qualities like justice (**9.36**).

The table displays many Pythagorean ideas. First, the number of pairs of basic opposites is ten. Second, the prominence of limit and unlimited, followed by odd and even, recalls the accounts of the generation of number in **9.19-9.22**. One and plurality, lined up respectively with limit and unlimited, recall another account of the generation of number and of the KOSMOS (**9.24**). Square and oblong bring to mind the properties of square and oblong numbers discussed previously (p. 94–95). The remaining pairs of opposites are diverse and not in all cases clearly related.

From the point of view of logic, each pair seems intended to consist of mutually exclusive items. Some pairs seem intended to exhaust their fields of application (all animals are either male or female, all whole numbers are either odd or even) and some do not (some numbers are neither square nor oblong). Some items admit degrees (moving, bent), while others do not. From the point of view of Pythagorean metaphysics, some of the pairs are basic (odd and even, cf. **9.19** and **9.20**; alternatively, limit and unlimited, cf. **9.21**), and some are derivative (one and plurality, cf. **9.20**). But the table leaves some important issues open. No effort is made to distinguish the types of opposition involved, and there is no explanation of the way in which these opposites are principles or of why these particular pairs of opposites are chosen instead of those which figure conspicuously in earlier cosmologies, such as dense and rare, hot and cold, or wet and dry. Indeed, if odd and even (or limit and unlimited) are the principles of all things, how can there be any other principles?

Things and Numbers

The Pythagoreans extended their program of accounting for phenomena in terms of number in surprising directions.

> **9.36** In numbers they thought they observed many resemblances to the things that are and that come to be . . . such and such an attribute of numbers being justice, another being soul and intellect, another being decisive moment, and similarly for virtually all other things . . . since all other things seemed to be made in the likeness of numbers in their entire nature.   (Aristotle, *Metaphysics* 1.5 985b28–33 = DK 58B4)

Further insight into this aspect of Pythagoreanism is found in the following passages, of which the first comments on **9.36**.

9.37 They supposed that requital and equality were characteristic of justice and found these features in numbers, and so declared that justice was the first number that is equal-times-equal. . . . They said that decisive moment is the number seven, since things which are natural appear to have their decisive moments of fulfillment in birth and growth by sevens. Humans, for example. They are born in the seventh month and teethe in as many months, and reach adolescence in the second span of seven years and get a beard in the third. . . . They said that marriage is the number five, because marriage is the union of male and female, and according to them the odd is male and the even is female, and this number is the first which has its origin from two, the first even number, and three, the first odd. . . . They declared intellect and essence to be the one, since he spoke of the soul as the intelligence. They said that because it is stable and similar in every way and sovereign, the intelligence is the unity and one.

(Alexander, Commentary on Aristotle's Metaphysics
38.10–39.20, not in DK)

9.38 Concerning what things are, they began to make statements and definitions, but treated the matter too simply. For they would define superficially and thought that the first thing an indicated term applies to was the essence of the thing, as if one were to suppose that double and the number two are the same because two is the first thing double applies to. But surely to be double and to be two are not the same; otherwise one thing will be many—a consequence they actually draw.

(Aristotle, Metaphysics 1.5 987a20–27 = DK 58B8)

Some of these cases reveal the reductionist reasoning found elsewhere, but the association of "decisive moment" with the number seven (**9.37**) is based on the wildest sort of speculative association, which is found in Neopythagorean treatments of other numbers.[47] One Pythagorean extended this approach to concrete substances.

9.39 Eurytus assigned what was the number of what, e.g., this is the number of a human, that is the number of a horse, like those who bring numbers into triangular and square figures, fashioning with pebbles the forms of plants. (Aristotle, *Metaphysics* 14.5 1092b10–13 = DK 45,3)

9.40 For example, suppose the number 250 is the definition of human being. . . . After positing this, he would take 250 pebbles, some green, some black, others red, and generally pebbles of all colors. Then he

---

47. Iamblichus, *Theologoumena Arithmeticae,* contains much of this kind of fanciful material. Some of the material in **9.37** may be due to Neopythagorean sources too.

smeared a wall with lime and drew a human being in outline . . . and then fastened some of these pebbles in the drawn face, others in the hands, others elsewhere, and he completed the drawing of the human being there represented by means of pebbles equal to the units which he declared define human being. As a result of this procedure he would state that just as the particular sketched human being is composed of, say, 250 pebbles, so a real human being is defined by so many units.

(Alexander, *Commentary on Aristotle's Metaphysics* 827.9–19 = DK 45,3)

In a procedure only distantly related to the reasoning given in **9.37**, Eurytus displays the number of a human being by placing pebbles on his diagram, thus showing that they are the smallest number that can fill in the shape of a human.

The Pythagoreans founded their account of the KOSMOS on numbers. But how did they think numbers are related to things? Aristotle makes several remarks on this subject (also **9.36**).

9.41 Because they noticed that many attributes of numbers belong to sensible objects, the Pythagoreans held that existing things are numbers—not separate numbers, but composed of numbers [literally, out of numbers]. Why so? Because the attributes of numbers are found in HARMONIA, in the heaven and in many other things.

(Aristotle, *Metaphysics* 14.3 1090a20–25, not in DK)

9.42 In making physical bodies (things possessing lightness and weight) out of numbers (which possess neither) they seem to be speaking about a different heaven and different bodies, not sensible ones.

(Aristotle, *Metaphysics* 14.3 1090a32–35, not in DK)

9.43 They supposed the elements of numbers to be the elements of all existing things.   (Aristotle, *Metaphysics* 1.5 986a1–2 = DK 58B4)

Aristotle expresses the Pythagorean view in four ways: (a) things are identical with numbers; (b) things are composed of numbers; (c) things resemble numbers; (d) the principles of numbers are the principles of all things. Some of these claims are puzzling. Regarding interpretation (a), even though four points determine the vertices of the simplest geometrical solid, how can the tetrahedron be identical with the number four? Likewise there may be a reason to associate justice with the first square number, but how can justice be the number four? Also identity is a transitive relation, but how can justice be a tetrahedron? Aristotle makes this objection too.

9.44 If all things must share in number, many things must turn out to be the same, and the same number must belong to one thing and to another. . . . Therefore, if the same number had belonged to certain things, these would have been the same as one another, since they would have had the same form of number.

(Aristotle, *Metaphysics* 14.6 1093a1–13 = DK 58B27)

Interpretation (b) involves other difficulties. If figures and physical objects are composed of numbers, then numbers must have size and weight. Thus, Aristotle:

9.45 The Pythagoreans say that there is one kind of number, the mathematical kind, only it is not separate, but they hold that sensible substances are constituted out of it. For they construct the entire heaven out of numbers, only not units, but they suppose the units to possess magnitude. But they seem to be at a loss about how the first one possessing magnitude was constituted.

(Aristotle, *Metaphysics* 13.6 1080b16–21 = DK 58B9)

9.46 In one way the Pythagoreans' approach has fewer problems than the previously mentioned ones, but in another way it has others of its own. Making number not separate removes many of the impossibilities, but it is impossible for bodies to be composed of numbers and for this number to be mathematical. For it is not true to speak of indivisible magnitudes, but even if this were very much the case, units, anyway, do not possess magnitude. How can magnitude be made up of indivisible things? But arithmetical number is made of units. And they say that existing things are number. Anyway they apply theorems to bodies as if they were composed of those numbers.

(Aristotle, *Metaphysics* 13.8 1083b8–19 = DK 58B10)

From these passages it appears that at least some Pythagoreans said that things are numbers. In Greek as in English, the statement "this stick is wood" can mean either (a) "this stick is identical with a particular piece of wood" or (b) "this stick is made of wood." (a) is a statement of identity and (b) is a statement of composition. Identity statements are transitive: if this stick is identical with a particular piece of wood and is also identical with a particular branch of the oak tree in my back yard, then that piece of wood is that branch. Composition statements are not transitive: if this stick is made of wood and that table is also made of wood, it does not follow that this stick is made of that table, or that table is made of this stick, nor does the identity statement "this stick is that table" follow. Both these uses of "is" are so familiar that we take such statements in the appropriate way without reflection. When Anaximenes says "everything is air" we take him to be making a composition statement, not an identity statement. There is no difficulty because Anaximenes' assertion is intelligible as a theory about the composition of the world, whereas the Pythagorean claim that things are numbers, if taken as a composition statement, is absurd. Although air is a material substance and so the right kind of thing for other things to be made of, numbers are different. Aristotle shares our discomfort at the thought that "things are numbers" could mean that they are composed of numbers. But if it is not a composition statement, it is natural to interpret it as an identity statement. But here too, we run into serious objections—in fact the objections Aristotle raises, the consequence that many different things will wind up with the same number and so are identical.

Aristotle criticizes Pythagorean philosophy on the grounds that it leads to absurd consequences, and he is surely correct if the theory asserts that numbers are identical with things or that things are composed of numbers. However, interpretation (c), that things resemble numbers, is not open to these objections and also has links with central features of Pythagorean thought.[48] There are many ways in which things may resemble numbers. 9.37 points out some ways in which qualities such as justice can be thought of as resembling numbers, i.e., by having some of the same properties as a particular number. More generally, numbers, geometrical figures, the physical KOSMOS, and musical scales are generated similarly: all come to be when limit is imposed on the unlimited. All are instances of order, perhaps even of sequential order, which exists in different realms. And they all have numerical aspects that are basic: the number of sides of a triangle, the number and distances of the heavenly bodies, the ratios of the lengths of strings. Moreover, the analysis of the generation of all these things in terms of limit being imposed on the unlimited gives a clear sense to interpretation (d), the principles of number are the principles of all things.

The Pythagoreans believed that number is fundamental to all things, that the basic features of all things are numerical, that numerical considerations are basic in understanding all things, that all things are generated in a similar way to numbers. These statements are all ways of claiming primacy for numbers, but they are different ways. The Pythagoreans noticed all these ways, but instead of keeping them distinct gathered them together into a single thought. One way of expressing the point is to say that they did not think that number is fundamental in many distinct and perhaps unrelated ways, some of which apply here and others there, but simply thought

---

48. The Pythagorean doctrine that things resemble numbers is a probable forerunner of Plato's doctrine that sensible things resemble or imitate Forms. Many of the philosophical problems inherent in the Pythagorean conceptions of the relations between things and numbers—issues of identity, resemblance, and predication—also arise for Plato, who struggles with them in such dialogues as *Phaedo*, *Parmenides*, and *Sophist*.

that number is fundamental and looked for evidence to support this claim. The difference is important. The Pythagoreans piled up evidence without calling attention to how different the bits of evidence are. They were not interested in analyzing different ways numbers are primary, only in establishing that numbers are in fact primary. They formulated their thesis vaguely, to accommodate the different relations they found between things and numbers, and to judge by the different ways Aristotle states their doctrine, they phrased it differently on different occasions. Also, to judge by Aristotle's criticisms, their vague notion of priority does not stand up to analysis, but as soon as the questions are put "in what way are numbers primary?" and "in what way are all things numbers?" it becomes necessary to specify once again all the different ways: different things are numbers, or imitate numbers, or resemble numbers, or are generated in the same way as numbers, etc.

These problems arise for the Pythagoreans because they based their physical system on numbers. How numbers are basic to the universe and things around us is less straightforward a matter than how a substance like air is, and the Ionian background offered little help towards drawing the necessary distinctions and analyzing connections at a sufficiently abstract level to identify the issues involved or offer a philosophically satisfactory account. What does it mean, for example, to say that the One is generated out of odd and even, or that the universe is composed of numbers, or that justice is the number four? What notions of generation, composition, and identity are in play—and if these are not precisely the notions in play, what relations are meant?

In fact, the Pythagoreans probably could not express their ideas accurately, given the state of the Greek language and the primitive state of philosophical analysis in their time. In the fifth century, Greek lacked most of the philosophical vocabulary needed to distinguish between sameness and resemblance (the same Greek word HOMOIOS meant both "same" and "similar"), identity and composition (the two uses of "is" discussed above), or origin and metaphysical structure. (In Greek, to say that one thing [A] is or comes "out of" another [B] can mean that what was once B is now A, or that A is made up of B, or that A depends on B, or that A can be analyzed into B.) These ambiguities need to be resolved before statements like the ones the Pythagoreans made about number can be fully understood, but nothing in earlier philosophy encouraged Pythagoras or his early followers to make fine distinctions. In fact, the philosophical work needed for the task was not undertaken before Socrates, Plato, and Aristotle, whose evident frustration with the Pythagoreans reflects the intellectual distance that separates him from ideas formulated only two or three generations before.

The Unity of Pythagoreanism

A general problem for understanding the Pythagoreans is why a religious movement dedicated to purifying the soul should have promoted mathematics and the study of the KOSMOS. In other words, how are the two sides of the movement related? Do they form a unity? I believe they do, and the connection between them may go back to the Founder. Other Greek cults promised their devotees immortality, but how can some souls be immortal while others are mortal, and how can attending religious rites make souls immortal? Milesian speculation on the nature of the KOSMOS and the composition of things including souls pointed to the view that souls are made up of the basic stuff of the universe and so, immortal. The issue is thus not how to gain immortality, but how best to use it. Pythagoras taught that the best and most important thing to do is to purify the soul, to rid it of pollution and disorder, because pure souls have the best afterlife, and perhaps ultimately attain a kind of divinity.

Distinctive to Pythagoreanism is idea that purification is not achieved solely by ritual means. It requires more than abstaining from meat and beans and more than obedience to the AKOUSMATA. It also requires eliminating the disorder which affects our soul when we lack clear knowledge of the KOSMOS. For the Pythagoreans (more precisely, the MATHEMATIKOI), this clear knowledge is not simply a matter of parroting a set of beliefs, saying a catechism of fixed doctrine without understanding. It involves the study of mathematics and the KOSMOS. The numerical basis of the KOSMOS implies that the KOSMOS is comprehensible to humans, and the knowledge of it which benefits our soul demands thought and understanding. Our soul becomes orderly (KOSMIOS) when it understands the order (KOSMOS) in the universe.[49] This is the inspiration that underlay the developments in Pythagorean thought and which gives the Pythagoreans much common ground with their Ionian predecessors as well as with their successors in mathematics, science, and philosophy.

Conclusion

Pythagoreanism was a two-faced movement that combined primitive ingredients with ideas still current today into a doctrine at home in the presocratic period. Its breadth of interest is typified by its concern with the individual soul on the one hand and with the structure of the universe on the other, and is represented by the ten pairs of fundamental opposites.

---

49. Plato, *Republic* 6 500c, (not in DK). The idea is nicely developed in Guthrie, *HGP*, vol. 1, pp. 206–12.

The Pythagoreans shared with their Ionian predecessors an interest in the physical world and the goal of explaining it through a small number of basic principles, as well as the confidence to base a theory on a breathtaking generalization from a limited range of evidence. Different was their proclamation of the fundamental importance of number in the world. Instead of basing other things on a material substance such as water or air, they explained them in terms of numbers. For this they are given credit for recognizing the importance of the quantitative aspects of phenomena and for the first reduction of quality to quantity (in their numerical account of the concordant musical intervals). On the other hand, the clear distinction between quantity and quality was not made until Aristotle, and in the absence of this and other relevant philosophical distinctions the Pythagoreans literally did not know what they were doing. However, their mathematical explorations made a lasting contribution. They were concerned to define mathematical concepts and invented the field of number theory. They were also involved in the development of geometry, and it is possible, but no more than that, that they created the notion of mathematical proof. Their cosmology is a blend of their mathematics, their musical theory, their religious ideas, and their mystical numerology. In its details it is noteworthy for removing the earth from the center of the universe and for postulating the harmony of the spheres. The main philosophical interest of their discussion of the universe is in its account of the origin, in which the KOSMOS resembles number, geometrical figures, and the musical intervals by being the product of the imposition of limit on the unlimited. Their failure to distinguish between the nature of numbers and the nature of material objects, however, leaves them open to charges that their cosmogony attempts the impossible, to make numbers the physical constituents of material things. Their doctrines of the soul's immortality, its rebirth into different living things, and the possibility of its ultimate release into a better existence have practical implications for how Pythagoreans should live their lives. The beliefs that a living being is composed of a body and a soul and that the soul is more important than the body would have an important legacy in ethical and metaphysical as well as religious thought. Finally, the bold conception of the universe in all its aspects—including the living and nonliving, the cosmological, musical and mathematical, and the ethical—as an intelligible, ordered whole, in a word a KOSMOS, was the ultimate basis of their thought and life.

10

Heraclitus of Ephesus

Fragments[1]

Group I. Contempt for the Lack of Understanding of the Many

10.1 (1)[2] This LOGOS holds always[3] but humans always prove unable to understand it, both before hearing it and when they have first heard it. For though all things come to be [or, happen] in accordance with this LOGOS, humans are like the inexperienced when they experience such words and deeds as I set out, distinguishing each in accordance with its nature and saying how it is. But other people fail to notice what they do when awake, just as they forget what they do while asleep.

10.2 (2) For this reason it is necessary to follow what is common. But although the LOGOS is common, most people live as if they had their own private understanding.

10.3 (17) For many, in fact all that come upon them, do not understand such things, nor when they have noticed them do they know them, but they seem to themselves <to do so>.

1. I translate all the fragments agreed to be authentic (except for DK 22B122, which is a single word without any context) and a few whose authenticity is disputed (which I mark with an asterisk). The wording of some fragments is disputed, as are their meaning and their proper order. General books on early Greek philosophy, including the present one, lacking much room to treat the problems or offer alternative readings, make things seem more certain than they are. For discussion of individual fragments, I recommend C. H. Kahn, *The Art and Thought of Heraclitus* (Cambridge, 1979); M. Marcovich, *Heraclitus* (Merida, Venezuela, 1967); and G. S. Kirk, *Heraclitus, The Cosmic Fragments* (Cambridge, 1954).

2. The numbers in parentheses are the numbers of the fragments in DK. (1) = DK 22B1.

3. The word "always," which occurs only once in the Greek, can go grammatically with either "holds" or "prove." Since Heraclitus holds both that the LOGOS is eternal and that other people do not understand it when he explains it to them, I have translated it twice. I believe the ambiguity is intentional. Heraclitus often exploits language in ways like this. Also, the first words, which I render as an absolute clause, can also be the object of "unable to understand." An alternative translation is "Humans always prove unable to understand this LOGOS which holds always."

10.4 (29) The best renounce all for one thing, the eternal fame of mortals, but the many stuff themselves like cattle.

10.5 (56) People are deceived about the knowledge of obvious things, like Homer who was wiser than all the Greeks. For children who were killing lice deceived him by saying "All we saw and caught we have left behind, but all we neither saw nor caught we bring with us."

10.6* (70) [Heraclitus judged human opinions to be] children's playthings.

10.7 (74) We should not be children of our parents.

10.8* (72) They are at odds with the LOGOS, with which above all they are in continuous contact, and the things they meet every day appear strange to them.[4]

10.9* (71) . . . the person who forgets which way the road leads.

10.10 (86) Divine things for the most part escape recognition because of unbelief.

10.11 (87) A fool is excited by every word (LOGOS).

10.12 (97) Dogs bark at everyone they do not know.

10.13 (104) What understanding (NOOS) or intelligence (PHREN[5]) have they? They put their trust in popular bards and take the mob for their teacher, unaware that most people are bad, and few are good.

10.14 (108) Of all those whose accounts (LOGOI, plural of LOGOS) I have heard, no one reaches the point of recognizing that that which is wise is set apart from all.[6]

10.15 (11) Every beast is driven to pasture by blows.

Also **10.20, 10.22**

Group II. Contempt for Predecessors

9.2 (40) Much learning ["polymathy"] does not teach insight. Otherwise it would have taught Hesiod and Pythagoras and moreover Xenophanes and Hecataeus.

4. Probably a recollection of **10.3**. Marcus Aurelius gives **10.9**, **10.8**, and **10.23** one after the other. He is probably relying on his memory and may be intentionally paraphrasing.

5. See p. 62 n. 6 on Xenophanes.

6. Grammatically, "all" can mean either "all humans" or "all things."

9.3 (129) Pythagoras the son of Mnesarchus practiced inquiry (HISTORIE) more than all other men, and making a selection of these writings constructed his own wisdom, polymathy, evil trickery.

10.16 (42) Heraclitus said that Homer deserved to be expelled from the contests and flogged, and Archilochus likewise.

10.17 (28) The knowledge of the most famous persons, which they guard, is but opinion. Justice will convict those who fabricate falsehoods and bear witness to them.

10.18 (39) In Priene was born Bias, son of Teutames, whose worth (LOGOS) is greater than the others'.

Also **10.5, 10.71**

Group III. Method

A. MISUSE OF THE SENSES

10.19* (46) [He said that] conceit is a holy disease[7] [and that] sight tells falsehoods.

10.20 (19) [Rebuking some for their unbelief, Heraclitus says,] Knowing neither how to hear nor how to speak.

10.21 (107) Eyes and ears are bad witnesses to people if they have barbarian[8] souls.

10.22 (34) Uncomprehending when they have heard, they are like the deaf. The saying describes them: though present they are absent.

B. SLEEP AND DEATH

10.23* (73) One ought not to act and speak like people asleep.

10.24 (89) For the waking there is one common world, but when asleep each person turns away to a private one.

7. A reference to epilepsy, which was called the holy disease.
8. A BARBAROS was originally anyone who did not speak Greek. Perhaps in Heraclitus' lifetime it began to have the negative overtones of "barbarian." Heraclitus probably uses the word here of people who do not understand the LOGOS.

10.25 (26) A man in the night kindles a light for himself when his sight is extinguished; living he touches[9] the dead when asleep, when awake he touches the sleeper.

10.26* (75) Sleepers are workmen and fellow-workers in what goes on in the world.[10]

10.27 (21) What we see when awake is death, what we see asleep is sleep.

Also **10.1, 10.74, 10.76, 10.89, 10.90, 10.113, 10.104, 10.107, 10.108, 10.109, 10.110, 10.111**

C. WISDOM AND INSIGHT

10.28 (78) Human nature has no insight, but divine nature has it.

10.29 (79) A man is called infantile by a divinity as a child is by a man.

10.30 (32) The wise is one alone; it is unwilling and willing to be called by the name of Zeus. [other translations, The wise is only one; it alone is unwilling. . . . One thing, the only wise, . . .]

10.31 (113) Thinking is common to all.[11]

10.32 (116) It belongs to all people to know themselves and to think rightly.

Also **10.14 10.44, 10.46**

D. EXPERIENCE AND INQUIRY

10.33 (101) I searched myself.

10.34 (35) Men who are lovers of wisdom must be inquirers into many things indeed.

Also **9.2**

E. THE SENSES

10.35 (55) All that can be seen, heard, experienced—these are what I prefer.

10.36 (101a) Eyes are more accurate witnesses than the ears.

9. The Greek word for "kindles" and "touches" is the same.
10. At best this is a paraphrase of Heraclitus' actual words.
11. See n. 6.

10.37 (7) If all things were smoke, nostrils would distinguish them.

10.38 (98) Souls smell [i.e., use the sense of smell] in Hades.

F. Difficulty of the Subject

10.39 (18) Unless he hopes for the unhoped for, he will not find it, since it is not to be hunted out and is impassable.[12]

10.40 (22) Those who seek gold dig up much earth but find little.

10.41 (84b) It is weariness to labor at the same things and <always> to be beginning [or, It is weariness to labor for the same <masters> and to be ruled].

10.42 (123) Nature loves to hide.

10.43 (93) The Lord whose oracle is at Delphi neither speaks nor conceals, but gives a sign.

G. The Goal

10.44 (41) Wisdom is one thing, to be skilled in true judgment, how all things are steered through all things.

10.45 (47) Let us not make random conjectures about the greatest matters.

10.46 (112) Right thinking is the greatest excellence, and wisdom is to speak the truth and act in accordance with nature, while paying attention to it.

Group IV. The Logos

10.1, 10.2, 10.8

10.47 (50) Listening not to me but to the Logos it is wise to agree that all things are one.

10.48 (10) Things taken together are whole and not whole, <something which is> being brought together and brought apart, in tune and out of tune; out of all things there comes a unity, and out of a unity all things.

10.49 (51) They do not understand how, though at variance with itself, it agrees with itself [or, how by being at variance with itself it agrees with

12. APORON ("without a path"), related to APORIA, "perplexity."

itself; more literally, how being [or, by being] brought apart it is brought together]. It is a backwards-turning [or, backwards-stretching][13] attunement like that of the bow and lyre.

10.50 (54) An unapparent connection (HARMONIA) is stronger than an apparent one.

10.51 (114) Those who speak with understanding (NOOS) must rely firmly on what is common to all[14] as a city must rely on law [or, its law] and much more firmly. For all human laws are nourished by one law, the divine law; for it has as much power as it wishes and is sufficient for all[15] and is still left over.

10.52 (8) What is opposed brings together; the finest harmony (HARMONIA) is composed of things at variance, and everything comes to be [or, occurs] in accordance with strife.

Group V. Fragments on Opposition

A. X Has Contrary Properties from Different Points of View

10.53 (61) The sea is the purest and most polluted water: to fishes drinkable and bringing safety, to humans undrinkable and destructive.

10.54 (13) Pigs rejoice in mud more than pure water.

10.55 (9) Asses would choose rubbish rather than gold.

10.56 (4) We would call oxen happy when they find bitter vetch to eat.

10.57 (37) Pigs wash themselves in mud, birds in dust or ash.

10.58 (82) The most beautiful of apes is ugly in comparison with the human race.[16]

10.59 (83) The wisest of humans will appear as an ape in comparison with a god in respect of wisdom, beauty, and all other things.

13. PALINTROPOS or PALINTONOS. The sources disagree here, and there is no scholarly consensus on which word Heraclitus used.
14. See n. 6.
15. Grammatically, "all" can mean either "all humans," "all things," or "all human laws."
16. Some consider this fragment spurious.

10.60 (124) The most beautiful KOSMOS is a pile of things poured out at random.

Also **10.88**

B. X HAS CONTRARY PROPERTIES TO THE SAME OBSERVER SIMULTANEOUSLY, IN DIFFERENT RESPECTS

10.61 (58) Physicians who cut and burn complain that they receive no worthy pay, although they do these things.[17]

10.62 (59) The track of writing [or, the path of the carding wheels[18]] is straight and crooked.

10.63 (60) The road up and the road down are one and the same.

10.64 (12) Upon those who step into the same rivers, different and again different waters flow.

10.65 (91) [It is not possible to step twice into the same river][19]. . . . It scatters and again comes together, and approaches and recedes.

10.66* (49a) We step into and we do not step into the same rivers. We are and we are not.[20]

10.67 (103) The beginning and the end are common on the circumference of a circle.

17. The text of this fragment is problematic. Another version (which is further removed from the manuscript readings) is "Physicians . . . demand pay, but deserve nothing." In any case, the point is that surgery and cautery, which heal patients, involve pain, as do the conditions they cure.

18. The manuscript reading GNAPHEON ("carding wheels") is emended by some editors to GRAPHEON ("writing").

19. The first clause of **10.65** contradicts **10.64**, which sees no difficulty about stepping into the "same" river. I follow KRS in thinking that the first clause of **10.65** follows Plato's interpretation (see pp. 142–44). (KRS prints **10.64** with **10.65** minus its first clause as a single fragment.) Since **10.66** is probably a paraphrase of Heraclitean ideas, not a direct quotation (see Kahn, op. cit. [p. 116 n. 1], p. 288), there is only one authentic river fragment. Much depends on whether the first clause of **10.65** is genuine, since **10.64** is the best evidence for the doctrine I hold fundamental to Heraclitus' thought, that identity is preserved by change.

20. See previous n.

10.68 (48) The name of the bow (BIOS) is life (BIOS), but its work is death.[21]

Also **10.47, 10.48, 10.49, 10.52, 10.78**

C. Opposite Qualities That Occur Successively

10.69 (126) Cold things grow hot, a hot thing cold, a moist thing withers, a parched thing is wetted.

10.70 (88) The same thing is[22] both living and dead, and the waking and the sleeping, and young and old; for these things transformed are those, and those transformed back again are these.

10.71 (57) Most men's teacher is Hesiod. They are sure he knew most things— a man who could not recognize day and night; for they are one.[23]

Also **10.86, 10.89**

D. Opposites Contrasted by Each Other; Each Is Necessary for the Recognition of the Other

10.72 (23) They [people in general] would not have known the name of justice if these things [unjust things] did not exist.

10.73 (111) Disease makes health pleasant and good, hunger satiety, weariness rest.

E. Transmutation of Elements

10.74 (36) It is death to souls to become water, death to water to become earth, but from earth comes water and from water soul.

---

21. The fragment exploits the identical spelling of the Greek words for bow and life; they differed in the accented syllables, but in Heraclitus' time accents were not yet written.

22. The word translated "is" more commonly means "is in." Perhaps Heraclitus means "the same thing is in us as both living and dead . . ."

23. The verbs translated "are sure," "knew," and "recognize" are almost synonyms and can all be translated "know," a translation that would emphasize the paradoxical suggestion of the fragment. M. M. Mackenzie's challenging interpretation of the fragment emphasizes the paradoxes. ("Heraclitus and the Art of Paradox," *Oxford Studies in Ancient Philosophy* 6 [1988]: 1–37.)

10.75 (31) The turnings of fire: first, sea; and of sea, half is earth and half fiery waterspout. . . . Earth is poured out as sea, and is measured according to the same ratio (LOGOS) it was before it became earth.

10.76* (76) Fire lives the death of earth and AER lives the death of fire, water lives the death of AER, earth that of water.

10.77 (30) The KOSMOS, the same for all, none of the gods nor of humans has made, but it was always and is and shall be: an ever-living fire being kindled in measures and being extinguished in measures.

Group VI. Cosmological Principles: The LOGOS at Work

All fragments in **Group V.E.**

10.78 (84a) Changing [or, by changing] it is at rest.

10.79 (125) Even the posset[24] separates if it is not being stirred.

10.80 (90) All things are an exchange for fire and fire for all things, as goods for gold and gold for goods [or, as money for gold and gold for money].

10.81 (64) Thunderbolt steers all things.

10.82 (53) War is the father of all and king of all, and some he shows as gods, others as humans; some he makes slaves, others free.

10.83 (80) It is necessary to know that war is common and justice is strife and that all things happen in accordance with strife and necessity.

10.84* (66) For fire will advance and judge and convict all things.

10.85 (65) Fire is want and satiety.

10.86 (67) God is day and night, winter and summer, war and peace, satiety and hunger, but changes the way <fire,> when mingled with perfumes, is named according to the scent of each.

10.87 (33) It is law,[25] too, to obey the counsel of one.

24. KUKEON, a potion made of ground barley, grated cheese, wine, and sometimes honey.
25. NOMOS, "law," "custom."

10.88 (102) To God all things are beautiful and good and just, but humans have supposed some unjust and others just.

10.89 (62) Immortal mortals, mortal immortals [or, immortals are mortal, mortals are immortal], living the death of the others and dying their life.

10.90 (20) When they are born, they are willing to live and to have their destinies, and they leave children behind to become their destinies.

Also **10.70, 10.104**

Group VII. Cosmology: Details

10.91 (94) The sun will not overstep his measures; otherwise, the Erinyes, ministers of Justice, will find him out.

10.92 (6) The sun is new each day.

10.93 (3) Its [the sun's] breadth is the length of the human foot.

10.94 (99) If there were no sun, as far as concerns all the other stars[26] it would be night.

10.95 (100) Seasons which bring everything. . . .

10.96 (120) Limits of dawn and evening are the Bear and opposite the Bear,[27] the limit of bright Zeus.

Also **10.61**

Group VIII. Religion

10.97 (5) They vainly purify themselves with blood when defiled with it, as if a man who had stepped into mud were to wash it off with mud. He would be thought mad if anyone noticed him acting thus.

10.98 (15) If it were not for Dionysus that they hold processions and sing hymns to the shameful parts [phalli], it would be a most shameless act;

26. This clause ("as far . . . stars") is omitted in one of the sources and may not be authentic.
27. The Bear is the constellation Ursa Major (the Big Dipper), and "opposite the Bear" refers to the star Arcturus, which was used as an indicator of the seasons.

but Hades and Dionysus are the same, in whose honor they go mad and celebrate the Bacchic rites.

10.99 (14) Nightwalkers, Magi, Bacchoi, Lenai, and the initiated. [These people Heraclitus threatens with what happens after death . . . .] For the secret rites practiced among humans are celebrated in an unholy manner.

10.100* (69) Sacrifices held by people who are wholly purified might take place in just one case. [So few are there who are not impure.]

10.101 (92) The Sibyl with raving mouth uttering mirthless [and unadorned and unperfumed phrases, reaches a thousand years in her voice on account of the god].[28]

10.102 (68) [Things seen and heard in sacred rites are introduced for the tendance of the soul in us and to keep within bounds the evils which birth has caused to grow about it, to set us free and release us from bonds. Hence Heraclitus rightly called them] cures [as tending to cure our troubles and the disasters attendant on generation.][29]

Also **10.43**

Group IX. The Soul

10.103* (67a) As a spider standing in the middle of its web notices as soon as a fly breaks any of its threads and quickly runs there as if grieved by the breaking of the thread, so the soul of a man, when any part of his body is harmed, rushes there quickly as if unable to endure the harm of the body, to which it is joined firmly and proportionally.

10.104 (77) It is death for souls to become wet.

10.105 (118) A gleam of light is a dry soul, wisest and best.

10.106 (117) A man when drunk is led by a boy, stumbling and not knowing where he goes, having his soul moist.

10.107* (136) Souls slain in war are purer than those that perish in diseases.

10.108 (24) Gods and humans honor those slain in war.

28. The bracketed material may contain Heraclitean ideas, although the wording is probably not authentic.
29. This is a testimonium containing only one word from Heraclitus.

10.109 (25) Greater deaths win greater destinies.

10.110 (27) Things unexpected and unthought of await humans when they die.

10.111 (63) They arise and become vigilant guardians of the living and the dead.

10.112 (16) How could one fail to be seen by that which does not set?

10.113 (96) Corpses are more fit to be thrown out than dung.

10.114 (45) You would not discover the limits of the soul although you travelled every road: it has so deep a LOGOS.

10.115* (115) The soul has a self-increasing LOGOS.

Also **10.21, 10.74, 10.125**

Group X. Politics

10.116 (121) Every grown man of the Ephesians should hang himself and leave the city to the boys; for they banished Hermodorus, the best man among them, saying "let no one of us excel, or if he does, be it elsewhere and among others."

10.117 (125a) May wealth never leave you, Ephesians, lest your wickedness be revealed.

10.118 (49) One person is ten thousand to me if he is best.

10.119 (52) A lifetime [or, eternity] is a child playing, playing checkers; the kingdom belongs to a child.

10.120 (44) The people must fight for the law³⁰ as for the city wall.

Group XI. Moral Thought

10.121 (43) Willful violence (HUBRIS) must be quenched more than a fire.

10.122 (119) A person's character [or, individuality] is his divinity [or, guardian spirit].

---

30. NOMOS: "law," "custom."

10.123 (110) It is not better for humans to get all they want.

10.124 (95) It is better to conceal ignorance.

10.125 (85) It is difficult to fight against anger, for whatever it wants it buys at
the price of soul.

Also **10.4, 10.13, 10.32, 10.46, 10.51, 10.87**

Dates and Life

Heraclitus was reportedly born c. 540 and lived sixty years—dates consistent with his references to Xenophanes, Pythagoras, and Hecataeus of
Miletus (c. 500 B.C.).[31] He belonged to an aristocratic family in Ephesus
and was entitled to hold a hereditary and possibly largely honorary "kingship," which he resigned to his brother. Xenophanes and Pythagoras had
both left Ionia, the one probably before Heraclitus' birth and the other
before Heraclitus was grown, so Heraclitus, as the only known presocratic
philosopher in the Ionian regions during his time, seems to have been an
isolated figure, and this fact may have something to do with his idio-
syncrasies and evident arrogance.

Many biographical anecdotes about Heraclitus are preserved, but practically all of them are spurious and based on his own fragments. For
example, the story that he died in a pile of cow manure where he had put
himself when suffering from dropsy, thinking that the warmth of the manure would evaporate the disease from him, is based on his statement "it is
death for souls to become wet" (**10.104**) and on his doctrine of exhalations
or evaporations by which water becomes fire (**10.75**).

Source Materials

Like the other Presocratics, Heraclitus is known to us through accounts of
his philosophy and fragments preserved in later sources. Although his book,
whose beginning is preserved (**10.1**) and which he deposited in the temple of
Artemis at Ephesus, has not survived as a whole, over one-hundred fragments survive. We are consequently better able to approach him, through
his own words and on his own terms, than we are his predecessors. This is
fortunate since the reports of Heraclitus' ideas in ancient writers are wildly
different from one another. Plato (in the *Theaetetus* and *Cratylus*) found in
Heraclitus the doctrine that "all things flow" (a statement not found in any

31. Especially **9.2, 10.16,** and **10.71**.

of Heraclitus' genuine fragments, though related to two important ones), which he interpreted as meaning that all things are always changing in all respects—the world is in continuous flux, and there is no stability or permanence in it. Aristotle, followed by Theophrastus, placed him in the tradition of the Ionian monists, with fire as his basic substance. The Stoics saw him as a forerunner of their own philosophy, in which fire is primary, the universe is governed by LOGOS, and in some sense fire, LOGOS, and god are identical, and so they interpreted him through their own system, attributing their views to him. In the third century A.D., Bishop Hippolytus of Rome found in him certain doctrines which he regarded as the origin of a Christian heresy.

The preserved fragments make it clear how Heraclitus could be interpreted in so many ways, all of them with a basis in the original but all of them partial and influenced by their authors' interests and beliefs. Most fragments are short, balanced, powerfully expressed. They have the ring of prophesies, riddles, similes, and metaphors which stand alone and demand careful attention each individually and in relation to one another. Many can be understood both metaphorically and literally or as applying to more than one subject (**10.74** talks of changes; it also tells about the human soul). In many cases, words and images are echoed vividly from fragment to fragment. The fragments cry out to be considered in each other's light, and the meaning that emerges is greater than the meanings of the fragments taken separately. They do not, in general, give the impression of being parts of a continuous prose exposition, but have much in common with the sayings of the Seven Sages and other maxims which survive in abundance in the literature of the Archaic Age (although Heraclitus' fragments exhibit more unity and probe more deeply than is common in such cases). A book of Heraclitus' writings in three sections (The Universe, Politics, Theology) circulated in later antiquity,[32] but may have been a compilation of Heraclitean materials rather than his original book. In any case, the divisions seem arbitrary[33] and untrue to Heraclitus, part of whose profound insight was that all things are one, which implies that such divisions are fundamentally incorrect.

In these circumstances some have decided to base their interpretations on the fragments alone (or virtually alone), ignoring the ancient testimonia or holding them guilty until proved innocent. This approach is flawed. First, many of the fragments are preserved in the same ancient reports that are considered dubious. But the authors of those reports had Heraclitus' book (or at least more information than we do), and so to reject the testi-

---

32. Diogenes Laertius, *Lives of the Philosophers* 9.5.
33. How would **10.51** and **10.86**, for example, be classified?

mony is to suppose that we understand Heraclitus better than the ancients did although we have less information than they had, and that we can reject their interpretations on the basis of the evidence they selected to support them. Second, if the ancient testimonia are misleading about Heraclitus, what becomes of our knowledge of the earlier Presocratics, which in the absence of abundant fragments depends almost entirely on the same authors? Further, the fragments occur in contexts determined by the interests of the writers who preserve them. To take them out of context and treat them as independent entities to be manipulated on their own risks losing valuable clues about their original context and meaning, and presupposes that the contexts in which they are preserved are so misleading that we do better without them.

Heraclitus appears different to virtually everyone who spends time with him, and the formidable and unique problems associated with his fragments and the ways they have been preserved do not encourage the hope that there will ever be a consensus about how to present the material, let alone about its meaning.[34] I have chosen to print the fragments without context, and arrange them by the topics I have chosen to discuss, with no pretense that they are in anything like the original order. This arrangement promotes brevity and focuses attention on Heraclitus, but is no substitute for close study of the source materials.[35] Further, though problems regarding text and meaning arise with most of the fragments, a chapter of this scope cannot hope to mention all, let alone treat them fully. The discussion that follows is meant to be merely suggestive, not exhaustive or authoritative.

Attitude towards Others

Heraclitus often expresses his low opinion of his fellow human beings **(Group I)**. He complains that people fail to understand him **(10.1)** and perhaps that they are hostile to his unfamiliar ideas **(10.12)**, also that they care more about their bellies than the truth **(10.4)**. They do not use their

34. To cite three approaches, DK abandons all hope of recovering the original arrangement and prints the fragments in the alphabetical order of the authors who quote them; Kahn believes that the fragments "were originally arranged in a significant order" and attempts "to present these incomplete and shattered fragments in the most meaningful order he can find" (p. 8); Osborne (op. cit., p. 116 n. 1) argues in favor of reading the fragments in the context in which they are preserved. (She argues this matter at length in the introduction to *Rethinking Early Greek Philosophy* [Ithaca, N.Y., 1987].)

35. Osborne (op. cit. n. 34) translates much of Hippolytus. A good deal of ancient context is given in the chapter on Heraclitus in *Early Greek Philosophy*, ed. J. Barnes (Harmondsworth, 1987).

senses (**10.1, 10.3, 10.20, 10.22, 10.13**) or intelligence (**10.3, 10.13**) correctly, they unreflectively and inconsistently (**10.1, 10.11**) listen to tradition, authority, and one another (**10.13**), and in the end they all make up their own minds and are content with their own thoughts (**10.2, 10.3**), which are for the most part worthless (**10.6, 10.20**), instead of recognizing that a single truth is present everywhere (**10.1, 10.8**) and common to all (**10.2**).

Heraclitus also attacks notable intellectual figures for their ignorance (**Group II**). Bias of Priene, one of the Seven Sages, is excepted from abuse (**10.18**), perhaps because he declared "most men are bad" (cf. **10.13**). It is interesting and perhaps significant that (in surviving fragments) Heraclitus does not attack the Milesian philosophers, to whom he is in fact indebted for many of his views.

Remarks on Method

As **10.1** makes clear, Heraclitus claims to have made a discovery of colossal importance—no less than the key to understanding everything. His notion of "everything" extends further than the Milesians', since it covers, in addition to the physical world, the practical world of ethics and politics, religion, and some more strictly philosophical realms as well. He calls this fundamental discovery the LOGOS, and believes that understanding the LOGOS is the most important thing a person can do. The chief task of this chapter will be to determine what he means by the LOGOS and how he understands it to account for all phenomena. Before turning to these questions it will be useful to consider his remarks on how to learn the LOGOS, which constitute the most extensive surviving reflections on philosophical method up to his time.[36]

Most people act as if asleep (**10.1, 10.23**), each with a private dream world, different from the common, public world we live in (**10.24**). Although surrounded by a part of the real world, which is common to all (the LOGOS is common [**10.2**]), they do not apprehend it (**10.3, 10.2, 10.1, 10.8, 10.10**) or comprehend it (**10.1, 10.3, 10.12**). Heraclitus suggests that we can escape from this state. For he contrasts sleeping and the dream world with waking and the real world, and the contrast suggests that we can wake up; the question is how.

In contrast to the normal human state of ignorance and unbelief, the divine has knowledge and insight (**10.28**), and is the only truly wise being (**10.30**). Neither this claim nor the observation that we are like babies in

---

36. The fragments and testimonia on the Milesians provide nothing on this topic. Xenophanes' comments on method are discussed above, pp. 66–68. The Pythagoreans' views must be inferred from (often hostile) testimonia, such as **9.32**.

comparison with god (**10.29**) means that we must remain wholly ignorant, any more than the thesis that understanding is common to all (**10.31**) means that we all possess the very insight Heraclitus denies we have (**10.28**). Rather, as children grow to maturity, we may grow in insight. Our ultimate goal is thinking (**10.31**), self-knowledge, and thinking rightly (**10.32**).[37] To the extent that we attain this insight and wisdom we transcend the human and resemble the divine (**10.28, 10.30**).

We gain insight mainly in two ways: inquiry into ourselves (**10.33**) and inquiry, through correct use of the senses (**Group III.E**), into the world around us. At first sight it appears that the senses cannot help us acquire this knowledge (**10.19, 10.20, 10.21, 10.22, 10.1** [near the end]). But note the qualifications: sight and hearing are unreliable to those with barbarian souls (**10.21**); some do not know how to hear or speak (**10.20**). Most people fall into these categories, but Heraclitus believes that a wise person can use the senses to gain accurate information. He prefers experiencing things for oneself (**10.36**), but rates hearing lower than sight (**10.36**), perhaps because we can be told falsehoods even by respected authorities (**10.13, Group III.B**). His comments on the sense of smell (**10.37**) indicate that we should use whatever sense is most appropriate in each situation. If all things were smoke, or in the darkness of the underworld (**10.38**), we could not see, but would distinguish things by smell.

To become wise we must learn to use the senses with insight or intelligence (NOOS).[38] We must also practice inquiry like the Milesian philosophers, but even more widely (**10.34**). Even so, mere learnedness is not the same as wisdom and insight (**9.2**). We must conduct our inquiry systematically (**10.45**), so as to promote right thought, speech, and action (**10.46**), and this requires us to grasp the unity and coherence of the universe and the cooperation of its parts (**10.44**).

Inquiry is difficult (**Group II.F**). It requires work (**10.34, 10.41**), patience (**10.40**), and hope (**10.39**). **10.39** may mean that unless you have an idea that there is a single principle that governs everything that takes place, you will never think of looking for it, and hence will never find it.

10.42 and **10.43** suggest reasons for the difficulty. The principles of nature as a whole, or the nature (the basic constitution) of each thing, are not obvious. They underlie or are behind all phenomena and must be grasped if we are to understand the phenomena, but we must get past the superficial aspects in order to grasp them. The phenomena are "signs" of the important underlying truths. They do not deliberately hide the truths so

---

37. "Thinking" (PHRONEEIN) and "thinking rightly" (SOPHRONEIN) are closely related in etymology as well as in sense.

38. According to **10.129**, perception is needed for our intelligence (NOUS, equivalent to NOOS) to attain its best condition, in which it is fully rational.

as to prevent us from discovering them, but their correct understanding (like the proverbially enigmatic oracular responses given at Delphi) demands careful interpretation.

The LOGOS

Heraclitus' great discovery is that all things that take place or come to be do so in accordance with a LOGOS (**10.1**), which is common (**10.2**) both because it applies everywhere and also because it is objective, and so available to all humans. A noun related to the verb LEGEIN, "to speak," LOGOS is a thing said, and hence a word, statement, or story. The close connection between what we say and what we write or think accounts for a further range of meanings: account, agreement, opinion, thought, argument, reason, cause. Perhaps from these last two meanings it gets other senses: relation, ratio, proportion. All these meanings were current in the fifth century. In the fourth it was also used to mean the faculty of reason, general principle, and definition.[39]

None of these meanings adequately describes Heraclitus' LOGOS. It is distinct from what people—even Heraclitus—say or think (**10.47**), so it is not a word, statement, account, opinion, etc., even a (or the) true one. "General principle" probably comes closest to his intent, but it is too abstract a notion, for Heraclitus associates the LOGOS with fire (cf. **10.1** with **10.81**) as the active nature in the universe. I have left LOGOS untranslated when it has its special Heraclitean meaning (**10.1, 10.2, 10.8, 10.47, 10.114, 110.115**). Elsewhere I have translated it and placed "LOGOS" in parentheses.

Given the world's vast diversity, if everything happens because of a single principle, that principle must function or be displayed in many different ways. It must be totally general, and so an explanation of a phenomenon in terms of the LOGOS will be at a very general level, and will link it to many other phenomena. Such accounts will be unfamiliar to the great majority of people who are unused to thinking in such ways. If Heraclitus "determines each thing according to its nature" and "says how it is" (**10.1**), it is not surprising that no one understands him.

The words just quoted suggest that Heraclitus believed that when properly used, language mirrors reality: the correct description or account of X accords with X's nature and says how X is, in that the account itself reflects the nature of X. This belief would account for Heraclitus' riddling and paradoxical expression: that is the only way to express accurately the surprising and complex natures of things and their interrelations. "Nature

39. The meanings of LOGOS are discussed at greater length by Guthrie, *HGP*, vol. 1, pp. 420–24.

loves to hide" (**10.42**), and accounts that are too straightforward cannot capture this essential feature of reality. Like reality itself, a correct account of reality needs to be interpreted (**10.43**).

One and Many

Heraclitus summarizes his discovery in the pregnant slogan "all things are one" (**10.47**), which he enlarges: "out of all things there comes a unity (one) and out of a unity all things" (**10.48**). These are general principles to be sure, and subject to widely differing interpretations. To see what Heraclitus means we need to look further, first at the remainder of **10.48**, which introduces three other ways of regarding phenomena. To the opposition between "one" and "all things" are added "whole" and "not whole," "brought together" and "brought apart," and "in tune" and "out of tune." All four pairs of opposites describe "things taken together." The real nature of the world is simultaneously and equally a unity and a plurality.

We can also understand the claim epistemologically: the world can be regarded either as composed of many distinct things or as a whole. An individual thing is a part of the world; the world as a whole is made up of parts that have their own identities. We tend to think of things separately, without paying attention to their interrelations and to the whole of which they are parts. This is a serious error. The correct way to view them involves understanding the whole and recognizing their part in it. This does not deny their individuality; but we can better appreciate a thing's individuality when we know how it is related to other things, and this knowledge is part of understanding that and how all things are one. Likewise, understanding the whole requires knowing how all its parts function, how they do and do not have identity in their own right ("wholes and not wholes"), how they do and do not join together ("brought together and brought apart"), and how they do and do not work together in various contexts ("in tune and out of tune"). Heraclitus emphasizes unity in diversity more than diversity in unity, for what constantly confronts us is diversity, and our first task is to grasp the underlying unity. This task is also the most difficult because it requires us to learn new ways of perceiving and thinking. Once it is accomplished, we can use the same tools to unpack the unity, to understand how the diversity exists and functions within it.

10.48 says that "things taken together" have opposite qualities. One opposite quality is due to the other: without differing elements there could be no harmony, for harmony is a relation among different things. Likewise, strife, which we think of as destructive, is responsible for the generation of things (**10.52**). **10.49** and **10.78** can be taken in both these ways: either things possess opposite qualities or they possess one quality because they possess its opposite. The second reading of these fragments makes the stronger and more interesting claim, and is supported by the images of the bow and lyre.

We are to imagine a strung bow or lyre which is not being used. The bow consists of a cord and a curved piece of wood. As we look at it, it appears stable and lifeless. What we fail to see is the connection (**10.50**), the tension that makes it a bow, not just a piece of wood and a cord. Moreover, the tension is "backwards turning" or "backwards stretching." The cord and the wood are under equal tension in opposite directions, the cord being pulled apart by the wood and the ends of the wood being pulled together by the cord. The bow's unity and ability to function depend on the tension between the wood and the cord ("out of many, one"), yet the tension cannot exist without the cord and the wood. Further, once we understand how bows function, we can do a better job of designing bows and choosing the type of wood and cord to use, according to their individual qualities ("out of one, many"). The case of the lyre is similar. The bow and the lyre are paradigmatic of how the world works and how we are to understand it. The moral can be applied to all complex things where the whole functions because of the relation of its parts, and the parts contribute to the working of the whole because of their own particular natures. But, as Heraclitus demonstrates, the LOGOS and the doctrine of unity and diversity operate in surprising ways and over a wider range of phenomena than we might expect.

Opposition

The LOGOS guarantees that all things are one, and that one thing is all. Heraclitus expresses this insight paradoxically, in terms of the unqualified opposites "one" and "all." His interest in opposition is wide, and the types of oppositions he treats illustrate how the LOGOS functions in many contexts.

In the first type of opposition (**Group V.A**) a single subject has opposite properties with respect to or in comparison with different types of beings. **10.53** is the clearest case.

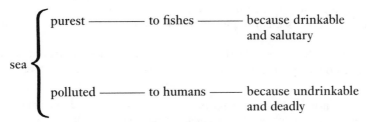

"Pure" and "polluted" are opposite characteristics that the sea has in a superlative degree. Full understanding of sea water involves knowing both that it is purest and that it is most polluted, but it is insufficient simply to assert that the sea has these opposite qualities; we need to unpack the assertion, pointing out that it has these different characteristics for different kinds of things, and explaining why. When we can do this, we know important things about sea water and also about humans and fishes. The other fragments in **Group V.A** can be interpreted along similar lines. Pigs, asses, and oxen have different preferences than humans do, so in each case something has opposite attributes. Mud is both more and less desirable than pure water: more desirable to pigs, less so to humans.

In **Group V.B** a thing has opposite properties in different circumstances. Here it is a matter of objective considerations, not of subjective preferences or judges with different constitutions. **10.61** envisages a case where a disease and the surgery that cures it cause the same kind of pain. In most cases things that cause pain are bad for us and we avoid them, but in some circumstances we choose to suffer something that causes pain because of its other desirable effects.

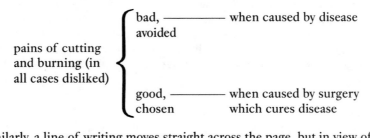

Similarly, a line of writing moves straight across the page, but in view of the shape of each individual letter, it is also crooked (**10.62**).[40] Both are essential aspects of writing. Two fragments included in this section can be taken differently, but make sense if analyzed along present lines. The road which goes up the hill, say the Panathenaic Way, is the same as the road which goes down it (**10.63**). A road that goes from X to Y also goes from Y to X. Both descriptions are correct but incomplete. Finally, **10.64** contrasts the same river with different waters. If I step into the same river at different times (presumably at the same place) the water that wets my feet is different each time. This is a consequence of the nature of rivers: they are moving water.

In **Group V.C** a single thing has opposite characteristics at different times. **10.69** may proclaim an inevitable law of nature: whatever is cold

---

40. On the manuscript reading (see p. 122 n. 18), **10.62** makes a similar point about carding wheels, though we do not know enough about these ancient devices to be able to understand how the fragment describes them.

must at some time become hot. Or, it may make the conceptual point that the only things which can become hot are cold; if they were already hot they could not become hot. It may also describe the physical functioning of the world. (Hot and cold were prominent in Milesian philosophy and play a role in Heraclitus' cosmology [**10.77**].) **10.70** contains some difficulties but its general point is similar to that of **10.69**. It begins with a paradox: a single thing has opposite characteristics; but it then resolves the paradox by explaining that the contrasted characteristics belong to the thing at different times because it changes. The difficulties arise in fitting the explanation to the given pairs of opposites.[41] In **Group V.C** so far we have seen cases where a definite subject now has one characteristic, now the opposite one. The unity of opposites consists in their successively belonging to the same subject. **10.71** extends this idea. Day and night are opposites which alternate, but here there is no subject that undergoes the change. In this case the regular alternation between opposite states is all that is needed to unify the opposites. (See also **Group V.E.**)

Group V.D makes an epistemological point. If all of us were always healthy, we would not know it, but would take it for granted in our ignorance of any alternatives. We would not even have a word for health, since the purpose of words is to distinguish things, to mark them off from others. If all things share a common quality, that quality will not have a name. The point here is that being able to conceive of, understand, and value correctly either of a pair of opposites requires being able to do the same for the other opposite as well.

Group V.E contains fragments important both for the treatment of opposition and for cosmology. **10.74** is least complicated and presents the following picture. Soul dies,[42] ceases to be, when it becomes water; water ceases to be when it becomes earth; but there are also processes in which earth becomes water and water becomes soul.

soul ↔ water ↔ earth

10.75 says the same thing more obscurely, with fire taking the place of soul and sea that of water.

fire ↔ sea ↔ earth

The fiery waterspout (a hurricane funnel illuminated by lightning) is the means by which water from the sea changes into fire.

41. For one suggestion, see p. 140.
42. Death here is not simply a metaphor for change. See **10.104** and p. 146.

10.75 emphasizes the idea of measure in change. Sea changes half into fire and half into earth. When earth changes to sea, a conservation principle is at work: e.g., two parts of sea become one part of earth, and similarly one part of earth turns into two parts of sea. **10.77** also emphasizes the notion of measured change and the eternity and stability of the overall situation. Since fire, sea, and earth are always being transformed into one another, each of them is always coming to be ("being kindled") and perishing ("extinguished"). All three major components of the KOSMOS are always in existence. The world's current structure is the way it always has been and always will be. Consequently, the world and its order had no origin. Our task is to understand it as it now is.

Group V.E differs from the groups already discussed in that it considers a single opposition, not a type of opposition found in many contexts,[43] and in that it presents not two but three contrasted states, each with its own identity and unique role.[44] As in **10.71**, there is no identifiable subject that takes on the different qualities and survives the change. Indeed, as the changes take place among the basic forms of matter, there can be no persisting subject of change. When fire becomes water, what was fire is now water, but neither the fire nor the water is present throughout the change. There is no way to describe "what was fire" except in terms of what it is at different times. Three factors play a role in analyzing such changes: (a) the different stages of the change (fire, water, earth), (b) the mechanisms or processes of change (e.g., rain, fiery waterspout), (c) the regularity, order, and measure of the change.

For Heraclitus, the opposites illustrate the principle of the LOGOS, "out of all things one, and out of one all things" **(10.48)**. Since opposite characteristics are normally considered distinct, separate, the furthest apart possible, they seem to present the hardest case for his theory. But if even opposites prove to be "one" the theory has survived an especially difficult challenge. Also, as many opposites are extremes that admit a range of intermediates, if the opposites prove to be "one" then a fortiori all the intermediates are unified too. If hot and cold are "one," so are tepid, lukewarm, etc. Heraclitus considers many kinds of opposition, some physical **(Group V.E)**, others conceptual **(Group V.D)**, some depending on the point of comparison **(Group V.A)** or the respect in which **(Group V.B)** or time at which **(Group V.C)** a thing is considered. He ranges more widely than the Milesians, who cared principally about the natural world. More-

43. For the identification of fire and soul, see p. 140.

44. In principle there could be any number, not just three. If Heraclitus had adopted Anaximenes' system, he might have had seven (see p. 53).

over, there is no single way to identify or analyze all the kinds of opposition he treats. This is why his enterprise is so difficult. Understanding how the LOGOS works requires finding and analyzing all the cases of unity in plurality and plurality in unity, and these turn up in unexpected settings. Hence the need to inquire into a vast number of things (**10.34**), to pay careful attention (**10.46**), and acquire the skill of thinking correctly (**10.46**, **10.44**). Hence too, learning many things by itself is not enough (**9.2**): it is equally important to know "the one." Finally, we must keep in mind the paradoxical spirit that pervades these fragments. Heraclitus aims to solve the puzzles he finds, but he also takes delight in the manifold complexities of the KOSMOS and the wonderful ways language can convey them.

Cosmological Principles: The LOGOS at Work

Two important features of Heraclitus' KOSMOS are that it is eternal (**10.77**) and that its principal material constituents are fire, water, and earth, which systematically and regularly change into one another (**10.75**). Paradoxically, the regularity of change guarantees stability (**10.78**). As with the river (**10.64**), the survival and very identity of the KOSMOS is dependent on this change. If the water stopped flowing, it would no longer be a river, but a long lake. If the basic forms of matter stopped changing, the stable, ordered, regulated KOSMOS would cease to exist. Likewise the "posset," a drink made of wine, barley, and grated cheese, separates into its components unless stirred (**10.79**). Unless it is kept in constant motion, i.e., change, it loses its stable identity.

Heraclitus calls water "sea" (**10.75**), thinking of the principal masses which constitute the KOSMOS. Water is found mainly in the sea. Earth is found mainly in the vast mass of it beneath our feet, which we call "the earth." Fire is mostly found (and in its purest form) in the heavens; even the bits of fire we see around us rise up in an effort to reach that place. Thus, like the Milesians[45] and Xenophanes, Heraclitus chooses familiar and plentiful materials for his basic forms of matter. Why air does not appear alongside the other three is unclear.[46]

Although the KOSMOS as a whole is ever-living (**10.77**), individual parcels

---

45. Anaximander is an exception to this generalization, but even for him, once the KOSMOS is generated, its main constituents are familiar substances: fire (especially in the heavens), AER (in the form of clouds), water (especially in the sea), and earth.

46. Given the prominence of air in Anaximenes as well as in the apparent structure of the KOSMOS, it is surprising that Heraclitus omits it. Kahn believes that air is a fourth basic form of matter for Heraclitus, but it is hard to find this doctrine in the fragments (aside from the dubious **10.76**).

of fire, water, and earth come to be and pass away, are born and die (**10.74**).[47] This may be the point of the obscure **10.89**, **10.90**, and **10.27** as well as of the strange claims that the dead become living and the old young (**10.70**).

Such a system gives no reason to award priority to any of the principal forms of matter. But in similar circumstances Anaximenes called air the basic material, and now Heraclitus declares fire primary: the KOSMOS is an ever living fire (**10.77**), and all other things are an exchange for fire (**10.80**). The two translations given of **10.80** imply different relations between fire and other things. On the first, the point is that other things can be valued in terms of gold, and exchange can go either way. So much gold is worth so much of something else. Thus, fire can become other things, but they in turn become fire again. So much fire becomes so much water and vice versa. The second translation recalls the ancient practice of coinage in which a gold coin was a piece of gold marked to indicate its weight; its weight determined its value. On this reading, the point of comparison is the persistence of the gold in the coins: the coins are gold. In the same way, other (nonfiery) objects are implied to be not distinct from fire, but actually made of fire. They are "coined" out of fire when fire takes on different forms, and will be "exchanged" for fire when the regular process of change brings them round once again into their fiery phase. Neither of these interpretations quite captures the nature of elemental change. Against the first, all things have been and will be fire, but no one who buys a nongolden thing with gold thinks that it has been or will be gold. Against the second, fire does not persist through its changes into water and earth; still, a coin of a given value used to be a lump of gold weighing so much, and what is now so much water used to be so much fire.

Still, however we interpret its identity with other things, fire gets priority among the basic materials, perhaps because the KOSMOS is ever-living (**10.77**). Unlike water and earth, fire has an active, controlling role in the KOSMOS ([**10.81**]: thunderbolt is a pure and highly active form of fire). This conception of fire links it closely with other central features of Heraclitus' philosophy. In the individual, the soul, which makes us alive and directs us, is fiery ("fire" and "soul" are used interchangeably in **10.74** and **10.75**). Further, fire as the all-controller (**10.81**) seems to be identified with the LOGOS, according to which all things happen (**10.1**).

The active nature of the universe is war and strife (**10.82**, **10.83**), which Heraclitus declares is justice, correcting Anaximander's opinion that the

---

47. **10.76** reflects Heraclitean ideas, although the mention of air is suspicious and the cycle of change it describes (earth → fire → air → water → earth) is incompatible with that found in **10.74** and **10.75**.

interplay of opposites which prevails in the world is injustice (**5.19**). Events in the KOSMOS, including transformations of one substance into another and changes between opposites, are a necessary and universal war and struggle which is needed to maintain the KOSMOS in a stable condition. Whatever results in a particular case—win or lose—it is part of the overall process that rules the universe with justice. Heraclitus identifies the justice, and therefore the strife and war in the universe, with fire (**10.84**).

Fire is also somehow identical with God (**10.85**, **10.86**). They both take on different appearances in different situations, but keep their own nature. In a sense, fire is the one behind the many, the unity in all the diversity of the KOSMOS. If **10.87** is correctly brought into the present discussion, then law too forms part of the same cluster of concepts.

We have seen that Heraclitus associates the LOGOS, fire, soul, war, justice, God, and perhaps law. In some sense they are the same, the ruling element in the universe, but precisely how they are the same is not clear. When I strike a match and create some fire, I am surely not bringing the eternal LOGOS or God into being. It will not do to demand strict conditions of identity in this context any more than it does when Heraclitus says that day and night are one (**10.71**). In different settings these concepts take on a variety of relations to one another, sometimes being virtually identical and sometimes being almost separate. For example, the burning match is not God, but is related to the cosmic fire (as a part? by resemblance? as an imperfect specimen? as a copy?), and in its small area of active existence it performs functions that both symbolize and are a part of the war and justice that rule the world.

Heraclitus, like the Pythagoreans, lacked conceptual tools and analytical techniques for analyzing such assertions.[48] Broad claims of sameness or identity were easy to make and hard to challenge. This state of philosophy and the Greek language suited Heraclitus' purposes: his approach to the unity of the KOSMOS through the LOGOS required associating ideas rather than analyzing or separating them. He needed to bring things together before bringing them apart again.

Some characteristics are favored over their opposites. War and strife (**10.83**) have opposites in peace and harmony, and it might seem that the KOSMOS is typified as much by peace as by war (cf. **10.86**). Likewise, from God's perspective, which is superior to the human one (**10.28**, **10.29**, **10.30**), all things are beautiful, good, and just, whereas mortals think some things have the opposite, negative qualities (**10.88**). The clear implication is that it is wrong to think anything ugly, evil, or unjust, at least when we have gained the correct view of things. (This is the best way to avoid conflict

48. See p. 112–13.

with **10.72**.) But why does God think that all things are just rather than that all are unjust or that some are just, others unjust? A possible answer to this serious question is that the order in the KOSMOS is not morally or aesthetically neutral, but good and beautiful. The word "KOSMOS" carries these positive connotations. A static world or a random world would be the opposite. Likewise, the word "LOGOS" has connotations of rationality, not irrationality, and is linked with other concepts of positive value, notably justice, but also law (which preserves things from anarchy) and soul (which is responsible for life, a condition with positive value).

On the interpretation favored here, Heraclitus puts equal weight on change and on stability, on plurality and on unity, on difference and on identity: stability is guaranteed by change; diverse individual things form a unity; identity is preserved through difference. Other readings are possible. In particular Heraclitus is frequently associated with a doctrine of radical change or "Heraclitean flux." This interpretation can be documented as far back as Plato,[49] who develops it in his dialogues *Theaetetus* and *Cratylus* on the basis of the river fragment (**10.64**), which he cites as follows.

> **10.126** All things move and nothing remains, and likening existing things to the flow of a river he says that you could not step twice into the same river.   (Plato, *Cratylus* 402a = DK 22A6)

For Plato's Heraclitus, all things are always changing in all respects.

> **10.127** There is nothing which in itself is just one thing: nothing which you could rightly call anything or any kind of thing. If you call a thing large, it will reveal itself as small, and if you call it heavy, it is liable to appear as light, and so on with everything, because nothing is anything or any kind of thing. What is really true is this: the things of which we

49. Plato in turn refers (jokingly?) to a vigorous Heraclitean movement in Ionia (Plato, *Theaetetus* 179d–180c, not in DK). Also, Aristotle reports that Plato "as a young man became familiar with Cratylus and the Heraclitean doctrines that all sensible things are always flowing (undergoing Heraclitean flux) and there is no knowledge of them" (*Metaphysics* 1.6 987a32–34 = DK 65A3). Aristotle elsewhere speaks of "the extreme doctrine of those claiming to be Heracliteans [Aristotle here coins a verb, "to Heraclitize"], which Cratylus held, who wound up thinking that he should say nothing, but only moved his finger, faulting Heraclitus for saying that it is impossible to enter the same river twice; for he thought it could not be done even once" (*Metaphysics* 4.5 1010a10–15 = DK 65A4). In what follows I challenge the view that Heraclitus was a Heraclitean in this sense. These extreme Heracliteans seem to have constructed their philosophy by giving a certain interpretation to Heraclitus' doctrines and carrying them to extremes.

naturally say that they "are," are in process of coming to be, as the result of movement and change and blending with one another. We are wrong when we say they "are," since nothing ever is, but everything is coming to be.

(Plato, *Theaetetus* 152d–e, not in DK, tr. Levett)

In Plato's treatment this theory is shown to imply such a radical instability in things that they cannot be described. They do not remain the same long enough for any description to apply. Indeed "every answer, on whatever subject, is equally correct, both 'it is thus' and 'it is not thus.' . . . <But> one must not use even the word 'thus'; for this 'thus' would no longer be in motion; nor yet 'not thus' for here again there is no motion."[50]

Plato's importance and early date give this interpretation an impressive pedigree, but it is fair to ask how well it fits what we know of Heraclitus from his fragments, how likely it is that Heraclitus intended all that Plato attributes to him, and whether the interpretation is due to a misunderstanding or exaggeration of Heraclitus' doctrine (either Plato's own or one that stems from Cratylus or other Heracliteans).

To begin, there is no reason to attribute to Heraclitus the implications that Plato draws, that language is impossible because there is insufficient stability in the world to secure references for words. This is Plato's elaboration and is not presented as held by Heraclitus or the Heracliteans.[51] On the other hand, Heraclitus' view that there is constant interchange among the three "elements" (**10.75, 10.77**) suggests that there is no long-term stability (in addition to the stability of the very process of change). The question is, did he believe that there is short-term stability, or that all things are constantly changing? The fragments do not supply a decisive answer. The existence of constant change among the "elements" requires that some water is at any moment changing into fire or earth, but not that all water is. Nor does the predominance of war and strife (**10.82, 10.83**) entail that all things are always in change, however compatible it is with such a view.

To some extent the answer depends on the changes involved. I see no reason to think that Heraclitus believed that anything large or heavy or white[52] is undergoing such rapid change that it immediately becomes small, light, or black. Thus, I see no reason to attribute "Heraclitean flux" to Heraclitus. On the other hand, he could well have believed in a weaker kind of flux, in which every object is continually undergoing changes, many of

---

50. Plato, *Theaetetus* 183a–b (not in DK), tr. Levett.

51. Plato, *Theaetetus* 181d–e (not in DK).

52. These are Plato's examples at *Theaetetus* 152d, 182d (not in DK).

which are too small to be noticed. There is nothing to disprove that he anticipated Melissus (**13.10**, sec. 3) in believing that "iron, which is hard, is worn away by contact with the finger, and gold and stone and anything else that seems to be strong." Such a view is compatible with a doctrine of universal change and also with the commonsense view that there is a good deal of stability in the KOSMOS. The iron ring, though constantly being eroded, lasts a long time, even though it will eventually cease to be. Such a theory about the nature of things is a natural development from the theories of earlier philosophers, for whom too the KOSMOS was a world of change and motion. Heraclitus did not extend the province of change, but came to the paradoxical realization that stability depends on change.

To return to the river fragment, we now see that it, like **10.78**, stresses identity that persists through, or because of, change. The fragment has always been interpreted as an example: the river is a paradigm. But of what? It is easy to take it as a paradigm for the KOSMOS as a whole, whose identity requires change, primarily the regular interchange of the "elements." It is harder to see it as a paradigm for each individual thing in the KOSMOS. The ring is being eroded; what is worn away is not replaced—though by compensation more iron may be being formed elsewhere. Finally, this interpretation attributes to Heraclitus a view which could easily be exaggerated or extended to the theory of Heraclitean flux.[53] In an obvious sense the Charles River is the same river today as it was yesterday (or a second ago), even though the water at each point of the river's course (or the totality of water in the river) is different at any two different times. In another sense, though, it is not the same river, and it is plain that someone like Cratylus could follow Heraclitus one-sidedly in maintaining that change is universal and stressing the differences this implies rather than the stability Heraclitus found.

Cosmology and Religion

We know few details of Heraclitus' cosmology. The reference to justice in **10.91** makes it likely that he saw the LOGOS at work in the movements of the heavenly bodies. His own astronomical theories are surprisingly naive (**10.92, 10.93, 10.94**). The following description of his astronomy gives a better picture than the surviving fragments.

> **10.128** Exhalations arise from earth as well as from sea; those from sea are
> bright and pure, those from earth dark. Fire is fed by the bright
> exhalations, the moist element by the others. He does not make clear

53. This interpretation is denied by KRS, which argues that Heraclitus did not believe in constant change.

the nature of the surrounding element. He says, however, that there are in it bowls with their concavities turned towards us, in which the bright exhalations collect and produce flames. These are the stars. The flame of the sun is the brightest and the hottest; the other stars are further from the earth and for that reason give it less light and heat. The moon, which is nearer to the earth, traverses a region which is not pure. The sun, however, moves in a clear and untroubled region and keeps a proportionate distance from us. That is why it gives us more heat and light. Eclipses of the sun and moon occur when the bowls are turned upwards; the monthly phases of the moon are due to the bowl turning round in its place little by little. Day and night, months, seasons and years, rains and winds and other similar phenomena are accounted for by the various exhalations. Thus the bright exhalation, set aflame in the hollow orb of the sun, produces day. The opposite exhalation when it has got the mastery causes night; the increase of warmth due to the bright exhalation produces summer, whereas the preponderance of moisture due to the dark exhalation brings about winter. His explanations of other phenomena are in harmony with this. He gives no account of the nature of the earth, nor even of the bowls.[54]   (Diogenes Laertius, *Lives of the Philosophers* 9.9–11, tr. Hicks = DK 22A1)

The evidence suggests that Heraclitus did not propose specific accounts for all the natural phenomena the Milesians were concerned to explain. His pressing need was to set out a general picture of how the LOGOS works; others could fill in the details. He followed the Milesian approach, accounting for phenomena in terms of understandable processes which do not include the willful actions of anthropomorphic gods.

He was like the Milesians too in not expelling the divine from his system. He even hints that the traditional religion is not wholly wrong, but expresses the truth incorrectly, and that religious practices have some benefits (**10.102**). Since God is the LOGOS that governs the world, the LOGOS is analogous to (but not the same as) Zeus, king of the gods, and father of gods and humans (**10.30, 10.82**). Certain cult practices are condemned (**10.97, 10.98, 10.99, 10.100**), especially those having to do with purification, though Apollo's enigmatic oracle receives respect (**10.43**) and perhaps the raving Sibyl as well (**10.101**).

54. This account, in which exhalations play an important role, is probably based on Theophrastus. But Heraclitus probably posited only one exhalation, to account for the change from water to fire (**10.75**), and Theophrastus mistakenly assimilated his theory to Aristotle's own two-exhalation theory. In any case, Heraclitus' own explanation of night (**10.94**) contradicts one of the functions **10.128** assigns to the "dark" exhalation.

The Soul

The conception of soul found most often in the Presocratics up to this point has been the "breath-soul," composed of air and having the function of rendering the body it inhabits alive. It departs at death, either to rejoin the cosmic air or (for the Pythagoreans) to be reincarnated. Heraclitus went further than his predecessors in integrating his view of the soul into his cosmology. The soul is fire, as is shown by the substitution of "soul" in **10.74** for "fire" in **10.75**. As the cosmic fire "steers all things" (**10.81**), so the soul directs us. As fire is extinguished when it becomes water, so life ends when the soul becomes wet (**10.104**). If the soul becomes moist, as when a person is drunk (Heraclitus can be surprisingly literal!), it is unable to perform its function of governing our actions (**10.106**)—our vitality is diminished. Conversely, the soul is at its best when dry and in its most fiery state (**10.105**).

Heraclitus believed in an afterlife depending on the soul's state at the moment of death (**10.104, 10.109, 10.110, 10.111**). **10.107** suggests that the soul's purity (degree of fieriness) determines what happens to it at death. Disease debilitates the soul along with the body and perhaps makes it wet, whereas the soul of a fighting soldier is (we may suppose) not affected by disease or drink, and is made especially fiery by vigorous activity and lust for battle. Heraclitus seems to hold that our soul will have an afterlife only if it is pure when we die. If it becomes wet, it dies too. Souls in general are not exempt from the cosmic cycle of change, and yet Heraclitus gives us hope—and a method—for attaining a good afterlife for our soul. If **10.111** refers to souls of those who die the best deaths, he may hold that they are absorbed into the cosmic fire and so play a part in governing the KOSMOS. On the other hand, the dead body is useless (**10.113**), cast off by its departed soul, decomposing and undergoing elemental change, but no longer the changes accompanying life and caused by the soul. The provocative assertion in **10.113**, which flouts Greek piety and respect for the human corpse,[55] shows how far his doctrines departed from ordinary belief.

The soul is more than a principle of life; it also (and this is new with Heraclitus) has cognitive functions.[56] In **10.21** the soul understands; it interprets the reports of the senses rightly or wrongly. Further, **10.21** may link thought and language. To interpret correctly the testimony of the senses, the soul must not be barbarian, it must speak the right language, the universal "language" of the LOGOS, so that it can interpret phenomena as

---

55. The concern for proper treatment of the dead body is made clear in Sophocles' *Antigone*.

56. See also **10.129**.

manifestations of the LOGOS. The soul also has some connection with anger (**10.125**, but the precise meaning is hard to make out).[57]

Finally, **10.115** and **10.114** describe the soul as having a "self-increasing LOGOS" and "so deep a LOGOS" that its limits cannot be discovered. These fragments may say much the same thing, but what it is is unclear. They may refer to the problem of self-consciousness in which it is possible to generate an infinite regress by regarding mind as both the subject and the object of thought. Or they may associate our soul with the vast amount of fire (i.e., the LOGOS) that governs the universe while itself being a part of the universe.

The following testimonium offers a physical account of the connection between intelligence and the LOGOS.

> **10.129** What surrounds us is rational (LOGIKOS, adj. derived from LOGOS) and intelligent. . . . According to Heraclitus, we become intelligent by drawing in this divine LOGOS by breathing, and though forgetful when asleep, we again become sensible when we awaken. For during sleep, our intelligence (NOUS) is separated from its natural contact with what surrounds us, since the passages of perception are shut, and only the attachment though breathing—like a root—is preserved. And being separated it loses the power of memory it previously had. When awake again it peeps out through the passages of perception as if through windows, and coming together with what surrounds us it takes on the power of reasoning. As coals when placed near the fire are altered and glow red, and when removed are extinguished, the portion of what surrounds us which dwells in our bodies as a stranger becomes practically irrational because of the separation, but in virtue of its contact by means of the great number of passages it comes to resemble the whole.[58]   (Sextus Empiricus, *Against the Mathematicians* 7.127, 129–130 = DK 22A16)

Political Thought

Heraclitus' belief that he alone understands the way the world works and his contempt for his fellow man presage the antiestablishment, antidemo-

---

57. Heraclitus thus anticipates the highest two parts of Plato's tripartite soul in *Republic*, book 4, the rational and the "spirited" (the Greek for this latter word is related to the word for "anger").

58. Although contaminated with Stoic ideas, such as the identification of the LOGOS with the air we breathe, this interpretation is securely grounded in Heraclitus' text (Sextus quotes three fragments in the immediate vicinity—one in 7.126 and two in 7.132–33) and is faithful to Heraclitus' ideas.

cratic political outlook prominent in his biography and in his fragments. The reports that he resigned a hereditary "kingship" in Ephesus and spurned the Ephesians' request to write laws for them[59] reflect a disgust at political life also expressed in **10.116** and **10.117**. In **10.118**, if it is meant to be a political statement, he rejects the basis on which democracy is founded (see also **10.87**) and proclaims himself an aristocrat in the true sense (the word translated "best" is ARISTOS). He does not esteem people for descent from powerful families, but values those who are truly "best" through their personal attainments, primarily their success in understanding and acting according to the LOGOS **(10.46)**. **10.13** further displays his antidemocratic bent: "the many are bad, the good are few."

A number of fragments mention law, crucially **10.51**, which speaks of a single divine law (the LOGOS) that is common to all. The inferential particles translated "for" show that **10.51** is an argument, but its structure is unclear. The LOGOS "nourishes" human laws: like other parts of the KOSMOS, they too are manifestations of the LOGOS. Heraclitus' low opinion of humans and their practices makes it surprising that **10.51** and **10.120** seem to call on people so strongly and without irony to rely on and defend human laws (or customs). Heraclitus is an unlikely candidate for a conventionalist, one who believes that local traditions should be upheld whatever they are. We expect him to hold that people should obey one person if he is best, but in what sense is it a law to do so **(10.87)**? Not, presumably, the actual city law; thus, the divine law or LOGOS, or its manifestation in an ideal city law. This in turn suggests a different reading of **10.51**, omitting "its" and taking the law in question to be the divine law. Cities must place complete reliance on the LOGOS[60] as the source of the best possible law code. They must strive to ground their own laws in the universal law of the LOGOS. **10.120** falls into line too. The law the people must champion is not the actual city law but the ideal one. If this interpretation is correct, Heraclitus' contribution to political thought is of fundamental importance. He grounds his views on law and politics in his cosmic theory (his references to war and injustice[61] can be reread in this light), the universal scope of the LOGOS thus providing a metaphysical basis for law and society. To our knowledge he is the first philosopher to extend the range of his philosophy to include these topics, even if the way he expresses his ideas precludes a sustained treatment of them.

59. Diogenes Laertius, *Lives of the Philosophers* 9.2 (= DK22A1).
60. The clause "and . . . reliance" can go grammatically with "a city must rely" as easily as with "those who speak with intelligence must rely . . . ".
61. See **10.82**, **10.83**, **10.88**, and **10.91**.

Moral Thought

Heraclitus made a fundamental contribution to ethics as well. The Milesians had not shown much interest in moral philosophy, and the moral reflection found in Greek literature before Heraclitus is not philosophical. Homer (above all), Hesiod, the poets of the Archaic Age (especially Solon, Tyrtaeus, and Theognis), and the Seven Sages had much to say about the best kind of life to lead, about virtues and vices, about moral choices and other topics studied by ethics, but there is little argument, little attention, to what we would call theoretical issues, little self-conscious analysis of ethical language. Much is at the level of prescriptions, frequently in maxims, of what one should do or not do, what sort of goals one should have, what sort of life to live. Aside from the promise of rewards and punishments for just or unjust behavior (as in Hesiod), there was no philosophical attempt to defend morality against immorality.

Heraclitus too states moral maxims (e.g., **10.2, 10.4, 10.17, 10.23, 10.46, 10.121, 10.123, 10.124**). But there is more. The chief questions of Greek ethics that the philosophers of the classical and hellenistic periods inherited from the earlier tradition were, What is the best life for a person? and What is the best kind of person to be? The answers Heraclitus provides to these questions are characteristically different from answers found in and before his time, and are bound up with his doctrine of the LOGOS. For Homer, some of the best human qualities were physical (strength, prowess in battle, beauty), some intellectual (good counsel, wiliness), others material (wealth). Others had to do with one's position (noble lineage, royal power), others with protecting and treating well one's family, followers, and city. The best life was a life spent in the active exercise of these qualities, many of which were not in a person's own power to attain and many of which were considered god-given.

For Heraclitus the most important thing to achieve in life is understanding of the LOGOS, which the most famous people from Homer to Pythagoras failed to grasp. Thus, none of Homer's heroes and none of the other paradigms of excellence from the earlier Greek tradition were really good or lived a good life. The supreme excellence is right thinking and wisdom, which consists in knowing "how all things are steered through all things" (**10.46**)—primarily an intellectual virtue, but one manifested in right actions. Heraclitus' wisdom is not only speculative; it has practical implications. Moreover, no one has this wisdom from birth, but whether we attain it or not depends on our own efforts (**10.34, 10.35, 10.39, 10.40, 10.42, 10.43**). Perfect wisdom is either beyond human reach or very difficult to attain (**10.28, 10.29, 10.30**), so the best human life may be one spent in search of perfect wisdom, investigating the world around us and ourselves as well (**10.33, 10.34**). Heraclitus has a motive for understanding the LOGOS, and justifies his claim that wisdom is the best human quality: it is divine, so that by attaining or striving to attain wisdom we become or strive to become godlike. Moreover, since for Heraclitus the divine is not the Olympian gods but the LOGOS itself, the nearer we are to being godlike, the more the LOGOS is actively, consciously, even self-consciously, in our soul. Moreover, since Heraclitus associates the LOGOS with the pure cosmic fire, he can maintain that the wisest soul is most fiery (**10.105**), and so reaps the benefits, both in this life and afterwards, of the best souls.

Finally, the famous **10.122** can be taken in different ways, but on any reading it has an important message. It may mean "A person's character is the immortal and potentially divine part of him or her," so that we must make great efforts to develop our character as best we can. It may also mean "A person's character, rather than an external divinity, is what determines what happens to him or her," so that we are responsible for our own lives (and for our soul's afterlife).

11

Parmenides of Elea

Fragments

11.1 (1)[1] The mares which carry me as far as my spirit ever aspired
were escorting me, when they brought me and proceeded along
    the renowned road
of the goddess, which [or, who[2]] brings a knowing mortal to all
    cities one by one.
On this path I was being brought, on it wise mares were
    bringing me,
straining the chariot, and maidens were guiding the way.   5
The axle in the center of the wheel was shrilling forth the bright
    sound of a musical pipe,
ablaze, for it was being driven forward by two rounded
wheels at either end, as the daughters of the Sun
were hastening to escort <me> after leaving the house of Night
for the light, having pushed back the veils from their heads with
    their hands.   10
There are the gates of the roads of Night and Day,
and a lintel and a stone threshold contain them.
High in the sky they are filled by huge doors
of which avenging Justice holds the keys that fit them.[3]
The maidens beguiled her with soft words   15
and skillfully persuaded her to push back the bar for them
quickly from the gates. They made
a gaping gap of the doors when they opened them,
swinging in turn in their sockets the bronze posts
fastened with bolts and rivets. There, straight through
    them then,   20
the maidens held the chariot and horses on the broad road.
And the goddess received me kindly, took my
right hand in hers, and addressed me with these words:

1. The numbers in parentheses are the numbers of the fragments in DK.
(1) = DK 28B1.

2. The pronoun can refer to either the road or the goddess.

3. The text is difficult here. The word translated "keys" can also mean "locks,"
and "that fit them" is a loose rendering of a word that means more literally
"alternating" or "in exchange for."

Young man, accompanied by immortal charioteers,
who reach my house by the horses which bring you,   25
welcome—since it was not an evil destiny that sent you forth
    to travel
this road (for indeed it is far from the beaten path of humans),
but Right and Justice. There is need for you to learn all things—
both the unshaken heart of persuasive [or, well-rounded[4]] Truth
and the opinions of mortals, in which there is no true
    reliance.   30
But nevertheless you will learn these too—that the things that
    appear
must genuinely be, being always, indeed, all things.[5]

11.2 (2) Come now, I will tell you—and bring away my story safely
    when you have heard it—
the only ways of inquiry there are to think:
the one, that it is and that it is not possible for it not to be,
is the path of Persuasion (for it attends upon Truth),
the other, that it is not and that it is necessary for it not to be,   5
this I point out to you to be a path completely unlearnable,
for neither may you know that which is not (for it is not to be
    accomplished)
nor may you declare it.

11.3 (3) . . . For the same thing is [or, is there] for thinking and for being.
    [or, For thinking and being are the same.]

11.4 (4) But gaze upon things which although absent are securely
    present in thought.
For you will not cut off what is from clinging to what is,
neither being scattered everywhere in every way throughout
    the KOSMOS
nor being brought together.

11.5 (5) For me, where I am to begin from is the same
    [literally, common],
for to there I will come back again.

4. The manuscript text of this word varies.

5. The last two lines of **11.1** are controversial. I follow Owen's text and interpretation ("Eleatic Questions," *Classical Quarterly* 10 [1960]:84–102). Other possibilities: "how what is believed would have to be assuredly, pervading all things" (KRS),
" . . . all of them passing through all [the tests]" (J. Lesher, "Parmenides' Critique
of Thinking," *Oxford Studies in Ancient Philosophy* 2 [1984]:1–30).

11.6 (6) That which is there to be spoken and thought of must be.
For it is possible for it to be,
but not possible for nothing to be. I bid you consider this.
For I bar your way from this first way of inquiry,
but next from the way on which mortals, knowing nothing,
two-headed, wander. For helplessness   5
in their breasts guides their wandering mind. But they are
    carried on
equally deaf and blind, amazed, hordes without judgment,
for whom both to be and not to be are judged the same and
not the same, and the path of all[6] is backward-turning.

11.7 (7) For in no way may this prevail, that things that are not, are.
But you, bar your thought from this way of inquiry,
and do not let habit born from much experience compel you
    along this way[7]
to direct your sightless eye and sounding ear and tongue,
but judge by reason the heavily contested refutation   5
spoken by me.

11.8 (8) There is still left a single story
of a way, that it is. On this way there are signs
exceedingly many—that being ungenerated it is also
    imperishable,
whole and of a single kind and unshaken and complete.[8]
Nor was it ever nor will it be, since it is now, all together, 5
one, continuous. For what birth will you seek for it?
How and from where did it grow? I will not permit you to say
or to think <that it grew> from what is not; for it is not
    to be said or thought
that it is not. What necessity would have stirred it up
to grow later rather than earlier, beginning from nothing?   10
Thus it must either fully be or not.
Nor will the force of conviction ever permit anything to
    come to be
from what is not, besides it [i.e., besides what is not]. For this
    reason, Justice has permitted it [i.e., what is]
neither to come to be nor to perish, relaxing her shackles,

6. The Greek is ambiguous between "all things" and "all mortals."

7. Alternatively, "born from much experience" can modify "this way."

8. I follow Owen's suggestion (reference in n. 5). In DK, the text of l.4 reads "for it is complete, unmovable and without end."

but holds <it> fast. But the decision about these matters lies
   in this: 15
it is or it is not. But it has been decided, as is necessary,
to let go the one way as unthinkable and nameless (for it is not
a true way) and that the other is and is real.
How could what is be in the future? How could it come to be?
For if it came into being, it is not, nor <is it> if it is ever
   going to be.   20
In this way, coming to be has been extinguished and destruction
   is unheard of.
Nor is it divided, since it all is alike;
nor is it any more in any way, which would keep it from holding
   together,
or any less, but it is all full of what is.
Therefore, it is all continuous, for what is draws near to
   what is.   25
But unchanging in the limits of great bonds,
it is, without start or finish, since coming to be and destruction
were banished far away and true conviction drove them off.
Remaining the same in the same and by itself it lies
and so stays there fixed; for mighty Necessity   30
holds it in the bonds of a limit, which pens it in all round,
since it is right for what is to be not incomplete;
for it is not lacking; if it were <lacking>, it would lack
   everything.
Thinking and the thought that it is are the same.
For not without what is, in which it is expressed,   35
will you find thinking; for nothing else either is or will be
except that which is, since Fate shackled it
to be whole and unchanging; wherefore it has been named all
   names[9] [or, all things]
mortals have established, persuaded that they are true—
to come to be and to perish, to be and not <to be>,   40
and to change place and alter bright color.
But since there is a furthest limit, it is complete
on all sides, like the bulk of a well-rounded ball,
evenly balanced in every way from the middle; for it must be not
   at all greater
or smaller here than there.   45

---

9. Some accept a different manuscript reading that would be translated as
"wherefore all things are a <mere> name."

For neither <is it the case that> what is not is—which would
    stop it from reaching
its like—nor <is it the case that> what is is in such a way that
    there could be more of what is
here and less there, since it is all inviolate;
for equal to itself on all sides, it meets with its limits uniformly.

At this point I stop for you my reliable account and thought   50
concerning Truth; from here on, learn mortal opinions,
listening to the deceitful ordering of my words.
For they made up their minds to name two forms,
of which it is not right to name one—in this they have
    gone astray—
and they distinguished things opposite in body, and established
    signs   55
apart from one another—for one, the aetherial fire of flame,
mild, very light, the same as itself in every direction,
but not the same as the other; but that other one, in itself
is opposite—dark night, a dense and heavy body.
I declare to you all the ordering as it appears,   60
so that no mortal opinion may ever overtake you.

11.9 (9) But since all things have been named light and night
    and the things which accord with their powers have been
        assigned to these things and those,
    all is full of light and obscure night together,
    of both equally, since neither has no share.

11.10 (10) You shall know the nature of the aether and all the signs in
        the aether
    and the destructive deeds of the shining sun's pure
    torch and whence they came to be,
    and you shall learn the wandering deeds of the
        round-faced moon
    and its nature, and you shall know also the surrounding
        heaven,   5
    from what it grew and how Necessity led and shackled it
    to hold the limits of the stars.

11.11 (11) . . . how earth and sun and moon
    and the aether which is common to all and the Milky Way and
    furthest Olympus and the hot force of the stars surged forth
    to come to be.

11.12 (12) For the narrower <wreaths> were filled with
     unmixed fire.
   The ones next to them with night, but a due amount of fire is
     inserted among it,
   and in the middle of these is the goddess who governs all
     things.
   For she rules over hateful birth and union of all things,
   sending the female to unite with male and in opposite
     fashion,   5
   male to female.

11.13 (13) First of all gods she contrived Love.

11.14 (14) Night-shining foreign light wandering round earth.

11.15 (15) Always looking towards the rays of the sun.

11.16 (16) For as each person has a mixture of much-wandering
     limbs,
   so is thought present to humans. For that which thinks—
   the constitution of the limbs—is the same
   in all humans and every one; for which is more is thought.[10]

11.17 (17) [That the male is conceived in the right part of the
     uterus has been said by others of the ancients.
     For Parmenides says:][11]
   <The goddess brought> boys <into being> on the right
   <side of the uterus>, girls on the left.[12]

11.18 (19) In this way, according to opinion, these things have grown
     and now are
   and afterwards after growing up will come to an end.

10. Other possible translations: "it is the same thing which the constitution of the
limbs thinks" (lines 2–3); "the full is thought" (l. 4), which can be understood to
mean that the *content* of what people think is "the full," i.e., the reality described in
The Way of Truth. The translation given in the text accords better with Theophrastus' account of Parmenides' views on the nature of thought (**11.20**), which
quotes **11.16**.
11. Context in Galen, *Commentary on Book 6 of Hippocrates' Epidemics*, II.46
(= DK 28B17).
12. I follow the text given in Gallop's edition (Toronto, 1984).

> And upon them humans have established a name to mark
> each one.

11.19 (not in DK) Such [or, Alone], unchanging, is that for which
as a whole
the name is "to be." (The "Cornford Fragment"[13])

Significance and Life

Parmenides' philosophy marks a turning point in the history of thought.
Neither his style of argument nor his astonishing conclusions could be
overlooked even by those who strongly disagreed with him. Like Heraclitus,
Parmenides pushed the limits of his thinking beyond the range of subjects
found in the early Ionian philosophers, though his ideas, like those of
Heraclitus, have implications for the entities and cosmic processes which
his predecessors proposed. If Heraclitus was the first person to approach
things philosophically instead of scientifically, Parmenides deserves recognition for introducing deductive arguments to philosophy and for acknowledging their compelling force, and for using this new tool to raise basic
philosophical questions: What conditions must existing things satisfy? Is
reality what our senses tell us it is? How we can tell? He was also the first to
undertake explicit philosophical analyses of the concepts: being and coming to be, change, motion, time, and space. And he was the first to use
these concepts to analyze the nature of a logical subject, and so in an
important sense he is the inventor of metaphysics.

The best piece of information about Parmenides' life[14] indicates that he
was born c. 515 and lived until at least 450 or so. He was from the Greek
city Elea in southern Italy, as was his follower Zeno, and their distinctive
philosophical opinions as well as their philosophical method gave rise to the
terms "Eleatic philosophy" and "the Eleatic school." Parmenides was sufficiently respected in Elea to have been asked to draw up a code of laws
which were still referred to with respect and were probably still in force
over five hundred years later.[15]

---

13. **11.19** is quoted by Plato (*Theaetetus* 180e) and Simplicius. Most editors, including DK, believe that it is a misquotation of **11.8** l. 38. Its authenticity was
defended by Cornford ("A New Fragment of Parmenides," *Classical Review* 49
[1935]:122–23) and has found influential support. **11.19** complements the claim in
11.8 lines 38–39 that all words really name the one existing thing, and mortals
invented the many names in their mistaken belief in a world of plurality
and change. The point of **11.19** is that the *correct* name for the one existing thing
is "to be."

14. Plato, *Parmenides* 127b–128d (= **12.1**).

15. Plutarch, *Against Colotes* 72, 1126A = (DK 28A12).

Parmenides' Poem

Parmenides' philosophy is in ways diametrically opposed to Heraclitus', whom he may have attacked in his writings.[16] He is called a pupil of Xenophanes and said to have had Pythagorean connections, but Parmenides went very much his own way in philosophy. He is best known for a poem written (like some of Xenophanes' poetry and all of Empedocles') in dactylic hexameter, the epic meter of Homer and Hesiod. We are fortunate to possess almost all of the most important section of the work, thanks to Simplicius, who in the sixth century A.D. copied it into his commentary on Aristotle's *Physics* "on account of the rarity of Parmenides' writings."[17] The poetic value of this philosophical work (except for the prologue) is very limited, but Parmenides may have chosen poetry instead of prose because it is easier to memorize, and also because hexameter verse, as the meter of epic poetry, connotes wisdom and authority, and is the vehicle of divine revelation (cf. **11.1**).

The poem falls into three parts. First (**11.1**), a prologue in which the goddess announces (lines 28–32) that she will tell Parmenides two things: (a) "the unshaken heart of persuasive (or, well rounded) truth," and (b) "the opinions of mortals in which there is no true reliance." These two topics occupy the remaining two parts of the poem, which are known as The Way of Truth and The Way of Mortal Opinions. Parmenides' philosophical importance is due almost entirely to The Way of Truth, of which many think almost all has survived (seventy-eight or seventy-nine lines are extant). The Way of Mortal Opinions, of which the surviving forty-four lines constitute only a few scraps, seems to have contained a cosmogony and cosmology.

The Prologue (11.1)

The prologue proclaims Parmenides a "knowing mortal" and says he received the kind attention of divinities, culminating in a revelation from a goddess. In this he is privileged among mortals. The imagery of light and dark is stressed, but it is not made quite clear whether he moves from darkness into light. The impressive barrier of the great door indicates the difficulty of the journey. Avenging Justice, the gatekeeper, allows only those sent by Right to enter. With the approval of Justice as well, Parmenides is

16. Parmenides' unmoving one existing thing forms a natural contrast with Heraclitus' world full of plurality and change (especially on the doctrine of Heraclitean flux—see pp. 142–44). There seem to be some verbal echoes of Heraclitus, for example, compare **11.5** with **10.67**.

17. Simplicius, *Commentary on Aristotle's Physics* 144.25–28 (= DK 28A21).

brought to the goddess, who promises to teach him two subjects: the truth, and unreliable human opinions. She summarizes the content of these unreliable opinions (lines 31–32): mortals believe in appearances; that is, they believe that what appears or seems to be really is, and that there is nothing else besides.[18] What this means is as yet obscure, but the indications are clear that the truth is not what we mortals believe, and that our trust in appearances will be called into question.

The content and style of Parmenides' thought go oddly with his portrait of his philosophy as a divine revelation. Revealed truth tends to be truth we would disbelieve except for its unimpeachable source, whereas The Way of Truth is not what we would expect a goddess to reveal to a mortal. It is, rather, a highly structured sequence of careful deductive proofs—the first such arguments in Western philosophy. Such arguments, we feel, should stand on their own, without needing the support of divine authority. The prologue may be just a literary show, but it may also recount a kind of mystical experience Parmenides actually had. I offer as a suggestion that this experience was the discovery of the power of logic, which is perhaps represented by the unnamed goddess. For the Greeks, many things aside from the Olympian gods were considered divine. In general, anything that exists independently of human will or effort, which is everlasting and has effects beyond human control, might be called divine—such things as rivers, love, and other powers in the universe. Deductive arguments have such power as well. If the premises of a valid deduction are true, the conclusion must also be true, and nothing in human power can make things otherwise. If we accept the premises we must accept the conclusion no matter how little we like it. Likewise for other logical relations. For example, if -A is the negation of A, then either A or -A is true; if one is false, it follows that the other is true. Now this describes Parmenides' arguments in The Way of Truth: arguments from apparently undeniable premises to conclusions unwelcome to common sense. And it is possible that reflection on the nature of such arguments led Parmenides to recognize their inescapable binding force. It is difficult for us to imagine the magnitude of this discovery (which is as profound and important as the Pythagorean discovery of the numerical basis for the concordant musical intervals[19]) but if the present suggestion is right, Parmenides considered it worthy of divine honor.

18. Lines 31–32 have been taken differently, with "these" (l. 31) referring not backwards, to "the opinions of mortals" (l. 30), but forward, to the final line and a half of the fragment, which then do not contain just a thumbnail sketch of the false opinions of mortals, but the Goddess's endorsement of the cosmology presented in The Way of Mortal Opinions as true.

19. See pp. 91–92.

The Two Ways

11.2 characterizes the two Ways of Inquiry the goddess reveals to Parmenides as the only conceivable paths of thought. They are both intelligible (unlike the confused ideas discussed in **11.6**), but are of unequal value. The first Way is called the Path of Persuasion, which attends upon Truth; the second is "completely unlearnable" and to be avoided (**11.7** l. 2). The two Ways are identified by important claims they make: the first Way is "that it is and that it is not possible for it not to be" (**11.2** l. 3); the second Way is "that it is not and that it is necessary for it not to be" (**11.2** l. 5).

Two questions arise immediately: (a) what is "it" of which it is declared that it is or is not, and (b) what do "is" and "be" mean? These questions can be answered fully only by those who have understood the doctrine of The Way of Truth. For example, at that point we see that the answer to (a) is that "it" is any possible entity—which turns out to be unique: the single existing thing, the only thing that can be spoken or thought of. Parmenides may have intended these initial accounts of the two Ways to be obscure, leaving (a) and (b) as puzzles for the reader (or hearer) to work out in the course of grasping the message of The Way of Truth.

Still, some further clarification is desirable. Parmenides not only does not state explicitly what "it" is; he does not even say "it." "It is" translates a single word, ESTI (the third person singular form of the present indicative of the verb "to be"). Greek does not require (as English does) subjects of verbs to be expressed when they can be understood from their context. In the present case, it is hard to see how a reader could infer from the context some of the answers that have been given to (a), such as "The One," "The One Being," "What is," "All that exists," "Being," and "Body or Corporeality."[20] Another suggestion is that ESTI is used impersonally, with no subject intended (so that the "it" corresponds to the "it" in "it is raining," which means "raining is going on"); but later in The Way of Truth ESTI does get a subject, which is identified in **11.6** lines 1–2 and described in **11.8**. The immediate context favors two proposals, "Any subject of inquiry" (inferred from **11.2** l. 2) and "Anything that can be spoken and thought of" (**11.6** lines 1–2, cf. closer to hand **11.2** lines 6–7), i.e., anything that can be the subject[21] of speech or thought. It will turn out that there is only one possible subject of inquiry and only one thing that can be spoken and thought of, and that these are identical.

---

20. Some of these proposals have further drawbacks. What, for example, could "Being is" mean? And "What is, is" (and perhaps "All that exists, is") is a tautology, which some have considered an unsuitable starting point for a metaphysical theory.

21. By "subject" I mean, roughly, "topic" or "subject matter"—what we speak or think of.

In question (b) more is at stake. The answers proposed do not come to the same thing, but result in (or from) different interpretations of Parmenides' philosophy. In what follows, I take it for granted that two desirable features of an interpretation are (1) that "is" and "to be" have the same meaning in **11.2** lines 3 and 5 and also in **11.3** l. 1, **11.4** l. 2, **11.6** lines 1–2 and 8, **11.7** l. 1, **11.8** l. 2, and frequently elsewhere in **11.8**, and (2) that Parmenides is not speaking nonsense (even if he speaks falsely). The chief contenders are that "is" is (1) existential, attributing existence to a subject, as in "there is a tiger in the zoo"; (2) predicative or copulative, assigning a predicate to a subject, as in "the tiger is hungry"; (3) a fusion (or confusion) of (1) and (2), in which "the tiger is hungry" entails not only that the subject, the tiger, has a certain predicate but also that the tiger exists; (4) veridical, asserting that the subject "is the case" or "is true," where the subject-place is held by a proposition, a description of a state of affairs, a name or a pronoun representing any of these, as in "that is true" or "it is true that tigers have four legs" (a rephrasing of what in Greek would look like "that tigers have four legs is").[22]

On interpretation (1) the two Ways assert, respectively, for a suitable subject x, (1.1) x exists and must exist, and (1.2) x does not and cannot exist. On interpretation (2) they assert (2.1) x has and must have at least one predicate, and (2.2) x does not and cannot have any predicates.[23] On interpretation (3) they assert (3.1) x exists and must exist, and x has and must have at least one predicate, and (3.2) x does not and cannot exist, and x does not and cannot have any predicates. On interpretation (4) they assert

---

22. For more possible meanings of "is," see Mourelatos, *The Route of Parmenides* (New Haven, 1970). Mourelatos favors what he calls the "is of speculative predication," which assigns to a subject a predicate that reveals the nature, reality, or essence of the subject (p. 56 ff.). On this interpretation, Parmenides claims that the essence of any subject is to be ungenerated, indestructable, unchanging, etc. I find the suggestion interesting, but difficult to work out in detail. (See D. Furley, "Notes on Parmenides," in *Exegesis and Argument*, ed. E. Lee, A. Mourelatos, and R. Rorty [Assen, 1973], pp. 1–15; and D. Furley, *The Greek Cosmologists*, vol. 1 [Cambridge, 1987], p. 37 n. 10.) I find the evidence presented for the occurrence of this use of "is" prior to Parmenides (Mourelatos, pp. 60–61) unconvincing.

23. An alternative interpretation—(2.1') x has and must have all predicates and (2.2') x lacks and must lack at least one predicate—is ruled out by **11.8**, where the subject of ESTI is said to lack several predicates (e.g. lines 22–23). However, (2.1) and (2.1') are identical (as are (2.2) and (2.2') if (as I argue later) there is only one possible predicate (see on **11.8** lines 34–41). In that case, the apparently negative assertions are "strictly speaking" wrong and (like apparently true affirmative assertions like "IT is one") to be understood as expressed in ordinary, misleading human language, not the philosophically correct language for which The Way of Truth prepares the way.

(4.1) something is true (or is the case) and cannot fail to be true (or to be the case), and (4.2) nothing is or can be true (or the case).

The second Way is "completely unlearnable" for the following reason: it is impossible to know or state that which is not (**11.2** lines 7–8). This argument can be given a reasonable sense on all four interpretations. (1) If something does not exist, we cannot know it or express it verbally, since there is no "it" to be known or expressed. (2) If something has no predicates, nothing can be (truly) said about it, and it cannot be known, since there is no way of recognizing it or becoming acquainted with it. Since it makes sense on (1) and (2), it also does on (3). Also on (4): if nothing is true or is the case, nothing can be known or truly stated since only what is true or is the case can be known or truly stated.

The import of Parmenides' thesis can be grasped if we consider an objection to (2) and (4). On (4), if nothing is true, then it is true that nothing is true, and so the argument does not prevent us from knowing *this*. Similarly for (2), if *x* has no predicates, we can know of *x* that it is predicateless. But the argument rules out this move. If "predicateless" is a predicate, then *x* cannot have even *that*. The second Way is unintelligible because nothing can be (meaningfully) asserted *or denied*.

Regarding (1) we might think that we can know and we do think that we can speak of nonexistent things, mermaids for example. But then asserting (or knowing) that mermaids have human heads implies that (some) nonexistent things have human heads, and Parmenides can object that nonexistent things cannot have heads at all. In fact, they cannot have any parts or attributes; no predicates can be true of them, because there is nothing there for them to be true of. Further (as before), if nothing is true of the nonexistent, it is not even true that it does not exist. Again, we have a fundamentally incoherent, inexpressible philosophical position.

The assumption driving the argument is that language and knowledge are grounded in reality. Propositions and knowledge-claims, whether existential ("*x* exists") or predicative ("*x* is *F*," where *F* is a predicate) presuppose the existence of their subject, i.e., that their subject-term refers to something that exists, and so the statement "*x* does not exist" is either false (because *x* exists) or fails to get off the ground (because it is about nothing).[24]

All four interpretations thus make sense in the context of **11.2**, but (4)

---

24. Referential theories of language have a powerful intuitive appeal, but lead to paradox: to say what is not is to say nothing, but to say nothing is not to speak at all (cf. Plato, *Theaetetus* 189a, *Sophist* 263b). Or, "to 'mean' something is to spear it with a spoken (winged?) word. Then to speak of what is not is to hurl a term at—what? It isn't there" (M. Furth, "Elements of Eleatic Ontology," in *The Pre-Socratics*, ed. A. P. D. Mourelatos [Garden City, N.Y., 1974], p. 255 n. 27).

does not fit **11.8**, which infers properties of the subject of ESTI (e.g., lines 3–4) that are extremely implausible on the veridical interpretation, which requires something like a proposition for its subject. **11.8** also tells against (2), and with it, (3), for it separates the claims that IT is without generation[25] and destruction (**11.8** lines 3, 40, argued at lines 6–21) from the claim that it does not suffer change (**11.8** l. 41, argued at lines 22–25), whereas on (2), these claims amount to the same thing. If "*x* is" means "*x* is *F*," then "*x* came to be" and "*x* will cease to be" mean "*x* came to be *F*" and "*x* will cease to be *F*," and these are ways of describing changes which *x* undergoes—coming to have or ceasing to have predicates.

The following discussion is based on the existential interpretation (1), though most of it can be reworked in terms of interpretations (2) and (3). However, this discussion of the various uses of ESTI is not meant to imply that Parmenides was conscious of these different possibilities. He was not, it is safe to say, since the earliest attempts to analyze different uses of the verb are found a century after Parmenides, in Plato's *Sophist* and several treatises of Aristotle.[26] Not the least of Parmenides' achievements is that The Way of Truth can be read in a way free of equivocation on different meanings of ESTI.[27]

But the two alternative Ways are not simply "it exists" and "it does not exist." The second clause in the account of each Way makes the alternatives even farther apart:

> it exists and must exist
> it does not exist and cannot exist

There is no possibility left for something which, say, does not exist but did or might exist, perhaps at a later time. This would allow for coming to be and destruction, which as we shall see are impossible (**11.8** lines 6–21).

The Way of Truth

11.6 begins with an argument for the claim "that which is there to be spoken and thought of must be" (lines 1–2), and takes the argument as further grounds for rejecting the second Way (l. 3). The argument starts from the premises (A): it is possible for what can be spoken and thought of to be, and (B): it is not possible for nothing to be. (A) and (B) imply (C):

25. I use this word as synonymous with "coming to be."
26. Especially *Categories*, *De Interpretatione*, *Posterior Analytics*, and *Metaphysics*.
27. For example, there is no need to see him moving from "*x* is not *F*" to "*x* is not," i.e., "*x* does not exist."

what can be spoken and thought of is not nothing. (C) implies (D): what can be spoken and thought of is something, i.e., it exists. The "must" in 11.6 l. 1 is the "necessity of consequence": given premises (A) and (B), the conclusion must follow.

Parmenides supposes an ordinary person[28] will grant premises (A) and (B). If we can coherently think of something, it is possible for that thing to exist, even if in fact it does not. This holds for mythical beasts, fictional characters, and the contingently nonexistent. If we can coherently conceive of a centaur or James Bond or the King of the United States, then it is possible for those things to exist. Likewise, (B) seems obviously true, although it contains a subtle fallacy, treating "nothing" as if it could intelligibly, even if falsely, be said to exist.[29] The two apparently innocuous premises yield a strong conclusion: whatever can be thought or spoken of exists.

At this point we may not realize how strong this conclusion is. It seems simply to grant existence to objects of thought, as if simply discussing or thinking of something guarantees it some kind of existence—not only real things like the Matterhorn which are "there to be spoken and thought of," but anything we can coherently conceive. That is not to say that the Republicans can get a Republican president just by wishful thinking, but that their thinking about a Republican president makes a Republican president exist in their minds, though not for that reason in the White House. Nothing has yet been said to rule out this interpretation, but it turns out that the conditions on what can be spoken and thought of are so strong that they exclude practically everything.

Parmenides next (11.6 lines 4–9) surprisingly introduces a third Way of Inquiry. The description of the two Ways launched in 11.2 as "the only ways of inquiry there are to think" is now seen to mean not that they are the only two Ways, but that they are the only intelligible Ways: the Way presented in 11.6 is not even intelligible, as is shown by the self-contradictory and so unintelligible description "to be and not to be are the same and not the same" (lines 8–9). Also, those who follow this Way seem unable to tell that it is unintelligible (lines 4–7).

The third Way is the Way of mortals, of ordinary people. But it is no

---

28. His philosophical forebears ought to agree too.

29. "*A*, which can exist, is distinguished from *B*, which (poor thing) cannot: invalid, for to say 'nothing cannot exist' is not to ascribe compulsory non-existence to anything but to say that it is necessarily (truistically) true that what doesn't exist doesn't exist, and this unexciting reformulation disables the argument. The fallacy is the so-called *de re* interpretation of modal statements" (Owen, op. cit. [p. 152 n. 5], p. 94 n. 2). I assume that Parmenides was unaware of the fallacy.

ordinary person who goes around saying "to be and not to be are the same and not the same." This must be intended to rephrase what we do think, in a way that brings out implications of our ordinary thoughts. What we do think is that there are many different things in the world, that these same things come into existence and cease to exist, and that they move and undergo other changes. In **11.8** Parmenides will disprove all these beliefs. Here he characterizes them so as to make us see that they are hopelessly confused and represent an incoherent view of reality. In particular they are infected with nonbeing, which has already been proved unthinkable and unutterable, so that any Way that makes any use of it is unintelligible.

11.7 (which may be the immediate continuation of **11.6**) says more about the beliefs of mortals: they imply "that things that are not, are," which rephrases the more complex expression of **11.6** lines 8–9. Parmenides fastens on the changes indicated above, in which a thing now is, now is not. In cases of destruction a thing now exists, now does not exist. In changes of quality, it now has, now lacks a given quality (now is hot, now is not hot). In denying that the third Way is a coherent way to think about the world, Parmenides challenges our views of reality, denying the most obvious aspects of the world around us, a world we believe in mainly because of our sense experience ("habit born from much experience" [**11.7** l. 3]). The senses (ridiculed in **11.7** l. 4) tell us that there are many things in the world and much change. Also, for the early Greek philosophers the most important features of the natural world are its diversity and change. Consequently Parmenides presents a radical challenge both to unreflective ordinary people and to the presocratic philosophical tradition.

Parmenides' description of our view of the world is so abstract up to now that it is easy to miss the sweeping breadth of his attack, and easy to fail to see where he is headed. However, his attack on the senses (**11.7** lines 3–4) is a warning note, as are his instructions (**11.7** lines 5–6) to accept the conclusions of his arguments (if we cannot refute them) rather than what sense perception and our habitual ways of thinking tell us. This last claim, it should be noted, involves the first explicit statement of the contrast between reason and the senses, which immediately became and has since remained one of the focal points of philosophical discussion. Moreover, Parmenides' preference of reason over the senses makes him the ancestor of rationalism (in some of its forms) and constitutes an important element in the historical background of Plato's Theory of Forms.

Next comes the account of the true Way. **11.8** is the longest continuous stretch of writing from any presocratic, and lines 1–49, in which Parmenides expounds his theory, contain the first elaborately structured series of deductive arguments in the history of Western philosophy. This is no accident. Parmenides' thesis is entirely contrary to our beliefs and experience, and he rejects the kinds of evidence on which ordinary knowledge-claims are based. Hence, he will not find support for his theories in ordinary mortal beliefs about the world and about how we come to know things; instead, he uses the divine power of logic to prove them and bases his proofs on truths no one could deny, such as premises (A) and (B) in the argument in **11.6** lines 1–2.

He begins by reminding us that there is only one Way left to consider (**11.8** l.1), and identifies a number of "signs" along the Way (**11.8** lines 2–6). These "signs," which point to the correct interpretation of "it is," are attributes he will discuss. To complete our journey along the Way we must understand all the signs, so that a full understanding of "it is" includes knowing all these features. What is, i.e., any legitimate subject of thought and discourse (from now on I shall call this subject "IT"[30]) is ungenerated, imperishable, whole, of a single kind, unshaken and complete, timeless, one, and continuous. To interpret these claims in the light of what follows, we see that Parmenides is claiming that anything we can coherently think of exists, but did not come to be and will not cease to be (argued at lines 6–21); it is undivided, unique, and changeless and uniform throughout ("whole," "of a single kind," "one," and "continuous," argued at lines 22–25), motionless ("unshaken," argued at lines 26–33), and possesses all attributes that can coherently be conceived to apply to anything ("complete," argued at lines 22–25, 42–49). The opening lines of **11.8** thus serve as a table of contents for most of the remainder of The Way of Truth.

11.8 lines 6–21. Ungenerated and Imperishable

This section falls into three parts. The first (lines 6–15), which contains three arguments to prove that IT is ungenerated, concludes (l. 14) apparently by asserting that it has eliminated destruction as well (doubtless because parallel arguments hold against the possibility of going out of existence). The second (lines 15–18) strongly reaffirms the dichotomy between what is and what is not, which forms the basis for the preceding arguments. The third (lines 19–21) argues for the timeless nature of IT, which provides a further argument against coming to be and destruction.

11.8 LINES 6–9. ARGUMENT 1

IT did not come into existence out of what is not. What is not cannot give rise to anything or foster the growth of anything. Since (as we know from

---

30. At present "IT" is only shorthand for "whatever can be legitimately spoken or thought of," with no suggestion intended that IT is unique or even a "thing" (as opposed, say, to a concept or mental idea). It will emerge from the argument that IT *is* unique, but otherwise unlike other familiar (real or mental) entities.

11.2 lines 7–8 and **11.3**) what is not cannot be intelligibly spoken or thought of, coming into existence out of what is not cannot be coherently conceived.

11.8 LINES 10–11. ARGUMENT 2

IT did not come into existence out of what is not, because if it did, it came into existence at a certain time. But there is no reason (necessity) for it to be generated at any one time rather than at any other, since that would mean that what is not has different attributes at different times. In particular, it would mean that what is not supplies a condition (necessity) for coming to be at one time but not at others. But what is not has no attributes at any time. Since there is no time at which IT should come into existence rather than at any other time, and since IT cannot come into existence at all times, there is no reason to suppose that IT came into existence at all. This is the second application of the Principle of Sufficient Reason we have seen.[31]

11.8 LINES 12–14. ARGUMENT 3

IT did not come into existence out of what is not, because what is not cannot give rise to anything except itself. This is the first enunciation of the principle "Out of nothing, nothing comes to be,"[32] which was implicit in earlier Greek thought, even as far back as Hesiod, and which afterwards, because of Parmenides, became a touchstone for subsequent Greek cosmogonies.

These arguments show that coming to be out of the sheer nonexistent is impossible, which is most obviously relevant in the first stage of a cosmogony. The arguments say nothing of more familiar cases of coming to be, which can be described in terms of changes among already existing things. The table comes to be when already existing wood, screws, and glue are treated and arranged in the right way. The baby comes to be when an existing sperm and an existing egg join in the right way in the right circumstances, and already existing food is transformed in the mother's body and passed on to the embryo in the appropriate way, etc. Nothing Parmenides has said so far excludes the possibility of the familiar world, just as long as we follow Xenophanes and Heraclitus in declaring it to be eternal.[33]

11.8 LINES 19–21. ARGUMENT 4: TIMELESS EXISTENCE

Another claim about IT is suggested in **11.8** lines 5 and 19–20. Since IT is now, IT never was nor will IT be (l. 5). Conversely, if IT came into existence

31. Anaximander provides the first, see p. 40.
32. This principle is usually known in its Latin form, "ex nihilo nihil fit."
33. See pp. 64, 139.

or if IT is ever going to be, IT is not. Parmenides excludes past and future tenses in describing IT. Just as it is timelessly true that $2 + 2 = 4$ (it is nonsense to say that $2 + 2$ used to be 4), so it is timelessly true to say that IT exists. No argument is offered for this interesting point, though the following Parmenidean considerations point to it. Parmenides holds that IT is eternal (a conclusion that follows from the facts that IT exists (l. 3), and that IT is without generation or destruction (lines 6–18) and is unchanging (lines 22–25). So at any given time IT is identical to the way IT is at any other time. All things that are ever true to say or think of IT are always true. Therefore, there are no time distinctions relevant to IT. But past and future tenses only make sense by contrast to each other and to the present, and if there is no possibility of any differences, there is no basis for any such contrast. "$2 + 2$ was 4" only makes sense if there is a possibility that at some time it is not then true that $2 + 2 = 4$. In the absence of such a contrast, there is no use for past and future, or even for the (tensed) present; all that is left is the timeless present. Further, the conception that all that is exists timelessly does away with time itself. There are no temporal distinctions, because there is temporal uniformity. IT exists fully, always. IT is held in shackles, bound fast (lines 14–15), unable to escape, or even to move. Moreover, parallel reasoning would imply that there are no spatial distinctions either, so that the concepts of space, place, and spatially distinct parts of IT do not make sense. IT (and therefore the universe) proves to be without time or space.

In its context, timelessness is presented as another obstacle to coming to be and destruction (cf. l. 21). The point will be that coming to be and destruction take place in time: at one time a thing exists and at another it does not. Timeless existence thus precludes the possibility of the different times needed for coming to be and destruction to take place.

11.8 lines 22–25. Undivided and Continuous

11.8 lines 6–21 show that IT is not generated from or destroyed into what is not. Lines 22–25 go on to prove some consequences: IT is undivided, IT is not any more or any less in any way, IT is all full of what is, and IT is all continuous. The premise from which this stretch of argument begins, "IT is all alike," restates the results of lines 6–21, that there is no generation or destruction. It is equivalent to "IT must fully be" (l. 11). Since IT all is fully or alike, IT is undivided: there are no gaps. The clearest application of this consequence has to do with existence in time: lines 6–21 show that IT has no absolute beginning or end; lines 22–25 show that IT has no intermediate beginnings or ends either. IT is temporally undivided and continuous, with no temporally separate stretches occurring one after the other. Further, since lines 6–21 rule out all generation and destruction, not only can IT not come to be or cease to be as a whole, but the same is true for any parts or attributes IT may have. Consequently, IT cannot change, in the sense of acquiring new parts or attributes or losing ones IT has. That would make IT more or less at different times in those respects ("more" in the sense that something more belongs to IT or is true of IT). "IT is all full of what is," in that at any time IT is complete, with all possible parts and attributes.

A further consequence seems to be that IT is unique, that there is only one existing thing. At any rate this is the best candidate in the fragments for an argument for monism.[34] IT is not more or less in any way, therefore IT holds together (equivalently, IT is all full of what is, and equivalently again, what is draws near to what is). Therefore, IT is all continuous.[35] I think Parmenides' idea is that since what is clings together, there cannot be more than one distinct thing. Whatever is, is uniform and has the same (i.e., all possible) attributes. It is not possible to say that one thing, or attribute, leaves off and another starts *here* and/or *now*.

The point can be argued as follows (though Parmenides does not put it this way).[36] If there is more than one existing thing, say there are two. (The point will hold no matter how many there are.) Call them *A* and *B*. *A* and *B* are different from one another. (If they were the same thing, we would have one thing, not two.) Therefore, each has at least one thing true of it that is not true of the other. (At the very least, it is true of *A* and false of *B* that it is identical with *A*.) Further if *A* and *B* exist in space, then *A* and *B* must occupy distinct regions of space, so that it is true of *A* and false of *B* that it is here, and false of *A* and true of *B* that it is there (where "here" and "there" designate the spatial locations of *A* and *B* respectively). But if anything is true of *B* and false of *A*, then *A* is lacking in that respect, and so is not "full." Once we have plurality, we violate the "full" and "not any more or any less" requirements as discussed above. Since "not full" and "more and less" are unintelligible notions, plurality is ruled out as well.

11.8 lines 26–33. Motionless

Since motion is one kind of change, change in place, lines 22–25, which claim that IT is changeless, already imply that IT is motionless. In fact,

34. Despairing of finding an argument for monism, J. Barnes (*The Presocratic Philosophers*, rev. ed. [London, 1982], p. 207) has maintained against a unanimous tradition that Parmenides was not a monist. He criticizes efforts to see 11.8 lines 36–37 as an argument for monism, but does not consider lines 22–25.

35. SUNECHES, the word for "continuous," is closely related in form and meaning to SUNECHESTHAI, the word translated "holds together"; notions of mathematical continuity are not here present.

36. See 11.8 lines 57–58 and discussion on p. 176 for evidence that Parmenides conceived of IT along these lines.

motionlessness is mentioned only at lines 29–30. The remainder of this section provides material to bolster the too brief arguments of the previous section. Lines 26–29 say that changelessness is a consequence of no coming to be or ceasing to be, which was an important element in the reconstruction of the argument for changelessness offered above. Lines 32–33 contain material used in the proof that IT is unique. In fact, these lines go farther: "IT is not lacking; if IT were lacking, IT would lack everything." This follows from the radical dichotomy between what is and what is not, strongly stated at l. 11: "it must fully either be or not (be)." If IT is lacking, then IT is infected with not-being. But if IT has *some* not-being, IT must completely not be.

The argument against motion does not depend on properties of space, only of time. The whole series of arguments so far has depended on temporal considerations, and subsequent proofs are based on the arguments against coming to be and ceasing to be.

11.8 lines 34–41. Linguistic Difficulties

At this point Parmenides goes back to his principle that it is impossible to think (or know or express) what is not (lines 35–36, cf. **11.2** lines 7–8, **11.3**). Since IT is unique (lines 36–37, cf. lines 22–25), there is only one legitimate subject of thought, speech, and knowledge, so all thinking has IT as its subject. But l. 34 says more. Not only is there only one intelligible subject, IT, there is also only one intelligible thought, that IT is. If any other statements could intelligibly be made about IT, they might conceivably be true or false, and that would lead to the difficulties noted previously. Moreover, what Parmenides has shown implies that many statements are unintelligible—those involving time, change, plurality, and motion. Strictly speaking, in referring to IT, we cannot use past or future, but only the timeless present. Even the tensed present is ruled out because it depends on the illegitimate contrast with past and future. In the same way we cannot strictly refer to IT in ways that depend on illegitimate contrasts with other illegitimate predicates. Strictly speaking, it is wrong to call IT changeless, motionless, or one, since "motionless," "changeless," and "one" are coordinate with the unintelligible notions motion, change, and plurality.

Parmenides now confronts a question raised by his doctrine. If, strictly speaking, the only intelligible thought or statement is "IT is," what happens when we think or utter other sentences? "The kids are running" is certainly a different sentence from "IT is," and it has a plural subject and a predicate that involves motion. What does Parmenides propose to do with that sentence, and for that matter with all the rest of language except for the one legitimate sentence? Further, we might try to turn his reasoning upside down. If there is an exact correspondence between what can be spoken or thought of and what is, don't sentences like "The kids are running" guarantee the existence of their subjects? Instead of restricting the range of legitimate subjects to IT, why not extend the range of existing things to anything we can think of, including Julius Caesar, the Wizard of Oz, my first billion dollars, and square circles? Simply by thinking of them or expressing them in an intelligible utterance we guarantee that they exist.

Parmenides has a straightforward reply to this last attack: anything infected with any nonbeing cannot exist at all; IT is the only subject not so infected, so IT is the only legitimate subject. But what, then, of the first question? How are we to deal with all but one of the vast number of apparently well-formed sentences that can be formed in an ordinary language? The answer is given in lines 38–41: all words name IT, even if the people who use them do not realize it. This thesis can be supported by a familiar line of reasoning: each word must name either IT or what is not; but IT is the only thing that is; what is not cannot be named; therefore, each word (despite appearances) names IT.

As the examples (lines 40–41) show,[37] the names in question are predicates. "It has been named all names" means that all (the indicated) names ("coming to be," etc.) are predicated of IT.[38] Since in **11.18** mortals are said to have given names to the subjects of these predicates, Parmenides seems to view language as consisting of names that can be formed into subject-predicate propositions. The "correct" language has only one subject, "IT," and one predicate, "is," which form one proposition.[39] The "incorrect" languages of mortals contain many names, but insofar as mortals use these names in significant speech, they form them into propositions that amount to the single correct proposition "IT is." Apparently all subject terms amount to "IT" and all predicate terms to "is." Although humans, misled by their senses, have created languages to describe the world the senses reveal to them, their languages (like the senses) mislead, and in that they relate to reality at all, what they say must express the only meaningful utterance, "IT is."

Strictly speaking, only one thought is intelligible, "IT is." Mortals are mistaken in using language to say other things. They cannot be doing the impossible, referring to what is not, so they are (despite what they think) referring to IT. This solution may not satisfy, but it invites a further question.

---

37. The examples are the predicates treated and eliminated so far ("alternating bright color" stands for the kinds of change ruled out in lines 22–25).

38. On the alternative translation "it has been named all things," the point will be the same, though not so well expressed. Since coming to be and the other "things" mentioned in lines 40–41 have been shown to involve what is not, they cannot be spoken or, therefore, predicated of anything, including IT.

39. In fact, this language consists of only one word, ESTI, a verb which implies its subject. See p. 160.

Occasionally Parmenides recognizes what can be spoken or thought of "strictly speaking." But even in describing IT, he frequently says things which, strictly speaking, he cannot say. In calling IT unchanging, for instance, he describes IT in terms of change, which is nonexistent and therefore inexpressible. Worse, he frequently speaks of what is not. In effect, he uses words to express concepts which he analyzes, showing that they are incoherent and so unintelligible, and then he forbids their use. This approach is dictated by the peculiar nature of his project. To eliminate virtually all our language and concepts he must begin in the world of our language and concepts and finish in another world where practically none of our language and concepts apply. In moving from the one world to the other, he uses and then discards words and concepts. At the end, he is left with only one expressible thought, but on the way there, and even afterwards in communicating to mortals who are not yet there, he must use many technically illegitimate words and concepts.

11.8 lines 42–49. Spatial Uniformity

The proof that IT is motionless depends on properties of time, not space, but it naturally brings up the question of the spatial extension of IT, the final topic discussed in The Way of Truth. The actual argument (lines 44–49) closely parallels the argument for temporal invariance (lines 22–25) and the consequences are similar: because IT is inviolate (i.e., complete), IT cannot be in any way (here, in any place) more or less; therefore, any spatial stretch of IT is identical with any other stretch. But there are no separate stretches, since that would require there to be stretches of what is not in between, and there is no such thing as what is not. Consequently, IT is spatially uniform ("not at all greater or smaller here than there" [lines 44–45], later rephrased as "equal to itself on all sides, it meets with its limits uniformly" [l. 49]). Spatial uniformity and temporal uniformity imply analogous results: IT is not only timeless, but also "spaceless" (there are no spatial distinctions); and timelessness and spacelessness too have analogous results: there is no time or space.

There are two obstacles to this interpretation: the prominent mention of limit at the beginning and end of this passage and the comparison of IT with a ball have led many to believe that IT is spherical. But if IT is spherical, and its (spatial) limit is the surface of the sphere, we are entitled to ask what lies outside (or inside[40])—and there is no answer, since it can be

---

40. On one interpretation of a spherical IT, IT is the spherical surface, not the entire bulk of the sphere enclosed by the surface. This interpretation has the advantage that a spherical surface is uniform, which cannot be said for the other case, where, for example, the center has different properties from the other points.

neither IT (which is all found in the sphere) nor what is not (which does not exist).[41] Also, though a spherical surface is uniform, it is possible to distinguish different areas and points on it, and so there *are* spatial distinctions. And once there are distinct points, there are things true of each point that are not true of any other, so that IT is not "full" (cf. the argument sketched above in the discussion of lines 22–25). These are strong reasons against believing that IT is spherical. And there is no need to follow that interpretation. For Parmenides uses the word 'limit' not of limits in space or time, but to express fixity and invariance, also expressed by the image of shackles (lines 13–14) and bonds (l. 26). And his comparison with the sphere stresses not its shape but its "completeness," i.e., being "evenly balanced," which in the context of the treatment of the spatial properties of IT corresponds to the property of being "not at all greater or smaller here than there." Like IT, a sphere is spatially uniform, but it is so in a different way. Parmenides emphasizes the similarity, but we should not be misled into thinking that the similarity goes further than it does or can.

11.4, whose original position in the poem is uncertain,[42] plays some role in the discussion of spatial properties. It seems to argue for spatial indivisibility (as **11.8** l. 22 argues for temporal indivisibility): IT is not spatially divided into bits separated by stretches of what is not.

Concluding Remarks on the Way of Truth

Parmenides' chief contributions to philosophy occur in The Way of Truth. The present account has been generous in its assessment of this section. It would be easy to fault Parmenides for expressing his ideas and arguments in difficult and obscure language, as well as for leaving large gaps in his thought. An obvious case occurs at **11.8** l. 14, where he concludes that IT can neither come to be nor perish, whereas the arguments up to that point attack only coming to be. He also fails to argue for his view that IT has timeless existence (**11.8** lines 5, 19–20). More importantly, there seem to be errors in the arguments. At **11.8** lines 22–25 he infers that since generation and destruction are impossible, so is change in qualities. But even if we agree that generation and destruction are inadmissible, since they involve what is

---

41. The idea that Parmenides had a conception of "Einsteinian," "curved" space (so that the question of what is outside does not arise) has been proposed (F. Cornford, "On the Invention of Space," in *Essays in Honor of Gilbert Murray* [Oxford, 1936], pp. 215–35) but is historically absurd.

42. We would expect it to have occurred somewhere in the middle of **11.8**, perhaps just before l. 42, but Simplicius, our source for **11.8**, seems to claim that he is quoting a continuous passage.

not, it is not clear why something cannot change from red to blue. The same comment holds for the argument against motion (**11.8** lines 26–33). Also, if, as suggested above, **11.8** lines 22–25 are meant to argue against plurality, the reasoning turns on moves from plurality to difference, from difference to lacking some possible attribute, and from lacking some possible attribute to being infected with what is not. But this last move is highly dubious: why should something's being red (or here) and so not blue (or not there) imply that it is infected with the unintelligible what is not? These are some of the most important flaws in Parmenides' argumentation. Other objections can be made against the arrangement of the arguments, since it is not always clear where one topic leaves off and another begins.

The reason for interpreting Parmenides charitably is that only in this way can we fully appreciate the interest, the potential, and the challenge of his ideas and arguments. Only if we make the effort to unravel his tortuous reasoning and fill in the gaps in ways congenial to his point of view can we hope to understand his enormous contribution to philosophy.[43]

The Way of Mortal Opinions

11.8 lines 50–52. Transition to The Way of Mortal Opinions

The goddess now proceeds to fulfill her promise (**11.1** lines 28–32) to expound the opinions of mortals. She makes it clear that this way is unreliable (**11.1** l. 30) and that her account is deceitful (**11.8** l. 52). Why does she deal in deceit in this way? The only clue in the text is found in the final two lines of **11.8**. She will expound the world "as it appears," i.e., the world as the senses present it to us, "so that no mortal opinion may ever overtake you." The Way of Mortal Opinions gives an account of the phenomenal world along familiar Milesian lines. However, it differs significantly from earlier theories, nonphilosophical as well as philosophical. Thus the goddess does not present Mortal Opinions in a straightforward way. Her starting point is the characterization she offers of Mortal Opinions: mortals believe "that the things that appear must genuinely be, being always, indeed, all things" (**11.1** lines 31–32). And her project in The Way of Mortal Opinions is to give the best possible account of the KOSMOS which appears to us and which mortals wrongly believe to constitute reality.

Earlier philosophers had attempted this task but their accounts were flawed. The goddess has presented what she asserts to be the truth. Now she presents a theory about the world of appearances that, as we shall see, is

---

43. One of Melissus' virtues is that he presents his version of Eleatic monism in a clearer and more systematic way. See chap. 15.

based on an error. For this reason, The Way of Mortal Opinions cannot win out over The Way of Truth. But if someone else proposed a different account of the world of appearances, it might be judged superior to The Way of Truth. Hence the need to give Parmenides the best possible account, "so that no mortal opinion (i.e., no other theory about the phenomenal world) may ever overtake you." If Parmenides can show that The Way of Mortal Opinions, which he knows to be false, is superior to all possible rival theories, then no such theory can threaten The Way of Truth.

11.8 lines 53–55. Foundations of The Way of Mortal Opinions

The Way of Mortal Opinions is based on a radical error. Humans posit, or rather, the best possible reconstruction of the world of appearance posits, a basic duality, and all other things in the KOSMOS and the history and development of the KOSMOS depend on these two basic things, or are reduced to these two things and their interactions, and "in this way they have gone astray."

In what precisely did they go wrong? They named two forms "of which it is not right to name one." This may mean (a) that their basic error was being dualists instead of monists, (Since only one thing exists, it is wrong to posit two principles. In fact, since both principles are different from the one existing thing, neither exists and neither of the two can be the basis of a correct account, but this is not Parmenides' point. Here he only calls attention to the incorrect number of principles.), (b) that they went wrong in naming *even* one of the two principles they named (Neither exists, so neither can be a principle.), and (c) that it was correct to name one, but not the other (One of the two principles, namely Fire, really exists and is identical with what The Way of Truth calls what is, and the other one, Night, does not exist, and is identical with what The Way of Truth calls what is not.).[44]

The Way of Mortal Opinions is importantly different from Milesian accounts, which are monistic in deriving the KOSMOS from a single principle. The Way of Truth has shown that true monism is incompatible with the world of appearances. No single principle can give rise to plurality and opposition;[45] at least two principles are needed, and Parmenides' dualistic cosmology puts opposition in the world from the start (**11.8 l. 55**). This

44. Interpretation (c), which seems incompatible with The Way of Truth, is Aristotle's interpretation (Aristotle, *On Generation and Corruption* 1.3 318b6–7 [= DK 68A42], *Metaphysics* 1.5 986b31–987a2 [= DK 28A24]).

45. Hence Milesian monism is mistaken. Anaximander illegitimately and obscurely derives hot and cold from the APEIRON (see pp. 36–37) and Anaximenes' monism involves air in a plurality of states (see p. 49).

minimal amount of error is thus ineradicable from any plausible account, even the best one, of the phenomenal world (interpretation [a] above) so even though the two forms the goddess reveals are not arbitrary, they remain fabrications designed to account for what does not really exist (interpretation [b] above).

11.8 lines 55–61, 11.9. The Basic Duality, Fire and Night

Just as what is has attributes called "signs" (11.8 l. 2), so the two principles of The Way of Mortal Opinions have opposing signs. Fire is mild, light (as opposed to dense), bright (so that it can be called light as opposed to dark), whereas Night is dark, dense, and heavy. No doubt other attributes hold as well. Fire will also be hot and dry, and Night cold and wet. Each of the two elements is distinct from the other and identical with itself,[46] its identity and difference being marked by the indicated "signs." Now for the first time we have true elements, distinct basic forms of matter that always preserve their own identity; they may intermingle with each other and form other substances, but under no conditions can they be transformed into each other.

The phenomenal world of Mortal Opinions is full of things composed ultimately of Fire and Night and endowed with properties that stem from the opposed "signs" of the two elements. 11.9 lines 3–4 can be taken as saying either that everything (that is, everything in the phenomenal world other than Fire and Night in their purest form) is a compound of the two elements or that the KOSMOS as a whole is full of the two elements (counting both their pure and their mixed forms). These interpretations both accurately characterize the world of Mortal Opinions.

Cosmology

The total amount preserved from The Way of Mortal Opinions is too small to enable us to form anything like a complete picture of the views it contained. The programmatic remarks in 11.10 and 11.11 indicate some of its contents: a cosmogony and cosmology treating the astronomical subject matter obligatory in any presocratic treatise. 11.14 and 11.15, which refer to the moon, form part of this section, as does 11.12, which is part of a description of the "wreaths" or rings which are the courses of the celestial bodies.

An interesting feature of the cosmology is the presence of "the goddess who governs all things" (11.12 l. 3), who is presumably identical with

---

46. Fire and Night thus are "lacking" or "incomplete" in a way incompatible with what fully is. See the discussion of uniqueness, p. 169.

Necessity (**11.10** l. 6), and who generates Love first of all gods (**11.13**). We seem to have a theogony as well as, or as part of, the cosmogony, and this reading is supported by ancient references to other gods in Parmenides (War and Discord) and to stories Parmenides told about the gods.[47] Unfortunately we do not know more.

The prominence Parmenides gives to Love ties in with his interest in sex (**11.12** lines 4–6) and embryology (**11.17**).

The final one of Parmenides' beliefs we will consider is his account of perception and thought, which attempts to find a physical basis for these psychological phenomena.

> **11.20** Most general theories of sensation are of two kinds. Some make sensation occur by like and other by the opposite. Parmenides, Empedocles, and Plato by like. . . . Parmenides made no general definition, but said only that there are two elements and knowledge is in accordance with the one which exceeds. For if the hot or the cold surpasses, the thought becomes different. Thought that is due to the hot is better and purer, but even this requires a certain balance. [Here Theophrastus quotes **11.16**.] For he speaks of sensation and thought as the same. This is why both memory and forgetfulness are produced from these through their mixture. But he did not at all determine whether or not there will be thought or what will be its arrangement if they are equal in the mixture. But that he makes sensation occur also by the opposite in its own right is clear from the passage where he says that a corpse does not perceive light, heat, and sound because the fire has left it, but it does perceive their opposites cold and silence. And in general everything that exists has some knowledge. (Theophrastus, *On Sensation* 1, 3 = DK 28A46)

This extract is given at length principally to show the level of Parmenides' thinking on these subjects and because it is the first detailed account we have of any treatment of these phenomena. Two implications of the discussion are that the soul, whose presence makes things alive, is fiery, and that human (and other) thought depends on the presence of Fire and Night. Thus, this account of thought makes sense only in the unreal world of Mortal Opinions and cannot be taken as a clue to how it is possible to have knowledge of the real world of Truth.

This last question is an important one to be sure. If the only thing that exists is the unique, unchanging, spaceless, timeless IT, then what is the status of Parmenides himself, the goddess, and the mortals whose opinions he disbelieves? Parmenides can dismiss the last group as part of the unreal

---

47. Cicero, *On the Nature of the Gods* 1.11.28 (= DK 28A37), Plato, *Symposium* 195c (not in DK).

world of opinions. And he can dismiss his own body in the same way. But how about his mind which is having the thoughts? Some have claimed that IT is identical with thought, translating **11.3** as "For thinking is the same as being," and **11.8** l. 34 as "thinking is the same as the object of thought" (where the only possible object of thought is IT). But apart from these two lines, which can easily be translated differently, there is no suggestion that IT thinks, and the whole approach Parmenides takes in The Way of Truth, as well as the absence in the earlier philosophical tradition of any tendency to consider thought as an entity, tell against this interpretation. I find it more plausible that he simply did not raise or answer this question, which may simply not have occurred to him.

11.18 appeared in Parmenides' poem "after he had related the ordering of perceptible things"[48] and serves as an appropriate conclusion to The Way of Mortal Opinions, stressing that the account covers what occurs "according to opinion," emphasizing change (growth), the time distinctions of past, present, and future, the names applied to all these illusory phenomena, and the fact that the names are the product of human decisions (not due to the nature of reality).

---

48. Simplicius, *Commentary on Aristotle's On the Heaven* 558.8 (= DK 28B19).

12

Zeno of Elea

Parmenides had argued that the world revealed by our senses is an illusion, that there is only one thing, and it does not change or move, never came into existence and will not cease to exist. These controversial views were defended by one man and accepted with modifications by another. These two philosophers, Zeno and Melissus, are the subjects of this chapter and chapter 15.

Life and Relation to Parmenides

Plato is the best source of information on Zeno's age and relation to Parmenides and the purpose and nature of Zeno's work.

12.1 (127a) Once Parmenides and Zeno came to Athens for the
    (b) Great Panathenaic festival. Parmenides was quite an elderly man, very grey, but fine and noble in appearance, just about sixty-five years old. Zeno was then almost forty, of a good height and handsome to see. The story goes that he had been Parmenides' young lover. . . .
    (c) Socrates and many others [were] eager to listen to Zeno's treatise, for he had then brought it to Athens for the first time. Socrates was then very young. Zeno himself read it to them. . . .
    (d) When Socrates had heard it, he asked Zeno to read again the first hypothesis of the first argument.
    (e) When he had read it, he said, "How do you mean this, Zeno? If things that are are many, they must therefore be both like and unlike, but this is impossible. For unlike things cannot be like, nor can like things be unlike. Isn't that what you are saying?"
    —ZENO: Yes.
    —SOCRATES: Now if it is impossible for unlike things to be like and like things unlike, it is also impossible for things to be many? For if they were many they would have impossible attributes. Is this the point of your arguments—to contend, against all that is said, that things are not many? And do you think that each of your arguments proves this . . . ?
(128a)   —ZENO: You have well understood the purpose of the whole work.
    —SOCRATES: I understand, Parmenides, that Zeno here wants to be identified with you by his treatise as well as his friendship, for he has written in the same style as you, but by changing it he is trying to make us think he is saying something else. For in your
    (b) poem you declare that the all is one and you do a good job of proving this, while he declares that it is not many, and furnishes many impressive proofs. Now when one of you says it is one and the other that it is not many, and each speaks so as to seem not to have said any of the same

things, though you are saying practically the same things, what you have said appears beyond the rest of us.

—ZENO: Yes, Socrates, but you have not completely understood the truth of the treatise. . . .

(c) It is actually a defense of Parmenides' argument

(d) against those who make fun of it, saying that if IT is one, the argument has many ridiculous consequences which contradict it. Now my treatise opposes the advocates of plurality, and pays them back the same and more, aiming to prove that their hypothesis, "if there are many things," suffers still more ridiculous consequences than the hypothesis that there is one, if anyone follows it through sufficiently. I wrote it in this spirit of competitiveness when I was young, and then someone stole it, so I did not even have the chance to consider whether it should be made public.[1]

(Plato, *Parmenides* 127b–128d; part = DK 29A11, part = DK 29A2)

Socrates was born in 469. The *Parmenides* makes Socrates "quite young" (127c) but old enough for philosophical discussion, hence its stage date is c. 450. If Parmenides and Zeno were then about 65 and 40 (127b), they were born c. 515 and c. 490.

If there is a historical basis for the setting of the *Parmenides*, Parmenides and Zeno may have come to Athens during the quadrennial Great Panathenaia (127a) to expound their philosophy in that public forum.[2] Plato informs us that this was the first appearance of Zeno's book in Athens (127c), but that it had been composed many years before (128e) and had been circulated in a pirated edition (128d).

Aside from his visit to Athens, the only story told about Zeno is that he plotted against a tyrant, was caught and tortured, but refused to name his fellow conspirators.

Zeno's Treatise

Zeno wrote his treatise to defend Parmenides' thesis (128c–d), here summarized as "there is one thing," against attempts to refute it by showing its

1. **12.1** must be handled cautiously. The conversation reported in the *Parmenides* certainly did not take place, and it is doubtful that Socrates even met the men from Elea. Still, the detailed information about the ages of Parmenides and Zeno is unlikely to be fiction, and they certainly could have visited Athens. In general, the setting is historically plausible. Great festivals were frequented by philosophers and other intellectual and literary figures wanting an audience for their works. And private readings of the sort Plato describes were no doubt common. Further, Plato's account of the purpose of Zeno's work and its relation to Parmenides' ideas is an interpretation, but for once Plato seems to be correct.

2. See p. 369.

absurd implications. Zeno set out to prove that the opposing view, "there are many things" (127e), entails greater absurdities. His book was a series of forty arguments, of which Plato claims to state the first (127d).[3]

Aristotle called Zeno the father of dialectic.[4] Dialectic for Aristotle is an important philosophical technique for sounding out ideas, typically the ideas of an opponent, by getting him or her to state a thesis and then asking questions to draw out its implications. Dialectical strategy, as discussed in Aristotle's *Topics*, consists in trying to show that the thesis has false or otherwise unacceptable consequences, and hence is false, while the opponent defends the thesis by trying to avoid such results. Many of Zeno's arguments derive mutually contradictory consequences from the hypothesis that there are many things (for example, the consequence that they are both like and unlike [127e]—an impossible and therefore false state of affairs).

Zeno was a master of arguments related to reductio ad absurdum or reductio ad impossibile ("reduction to absurdity, or to the impossible") arguments. To refute thesis A, show that A entails B, which is known to be impossible or absurd, therefore false. Since B is false and follows from A, A must be false as well. Thus A is refuted. In the example given, the thesis that there is a plurality yields two consequences: they are like and they are unlike. But it is impossible for something to be like and unlike. Therefore, the thesis entails an impossibility and hence it is false.

Zeno's arguments do not explicitly make the moves from "B is impossible" to "B is false" to "A is false," nor does the account of their purpose ("to prove that their hypothesis that there are many things suffers still more ridiculous consequences than the hypothesis that there is one, if anyone follows it through sufficiently" [128d]) require these moves. But since the arguments "contend, against all that is said, that things are not many" (127e), they have the force even if not the form of reductio arguments. Zeno did not invent this form of argument,[5] but he brought it to new heights and prominence.

Some of Zeno's surviving arguments are directed against plurality, some against motion, one against place, and one against the sense of hearing. Plato's statement that Zeno's arguments were all aimed against plurality (128d) need not trouble us, for describing Parmenides' opponents as

3. Proclus, *Commentary on Plato's Parmenides* 694.23–25; Elias, *Commentary on Aristotle's Categories* 109.17–30 (both = DK 29A15).

4. Aristotle, fr. 65 (Rose), quoted in Diogenes Laertius, *Lives of the Philosophers* 8.57 (= DK 29A10), 9.25 (= DK 29A1).

5. Reductio arguments are common in Parmenides and underlie Xenophanes' arguments against the gods of popular belief and Anaximander's argument that the earth stays still in the middle of the universe. See pp. 40, 60–61.

pluralists may be shorthand for saying that they deny all Parmenides' claims, just as it is shorthand to say that Parmenides believed in the one (128d).[6] Alternatively, the arguments about motion, place, and hearing, of which we have only summaries, may have been aimed at plurality. For example, motion requires a plurality of times and places, so by arguing against motion Zeno is arguing against one reason to believe in a plurality of times and places. Zeno's book could have made the connection clear.

In the rest of this chapter I will set out the arguments and discuss them briefly. In several cases I give Aristotle's comments, which provide a useful perspective. Zeno's paradoxes are extremely suggestive philosophically and in this century have received much attention from philosophers of mathematics and logicians. They raise mathematical issues that could not be settled until the concepts of the infinitesimal and the mathematical infinite were worked out in the nineteenth century by Bolzano and Cantor, and they raise philosophical issues on which there is still no general agreement.[7]

Arguments against Plurality

Argument 1

According to Plato (127d), Zeno's first hypothesis of his argument against plurality states that "If things are many, they must be both like and unlike," and the argument proceeds to claim that it is impossible for what is like to be unlike and for what is unlike to be like; therefore there cannot be many things. I reconstruct the argument as follows. If there are many things, there are at least two. Pick two of them, A and B. A is unlike B because A differs from B in at least one way (A is different from B, but B is not different from B). Likewise, B is unlike A. But A is like A (since A is not different from A in any way), and B is like B. Therefore, A and B are both like and unlike.

This is not yet a good argument; there is no contradiction unless something is like and unlike the same thing. The argument can be improved to show this. As before, A and B are unlike each other. But A is like B (and B like A) in that both are existing things. Thus A is both like and unlike B.

---

6. Since the bulk of the *Parmenides* is a dialectical exploration of various "hypotheses" related to the view that "if there is a one" or "if one is," Plato's way of expressing Parmenides' claim may be affected by his purpose in the dialogue.

7. Bertrand Russell's interest in Zeno (e.g., *The Principles of Mathematics* [London, 1903], chs. 42–43; *Our Knowledge of the External World*, 2d ed. [London, 1926], ch. 6) led to further studies, especially A. Grünbaum, *Modern Science and Zeno's Paradoxes* (London, 1968), and the papers collected in W. Salmon, *Zeno's Paradoxes* (Indianapolis, 1970).

But again, the contradiction is only apparent, since A is not both like and unlike B in the same respect. The argument fails.[8]

I begin with this bad argument to show that not all of Zeno's reasoning is sound, and not all of his ideas profound. With Zeno, as with the other Presocratics, it is a mistake to assume that there are brilliant ideas everywhere, however plentiful they may be. Also, this argument gives insight into the level of argument and standards of reasoning that prevailed in the early fifth century, shortly after deductive reasoning was introduced to philosophy and long before the rules of logic were worked out.

Argument 2

12.2 Zeno stated that if anyone could make clear to him what the one is, he would be able to speak of existing things.

> (Eudemus, *Physics* fr. 7, quoted in Simplicius, *Commentary on Aristotle's Physics* 97.12–13 = DK 29A16)

Ordinary people believe that there are many things, there is a plurality which is made up of many individuals, units, or "ones." Some of Zeno's attacks on plurality proceeded by showing that the units or "ones" on which the conceptions of plurality are founded involve logically unacceptable features.

A number of these arguments are preserved. One argues for the antinomy that if there are many, they are both small and large (in fact, it argues the stronger thesis that they are so small as to have no size and so large as to be unlimited in size) by showing that there cannot be a plurality because each member of the plurality has these contradictory attributes. This strategy accords with Zeno's challenge to his opponents in **12.2**. Argument 2 has two stages.

Argument 2A

Zeno begins from the thesis that there are many things. He then argues that each of the many is "the same as itself and one," and from that he concludes that each of the many has no size. The argument for this conclusion is not preserved.

Argument 2B

The proof of the other limb of the antinomy, "So large as to be unlimited in size," also has two stages.

8. Perhaps not too much weight should be given to this conjectural reconstruction of Zeno's argument. It may be possible to find a stronger argument for the hypothesis.

ARGUMENT 2B1

It begins by arguing that "anything with no size, thickness or bulk does not exist."[9]

> **12.3** For if it should be added to something else that exists, it would not make it any bigger. For if it were of no size and was added, it [the thing it is added to] cannot increase in size. And so it follows immediately that what is added is nothing. But if when it is subtracted, the other thing is no smaller, nor is it increased when it is added, clearly the thing being added or subtracted is nothing.   (Zeno, DK 29B2)

Argument 2B1 works in the case of three-dimensional bodies (cf. "thickness, bulk"), and so tells against opponents who have in mind the many objects in the physical world perceived by the senses. Since the conclusion is unacceptable, the many existing things cannot be nothing. Therefore, each must have some size.

ARGUMENT 2B2

Zeno next shows that anything with size is unlimitedly large.

> **12.4** But if it exists, each thing must have some size and thickness, and part of it must be apart from the rest. And the same reasoning holds concerning the part that is in front. For that too will have size and part of it will be in front. Now it is the same thing to say this once and to keep saying it forever. For no such part of it will be last, nor will there be one part <of any such part> not related to another. Therefore, if there are many things, they must be both small and large; so small as not to have size, but so large as to be unlimited.   (Zeno, DK 29B1)

Argument 2B2 depends on a characteristic Zenonian infinite regress. Take any one of the many existing things. It has size. Therefore, one part of it ("the part that is in front") can be distinguished from ("must be apart from") the rest. Let $A1$ be the original thing and $A2$ the part distinguished from the rest. $A2$ exists (or else it is not a part of $A1$), and so has size. But in the same way we can distinguish a part of $A2$ (call it $A3$) which exists and has size. And this process has no end, since we never reach a part with no subparts.

---

9. Quotation from Simplicius, *Commentary on Aristotle's Physics* 139.9–11 (= DK 29B2). It is Simplicius' summary of Zeno's argument and occurs immediately before he quotes **12.3**.

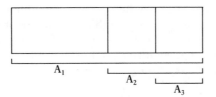

Argument 2 concludes that the many are (a) so small as not to have size, and (b) so large as to be unlimited. The first limb (2A) proves that each of the many has no size, which we may take as equivalent to (a), although it does not mention smallness. The second limb (2B) (which does not mention largeness) works by dividing up an existing thing (*A1*) of limited size. It does not prove (b), but that if there are many, each has an unlimited number of parts. Zeno argues that anything composed of parts is composed of an infinite[10] number of elements, each with positive size. If the sum of an infinite number of positive magnitudes is infinite, it follows that the sum of the parts of *A1* is infinite in size, so that *A1*, which consists of all its parts, is "so large as to be unlimited." I shall postpone criticism of this argument.

Argument 3

Yet another argument against plurality asserts that "the same things are limited and unlimited." The verbatim report of this argument goes as follows.

> **12.5** (a) If there are many, they must be just as many as they are and neither more nor less than that. But if they are as many as they are, they would be limited. (b) If there are many, things that are are unlimited. For there are always others between the things that are, and again others between those, and so the things that are are unlimited.   (Zeno, DK 29B3)

The first limb (a) of Argument 3 claims that the many things are "just as many as they are and neither more nor less than that," and therefore limited. The operative principle (though Zeno does not state it) seems to be that there is a definite number of them, and any definite number is a finite number, so there is a limited number of things.

10. "Unlimited" and "infinite" translate APEIRON. I use whichever seems appropriate, but both English words represent a single unclarified notion. Partly as a result of reflecting on Zeno's paradoxes, Aristotle (*Physics*, books 3, 6) developed a more precise notion of APEIRON, in which it is appropriately translated as "infinite."

There are different interpretations of the second limb (b). (1) If Zeno is still talking about three-dimensional things with size, it is not clear why he thinks "there are always others between the things that are." Why can't two objects simply touch one another? (2) The ancient commentator who preserves the argument says, "in this way he proved the unlimited in quantity on the basis of dichotomy [division in two],"[11] a process of division similar to that found in Argument 2B2. In that case, the argument may suppose two adjacent existing things *A1*, *B*, with *A1* subdivided as before into *A2*, *A3*, etc.

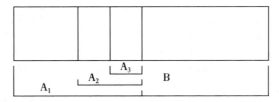

The argument shows that there are no adjacent *least* parts, so that a plurality of existing things requires an infinite number of them. (3) Zeno is talking not of three-dimensional objects, but of mathematical points on a line. Here it is true that between any two distinct points there is a third, and indeed there is an infinite number of points on a line. Thus Zeno discovered a property of densely ordered sets. But there is no evidence that he intended this interpretation of his paradox.

Arguments against Motion

Zeno pressed the Eleatic attack on motion much further than Parmenides had done in his brief argument (**11.8** lines 29–30). Aristotle preserves four of his five arguments on motion which he prefaces with the following statement:

> **12.6** Zeno's arguments about motion which present difficulties for those who
> try to solve them are four.
> (Aristotle, *Physics* 6.9 239b9–11 = DK 29A25)

The first two are essentially the same and will be treated together. The first is called "The Dichotomy," from the process of division employed, or "The Stadium," from a particular use of the argument, perhaps made by Zeno himself, to show that it is impossible to cross a stadium. The second is called "The Achilles" and is familiar as "Achilles and the Tortoise."

11. Simplicius, *Commentary on Aristotle's Physics* 140.33–34 (= DK 29B3).

The Dichotomy or Stadium

12.7 First is the argument which says that there is no motion because that
which is moving must reach the midpoint before the end.
(Aristotle, *Physics* 6.9 239b11–13 = DK 29A25)
(continuation of **12.6**)

The argument is spelled out more fully elsewhere.

12.8 It is always necessary to traverse half the distance, but these are infinite,
and it is impossible to get through things that are infinite . . .
(Aristotle, *Physics* 8.8 263a5–6, not in DK)

In moving from A to B (where A and B are different points), we must reach
$A1$, the halfway point, before reaching B. Then we must move from $A1$ to
B. In so doing we must reach $A2$, the halfway point, before reaching B.
Then we must move from $A2$ to B. There is an infinite number of such
steps A–$A1$, $A1$–$A2$, etc.

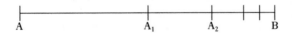

(Equivalently, there is an infinite number of halfway points $A1$, $A2$, etc.)
But it is impossible to cross an infinite number of distances (or to come
into contact with an infinite number of points), so the motion from A to B
cannot be completed. Therefore, motion is impossible. The argument can
also be taken to say that before reaching $A1$ we must reach the halfway
point of the interval A–$A1$, etc., so that not only can we not complete a
motion, we cannot even begin.

The Achilles

12.9 The second is the one called "Achilles." This is to the effect that the
slowest as it runs will never be caught by the quickest. For the pursuer
must first reach the point from which the pursued departed, so that the
slower must always be some distance in front. This is the same argument
as The Dichotomy, but it differs in not dividing the given magnitude
in half. (Aristotle, *Physics* 6.9 239b14–20 = DK 29A26)

In the Stadium the distance is divided into two equal parts each time; the
Achilles points out that the same situation arises for division into other
constant proportions as well.

It is natural to think that the argument must be flawed: it has a true
premise and a false conclusion. After all, motion does occur, and yet when

we move from one point to another we do reach the halfway point before the final destination. We may feel sympathy for Antisthenes the Cynic who, "since he was unable to contradict Zeno's arguments against motion, stood up and took a step, thinking that stronger than any opposition in arguments was a demonstration through what is obvious."[12]

One approach is to point out that some infinite series have finite sums. In particular, the series $\frac{1}{2} + \frac{1}{4} + \frac{1}{8} + \dots$ sums to 1. If Zeno thought that it is impossible to cross an infinite number of distances because their sum is infinite, he is just wrong for the particular infinite sets of distances involved in The Stadium and The Achilles (also for the magnitudes in Argument 2B2).

Aristotle takes another approach.

> 12.10 For this reason Zeno's argument falsely assumes that it is impossible to traverse or come into contact with an infinite number of things individually in a finite time. For both length and time and generally everything that is continuous are called infinite in two ways: infinite in division and infinite with respect to their extremities. Now it is impossible to come into contact with things infinite in quantity in a finite time, but it is possible to do so with things that are infinite in division. For time itself too is infinite in this way. And so, it follows that it traverses the infinite in an infinite and not a finite time, and comes into contact with infinite things in infinite, not finite times.
>
> (Aristotle, *Physics* 6.2 233a21–31 = DK 29A25)

Aristotle understands Zeno to argue that traversing an infinite number of distances is impossible because it would take an infinite amount of time. He accuses Zeno of confusing two distinct notions of infinity: what is infinite in respect of its extremities (its end points are infinitely far apart), and what is infinite in respect of divisibility (it can be divided without limit). The continuous distance *A–B* is infinite in respect of divisibility (hence the process of division by dichotomy is possible) but not in respect of its extremities. The time it takes to move from *A* to *B* is also infinite in respect of divisibility but not in respect of its extremities. Time is continuous, and an interval of time can be divided into parts and subparts in the same way distance can. If it takes N seconds to move from *A* to *B*, it takes $\frac{N}{2}$ seconds to move from *A* to *A1*, $\frac{N}{4}$ seconds to move from *A1* to *A2*, etc. So there is no need to suppose that the infinite number of distances needing to be passed in getting from *A* to *B* will take an amount of time that is infinite in extent, only one that is (harmlessly) infinitely divisible. Moreover, though this additional point is not made by Aristotle nor is it necessary for his argument, the total time taken to move from *A* to *B* is $\frac{N}{2}$ sec. + $\frac{N}{4}$ sec. + $\dots = N$ sec.

Referring to the previously quoted passages, he says

12. Elias, *Commentary on Aristotle's Categories* 109.20–22 (= DK 29A15).

12.11 This solution is sufficient to use against the person who raised the
question (for he asked whether it is possible to traverse or count infinite
things in a finite time), but insufficient for the facts of the matter and
the truth.   (Aristotle, *Physics* 8.8 263a15–18, not in DK)

In **12.10** Aristotle assumes without proof that "it is impossible to come into
contact with things infinite in quantity in a finite time," where "contact"
means a discrete physical act of touching. Obviously, if each act of "touching" takes the same amount of time, the amount of time needed to touch
an infinite number of things will be infinite, which is to say they cannot all
be touched in a finite time. This objection fails too if each "touch" takes
only half the time of the previous one. But then is there any objection to an
infinite number of acts of touching in a finite time? Aristotle thought there
is: the question of total elapsed time is irrelevant; it is still impossible to
"touch" an actually infinite number of points. This is not to say that he
withdraws his former refutation. Rather, he reopens the question in the
light of his own (not Zeno's) distinction between the actual and the potential infinite. At this point, the discussion is already beyond what Zeno
intended by it, as Aristotle acknowledges in **12.11**, and has reached an area
still under debate: whether and in what sense it is possible to complete an
infinite number of discrete physical acts, or whether the very notion of
doing so is self-contradictory.

The Flying Arrow

12.12 The third argument is the one just stated, that the arrow is stopped
while it is moving. This follows from assuming that time is composed of
"nows." If this is not conceded, the deduction will not go through.
                    (Aristotle, *Physics* 6.9 239b30–33 = DK 29A27)

Aristotle refers to the following passage:

12.13 Zeno makes a mistake in reasoning. For if, he says, everything is always
at rest when it occupies a space equal to itself, and what is moving is
always "in the now," the moving arrow is motionless.
                    (Aristotle, *Physics* 6.9 239b5–7 = DK 29A27)

I reconstruct the argument as follows. Anything that occupies a space equal
to itself is at rest. At each instant ("now") an arrow in flight occupies a
space equal to itself, and so is at rest. Therefore, during the whole of its
flight it is at rest. Therefore, it is motionless. The point of saying that
"what is moving is always 'in the now'" is to exclude the possibility that the
arrow moves between the instants at which it is at rest.

Aristotle objects from the point of view of his own theory that time is continuous and not composed of instants. He holds it is wrong to say that something is either at rest or in motion at an instant, because rest and motion alike take place over an interval of time. An instantaneous photograph reveals its subject's position but not whether it is moving or still.

Another objection can be made to the move from "motionless at every instant of its flight" to "motionless over the whole of its flight," which commits the fallacy of moving from "each of the parts of X is F" to "X is F."[13]

The premise "anything that occupies a space equal to itself is at rest" can also be resisted in the absence of a reason to suppose that a thing in motion does not occupy a space equal to itself, at any instant of its motion.

Finally, it has been held[14] that this argument is aimed at a theory that time is composed of instants and a corresponding conception of motion as "cinematographic," moving in jerks with one "still frame" for each discrete instant. Those who uphold this interpretation tend to see the argument as sound,[15] but the argument does not depend on such a theory of time, and there is no evidence that such a theory had been proposed.

The Moving Rows

12.14 The fourth argument is about the equal bodies moving in a stadium past equal bodies in the opposite direction, the one group moving from the end of the stadium, the other from the middle, at equal speed. He claims in this argument that it follows that half the time is equal to the double. The mistake is in thinking that an equal magnitude moving with equal speed takes an equal time in passing something moving as it does in passing something at rest. But this is false. Let A's represent the equal stationary bodies, B's represent the bodies beginning from the

---

13. We may rebut this move in kind: it is in motion over the whole of its flight, therefore, it is in motion at each instant. Indeed, something can be moving, or in motion, at an instant (a car can be going 60 m.p.h. at noon precisely), but that does not mean that it covers any amount of distance in an instant. If it goes at constant velocity and takes a minute to go a mile, it covers parts of the mile in proportional parts of the minute, but an instant (with duration zero) is not a part of the minute; the minute is the sum of seconds, but not of instants.

14. This is the view of H. Lee (*Zeno of Elea* [Cambridge, 1936]), G. Owen ("Zeno and the Mathematicians," in *Studies in Presocratic Philosophy*, vol. 2, ed. R. Allen and D. Furley [London, 1975], pp. 143–65; originally in *Proceedings of the Aristotelian Society* 58 (1957–58): 199–222, and reprinted elsewhere), KR, and Guthrie (*HGP*).

15. If the arrow is at rest in each still frame and there is no time in between successive still frames for the arrow to move, then the arrow does not move at all.

middle of the A's, equal in number and size to the A's, and C's represent the bodies beginning from the end, equal in number and size to these and having the same speed as the B's. It follows that the first B is at the end at the same time as the first C, as they [the B's and C's] move past each other, and the <first> C has passed by all the B's but the B's have passed half the A's. And so the time is half. For each of them is next to each thing for an equal time. It follows simultaneously that the B's have passed by all the C's, for the first C and the first B will be at the ends at the same time, because both have been next to the A's for an equal time.   (Aristotle, *Physics* 6.9 239b33–240a17 = DK 29A28)
(continuation of **12.12**)

The following diagram[16] represents the starting point of the movement.

D
$$\begin{array}{l} A\ A\ A\ A \\ B\ B\ B\ B \rightarrow \\ \leftarrow C\ C\ C\ C \end{array}$$
E

A: stationary bodies
B: bodies moving from D to E
C: bodies moving from E to D
D: beginning of stadium
E: end of stadium

The B's and C's move in opposite directions at the same speed. The finish of the movement will correspond to the following diagram

D
$$\begin{array}{l} A\ A\ A\ A \\ B\ B\ B\ B \\ C\ C\ C\ C \end{array}$$
E

In the time of the movement, the leftmost C passes all four B's, whereas the rightmost B passes only half the A's and also all four C's. So far, so good. However, from this situation, according to Aristotle, Zeno wrongly infers that the time the rightmost B takes to pass the two A's is half as long as the time the leftmost C takes to pass all four B's. This conclusion depends on the premise "each is alongside each for an equal time," i.e., each C is alongside each B for the same length of time each B is alongside each A. According to Aristotle, the argument depends on a fallacy: since the B's and C's are moving in opposite directions, a B takes only half as long to get past each C as it does to get past a stationary A. The fallacy is so obvious that some have held that Zeno could not have committed it, but such

16. The diagram is given by Simplicius (quoting Alexander), *Commentary on Aristotle's Physics*, 1016.19–24 (= DK 29A28).

judgments are dangerous. Equally elementary errors about relative terms occur in Plato's dialogues written half a century later. Further, the fact that it is a fallacy does not entail that Zeno himself was taken in by it. We recall that he wrote his book "in a spirit of contention" (**12.1**, 128d).

This argument becomes more historically and philosophically significant if the "bodies" are smallest, indivisible bodies ("atoms"), and the moving bodies are alongside the stationary ones for a smallest, indivisible unit of time. Zeno then has a valid argument against a mistaken ("atomistic") conception of time.[17] However, there is no hint in the sources that Zeno intended the argument in this way.[18]

Two Remaining Paradoxes

The Place of Place

This argument is reported variously.[19] Its gist is:

> **12.15** If place exists, where is it? For everything that exists is in a place. Therefore, place is in a place. This goes on to infinity. Therefore, place does not exist.

The target of this infinite regress argument is the existence of place: nothing that exists can have a location. Zeno thus strikes another blow against our ordinary conception of the world in which things do have places.

There are several responses. Aristotle and his followers simply denied the premise that everything that exists is in a place. "For no one would say that health or courage or ten thousand other things were in a place."[20] We

---

17. This sort of interpretation is given by Lee (op. cit. [p. 190 n. 14]), KR and Owen (op. cit. [p. 190 n. 14]). "If we say that the first *B* can pass twice as many *C*s as *A*s in a given time, what we say entails that if in a given time it passes one *C* it also passes half an *A*. But suppose now that any *A* (and therefore any *B* or *C*) is an *infinitesimal* quantity. Then the *B* cannot pass half an *A*: it must pass all or nothing. And since *ex hypothesi* it *is* moving past the *A*s, it must pass a whole *A* in the time that it passes one *C*. Yet, as we set up the problem, it would pass twice as many *C*s as *A*s in a given time. So when it passes one *C* it also passes two *C*s" (Owen, op. cit. [p. 190 n. 14]), p. 151).

18. Guthrie (*HGP*), Barnes (*The Presocratic Philosophers*, rev. ed., [London, 1982], p. 291), and KRS reject the interpretation for this reason.

19. Simplicius, *Commentary on Aristotle's Physics* 562.3–6 (= DK 29B5, in DK vol. 2, p. 498); Aristotle, *Physics* 4.3 210b22–23, 4.1 209a23–25; Eudemus, *Physics* fr. 42, quoted by Simplicius, *Commentary on Aristotle's Physics* 563.25–28 (all three testimonia = DK 29A24).

20. Eudemus, fr. 78 (Wehrli) (= DK 29A24).

can then admit that three-dimensional objects have places, but deny that the place of such an object is the kind of thing that has a place.

Another reply is to accept the premise and the conclusion that place is somewhere, but to declare that the place of the place of X is just the place of X, so the infinite regress becomes harmless.

The Millet Seed

This argument is preserved in a "theatrical version," a dialogue between Zeno and the Sophist Protagoras, which is probably not the way it originally appeared.

12.16 ZENO: "Tell me, Protagoras, does a single millet seed make a noise when it falls, or one ten-thousandth of a millet seed?"—PROT. "No."

ZENO: "Does a bushel of millet seeds make a noise when it falls, or doesn't it?"—PROT. "It does."

ZENO: "But isn't there a ratio between the bushel of millet seeds and one millet seed, or one ten-thousandth of a millet seed?"—PROT. "Yes there is."

ZENO: "So won't there be the same ratios of their sounds to one another? For as the things that make the noise <are to one another>, so are the noises <to one another>. But since this is so, if the bushel of millet seeds makes a noise, so will a single millet seed and one ten-thousandth of a millet seed."

(Simplicius, *Commentary on Aristotle's Physics*
1108.18–25 = DK 29A29)

This argument supports Parmenides by proving one of the senses unreliable. (Analogous arguments hold against the other senses.) Aristotle treats it in connection with the question how much force it takes to shift a heavy weight.

12.17 It does not follow that, if a given motive power causes a certain amount of motion, half that power will cause motion either of any particular amount or in any length of time: otherwise, one man might move a ship, if the power of the ship haulers is divided into their number and the distance which all of them move it.

(Aristotle, *Physics* 7.5 250a16–19, not in DK)

Likewise there is a threshold below which no sound is made. We would explain these states of affairs in terms of friction and the elasticity of air, but Aristotle's criticism is to the point.

Evaluation

The surviving arguments all bear out the account of the purpose of Zeno's book given in **12.1**. Though they do not all explicitly attack the hypothesis that there are many things, they all assail elements of our ordinary beliefs that the world contains many things and is full of motion and apprehensible by the senses.

It has been held that some of the arguments tell against Parmenides as much as they do against his critics. Indeed, the conclusion of Argument 2, that if each of the many existing things has size it is unlimited in size, contradicts Parmenides' claim that IT is limited. But the contradiction arises only if IT has size, i.e., spatial extension, and the last chapter gave reasons against this view. The nonspatial interpretation of IT is therefore strengthened by Zeno's argument refuting the possibility of an extended but limited existing thing.

Zeno had a unique role in early Greek philosophy. He did not put forward distinctive views of his own or extend Parmenides' ideas or support them by improved arguments. In the Eleatic team, he played on the defensive side. His arguments are of varied quality. Aristotle's criticisms show that the paradoxes received attention in antiquity, and that Aristotle thought most of them obviously unsound, and believed he had adequate solutions.

That is not to say that Zeno is unimportant. His puzzles drove Aristotle to sharpen the conception of the infinite and related ideas. He made later Presocratics (the Atomists and possibly Anaxagoras[21]) sensitive to issues about the minimal size of matter. Zeno's method of argument had a dual legacy in antiquity. His general strategy of constructing arguments on both sides of an issue (e.g., that if things are many, they must be both like and unlike) was taken up by Protagoras and became perhaps the most notable weapon in the arsenals of the fifth-century Sophists. His methods of abstract argument were followed in certain fifth-century texts and influenced Plato (the *Parmenides* is a notable example). Insofar as he deserves the title of father of dialectic, he sired an offspring with a long and vigorous life in philosophy and other fields. Finally, his paradoxes, especially those concerning motion, were important because they forced people for the first time to pay attention to the way they conceived of time, space, and motion, and either to accept Zeno's conclusions or refute them. Frequently refuta-

---

21. Zeno may have been influenced by Anaxagoras rather than vice versa. Our view on this issue depends on what we make of the statement that Zeno wrote his work while a young man (**12.1**, 128d) and on what view we take of the date of Anaxagoras' treatise (see p. 201). For Zeno and the Atomists, see pp. 310–12, 315–16.

tion was only possible after relevant concepts had been defined precisely and appropriate distinctions drawn. In this century, these paradoxes have provoked a great deal of controversy among mathematicians and philosophers over the nature of space, time, and the infinite. In fact, they do raise fundamental questions in these areas, and the attempt to understand them fully has led to much valuable philosophical work.

13

Anaxagoras of Clazomenae

Fragments

13.1[1] (1)[2] 1. All things were together, unlimited in both amount[3] and smallness.

2. For the small too was unlimited.

3. And when (or, since) all things were together, nothing was manifest on account of smallness.

4. For AER and AITHER dominated all things, both being unlimited.

5. For these are the largest ingredients in the totality, both in amount and in size.[4]

13.2 (2) 1. For both AER and AITHER are being separated off from the surrounding multitude

2. and what surrounds is unlimited in amount.

13.3 (3) 1. For of the small there is no smallest, but always a smaller

2. (for what is cannot not be).[5]

3. But also of the large there is always a larger,

4. and it is equal in amount to the small.

5. But in relation to itself, each is both large and small.

13.4[6] (4) 1. These things being so, it is necessary to suppose that in all things that are being mixed together there are many things of all kinds, and

1. **13.1–13.9** and **13.11–13.17** are all quoted by Simplicius—ample evidence that he had the text (or at least some of the text) of Anaxagoras before him. Guthrie (*HGP*, vol. 2, pp. 332–38) and Barnes (*Early Greek Philosophy* [Harmondsworth, 1987], pp. 227–34) quote the full context.

2. The numbers in parentheses are the numbers of the fragments in DK. (1) = DK 59B1.

3. I translate PLETHOS throughout as "amount." Other possible translations of this nontechnical word are "number," "multitude," and "quantity."

4. The authenticity of **13.1** sec. 5 has been cast into doubt by Sider (D. Sider, *The Fragments of Anaxagoras* [Meisenheim am Glan, 1981], pp. 49–50), who thinks it was written by Simplicius to explain what Anaxagoras means in sec. 4 by the word here translated as "dominated."

5. Many accept Zeller's emendation of the line to read "for what is cannot through division [literally, "by cutting"] not be," i.e., it cannot be divided up into parts that do not exist.

6. Many editors divide **13.4** into two or three separate fragments.

seeds of all things, having all kinds of shapes and colors and flavors;

2. and that humans too were compounded and all the other animals that possess life;

3. and that there are inhabited cities and cultivated fields for the humans just as with us,

4. and that there are for them a sun and a moon and the rest just as with us,

5. and that the earth grows many things of all kinds for them, of which they gather the most useful into their dwelling and use it.

6. I have said these things about the separating off, because [or, that] it would have occurred not only with us, but elsewhere too.

7. But before these things separated off, when [or, since] all things were together, not even any color was manifest,

8. for the mixture of all things prevented it—the wet and the dry, the hot and the cold, the bright and the dark, there being also much earth in the mixture and seeds unlimited in amount, in no way like one another.

9. For none of the other things are alike either, the one to the other.

10. Since this is so, it is necessary to suppose that all things were in the whole.

13.5 (5) It is necessary to know that although [or since] these things have been separated apart in this way, all things are not at all less or more (for it is not to be accomplished[7] that they are more than all), but all things are always equal.

13.6 (6) 1. And since the portions of both the large and the small are equal in amount, in this way too all things would be in everything;

2. nor can they be separate, but all things have a portion of everything.

3. Since there cannot be a smallest, nothing can be separated or come to be by itself,[8] but as in the beginning now too all things are together.

4. But in all things there are many things, equal in amount, both in the larger and the smaller of the things being separated off.

13.7 (7) . . . and so we do not know either in word or in deed the amount of the things being separated off.

13.8 (8) The things in the single KOSMOS are not separate from one another, nor are they split apart with an axe, either the hot from the cold or the cold from the hot.

7. "To be accomplished" translates ANUSTON, an unusual word which Parmenides also uses (**11.2** l. 7). Here it means something close to "possible."

8. "By itself" means "separate from other things," not "through its own agency."

13.9 (9) 1. As these things are thus rotating and being separated off by both force and speed,

2. the speed causes the force,

3. and their speed is like the speed of nothing now found among humans, but altogether many times as fast.

13.10 (10) For how could hair come to be from not hair or flesh from not flesh?[9]

13.11 (11) In everything there is a portion of everything except Mind, but Mind is in some things too.

13.12 (12) 1. The rest have a portion of everything, but Mind is unlimited and self-ruled and is mixed with no thing, but is alone and by itself.

2. For if it were not by itself but were mixed with something else, it would have a share of all things, if it were mixed with anything.

3. For in everything there is a portion of everything, as I have said before.

4. And the things mixed together with it would hinder it so that it would rule no thing in the same way as it does being alone and by itself.

5. For it is the finest of all things and the purest, and it has all judgment about everything and the greatest power.

6. And Mind rules all things that possess life—both the larger and the smaller.

7. And Mind ruled the entire rotation, so that it rotated in the beginning.

8. And at first it began to rotate from a small area, but it <now> rotates over a greater range and it will rotate over a <still> greater one.

9. And Mind knew all the things that are being mixed together and separated off and separated apart.

10. And Mind set in order all things, whatever kinds of things were to be—whatever were[10] and all that are now and whatever will be—and also this rotation in which are now rotating the stars and the sun and

---

9. Some doubt the authenticity of this fragment. It has even been suggested that it may be a fabrication of the source a scholium (note in the margin of a manuscript) on the text of the Church Father, Gregory of Nazianzus, which is strongly influenced by Aristotle's interpretation of Anaxagoras. (M. Schofield, *An Essay on Anaxagoras* [Cambridge, 1980], pp. 138–43). But even on this view, the ultimate source (Aristotle) of the interpretation is quite likely to be correct, since he is thought to have had access to Anaxagoras' book and is unlikely to have misunderstood an obvious point like the one in question here. It is therefore reasonable to take **13.10** as Anaxagorean in thought even if (possibly) not in word.

10. I omit the phrase "but are not now," which DK prints here. It seems to be a variant of the following phrase, "all that are now." I follow Schofield's interpretation of sec. 10 (op. cit. [p. 198 n. 9], p. 4 and n. 1).

the moon, and the AER and AITHER that are being separated off.
11. This rotation caused the separating off.
12. And the dense is being separated off from the rare and the hot from the cold and the bright from the dark and the dry from the wet.
13. But there are many portions of many things.
14. And nothing is being[11] completely separated off or separated apart one from another except Mind.
15. All Mind is alike, both the larger and the smaller.
16. But nothing else is like anything else, but each single thing is and was most plainly those things of which it contains most.

13.13 (13) 1. And when Mind began to cause motion, separating off proceeded to occur from all that was moved,
2. and all that Mind moved was separated apart,
3. and as things were being moved and separated apart, the rotation caused much more separating apart to occur.

13.14 (14) Mind, which is always, is very much[12] even now where all other things are too, in the surrounding multitude and in things that have come together in the process of separating[13] and in things that have separated off.

13.15 (15) The dense and the wet and the cold and the dark came together here, where the earth is now, but the rare and the hot and the dry went out into the far reaches of the AITHER.

13.16 (16) 1. From these things as they are being separated off, earth is being compounded;
2. for water is being separated off out of the clouds, earth out of water, and out of the earth stones are being compounded by the cold,
3. and these [i.e., stones] move further out than the water.

13.17 (17) 1. The Greeks are wrong to accept coming to be and perishing,
2. for no thing comes to be, nor does it perish, but they are mixed together from things that are and they are separated apart.

11. This translation preserves the present tense of the original. Since Anaxagoras cannot mean that Mind (which is already separate from everything else [**13.12** sec.1]) is being separated, or that nothing else undergoes separation (**13.12** sec. 9), he must mean that nothing else attains the complete state of separation that Mind has.
12. The manuscript reading does not make good sense here. In "which is always, is very much," I follow the text of DK.
13. "Come together in the process of separation" is an interpretive overtranslation of PROSKRINESTHAI, which means literally "separate towards." For discussion, see pp. 225–26.

3. And so they would be correct to call coming to be being mixed together, and perishing being separated apart.

13.18 (18) The sun puts the shine in the moon.

13.19 (19) We call Iris [rainbow] the brightness in the clouds opposite the sun.

13.20 (21) On account of their [the senses'] feebleness we are unable to discern the truth.

13.21 (21a) Appearances are a sight of the unseen.

13.22 (21b) [We are less fortunate than animals in all these respects] but we make use of our own experience and wisdom and memory and skill, and we take honey, milk <cows>, and laying hold <of animals> we carry them and lead <them>.[14]

13.23 (22) The white of the egg is bird's milk.

Life and Writing

Anaxagoras was born c. 500 and died c. 428. He was an Ionian, and his philosophy marks a return to the philosophical and scientific interests and style of the Milesians,[15] though he was also keenly aware of and deeply influenced by Eleatic philosophy. He reportedly predicted the fall of a meteorite which occurred at Aegospotami (in the Gallipoli peninsula) in 467 (**13.31**). He moved to Athens, where he lived for thirty years. While there he was an associate of Pericles, the great Athenian statesman. This political connection and his scientific views led to his prosecution and conviction (probably c. 450)[16] for impiety, on the grounds that he believed the sun to be not a god but a fiery stone. Anaxagoras thus has the honor of being the first philosopher prosecuted at Athens[17] (Socrates would follow;

14. It is debated how much of this material is Anaxagoras and how much is due to the source (Plutarch, *On Chance* 3 98F).

15. The claim that he was Anaximenes' pupil (Diogenes Laertius, *Lives of the Philosophers* 2.6 = DK 59A1), though chronologically impossible, is true to the spirit of his thought.

16. Some ancient testimonia imply a date of c. 430.

17. This title may belong to Protagoras, but the story of his banishment is less secure. See p. 364.

Aristotle fled to avoid prosecution). Forced to leave Athens, he lived the rest of his life in Ionia, in the city of Lampsacus near Troy, where he was honored after his death with an annual holiday for children.

He had a reputation for single-mindedly pursuing intellectual inquiry to the extent that (unusual for a Greek of this period) he had no concern with politics or worldly affairs. His commitment to inquiry is displayed in the following incident.

> **13.24** Once a ram with one horn was brought to Pericles from his country estate, and when the soothsayer Lampon saw the horn growing strong and solid from the middle of the forehead, he said that though there were two contending factions in the city (those of Thucydides and of Pericles), the one who obtained the head would gain power. But Anaxagoras had the skull cut open and showed that the brain had not completely filled its place, but was drawn together in a point like an egg in the very spot in the entire cavity where the root of the horn had its origin. (Plutarch, *Life of Pericles* 6 = DK 59A16)

He wrote a single work, *Physica* ("Studies of Nature"), in plain clear prose, which treated the nature of matter, its original condition (since for Anaxagoras the KOSMOS had a beginning), the entity (NOUS) that initiated and governed the cosmogonic process, that process itself, and (possibly in considerable detail) the KOSMOS as it is now.

Relations to Other Philosophers

Anaxagoras was decidedly younger than Parmenides (born c. 515) and somewhat older than Zeno and Empedocles (both born c. 490). Parmenides' influence on Anaxagoras is strong, but his relations with the other two philosophers are not clear. The best evidence for the date of Zeno's work is the statement that he wrote his treatise at a young age.[18] Anaxagoras' alleged prediction of the meteorite of 467 may mean that his book had been published by that date.[19] This information does not provide a basis for deciding who wrote first, though I believe that Zeno wrote first and that Anaxagoras constructed his theory partly in response to him.[20] As for his relation to Empedocles, the key text runs as follows.

> **13.25** Anaxagoras . . . was in age prior to him [Empedocles], but in works posterior . . . (Aristotle, *Metaphysics* 1.3 984a11–13 = DK 59A43)

18. Plato, *Parmenides* 128d (= **12.1**).
19. See p. 229 and p. 229 n. 82.
20. See p. 218. Some prefer the reverse ordering.

Taken straightforwardly this assertion indicates that Anaxagoras wrote later than Empedocles, although even in antiquity interpretations were floated that Aristotle meant that Anaxagoras was inferior to Empedocles[21] or that Anaxagoras was "more up to date" than Empedocles, hence superior.[22] Aristotle's statement is thus inconclusive, but Diogenes Laertius reports that Empedocles "heard" Anaxagoras,[23] and the evidence on balance favors an earlier date for Anaxagoras' work.[24] It is reasonable, though, to regard Anaxagoras and Empedocles as contemporaries who in constructing their physical systems were largely concerned with the same problems, which stem from Parmenides. I shall not attempt to point out instances where one of these philosophers may have influenced the other, but I will from time to time show points of similarity and difference between the two systems.

Anaxagoras accepts Parmenides' absolute division between what is and what is not (**13.3** sec. 2) and his consequent denial of coming to be and perishing (**13.17**). Like Empedocles he holds that what appear to be cases of coming to be and perishing are really instances of mixture and separation of existing things. But there is a difference. For Empedocles mixing is sometimes the cause of a compound's coming to be and sometimes the cause of its perishing, and similarly for separation (**14.19** lines 3–5), but for Anaxagoras coming to be is simply mixture and perishing is simply separation.[25]

The ban on coming to be and perishing permeates Anaxagoras' system further than it does Empedocles'. For Empedocles, genuine types of substances like blood and flesh are formed out of the four elements and dissolve into them. Anaxagoras prohibits even this sort of coming to be and

---

21. Alexander, *Commentary on Aristotle's Metaphysics* 27.28–28.3 (not in DK). This reading is rendered less plausible by Aristotle's apparent contempt for Empedocles. For references, see chap. 14, p. 297 n. 89. Noteworthy in this connection is Aristotle's description of Anaxagoras as "like a sober man in contrast with the random talk of his predecessors" (*Metaphysics* 1.3 984b17–18 = DK 59A58), where the predecessors seem to include Empedocles (cf. 1.4 984b31–985a10 = DK 31A39).

22. Alexander, *Commentary on Aristotle's Metaphysics* 68.25–69 (not in DK).

23. Diogenes Laertius, *Lives of the Philosophers* 8.56 (= DK 14, 5).

24. See D. O'Brien, "The Relation of Anaxagoras and Empedocles," *Journal of Hellenic Studies* 88 (1968): 93–113.

25. More precisely, perishing is "being separated apart" (**13.17**). Specifically, the destruction of a compound such as an animal is the (not necessarily complete) separation apart of some or all of its component parts (its limbs, tissues, etc., and the Basic Things of which they are composed). For the difference between "separation apart" and "separation off," see p. 224–25.

perishing: the blood or flesh must have been there all along, even if it was not detectable (**13.10**). Counter to appearances there is a portion of everything in everything (**13.6** sec. 2). The food we eat changes into blood, flesh, etc., but these substances do not come to be in either a Parmenidean or an Empedoclean sense. They were already in the food, but in quantities so small as to be invisible (**13.12** sec. 16). When the food is digested, the (invisible) blood in it becomes (visible) blood in us by a process of separation and mixture. A similar account holds for qualitative changes. When hot food cools, it is not because the hot in it perishes and there comes to be cold that previously did not exist. There was cold already in the hot food, but in an amount too small to be perceptible. Cooling is a process in which the imperceptible cold becomes perceptible and the perceptible hot imperceptible.

Thus, Anaxagoras takes seriously the Parmenidean conditions that existing things (which for Anaxagoras include "things" like hot and cold) are permanent, and that change cannot involve coming to be or perishing, though he does admit plurality and motion. It is plausible to interpret his theory as a response to the Eleatic challenge that takes this starting point. He escapes coming to be and destruction by positing a vast number of different kinds of things and by developing an elaborate theory of matter that accounts for the phenomena we observe in the world around us and for the origin of the KOSMOS itself without violating this central Eleatic thesis.

Entities and Principles of Anaxagoras' System

Anaxagoras' accounts of the origin of the KOSMOS and of the nature of mind and matter are intimately related and inseparable from one another. They are founded on five kinds of entities and six basic principles. The five kinds of entities are (a) ordinary macroscopic objects, (b) Basic Things, (c) Portions, (d) Seeds, and (e) Mind. The six principles are the following.

P1. There is no coming to be or perishing.
P2. There are many (perhaps unlimitedly many) different types of Basic Things.
P3. There is a Portion of everything in everything.
P4. Each thing is most plainly those things of which it contains the largest Portions.
P5. There are no smallest Portions.
P6. Mind (NOUS) is unmixed with other things and has the following functions: (a) it knows all things, (b) it rules all things, (c) it sets all things in order, and (d) it causes motion.

I shall discuss these entities and principles, and then sketch out the cosmogony and cosmology Anaxagoras based on them.

The entities include (a) ordinary perceptible objects, such as lumps of gold, human beings, and the earth. The other kinds of entities are posited to account for the generation, existence, and behavior of these. Ordinary objects—including both organic, differentiated things such as animals and also apparently uniform, homogeneous things such as a lump of gold—are "mixtures" of Basic Things and Seeds (**13.4** sec. 1).

(b) Basic Things are the materials out of which macroscopic objects (also Seeds—see below) are composed. An animal is composed of flesh, blood, and bone (among other things), and these are Basic Things. Perceptible qualities too, such as hot and cold, wet and dry, and colors and flavors, are Basic Things. An animal is composed, then, not only of flesh, etc., but also of Basic Things which endow it with qualities. I shall discuss Basic Things at greater length below in connection with P2.

(c) The Portion of a Basic Thing (X) in something (Y) is, roughly speaking, the amount of X in Y. It is most helpful in understanding Anaxagoras to resist the thoughts that Portions can be separated (as all the bones of an animal can be gathered and separated from the rest of its parts) and that Portions are parts, pieces, or discrete bits (see discussion of P3, P4, and P5 below). We would do well to think of liquids mixed together (neglecting their molecular structure) rather than mixtures like salt and pepper. One way of putting the point is that the Portion of X in Y is not "how many" bits of X there are in Y, but "how much" X. Anaxagoras holds not only that an animal contains Portions of flesh, bone, and blood, but that everything contains a Portion of *everything* (P3). There are Portions of wood and diamond in a human and Portions of hot and wet in ice, although the smallness of these Portions makes them undetectable (P4). One of the most distinctive and difficult features of Anaxagoras' system is that each Portion has Subportions of everything, so that there are no pure substances (no cases where a Basic Thing is found without any Portions of other Basic Things), and no end to the analysis of anything into Portions.

(d) The extant fragments mention Seeds twice, once as existing "in all things that are being mixed together" (**13.4** sec. 1) and once as existing in the original mixture of all things prior to the beginning of the KOSMOS (**13.4** sec. 8). I suggest that the Seeds are different from both the Basic Things and the Portions, that they are microscopic particles of Basic Things (including "things" like earth and flesh and also "things" like hot and cold) that are too small to be seen (cf. **13.1** sec. 3). They occur in all macroscopic objects, possibly in all Portions too. By P3, each Seed contains a Portion of everything.

(e) For Anaxagoras' doctrine of Mind, see pp. 219–23.

Anaxagoras is thus committed to separable, countable objects both macroscopic and microscopic. The macroscopic entities include macroscopic amounts ("pieces") of Basic Things, such as a lump of gold, a pint of blood, or a bone, and complex entities, such as animals, which are composed of pieces of more than one Basic Thing (e.g., bone, flesh, and blood). The microscopic objects, "Seeds," are pieces of Basic Things too small to be seen. They have the same structure as the macroscopic pieces do. He is also committed to nonseparable, noncountable amounts of the Basic Things, the Portions. I shall say more about the nature and interrelations of these types of entities in connection with P1 and P6, but first I shall give a rough illustration of how Anaxagoras viewed the structure of an ordinary macroscopic object.

The element mercury is found in nature chiefly in the form of a sulfide called cinnabar, which is often accompanied by some uncompounded mercury. A lump of the associated ore thus contains some mercury in the form of mercury sulfide and some in the form of small globs of pure mercury scattered across the surface. In Anaxagorean terms, the Portion of mercury in the lump is the total amount of mercury in it—all the mercury in the globs and in the mercury sulfide. The globs correspond to Anaxagoras' Seeds (though the Seeds are too small to be seen). There is also a Portion of sulfur in the lump—all the sulfur in the mercury sulfide. Neither the mercury nor the sulfur in the mercury sulfide is recognizable as such, and we cannot extract the mercury or the sulfur from the mercury sulfide by mechanically separating little pieces of mercury and little pieces of sulfur out of it, yet both are there as ingredients.

Anaxagoras complicates this picture by maintaining (P3) that the Portion of sulfur in the lump contains a Portion of mercury (and also Portions of all other Basic Things too) and the Portion of mercury in the lump contains a Portion of sulfur (as well as Portions of all other Basic Things). This holds for the mercury in the globs too—even microscopic globs that he calls Seeds are not pure mercury but contain Portions of all the Basic Things, though they contain more mercury (a larger Portion of it) than anything else (P4). Further, each of the Portions of Portions contains Portions of all Basic Things and so on without limit (P5). This theory raises a number of questions which I shall take up in considering the basic principles of the system.

P1. There is no coming to be or perishing (**13.17**). What ordinarily pass for such events are cases of mixture and separation of things that already are and will continue to be. This is true uncontroversially for things like tables, which are made by fastening together ("mixing" in a certain way) pieces of wood, glue, and other materials that already exist. Anaxagoras claims it also holds for plants and animals, which come from seeds[26] containing all the materials (blood, flesh, etc., or bark, sap, etc.) found in the mature individual, and which grow by assimilating the same sorts of materials from the nutrients the plant or animal ingests. This view is found in the following passage and in **13.27**.

> **13.26** In the same seed there are hairs, nails, veins, arteries, sinews and bones. They are unapparent because of the smallness of their Portions, but as they grow they gradually separate apart. . . . He made these claims not only for bodies but also for colors. For black is in white and white is in black.[27] He posited the same for weights, supposing that light is mixed with heavy and vice versa.
>
> (Scholium on Gregory Nazianzus, *Patrologia Graeca* vol. 36, col. 911 = DK 59B10)

The same also holds for other kinds of changes: from hot to cold, from black to white, and from light to heavy (**13.8**, **13.26**), and also for changes in substance: from bread to hair and flesh (**13.10**).

P2. There are many (perhaps unlimitedly many) different types of Basic Things. By Basic Thing, I mean roughly what corresponds to Empedocles' four elements, even though Anaxagoras' system leaves no room for true elements (see discussion of P3). A survey of the fragments yields the following list of Basic Things.

> wet and dry (**13.4** sec. 8, **13.12** sec. 12, **13.15**)
> hot and cold (**13.4** sec. 8, **13.8**, **13.12** sec. 12, **13.15**)
> bright and dark (**13.4** sec. 8, **13.12** sec. 12)
> dense and rare (**13.12** sec. 12, **13.15**)
> AER, AITHER (**13.1** sec. 4, **13.2** sec. 1, **13.12** sec. 10)
> earth (**13.4** sec. 8, **13.16** secs. 1–2)
> cloud, water, stones (**13.16** sec. 2)
> hair, flesh (**13.10**)

Anaxagoras also speaks of Seeds as ingredients.

> seeds of all things with all kinds of shapes and colors and flavors (**13.4** sec. 1)
> seeds unlimited in amount, in no way like one another (**13.4** sec. 8)

26. Aristotle, *Generation of Animals* 4.1 763b30 (= DK 59A107). Anaxagoras was interested in questions of biology, including reproduction, but we do not know enough about his views on these matters to be able to say whether he thought of human sperm as being a Seed in his technical sense of the word. He uses the same word, SPERMA for both.

27. See **13.33**.

The items Anaxagoras mentions reveal his intellectual heritage and his determination to embrace it and to go beyond. The pairs of opposites represent his Milesian forebears. AER, AITHER,[28] and earth, along with clouds, water, and stone are reminiscent of Anaximenes (**6.2**). Hair and flesh mark a departure from tradition. These examples suggest a range of substances that others had not considered basic. The testimonia mention other Basic Things, including gold, bone, veins, sinews, fingernails, feathers, horn, wood, bark, and fruit.[29] Further, on the interpretation of Seeds given above (p. 204), colors, flavors, and possibly shapes (thus, presumably, all perceptible qualities) are yet other Basic Things. Anaxagoras seemingly gives equal billing to all perceptible properties, a novel extension of the Milesian tendency to treat "the hot" and "the cold" as entities.

Aristotle several times discusses Anaxagoras' "elements."[30] The most important passage for present purposes is the one that identifies these "elements" as "the homoeomeries and the opposites,"[31] terms which cover all the Basic Things listed above. Aristotle defines homoeomeries[32] (literally, "similar part") as "things whose part is synonymous with the whole."[33] In Aristotle's physical theory, earth, bone, and gold are homoeomeries.[34] Any part of a mass of earth or a lump of gold or a bone is also called earth or gold or bone. By contrast, in nonhomoeomerous substances, such as faces or trees, there are parts (the nose, the roots) which are not called by the same name as the whole.[35] It is almost certain that Anaxagoras did not use the words "homoeomery" or "homoeomerous," and it is likely that

---

28. Aristotle (*On the Heaven* 3.3 302b4–5 = DK 59A43) says that Anaxagoras used this word for "fire," but I suspect that this is Aristotle's conjecture.

29. Simplicius, *Commentary on Aristotle's Physics* 27.14 (= DK 59A41), 460.16–19 (= DK 59A45), quoted in **13.27**.

30. Although the element is alien to Anaxagoras' system (see p. 212), Aristotle can perhaps be forgiven for employing it.

31. Aristotle, *Physics* 1.3 187a25 (= DK 31A46). Aristotle more often says just that the homoeomeries are Anaxagoras' elements: *Physics* 3.4 203a20–22 (= DK 59A45), *On the Heaven* 3.3 302a31–32 (= DK 59A43), *On Generation and Corruption* 1.1 314a17–19 (= DK 59A46).

32. Singular, "homoeomery"; the adjective is "homoeomerous."

33. Aristotle, *On Generation and Corruption* 1.1 314a20 (= DK 59A46).

34. For some purposes Aristotle distinguishes "elements" (earth, water, air, and fire) from homoeomeries. In these contexts, the homoeomeries are *nonelemental* homoeomeries. Some commentators have wrongly fixed on this special usage; the more general use is needed to account for the examples in Anaxagoras' fragments.

35. The distinction is first set out clearly by Plato (*Protagoras* 329d, not in DK), though he does not use the word "homoeomerous."

Aristotle coined them[36] and applied them to those Anaxagorean Basic Things that in Aristotle's theory are homoeomeries.[37] Since, as P3 implies, there are no true homoeomeries in Anaxagoras' system, Aristotle's use of the term is confusing.[38]

The other type of Basic Things according to Aristotle are "the opposites." This term covers the pairs "wet and dry," etc. listed above. **13.4** sec. 1 mentions "Seeds of all things with all kinds of shapes and colors and flavors." On my interpretation of Seeds, **13.4** sec. 1 commits Anaxagoras to yet more Basic Things, which from Aristotle's point of view also come under the heading of "the opposites." For Aristotle, all colors are mixtures of the opposites black and white. Likewise, flavors are mixtures of the opposites sweet and bitter.[39] **13.4** sec. 1 also mentions shapes, but these are harder to fit into this account. Anaxagoras may have considered them to be mixtures (in some sense) of straight and round, which might be thought opposites, but he may not be claiming that shapes are among the Basic Things. **13.4** sec. 1 need only be saying that the *Seeds* have shapes[40] (which

---

36. Guthrie, *HGP*, vol. 2, p. 325.

37. The occurrence of the term "homoeomeries" in this context therefore means "what we Aristotelians call homoeomeries"; it does not mean "what Anaxagoras called homoeomeries" or even "what Anaxagoras believed to be homoeomerous as *we Aristotelians* use the term." It would be wrong to attribute to Anaxagoras, on the basis of the testimony of Aristotle or from the passages of Simplicius that make the same point (*Commentary on Aristotle's Physics* 460.4–10 = DK 59A45, 27.4–7 = DK 59A41, 27.23–28 = DK 60A5, 65.1–3 = DK 59B3, 155.24–26 = DK 59B1, 156.9–13 = DK 59B5), any theory of the structure of matter, in particular a "principle of homoeomereity," that "things" (sc., "things" like a lump of gold or a clod of earth) are made of parts that are like one another and are also like the whole. These parts are the elements out of which all things are made" (G. Kerferd, "Anaxagoras and the Concept of Matter before Aristotle," in *The Pre-Socratics*, ed. A. Mourelatos [Garden City, N.J., 1974], p. 491).

38. One way of explaining Aristotle's point is to say that in using these terms to describe Anaxagoras' theory he is employing their denotations, not their connotations.

39. Aristotle, *On Sense and Sensible Objects* 3–4 (not in DK).

40. The Greek of **13.4** sec. 1 is tantalizingly ambiguous. It can mean that there are (A) (1) many things of all kinds, (2) Seeds of all things—Seeds that have all kinds of shapes, all kinds of colors, and all kinds of flavors, or (less likely) (B) (1) many things of all kinds, (2) Seeds of all things—Seeds that have all kinds of shapes, (3) colors, (4) flavors. It cannot mean that there are (C) (1) many things of all kinds, (2) Seeds of all things, (3) all kinds of shapes, (4) colors, (5) flavors. I assume that if a Seed can have a particular color or flavor, then that color or flavor is a Basic Thing.

they must, having spatial extension). However this issue is decided, Aristotle's testimony on the types of Anaxagoras' Basic Things confirms the evidence of the fragments.[41]

It sounds odd to modern ears that qualities ("the opposites") should be put on the same footing as substances. (Aristotle, who first clearly distinguished substances from qualities, would agree with us.) But here Anaxagoras continues the Milesian tradition of considering opposites as principles.[42] He views an object, say, a hot lump of gold, as a lump that is, say, gold, hot, heavy, yellow, dry, etc. It contains gold, but also hot, heavy, yellow, dry, etc. (I neglect for the moment the complications introduced by P3.) The way the lump appears is determined by the Basic Things that predominate in it (P4). This way of looking at things is interestingly different from our own and is a conceivable view for Anaxagoras to have proposed.[43] Indeed, it has some plausibility. If we point out that hot is never found by itself, he will agree: in hot as in everything else, there is a Portion of everything (by P3). Still, we might say, there are independently identifiable pieces of bread, earth, and gold, but not so for pieces of hot. Anaxagoras has a reply to this attack too: true, hot is never found except as a hot piece of bread or gold, etc. But equally bread is never found without being hot or cold or some mixture of the two. Just as qualities are not found except in conjunction with substances, so substances are not found without qualities. It is misleading, then, to identify a certain body simply as a lump of gold on the grounds that gold predominates. The gold has a certain color, texture, shape, temperature, etc., so a full description of it will acknowledge the predominance not only of gold but also of dense, cold, etc. Presumably this is the reason for the plural ("things") in **13.12** sec. 16.

41. Some (e.g., G. Vlastos, "The Physical Theory of Anaxagoras," in *Studies in Presocratic Philosophy*, vol. 2, ed. R. Allen and D. Furley [London, 1975], pp. 323–53; reprinted from *Philosophical Review* 59 [1950]: 31–57; Schofield, op. cit. [p. 198 n. 9]; B. Inwood, "Anaxagoras and Infinite Divisibility," *Illinois Classical Studies* 11 [1986]: 17–33) hold that the opposites are the only Basic Things out of which everything else including the "homoeomeries" are made. This admittedly simpler interpretation is bought at the price of rejecting the Aristotelian evidence that supports the present interpretation, and overlooking or discounting the evidence in Anaxagoras' fragments that AER, AITHER, earth, hair, etc., have the same standing as hot, cold, etc.

42. See p. 46.

43. After Aristotle, such a view could not be proposed without an elaborate metaphysics to justify it, but there is no reason why the theory could not have been put forward in the fifth century, before distinctions had been made between substance and attribute and between essence and accident, and before the issues had been raised explicitly that led to those distinctions.

It would be unwise and also alien to the spirit of presocratic thought to attempt a complete enumeration of the Basic Things. Aristotle asserts that they are infinitely or unlimitedly many,[44] which would indeed follow if Anaxagoras acknowledged all possible shapes or colors as Basic Things.

However, not all entities belong at this level. The sun, moon, and stars are fiery stones.[45] Some things, such as humans and animals, are "compounded"[46] of these Basic Things (**13.4** sec. 2). Cities, fields, and dwellings (all mentioned in **13.4**) will be constructed out of the Basic Things in yet different ways.

P3. There is a Portion of everything in everything (**13.6** sec. 2, **13.11**,[47] **13.12** secs. 1, 3, cf. **13.8**). By this oft-repeated claim Anaxagoras asserts that there is *some amount* of everything in everything. There is some flesh in bread, some gold in lead, some hot in ice, etc. This is not to say that a piece of ice contains a hot spot, that it is always possible to isolate or identify Portions, only that they are there—like a drop of black paint mixed uniformly throughout a bucket of white paint.[48]

This claim provides for all possible changes. When a hot object becomes cold, the cold does not come into existence (P1 rules this out), but was already in the object and perhaps in the environment. The cooling of an object is the concentration of cold in it to the point that it overpowers the hot (see discussion of P4 below). Likewise for substantial change.

> **13.27** Seeing that everything comes to be from everything—if not imme-
> diately at least in sequence (for air comes from fire, water from air,
> earth from water, stone from earth, and fire again from stone, and when
> the same food, such as bread, is assimilated, many things of different
> kinds come to be: flesh, bones, veins, sinews, hairs, nails, and in some
> cases feathers and horns, and like grows by means of like)—for these
> reasons he supposed that in the food, even in water if trees are nour-

44. Aristotle, *Metaphysics* 1.3 984a13 (= DK 59A43).

45. Hippolytus, *Refutation* 1.8.6 (= DK 59A42).

46. The term "compounding" is not restricted to organic entities like animals, but seems to be synonymous with "separating off," which describes the formation of macroscopic pieces of Basic Things. The formation of earth out of water is "compounding" in **13.16** sec. 1 and "separating off" in **13.16** sec. 2.

47. Mind is the sole exception. See pp. 219–20.

48. This doctrine does not commit Anaxagoras to a view that there are countable or discrete Portions or particles of flesh in bread, a view which would conflict with P5. Like Empedocles (see p. 265), Anaxagoras does not seem to have been concerned with the ultimate structure of matter, but, possibly unlike Empedocles, Anaxagoras has a theory which is inimical to there being *any* ultimate structure.

ished by this, are wood, bark, and fruit. This is why he claimed that all
things are mixed in all things.

(Simplicius, *Commentary on Aristotle's Physics*
460.12–19 = DK 59A45)

Since Simplicius seems to have had access to Anaxagoras' book, there is
every reason to accept his account as faithful to Anaxagoras' thought. **13.27**
settles two issues which have provoked a great deal of discussion. First, the
charge that Anaxagoras' theory is uneconomical. Since a given substance
can become only a limited number of other things (cheese can become
bone and blood, but not chalk), it would be better to hold that it contains
Portions of only some things, not of everything.[49] The reply to this charge
is twofold. (a) As **13.27** shows, Anaxagoras was concerned to account not
only for the changes the cheese undergoes but also for subsequent changes
as well. Some of the bread we eat becomes flesh, but some is excreted with
our wastes and can fertilize the earth and so become nourishment for a
tree. To cover all such possibilities it is necessary to postulate a Portion of
everything in everything. (b) To investigate all the possible changes of any
particular thing would be a very difficult task quite unlike any research
undertaken by any Presocratic. Moreover, it is neater, more memorable, and
intellectually more (not less) economical simply to make the general pronouncement "a Portion of everything."

Second, it determines the scope of the two occurrences of "everything"
in P3. They do not cover all entities: it is implausible to hold that Anaxagoras meant that, say, a rosebush contains a Portion of an octopus. Yet it is
natural to think that both have the same scope,[50] or that in each occurrence
"everything" covers as wide a range of entities as Anaxagoras' theory allows. The most plausible interpretations of P3 in the context of Anaxagoras' theory are that it means that (A) there is a Portion of every Basic
Thing in every Basic Thing (including flesh and gold, and also hot and
cold) or (B) there is a Portion of every Basic Thing in every Basic Thing
and in every macroscopic entity and Seed. But any macroscopic object is a
mixture of Basic Things and so has a Portion of at least one Basic Thing,
and any Seed is a microscopic piece of a Basic Thing, which means that it
has a Portion of that Basic Thing. If (as I maintain below) any Portion of

---

49. Cornford makes this thesis the basis of his interpretation of Anaxagoras' theory
(F. Cornford, "Anaxagoras' Theory of Matter," in *Studies in Presocratic Philosophy*,
vol. 2, pp. 275–322; reprinted from *Classical Quarterly* 24 (1930): 14–30 and 83–95.
50. On the interpretations of Cornford and Vlastos, they have different scopes:
Anaxagoras means that there is a Portion of every opposite in every *thing*.
(F. Cornford, op. cit. [p. 211 n. 49], G. Vlastos, op. cit. [p. 209 n. 41]).

any Basic Thing contains Portions of all Basic Things, interpretation (A) entails interpretation (B). But as interpretation (B) also entails interpretation (A), the two interpretations are equivalent. That "the opposites" are in everything has not to my knowledge ever been doubted, and seems confirmed by **13.8**. **13.27** makes it clear that Basic Things like flesh are in everything too.

But what does Anaxagoras mean by "in everything"? At the least he must mean in every macroscopic piece of every Basic Thing—in every lump of gold or pint of blood, for example—therefore also in other macroscopic and microscopic entities (for example, an animal or a Seed). I think he also intends P3 to apply to the Portions of Basic Things mentioned frequently in the fragments (otherwise it is hard to see what motivates P5). Thus, in every lump of gold is a Portion (i.e., an amount) of water, and in that Portion of water there is a Portion of gold. P3 therefore amounts to the claim that in every piece or Portion of every Basic Thing there is a Portion of every Basic Thing.

A corollary of P3 is that it is impossible to purify anything completely, so no pure substances are found in nature. Any piece of flesh has Portions of all Basic Things—and this is true no matter how small a piece we take. Anaxagoras took this point seriously, as P5 shows.

It follows that there is no place in Anaxagoras' system for elemental or pure substances,[51] and on this point his theory is different from modern chemistry, which holds that impure substances—iron ore, for example—are combinations of pure substances (iron, oxygen, etc.), and that it is possible in theory to isolate samples of these pure substances, that it is possible to give a precise account of a thing's composition in terms of the pure substances that constitute it (so much iron, so much oxygen, etc.), and further, though it may be possible to give a further account of the pure substances (in terms of subatomic particles, for example), the analysis of anything stops somewhere. The analysis of iron ore will stop at the level of iron and oxygen. The analysis of iron itself will stop, perhaps at the level of protons, neutrons, and electrons. But wherever the analysis stops, we have reached the materials out of which the original thing is composed. For Anaxagoras, though, there are no components of this sort. P3 implies that there is no such thing as pure gold, water, or blood, and even in theory there cannot be any such thing. Analysis of a lump of flesh or gold is in a sense pointless, since at every stage we still have Portions of everything.

This last consideration points to a potential awkwardness. If flesh and gold both have Portions of everything in them, what makes flesh different from gold? Alternatively, if there is no difference between flesh and gold,

---

51. Aristotle is thus wrong to say that the homoeomeries and the opposites are "elements" for Anaxagoras (references in p. 207 n. 31).

Anaxagoras fails to account for the diversity of things in the world, which is a serious flaw in a pluralist of his sort. He addresses these issues in P4.

P4. Each thing is "most plainly those things of which it contains most" (**13.12** sec. 16), i.e., of which it has the largest Portions. Although (by P3) there are no cases of pure substances, we identify a macroscopic[52] piece of gold as gold, or a bone as bone, because of the Basic Things of which it contains most. There is more gold in a piece of gold than there is water (although by P3 there is water too). The word "most" points to a quantitative view. A lump of gold is identified as gold because it contains more gold than anything else—as if it were made, perhaps of 60% gold and 40% everything else, or perhaps 40% gold and 60% everything else, but each other ingredient constitutes less than 40% of the total. This is of course not to commit Anaxagoras to the view—which P5 denies—that all the gold could be isolated, or to the view that there are least particles of gold and other Basic Things in the lump.

This move, though intuitively plausible, requires careful treatment. First, it must account for the properties of the lump, which is not only gold but also heavy, yellow, dry, and (at a given moment) cold.[53] Anaxagoras will say that the lump contains more heavy than light, more yellow than other colors, etc. It would be difficult or impossible to place all the properties of the lump of gold, including its being gold, on a single balance sheet that totals to 100%, but this is perhaps not a serious objection. Anaxagoras might be content with saying simply that it is yellow because it contains more yellow than any competing quality (where the competitors of yellow are the other colors), and likewise for the rest. In the cases of opposites, there is only one competitor.

Second, what does it mean to say that a lump of gold is composed chiefly of gold? If gold is that which is composed chiefly of gold, then to say that a lump of gold is composed chiefly of gold amounts to saying that it is composed chiefly of that which is composed chiefly of gold. And this puts Anaxagoras on the path to an infinite regress: gold turns out to be that which is composed chiefly of that which is composed chiefly of that which

---

52. There can, of course, also be bits of gold (i.e., bits in which there is more gold than other Basic Things) too small to be seen. I take it that P4 offers an account of macroscopic objects that can be applied straightforwardly to microscopic ones.

53. Gold can change in many of its properties. For example, it can change from cold to hot. It can even be melted and so become wet. Failure to account adequately for this consideration vitiates some interpretations of Anaxagoras, notably those of Cornford and Vlastos, in which the nature of other things than the opposites is determined by the relative proportions of the opposites occurring in them (Cornford, op. cit. [p. 211 n. 49], p. 311, Vlastos, op. cit. [p. 209 n. 41], p. 338).

is composed chiefly of. . . . And the same is true for any other substance, such as flesh or bone. But then an even worse result follows. All things turn out to be the same: flesh and blood, hot and cold, as well as gold prove to be that which is composed chiefly of that which is composed chiefly of. . . . To solve this problem, it has been suggested[54] that Anaxagoras means that an (impure) lump of gold has (pure) gold in it. Of course P3 implies that pure gold does not actually exist, but this is not a contradiction, for Anaxagoras need not hold that pure or elemental gold actually exists or could in theory be separated out from actually existing impure gold. It is enough if he treats it as what might be called a factor of analysis (as an economist treats supply and demand, not thinking that they can exist separately, but finding it desirable to treat them separately for purposes of analyzing complex actual phenomena).

What, then, *is* gold, apart from its perceptible properties? One answer is: nothing—gold is just its perceptible properties; identify all the thing's perceptible properties and there is nothing more to identify.[55] Another is: something—gold is not identical with any or all of its perceptible properties; they can change (the gold can be heated or cooled, melted, painted another color, etc.), but the gold persists.[56] It is clear from the discussion of P2 that Anaxagoras favors the second reply. Basic Things include substances like gold as well as perceptible properties, and Anaxagoras' theory covers changes in substance as well as changes in quality.[57]

P4 implies that change is a matter of reconstitution. When X ceases to be (an) F and comes to be (a) G, the Basic Things that make something be (a) G come to predominate over those that make it be (an) F. How this happens is obscure. Since (by P5) there are no smallest Portions, change cannot occur through rearrangement of least particles. It must therefore be due to processes which concentrate smaller Portions so that they become larger Portions. For example: in digestion, the bone, flesh, etc., that are in a piece of bread, but not present in large enough Portions to be visible, are

54. This suggestion as well as the regress argument is due to Strang (C. Strang, "The Physical Theory of Anaxagoras," in *Studies in Presocratic Philosophy*, vol. 2, pp. 361–80; reprinted from *Archiv für Geschichte der Philosophie* 45 [1963]: 101–18.

55. This is the view of Vlastos, op. cit. (p. 209 n. 41), p. 337.

56. Descartes considers a ball of wax: all of its sensible qualities can change into their opposites when it is heated, and yet it remains wax (R. Descartes, *Second Meditation*).

57. Regarding the further question of what relation gold has to its properties—whether, for example, some are essential, so that if *they* change the gold does not remain gold—there is nothing in the evidence to indicate that it occurred to Anaxagoras.

"brought out" so as to become the dominant elements in certain smaller parts, so that they can be added to the bone and flesh already found in our bodies.

I suggest that the Seeds play a role in this process. The bread contains Seeds of bone, flesh, and all other Basic Things (**13.4** sec. 1), microscopic bits of bone, flesh, etc., that will develop into macroscopic pieces of bone, etc., if provided with the appropriate ingredients and environment. In effect, they are focal points for accretion from which visible amounts of bone, etc., can grow. Growth takes place through the process of digestion, which somehow rearranges the Portions of Basic Things so that more bone is added to the Seed of bone, and the Portion of bone in the bread becomes correspondingly smaller.

This view of change goes only so far. It accounts for why one thing (or, in the case of food, part of one thing) can turn into another, but Anaxagoras owes us an account, or rather an accounting of what happens to the Portions dominant in the original thing. Consider a simplification of what happens when we eat bread. Some turns to bone, some to flesh, and the rest becomes bodily wastes which we excrete. Anaxagoras accounts for its becoming bone and flesh by saying that there were bone and flesh in the bread to begin with. Conversely, he would say that in any bit of bone that results from the change, there are Portions of bread (or, more probably, wheat[58]), but Portions smaller than the Portions of bone, i.e., there is some bread (or wheat), but less bread than bone. The question he needs to face is what happens to all the bread. On the account just given, the Portions of bread in the stuff that does not turn to bone or flesh should become even larger than previously. Digestion would resemble a kind of process of purifying or concentrating. There is no possibility of reaching pure bread, bone, or flesh, but the result of digesting an amount A of bread would be, on the one hand, amount B of flesh and amount C of bone in which the flesh and bone are respectively more concentrated than in the original amount of bread, and, on the other hand, an amount D (such that $B + C + D = A$) of a material in which there is a higher concentration of bread than in the original amount of bread. But Anaxagoras will have realized that the waste products of digestion are not a more highly concentrated form of bread, or of any other food, for that matter. Presumably, then, this is not how he would have explained digestion or other processes of change.

In order to avoid this problem, he needs to explain how, when X becomes

---

58. Wheat seems a better candidate for a Basic Thing than an artificial product like bread (the example used by Simplicius), but wheat, too, seems to be a composite of various different sorts of more basic components. The point at issue, however, does not depend on the particular example.

Y, what was formerly present in a smaller quantity (*Y*) comes to be present in a larger quantity and conversely how what was formerly present in the greatest quantity (*X*) comes to be present in a smaller quantity (cf. **13.12** sec. 16). This explanation must satisfy Parmenides' requirement that there is no coming to be out of or perishing into what is not. Since it seems unlikely that Anaxagoras can offer a satisfactory account, this is a serious weakness in his theory.

P5. There are no smallest Portions (**13.1** secs. 1–2, **13.3** sec. 1, **13.6** sec. 3). P5 is needed for P3 to get off the ground. For if *A* and *B* are Basic Things, then P3 says that in a piece of *A* there is a Portion (*B*$_1$) of *B*, and further that in *B*$_1$ there is a Portion (*A*$_2$) of *A*, and in *A*$_2$ a Portion (*B*$_2$) of *B*, and so on. P5 enables this sequence to continue without end. It guarantees that no matter how small a piece or Portion of something may be, it contains smaller Subportions of other things, so that we never reach pure bits of gold, flesh, etc., (cf. **13.6** sec. 3). This interpretation requires that there are Portions of Portions, and that if *A* contains a Portion *P*$_B$ of Basic Thing *B*, then *P*$_B$ is smaller than *A*. It does not require that *A* be divisible into separate parts such that *P*$_B$ is a part of *A*, but it does require that *P*$_B$ exist, as well as the Subportions of *P*$_B$, which are in turn smaller than *P*$_B$. This interpretation does not commit Anaxagoras to a doctrine of the infinite physical divisibility of matter,[59] but it does commit him to something analogous, which might be called infinite analysibility of things into Portions and Subportions, with a partial ordering by size, such that if *A* is a piece or Portion of a Basic Thing, then any Portion or Subportion of *A* is smaller than *A*.

Here above all Anaxagoras conflicts with modern ideas. P5 implies that things are not composed of ultimate indivisible pure particles: there are no atomic building blocks of matter. As the relation with P3 shows, for Anaxagoras the doctrines of no elements and no smallest particles go hand in hand.

Anaxagoras argues for P5 in **13.3** secs. 1–2. The argument is sketchy and needs to be supplemented. I think it most plausible to bring in P3. Suppose *A* has smallest Portions. Let *B* be a smallest Portion of *A*. By P3, *B* contains Portions of everything. Let *C* be one of these Portions. Clearly, *C* exists. But *C* is smaller than *B*, and *B* is the smallest Portion of *A*. Therefore *C*

59. In this respect I agree with M. Schofield, op. cit. (p. 198 n. 9) and B. Inwood, op. cit. (p. 209 n. 41) against the traditional view that the passages cited in support of P5 imply a doctrine of infinite divisibility. If Anaxagoras' notion of Portions does not involve physically distinguishable parts, there is no need to introduce infinite divisibility into his system.

cannot exist. But "what is cannot not be" (sec. 2), therefore, the hypothesis that A has smallest Portions must be abandoned.

The claim in **13.3** sec. 3, similar to that in sec. 1, is proved by a parallel argument. Suppose A is a lump of gold. Then the largest Portion (A_1) of A is gold. Let B_1 be the Portion of A_1 that is something else, say water. Then B_1 is smaller than A_1. But B_1 contains a Portion (A_2) of gold. $A_1 + A_2$ is larger than A_1. Likewise, A_2 contains a Portion B_2 of water, B_2 contains a Portion A_3 of gold, and $A_1 + A_2 + A_3$ is larger than $A_1 + A_2$. And so on. There are other ways of generating the infinite series, but the result is the same: P3 and P5 entail not only that there are no smallest Portions of matter, but also that we can never identify the total quantity of any Basic Thing in anything, and further that all the ingredients of a thing (in the example, the gold and water in a lump of gold) have Portions equal in number (sec. 4). The fragment ends obscurely (sec. 5).[60] I tentatively suggest that it means that, for example, the gold in a lump of gold is large (as in sec. 3) and also small (as in sec. 1): it constitutes a large Portion of the lump, but the Portions of gold in the Portions and Subportions of, say, water are as small as you like.

Anaxagoras' doctrine that there are no smallest Portions can be seen as a response to Zeno's attack on division of anything into parts (see above, pp. 52, 56). According to Zeno, if the division of a finite-sized object can be carried out infinitely, then the end products left when the division is completed will be infinite in number and will have either no size or positive size. But infinity times zero is zero, and infinity times any positive size, no matter how small, is infinite. Neither way do we get back to the original finite object. Anaxagoras denies that the process of analysis[61] will ever yield Portions of no size, for he accepts the Zenonian point that that would mean that what is could cease to be (**13.3** sec. 2). But that does not entail that the end products have positive size. Anaxagoras correctly sees that an infinite process of division is not like a very long process of division, that analyzing something into an infinite number of Portions is not like analyzing it into a very large number of very small Portions. "Of the small there is no smallest but always a smaller," and "of the large there is always a larger." In both

60. I accept the authenticity of **13.3** sec. 5, though some deny it.

61. By "analysis" I mean the manner of considering the Portions and Subportions of Basic Things in a given entity. This is presumably a notional activity, unlike division, which (following Zeno) I intend as a physical activity of breaking up an object into separate parts. My thesis is that there are close similarities between Zenonian infinite division and Anaxagorean infinite analysis, and that the difficulties Zeno raises for infinite division also apply to infinite analysis, and that Anaxagoras found a way to evade them—a way that can be also applied straightforwardly to cases of infinite division into separate parts.

these statements the word "always" is meant seriously. An infinite process of division or analysis has no end; it cannot be completed. There *are* no end products, since however far the division or analysis proceeds it can always go farther. And at each stage we have a definite, finite number of parts or Portions, each with a definite, positive size or amount, and the parts or Portions if reassembled reconstitute the original thing (**13.5**). It appears, then, that Anaxagoras was the first to recognize one of the most important properties of the infinite and to build it into the foundations of his system.

The nature of this "response to Zeno" deserves a comment. Anaxagoras does not refute or contradict either of the limbs of Zeno's argument; rather he finds a way round them. Zeno's dilemma, that the end products have either no size or some positive size, is a false one, since there are no end products. I find it more plausible that Anaxagoras developed his doctrine of infinite divisibility after thinking about Zeno's arguments than that Zeno composed those arguments in response to Anaxagoras—since they would leave Anaxagoras' theory intact.

The infinite analysibility of things brings paradoxical consequences. First, "all things are not at all less or more . . . but all things are always equal" (**13.5**): all things can equally be analyzed without limit; they have an equal number of Portions. Anaxagoras thus has a way to compare infinite classes. **13.5**, then, may mean that any ingredient (e.g., gold, water) of a thing (e.g., a lump of gold) can be treated as consisting of all the gold or water in the lump as a whole, or as the Portions and Subportions of that ingredient found in the whole lump and in the other Portions.

Second, even though there is more gold than water in a lump of gold (i.e., the Portion of gold in it is larger than the Portion of water[62]), there are as many Portions of water as of gold. "The Portions of both the large and the small are equal in amount" (**13.6** secs. 1, 4)—there are as many of the one as of the other,[63] since every Portion of gold contains a Portion of

---

62. Cf. **13.1** sec. 5.

63. Although elsewhere (e.g., **13.1** sec. 5, **13.2** sec. 2) he talks of the "amount" of one or more "things," by which he means how much of them, in **13.3** sec. 4 and **13.6** secs. 1 and 4, Anaxagoras talks of the "amount" of Portions, by which he means the number of them, how many they are. Likewise, in **13.4** sec. 8, the "Seeds unlimited in amount" will be unlimited in numbers. The Greek word PLETHOS can mean either "how many" or "how much," depending on the context, and since on the present interpretation of Portions it does not make sense to ask "how much," I understand the word in its other sense. On this way of taking the passages, there is no contradiction between **13.1** sec. 5 (which says that there are more AER and AITHER than any other "thing") and **13.6** secs. 1 and 4 (which say that there are as many Portions of one Basic Thing as of another).

water and vice versa. Anaxagoras repeats this point frequently, as if he realized that it is difficult to grasp: he once puts it picturesquely, saying that things are not "split apart with an axe" (**13.8**).

P6. The Nature of Mind. Mind forms the only exception to the principle "a Portion of everything in everything" (**13.11**, **13.12** secs. 1, 14). The special status of Mind is reflected in its principal functions: knowing, ruling, setting things in order, and causing motion. Unlike Empedocles' four elements, which have psychological as well as physical attributes, Anaxagoras' "things" are conceived in wholly physical terms. And unlike Empedocles' motive-forces Love and Strife, Anaxagoras' Mind is devoid of moral aspects. For Anaxagoras, all changes are due to mixture and separation, which result from motion, and motion is ultimately caused by Mind. Mind's ability to cause motion in "things" is the basis of its power to put them in order and rule them. It rules them by putting them in order, and it puts them in order by causing them to move. This interpretation results from an examination of Anaxagoras' remarks on Mind.

Mind is the only exception to the principle "a Portion of everything in everything." **13.11** says that there are some things (inanimate things) that do not contain a Portion of Mind, and **13.12** secs. 1 and 4 say that Mind is not mixed with anything else. So even in animate things, which do have a small amount of Mind (cf. **13.12** sec. 15 with sec. 5), the Portion of Mind they possess is pure, with no Portions of anything else. Anaxagoras argues for the purity of Mind as follows (**13.12** secs. 1–4): Mind rules the way it does; if it were mixed with other things it could not do so; therefore, it is unmixed. To understand this argument we need to find out more about how Mind rules.

In the first place, Mind rules all things—both animate things (**13.12** sec. 6) and the entire KOSMOS and everything in it (**13.12** secs. 7 ff.). It can rule all things because it is always and everywhere, in all things (**13.14**), and is thus unlimited (APEIRON) (**13.12** sec. 1) in time and space (being present in the unlimited amount of the surrounding multitude [**13.2**] as well as in the unlimited Portions and Subportions of things). Further, since all Mind is alike (**13.12** sec. 15), it is unbounded (recall that APEIRON means "unbounded" as well as "unlimited") in that it has no internal boundaries: no part is different from another. Moreover, being unmixed with other things, it is not affected by the fact that other things are mixed: it is in a condition to operate on all other things at any time.

I suggest that Mind's unique power of ruling is due to its unique purity and fineness. Anything else has positive size and contains limitless numbers of Portions of other things. Since Mind is free of such extraneous baggage it can penetrate and permeate other things right through all their unlimited Portions. Mind's unlimited spatial extent, its extreme fineness, and its lack of mixture with other things suggest that Anaxagoras is striving towards the notion of immaterial existence.[64] He lacks the vocabulary and concepts to say that Mind is a pure immaterial force that acts on everything, everywhere. Still, in calling Mind "finest of all things" he is giving it a material attribute. He conceives of Mind as so fine that it penetrates and permeates other things and somehow causes them to move by its presence. Also, like Empedocles' Love and Strife, Anaxagoras' Mind is extended in space and must be physically present to something in order to affect it.

Despite this awkwardness, Anaxagoras was the first philosopher to distinguish clearly between the mover and the moved. Earlier thinkers had conceived of their originating principles as responsible simultaneously for both the material composition and the organization of the KOSMOS. Anaximenes' AER, for example, is always in motion and so causes change,[65] and Heraclitus' fire is somehow identical with soul, god, and the LOGOS. Empedocles comes much closer, distinguishing between Love and Strife on the one hand, and the four elements on the other. But the action of Love and Strife is partly psychological, and in some sense Empedocles makes Love and Strife material and parts of the mixtures they cause.[66] By insisting that Mind is wholly unmixed with other "things" although physically present throughout them, Anaxagoras clearly distinguishes between what causes motion and what is moved—and this is a great conceptual advance. Even if it frequently happens that a material object causes motion, as when my hand makes a book move, the distinction between mover and moved is there, and the same applies even when something moves itself. When I cause myself to move, in a sense mover and moved are identical, but the two aspects of the self-mover can be distinguished in thought even if not physically. Anaxagoras believes that all motion of material things is ultimately traceable to the action of Mind (which is only barely material), and he would doubtless say that when I move myself, a more careful description of the event would make clear that my mind (the small part of the totality of Mind which is in me and constitutes me as a living, sentient, and thinking being) is the mover and my material body is the moved. Thus, the basis of Mind's rule over all things is its power of causing them to move, and to move not in a random fashion but in a way that sets them in order (**13.12** sec. 10). DIAKOSMEIN, translated "set in order," is closely related to KOSMOS. Mind rules things by moving them so that they form a KOSMOS, an orderly, beautiful arrangement.

64. According to Guthrie, Anaxagoras' Mind is immaterial (Guthrie, *HGP*, vol. 2, pp. 276–78).

65. See pp. 52, 56.

66. Aristotle, *Metaphysics* 12.10 1075b2–4 (not in DK).

The final thing that needs to be accounted for is why Anaxagoras identifies the source of change as Mind rather than a vortex (as with the Atomists) or some other mechanism. "Mind" (NOUS) is the word standardly used by philosophers for the highest form of reason,[67] so that it is found (if at all) only in humans among mortal creatures. Anaxagoras, however, believing that not only the lower animals but even plants have a certain amount of sensation and thought and feel pleasure and pain,[68] holds that each living thing has a share of Mind. Now living things are sources of motion and change (even down to the level of plants, which convert soil and water into roots, stems, and leaves) so Anaxagoras will hold that those motions and changes are due to the activity of Mind. Thus, in identifying Mind as his universal cosmic principle of change, Anaxagoras chooses something already considered responsible for some changes in the sphere of humans and other living things.

The claim that Mind "has all judgment about everything" (**13.12** sec. 5) suggests strongly that it is not just a mechanical agent. This idea is strengthened even further by statements that Mind "knows all things that are being mixed together and separated off and separated apart" (**13.12** sec. 9) and that Mind "set in order all things"—past, present and future (**13.12** sec. 10), which may mean that it knows all these things in advance and brings about their ordering deliberately and with foresight. If so, we can better appreciate Mind's intellectual aspect. It produces motion and so causes things to change in ways it foresees and thus controls. With unparalleled power and omniscience Mind brings about the results it desires, through the appropriate mechanical mixtures which it controls, so that the KOSMOS as it is now and has been and will be, is under Mind's control and is arranged as Mind wishes. That the cosmic Mind has desires may be inferred from the desires that humans experience by virtue of being possessed of a small Portion of Mind.

Once we speak of Mind as desiring, or desiring particular states of affairs and bringing about events so as to achieve its desires, we are in the realm of teleology, in which the reason why something happens or is the case is that the resulting state of affairs is a goal, and events happen and things come to be in order to achieve that goal. It is easy to assume that

---

67. E.g., Plato, *Republic*, books 6–7; Aristotle, *Metaphysics* 12.9 and *Posterior Analytics* 2.19. See also the articles of K. von Fritz, "*NOUS, NOEIN*, and their Derivatives in Pre-Socratic Philosophy (excluding Anaxagoras)," in *The Pre-Socratics*, ed. A. Mourelatos [Garden City, N.Y., 1974], pp. 23–85; reprinted from *Classical Philology* 40 (1945): 223–43, and 41 (1946): 12–34; and "*Nous and Noein* in the Homeric Poems," *Classical Philology* 38 (1943): 79–93.

68. Pseudo-Aristotle, *On Plants* 1.1 815a15–18, b15–22 (= DK 59A117).

Mind acts teleologically. According to Plato, Socrates made this assumption when he first learned of Anaxagoras' philosophy.

> **13.28** Once I heard someone reading out of a book by Anaxagoras, as he said, and saying that it turns out to be Mind that causes order and is the cause of all things. I was delighted at this account of causation and I thought it was somehow good that Mind was the cause of everything, and I believed that if it is so, Mind in producing order puts all things in order and establishes each thing in whatever way is best. . . . I thought I had found in Anaxagoras a teacher about causation in things who was after my own mind,[69] and that he would tell me first whether the earth is flat or round, and then would go on to explain in detail the cause and necessity, stating what was better, and that it was better that it be like this. If he revealed this to me I was prepared never to desire any other kind of causation again. I was also prepared to find out in the same way about the sun and moon and the other stars, their relative speeds and turnings and other characteristics—how it is better that each of these act and be affected as they are. For I would never have supposed that after declaring that they are set in order by Mind, he would have introduced any cause for them other than that it is best for them to be as they are.
>
> So I thought that by assigning what is best for each of them as a cause for each he would explain what is best for each and the common good for all. And I would not have abandoned my hopes for a great deal, but taking the books with all haste I read them as quickly as I could in order to know as soon as possible what is best and what is worse. But I was quickly deprived of this wonderful hope, friend, when as I proceeded to read I saw that the man did not make use of Mind at all and did not attribute to it any causation in putting things in order, but used as causes AERS and AITHERS and waters and many other things as well that were out of place.   (Plato, *Phaedo* 97b-98c = DK 59A47)

Aristotle shares Socrates' disappointment. On the one hand he praises Anaxagoras' distinction between Mind and the matter on which it works.

> **13.29** When someone said, then, that just as Mind is found in animals, so it is found in nature as the cause of the world and of all its order, he seemed like a sober man in comparison with his predecessors who spoke at random. . . . Those who believed this posited as a principle of things that which is at the same time the cause of beauty and the kind of cause from which things acquire movement.
>
> (Aristotle, *Metaphysics* 1.3 984b15–22 = DK 59A58)

69. NOUS: a play on the word.

The reference to beauty implies that Mind is a teleological as well as a motive principle, though Aristotle says elsewhere that Anaxagoras was unclear on the distinction between thinking of Mind as the cause of movement and as a teleological principle.[70] However, like Socrates, Aristotle says that Anaxagoras failed to make proper use of Mind as a cause.

> **13.30** They make hardly any use of their causes except to a small extent. For Anaxagoras uses Mind as a mechanism for the making of the KOSMOS, and when he is at a loss to say through what cause something necessarily is, then he drags Mind in, but in all other cases he makes anything rather than Mind the cause of what happens.
> (Aristotle, *Metaphysics* 1.4 985a17–21 = DK 59A47)

Whether or not Anaxagoras intended the teleological implications of making Mind his principle of movement must remain an open question. Although Mind's intellectual and directive powers may be manifested in a general supervision and control of events in the KOSMOS, the criticism of philosophers who had access to his work proves that he made little or no use of these considerations in discussing the origins and working of the world. Their verdict is borne out by what survives of his cosmogony.

Cosmogonic Mechanisms and Principles

Anaxagoras began his book[71] with the pronouncement "In the beginning, all things were together" (**13.1** sec. 1, **13.4** sec. 7) in so complete a mixture that nothing was distinct in any part (**13.4** secs. 7–8). For some thing, or part of the totality of all things, to be identifiable by any definite characteristic, it must have a macroscopic size and contain a greater quantity of that characteristic than of anything else.[72] In the beginning, therefore, no macroscopic part of the mixture of all things had a sufficient concentration of any single "thing" for that "thing" to be manifest (**13.1** sec. 3). Nevertheless, all "things" were in the mixture—the hot and the cold, earth, etc. (**13.4** sec. 8).

The beginning occurred when Mind, which permeated the mixture, caused a rotation to begin (**13.12** secs. 7–8). Friends of the Eleatics will immediately object: "What necessity would have stirred it up to grow later

---

70. Aristotle, *Metaphysics* 1.7 988b8–11 (not in DK)

71. Simplicius, *Commentary on Aristotle's Physics* 155.26 (= DK 59B1), 164.15 (not in DK), 460.26 (= DK 59A45), *Commentary on Aristotle's On the Heaven* 608.21 (not in DK).

72. Or greater than that of any competitor. See p. 213.

rather than earlier?" (**11.8** l. 10). For if Anaxagoras is not to violate the Principle of Sufficient Reason, he needs to specify some feature of Mind itself or of the state of mixture of all things that accounts for why the rotation began at one time rather than another, and there is no reason to think that he did so.

The rotation began in a small area (**13.12** sec. 8). As time went on, two things happened: (a) ever increasing expansion of the region in which the rotation occurs (**13.12** sec. 8), and (b) separation of identifiable things out of the mixture (**13.12** secs. 11–12, **13.13** secs. 1–2). Moreover, the mechanical process of rotation caused the separating to occur (**13.12** sec. 11, **13.13** sec. 3), by what we would call centrifugal or centripetal force (**13.9** secs. 1–2). (The distinction between the speed and the force that the speed causes is noteworthy.) Most likely the speed increased in proportion to the size of the revolving mass, since it is most reasonable to suppose that the original rotation not only occupied a small volume but was also slow. Like Empedocles (**15.149**), Anaxagoras believes in a cosmogonic vortex in which like is gathered to like. In this way, things were separated off from the indistinct mass of all things together and took on definite characters.

This process doubtless worked similarly to other cases of change in which substances or qualities emerge out of others, such as digestion (see above, pp. 214–15). Although in the beginning there were no sufficiently large concentrations of Basic Things to form distinct macroscopic objects, there were microscopic concentrations, Seeds, of all Basic Things (**13.4** sec. 8).[73] The "like to like" effect of the vortex caused a rearrangement of the Portions of Basic Things in the whole indistinct mass so that some of the Seeds grew to have macroscopic size. Since the Portions of AER and AITHER in the original mixture were the largest (**13.1** sec. 5), they were more available than other Basic Things to be added to the Seeds of their kind, and hence it seems that AER and AITHER were the first distinguishable things to be separated out of the original mass. Other kinds of things were separated out of the residue of the original mass and out of the AER or AITHER as the vortex motion continued to rearrange the Basic Things present in their Portions.

Anaxagoras most frequently speaks of things "separating off" from the

73. That the Seeds are unlike one another (**13.4** sec. 8) is easily explained in terms of differences in their constituent Portions of Basic Things. Infinite analysibility (cf. p. 217 n. 61) and the limitless possibilities of variation in the Portions of Basic Things that are not manifest allow ample room for the differences mentioned. These relatively simple accounts of the original mixture and of Seeds are incompatible with the view that Anaxagoras' substances are homoeomerous in Aristotle's sense. Once this view is exploded (see p. 212 n. 51), the present accounts become possible.

mixture, but he also says that they "separate apart," which does not appear to be just a synonym of the more common term (cf. **13.12** sec. 9, **13.13**). Perhaps "separating off" refers to the process by which one kind of thing emerges from a different kind of thing,[74] as flesh emerges from bread or any "thing" does from the original mixture, and "separating apart" refers to actual spatial separation, for instance, the tendency of earth towards the center of the vortex and of AITHER to the periphery. The primary cosmogonic processes, then, are processes of separating, both qualitative and spatial, as we would expect, given the initial state in which all things were mixed together.

Anaxagoras also recognizes a tendency in the opposite direction. A number of places speak of "mixing together" (**13.4** sec. 1, **13.12** sec. 9, **13.17** secs. 1–2), which in one place (**13.4** sec. 1) appears to be a complementary description of separating off. When, say, a lump of gold is formed out of the original mixture or when flesh is formed out of bread, the scattered Portions of gold or flesh are mixed together until they are sufficiently concentrated ("compounded" [**13.16** sec. 1]) to form an identifiable bit of the "thing" in question.[75]

The other three occurrences of the term, though, refer to the mixing together of different "things." The important occurrences are found in **13.17**, which says that coming to be is really a matter of being mixed together, and perishing is really a matter of being separated apart. In that this doctrine applies to the coming to be and perishing of Basic Things like gold and flesh, the point is the same as already discussed. But since Anaxagoras offers **13.17** as a general interpretation of coming to be and perishing, it should apply more widely. In **13.4**, he speaks of humans and other living beings as "compounded"—obviously, out of Basic Things. The coming to be of a human, then, involves a "compounding" of flesh, bone, etc., and **13.17** requires us to see this "compounding" as a case of "mixing together."[76]

Anaxagoras clearly recognizes mixing together as a process in the world, though he does not explain its relation to the primary processes of separating off and separating apart. **13.14** may contain a hint of how to understand this process. It speaks of separating off and also of "separating towards"—in the translation given, this unusual compound is translated

---

74. For "separation off" in Anaximander, see p. 37.

75. The corresponding feature of Empedocles' system is that Strife, which has the effect of separating the four elements, by that very fact also has the effect of uniting each to its like.

76. Like "mixing together," "compounding" applies to Basic Things as well as other entities (**13.16** sec. 1).

"have come together in the process of separating." It is possible that as different "things" are separated off or apart, the force of the motion throws them together in such a way that they join together and form a compound. Mixing together or "separating towards," then, would not be a different process, but a by-product of the two processes already identified. It would not necessarily take place at random or by chance, since the particular compounds that occur may have been foreseen and therefore perhaps intended by Mind, which is the ultimate cause of such compounds.

It is as well that Anaxagoras makes room for processes of combination. If separating off and separating apart were the only processes in the KOSMOS, it would be hard to explain many of the events taking place around us which obviously involve combination, so that the theory would be open to empirical objections. It might be vulnerable to a theoretical objection too. Separating off and separating apart are processes of differentiation—qualitative and spatial. If differentiation proceeds far enough, will things not become so distinct that the changes observed in the KOSMOS, the very changes Anaxagoras' system is designed to explain, can no longer to take place? The principle "a Portion of everything in everything" guarantees that differentiation is never complete. But the principle "each single thing is and was most plainly those things of which it contains most" (13.12 sec. 16) again leads to a difficulty. For as the processes of differentiation continue, each thing will come to have greater and greater quantities of what it "is most plainly," and correspondingly less of the others. In these circumstances it will presumably be increasingly difficult for the other things in it to be mixed together so as to be the greatest quantity in any part of the thing, so changes will become more difficult. A case in point can be taken from our present world. Bread can turn into flesh, but not into gold. Anaxagoras should account for this fact by saying that while there are equal numbers of Portions of flesh and gold in the bread, and although neither is present in sufficiently large an amount as to be visible, still the amount of flesh far exceeds that of gold. The Portion of flesh is far bigger than the Portion of gold. The more there is of one "thing" in another "thing," the easier it should be for the one to change into the other. So, if differentiation is carried out far enough without any compensating combination, there is danger that the "things" in the KOSMOS will become separated off and separated apart so far by the ever increasing force exerted by the ever increasing rotation that change (aside from motion itself) will cease to occur. Mixture is needed, then, but we may wonder whether the mixtures that are merely by-products of the primary processes of separation are enough to stem the tide.

There are two ways Anaxagoras might have guaranteed continued mixture. First, he might have denied these implications of the quantitative principle (**13.12** sec. 16), saying that as long as there is a Portion of everything in everything (i.e., forever), it is possible to account for all the change we like. His answer here would depend on the explanation he gives of how it is possible for what is present in smaller quantities to come to be present in larger quantities.[77]

Second, he might have held that the amount of matter available to be differentiated is unlimited in extent (not just in divisibility), so there is always more undifferentiated material being brought into play. He may well have believed that this was the case. **13.12** sec. 8 suggests that there is no limit to the volume of material available to undergo the rotatory movement which causes differentiation, and **13.2** sec. 2 can be taken as making this very point. But the interpretation of both passages is uncertain,[78] and the view under consideration would imply not only that the KOSMOS expands at the periphery but also that the matter at the periphery, as it becomes differentiated through the processes of separating out and separating apart, will be affected by the tendency of rotational movement to bring like to like. The vortex action will continually bring more freshly separated earth to the center. But there is no sign or any likelihood that Anaxagoras believed that this was happening. It is therefore necessary to leave this issue unsettled, while acknowledging that it raises one or more difficulties for Anaxagoras' system as we know it.

Anaxagoras' Cosmogony

Mind initiated a rotatory movement, which caused a force (**13.9** sec. 2) that separated things off from the original mixture (**13.12** sec. 11) and separated them apart (**13.13** sec. 3). As time went on, the rotating area increased (**13.12** sec. 8), as apparently did the speed, and consequently the force and the differentiation. At present the speed of the rotation is much faster than anything found on earth (**13.9** sec. 3).

13.1, which describes the beginning of the cosmogony, contains an apparent contradiction. In the beginning "AER and AITHER dominated all things . . . the biggest ingredients . . . both in amount and size" (sec. 4–5). But since "each single thing is and was most plainly those things of which it contains most" (**13.12** sec. 16), AER and AITHER must have been apparent in the original mixture, and yet Anaxagoras insists that "nothing

77. For difficulties in this area, see pp. 215–16.
78. **13.2** sec. 2's "unlimited in amount" is Anaxagoras' normal way of referring to the property of infinite analysibility (cf. **13.6** sec. 1), and (*re* **13.12** sec. 8) anyone who knew Zeno would know that there can be a bounded infinite sequence, as in the paradox of the stadium.

was manifest" (**13.1** sec. 3). I offer the following as a possible solution. In the Greek, the verb "dominated" (**13.1** sec. 4) is singular, though we would expect it to be plural as it has two subjects, AER and AITHER. I suggest that AER and AITHER are here treated together as a single subject: AER-and-AITHER. Now if AITHER is hot, dry, rare, and bright, and AER is cold, wet, dense, and dark,[79] AER-and-AITHER would not be marked by any of these qualities, nor would AER or AITHER be distinguishable. The Portions of AER and of AITHER, like the Seeds of all other Basic Things, were so small in the original mixture as to be indistinguishable (**13.4** sec. 7–8), though even so they were the largest ingredients (**13.1** sec. 5).[80] This is why they were presumably the first to separate off (**13.2** sec. 1)[81] and so become distinguishable.

The vortex action will also have separated them apart, so that the lighter AITHER went towards the periphery and the heavier AER towards the center. The separating apart of the different constituents of the KOSMOS is also found in **13.15**, which, as we would expect, has the wet, cold, and dark moving to the center ("here") and their opposites to the periphery ("to the far reaches of the AITHER"). These processes still continue, with heavier things being separated off from lighter ones. Out of AER (in the form of clouds) are separated off by the force of the vortex successively denser "things" (**13.16** secs. 1–2).

An important exception to the rule that dense things move to the center is formed by the heavenly bodies which Anaxagoras conceives not as pure, light fire, but as fiery stones. It seems that the speed of the vortex is sufficient in some cases to pick up stones from the earth and whirl them round in the air. Probably only stones are compact enough to undergo this type of motion. It is certainly possible to throw a stone farther up than a handful of water or loose earth (cf. **13.16** sec. 3).

The gross structure of the KOSMOS is therefore efficiently explained by the vortex with its effects of separating off and separating apart. Moreover, Plato's and Aristotle's complaints (**13.28**, **13.30**) are seen to be justified. Mind initiates movement, but afterwards mechanical explanations prevail.

---

79. See p. 50.

80. See p. 96 n. 4. The point holds even if **13.1** sec. 5 is not authentic, since it is implied in sec. 4.

81. That they were first to separate off may be supported by **13.2**, which Simplicius (*Commentary on Aristotle's Physics* 155.30 = DK 59B2) says came "a little after" **13.1**, which was the beginning of Anaxagoras' work (see p. 196 n. 1). However, I hesitate to press this interpretation of **13.2**, which requires the present tense of the fragment "are being separated" to be taken as an "historical present," i.e., as equivalent to a past tense.

Cosmology

It remains to look at a few of Anaxagoras' most interesting theories about the present world. Anaxagoras' notorious belief that heavenly bodies are masses of stone enabled him to explain meteorites—stones that fall from the sky.

> 13.31 A huge stone fell from the sky at Aegospotami. . . . And it is still displayed, since the people of the Chersonnese revere it. It is said that Anaxagoras predicted that when there occurred a slip or shaking of the bodies fastened in the heaven one of them would be torn off and be thrown down and fall. Each of the stars is not in its natural place, since they are made of stone and heavy, and shine because of the resistance and breaking of the AITHER. They are dragged by force, held tight by the vortex and force of the rotation, as at the beginning when cold and heavy things were being separated off from the whole they were kept from falling to the earth. (Plutarch, *Lysander* 12 = DK 59A12)

The event took place in 467 and Anaxagoras was closely associated with it. 13.31 also gives valuable information on the mechanism of the rotation of the heavenly bodies and the source of their brightness. Although it is frequently declared absurd that Anaxagoras could have predicted the fall of a meteorite, he may well have said that the earthen bodies held aloft by the cosmic vortex can sometimes slip and fall to earth. If this assertion (which might loosely be called a general prediction) were widely known when the famous meteorite fell, it would be but a small step to credit Anaxagoras with predicting the event.[82]

Anaxagoras asserts that the moon's light is derived from the sun (13.18). He gives the correct explanation of lunar as well as solar eclipses, and he recognizes that rainbows are an effect of sunlight on moisture in the air (13.19). He surprisingly maintains the primitive view that

> 13.32 The earth is flat and stays aloft (a) because of its size, (b) because there is no void, and (c) because AER is very strong and so able to support the earth, which rides upon it.
> (Hippolytus, *Refutation* 1.8.3 = DK 59A42)

The second reason given here has Eleatic echoes, but the third (which goes strangely with Anaxagoras' opinions on the cosmological role of the vortex) is pure Anaximenes (see 6.7, 6.8, 6.9). Following the Ionian tradition,

---

82. It would be unsafe to ignore the possibility that Anaxagoras' theory was prompted by the meteorite, and that later on people who did not know the order of events gave Anaxagoras credit for predicting it.

Anaxagoras also has theories about lightning and other meteorological phenomena, about earthquakes, the origin of the saltwater sea, the flooding of the Nile, the origins of life, and many questions having to do with biology. Noteworthy among them is his view that the brain is the seat of sensation.[83]

He also speaks of human life "elsewhere" (**13.4** secs. 3–6), and he believes that his cosmogonic principles are such that life and the KOSMOS as we know it are not generated uniquely here "with us." The present tenses (**13.4** secs. 3–5) indicate that he is not thinking of a series of worlds that succeed one another in time—as in Empedocles' cosmic cycle—but of other places where life is similar to ours right now. This ingenious idea does not fit well with his cosmogony, however. There is only one vortex and therefore only one earth at the center. Accordingly, if Anaxagoras means that there are other worlds contemporary with our own, it is hard to see where they would be located. The most plausible suggestion is that he is thinking of different regions of *this* world—remote and perhaps inaccessible from the region inhabited by and known to the Greeks.

Epistemology

The Eleatic challenge attacked the reliability of the senses as well as our ordinary conceptions about the nature of the world. Anaxagoras developed a physical system which responded to the Eleatics, but he also needs to say something about the status of the senses. Quite clearly, they do not reveal to us all that Anaxagoras says is true about the world.

Unlike Empedocles, he holds that sensation is produced by unlikes acting on unlikes. Something feels hot to the touch when our hand is cold relatively to it. He also holds that since it results from the action of opposites, all sensation involves pain. Since he recognizes that we do not always feel pain when using our senses, he is committed to belief in the fallibility of the senses, more specifically in their frailty. It is not that they misreport what is the case, but that they may fail to report it. Anaxagoras states this view generally (**13.20**). Sextus Empiricus, who quotes **13.20**, also paraphrases an example which Anaxagoras used to support the general claim.

> **13.33** He offers as evidence of their [the senses'] untrustworthiness the gradual change of colors. For if we take two colors, black and white, and then pour out one into the other a drop at a time, our vision will not be able to distinguish the gradual changes, even though they exist in reality.
> (Sextus Empiricus, *Against the Mathematicians* 7.90 = DK 59B21)

---

83. See Guthrie, *HGP*, vol. 2, pp. 304–18, for discussion and references.

Similar examples can be constructed to make the same point about the other senses too.

The weakness of the senses implies that we cannot perceive the complete nature of things, but that is not to say that they are totally misleading and useless for understanding reality. What they tell us has some relation to reality, as the famous **13.21** makes clear. "Appearances are a sight of the unseen" can equally be translated "Phenomena are a vision of what is not manifest." We do not know more about how Anaxagoras thought it was possible to achieve knowledge of the world from our weak senses. Doubtless he held that our mind plays an important role, since the cosmic Mind knows all things (**13.12** sec. 9) and our mind is similar in nature to it (**13.12** sec. 15). Still, it is unclear whether Anaxagoras worked out a precise theory of how senses and mind cooperate to make knowledge possible.

Conclusion

Anaxagoras' physical theory is more complex than those of his predecessors, but comparable to those of Empedocles and the Atomists, who also wrote in response to the Eleatics. Anaxagoras has close connections with his Ionian forebears, as witnessed by his interest in cosmogony and cosmology, the absence of any religious or mystical tendency in his writing, and his determination to give a plausible account of the world around us in terms of a rationally comprehensible set of principles.

The complexities of his system can be attributed to the effects of Eleatic philosophy, which established requirements that Anaxagoras went to great lengths to meet. He did not accept all of Parmenides' views on the nature of reality (which would make cosmogony and cosmology impossible), but was apparently convinced (as were Empedocles and the Atomists) by Parmenides' rejection of coming to be and destruction, and aimed to construct an account of reality that avoids coming to be and perishing and also accounts for the origin and present constitution and functioning of the KOSMOS.

The present century has seen a greater number of radically different interpretations of Anaxagoras than of any other Presocratic with the possible exception of Empedocles—a remarkable fact given the small number of fragments on which interpretations can be based. Indeed, at present there is no consensus on many of Anaxagoras' central doctrines, such as the kinds of Basic Things, the nature of the Portions and Seeds, whether matter is infinitely divisible, and whether the original mixture of all things was uniform. The interpretation I have presented is based closely on the fragments, in some cases supplemented by appeal to important testimonia, but it should be regarded as an exploration of Anaxagoras' subtle ideas rather than a definitive account.

14

Empedocles of Acragas

Fragments

Introduction and Programmatic Remarks

14.1 (112)[1] Friends who dwell in the great city on the yellow Acragas
on the heights of the citadel, you whose care is good deeds,
respectful havens for strangers, untouched by evil,
hail! I go about among you, an immortal god, no longer mortal,
honored among all, as it seems,   5
wreathed with headbands and blooming garlands.
Wherever I go to their flourishing cities,
I am revered by the men and women. And they follow together
in tens of thousands, inquiring where lies the path to profit,
some in need of prophecy, while others,   10
pierced for a long time with harsh pains,
asked to hear the voice of healing for all diseases.

14.2 (114) Friends, I know that truth is in the words
I will speak. But very difficult for men and exceedingly jealous
is the invasion of belief into their minds.

14.3 (1) But listen, Pausanias, son of wise-minded Anchites.

14.4 (4) But it is highly typical of evil people to disbelieve what
prevails [i.e., is the truth];
but <you>, learn how the trustworthy reports from our Muse
command,
by splitting apart the account (LOGOS) in your entrails.[2]

14.5 (5) [Empedocles advised Pausanias] to cover up [his
teachings] within a voiceless heart (PHREN).[3]

(Context from Plutarch, *Table Talk* 8.8.1 728E.)

---

1. The numbers in parentheses are the numbers in DK. (1) = DK 31B1.
2. Reading *pélei* and *diatmēthéntes* with the manuscripts.
3. See p. 62 n. 6 on Xenophanes.

14.6 (110) If you fix them in your strong intelligence
and gaze upon them propitiously with pure attention,
these things will all be very much present to you all your life long
and from them you will obtain many others. For these very
  things
grow into each kind of character, depending on each person's
  nature. 5
But if you reach out for other kinds of things, the millions
of evils that are found among men which blunt their thoughts,
indeed they will leave you immediately as time revolves,
longing to come to their own dear kind.
For know that all things possess thought and a portion of
  intelligence. 10

14.7 (111) You will learn all the drugs there are for evils and a
  safeguard against old age,
since for you alone I am bringing all these things to pass.
You will stop the force of tireless winds which rush
over the earth and devastate the plowed fields with their blasts.
And, if you wish, you will arouse their breath again. 5
You will change black rain to seasonable dryness
for people, and summer drought you will change
into tree-nourishing waters which pour from the sky.
And you will bring the strength of a dead man back from Hades.

14.8 (2) Narrow are the means of apprehension spread throughout
  the limbs.
Many unhappy things burst in which blunt the thoughts.
People see a tiny part of life during their time
and swift-fated they are taken away and fly like smoke,
persuaded only of whatever each of them has chanced to meet 5
as they were driven everywhere; but everyone boasts that he
  discovered the whole.
But these things are not in this way to be seen or heard by men
or grasped with the mind. But you, since you have turned aside to
  this place,
will learn; mortal cunning has reached no further.

14.9 (38) But come, I shall first tell you the beginning . . .
from which all that we now look upon came to be clear,
earth and the sea with many waves and moist air
and the Titan AITHER, squeezing all things round about in a
  circle.

14.10 (113) But why do I insist on these matters as if I were
accomplishing something great,
if I am superior to mortal humans who perish many times?

14.11 (24) Joining high points of my story one to another,
not to complete a single path.

14.12 (25) For indeed it is a fine thing to tell twice what one must.

14.13 (132) Blessed is he who possesses wealth of divine intelligence
but wretched whose concern is a dim opinion about the gods.

14.14 (133) It is not possible to reach and approach [the divine] with
the eyes
or grasp <it> with our hands, by which the most powerful
highway of persuasion strikes the minds of men.

14.15 (131) For if, immortal Muse, for any ephemeral creature
it pleased you that our concerns should come to your thoughts,
be present once again to me, Kalliopeia, now as I pray,
as I reveal a good account about the blessed gods.

14.16[4] (3a) But, gods, avert madness from my tongue,
and lead a pure stream from holy mouths.
And you, much-remembering maiden Muse with white arms,
I entreat—bring <to me> the things it is right for creatures
of a day
to hear, driving your easily-steered chariot from the halls of
Reverence.

14.17[5] (3b) Nor will the blossoms of fair-famed honor from mortals
compel you to take them up, on the condition that you say in
rashness more than is holy—
and <only> then sit upon the summits of wisdom.
But come, look with every means of apprehension, in whatever
way each thing is clear,
not holding any sight more in trust than <what comes>
through hearing,

---

4. I divide DK fr. 3 into two fragments, since it is implausible to identify the
addressee of lines 6 ff. as the Muse.

5. See previous n.

or loud-sounding hearing above the things made clear by the
  tongue,
and do not at all hold back trust in any of the other members,
whatever way there is a channel for understanding, but
understand each thing in whatever way it is clear.

14.18 (115) There is an oracle of Necessity, an ancient decree of
  the gods,
eternal and sealed with broad oaths,
that whenever anyone pollutes his own dear limbs with the sin
  of murder,[6]
. . . [7] commits offense and swears a false oath—
divinities (DAIMONES) who possess immensely long life[8]—   5
he wanders away from the blessed ones for thrice ten thousand
  seasons,
growing to be through time all different kinds of mortals
taking the difficult paths of life one after another.
For the force of AITHER pursues them to the sea
and the sea spits them out onto the surface of the earth, and the
  earth into the rays   10
of the shining sun, and he [the sun] casts them into the vortices
  of AITHER.
One receives them after another, but all hate them.
Of them I am now one, a fugitive from the gods and
  a wanderer,
putting my reliance on raving Strife.

Physical Principles

14.19 (17) I will tell a double story. For at one time they grow[9] to be
  only one
out of many, but at another they grow apart to be many out
  of one.

6. Reading *phónoi* with most editors.

7. The first part of this line is not preserved.

8. This line probably elaborates "anyone" in l. 3.

9. The verbs in lines 1 and 2 usually and those in line 5 sometimes are translated in the past tense. The verbs occur in the aorist, a tense that usually refers to the past but is also used to express general or often recurring truths, as here. In such cases, it comes into English as a present tense.

Double is the coming to be of mortal things, and double is
    their failing.
For the coming together of all things produces one birth and
    destruction,
and the other is nurtured and flies apart when they grow apart
    again.   5
And these never cease continually interchanging,
at one time all coming together into one by Love
and at another each being borne apart by the hatred of Strife.
Thus in that they have learned to grow to be one out of many
and in that they again spring apart as many when the one grows
    apart,   10
in that way they come to be and their life is not lasting,
but in that they never cease interchanging continually,
in this way they are always unchanging in a cycle.
But come, listen to my words, for learning increases wisdom.
For as I previously said, while declaring the bounds of
    my words,   15
I will tell a double story. For at one time they grew to be
    only one
out of many, but at another they grew apart to be many
    out of one:
fire and water and earth and the immense height of air,
and deadly Strife apart from them, equal in all directions
and Love among them, equal in length and breadth.   20
Behold her with your mind, and do not sit with your eyes
    staring in amazement.
She is also recognized as innate in mortal limbs.
Through her they have kindly thoughts and do peaceful deeds,
calling her by the appellation Joy and also Aphrodite.
No mortal man has seen her spinning   25
among them. But listen to the undeceitful course of my
    account.
For these [the four elements] are all equal and of the same age,
but each rules in its own province and possesses its own
    individual character,
but they dominate in turn as time revolves.
And nothing is added to them, nor do they leave off,   30
for if they were perishing continuously, they would no
    longer be.
But what could increase this totality? And where would it
    come from?

And how [or, where] could it perish, since nothing is empty of
   these?
But there are just these very things, and running through one
   another
at different times they come to be different things and yet are
   always and continuously the same.   35

14.20 (6) Hear first the four roots of all things:
Shining Zeus and life-bringing Hera and Aidoneus
and Nestis who with her tears moistens mortal Springs.

14.21 (21) But come, behold this witness of my previous discourse,
if anything in the foregoing was feeble in form:
the sun, brilliant to see and hot everywhere,
all the immortal things that are drenched in the heat and
   shining light,
and rain in all things, dark and cold,   5
and from earth stream forth things rooted and solid.
In Anger they are all separate and have their own forms,
but they come together in Love and yearn for one another.
For from these come all things that were and are and will be in
   the future.
Trees have sprouted and men and women,   10
and beasts and birds and fishes nurtured in water,
and long-lived gods highest in honors.
For there are just these things, and running through one
   another
they come to have different appearances, for mixture changes
   them.

See also **14.49**

14.22 (22) For all these things—shining sun and earth and heaven
and sea—have links with their own parts,
all that are split off and have come to be in mortal things.
In the same way, all that are more fitted for mixture
are made alike by Aphrodite and love one another.   5
But enemies are those which are furthest separated from one
   another
in birth and mixture and moulded forms,
in every way unaccustomed to be together and very bitter

through their birth in Strife,[10] because it brought about
their birth.

14.23 (16) For they are as they have been previously[11] and will be, and
never, I think,
will endless time be empty of both of these [i.e., Strife
and Love].

14.24 (20) This is very clear in the mass of mortal members:
sometimes all the limbs coming together through Love
into one—those whose lot it is to become a body—at the peak
of flourishing life,
while at other times, split apart through evil Quarrels
they wander each kind separately on the furthest shore
of life.   5
And it happens the same way for bushes and water-homed
fishes
and mountain-dwelling beasts and wing-propelled birds.

14.25 (116) <The Grace [i.e., Love]> loathes Necessity, hard
to endure

14.26 (125) For from living forms it [? Strife] was making dead ones,
changing them.

14.27 (71) If your faith in these matters were at all faint—
<about> how when water, earth, AITHER and sun
are mixed, as many shapes and colors of mortals came to be
as now have come to be, fitted together by Aphrodite . . .

14.28 (23) As when painters decorate votive offerings—
men through cunning well taught in their skill—
who when they take the many colored pigments in their hands,
mixing in harmony more of these and less of those,
out of them they produce shapes similar to all things,   5
creating trees and men and women
and beasts and birds and fishes nurtured in water
and long-lived gods highest in honors.
So let not deception compel your mind (PHREN) to believe that
there is from anywhere else

10. Reading *neikeogennéteisi.*
11. Reading *ésti gàr hōs páros ên* (Lloyd-Jones).

a source of mortal things, all the endless numbers of   10
things which have come to be manifest,
but know these things distinctly, having heard the story
    from a god.

14.29 (73) As then Cypris, busily working on shapes [or, kinds of
    things] moistened earth in rain,
and gave it to swift fire to strengthen . . .

14.30 (75) . . . all of them that are dense within, while their exterior
    parts are formed in a loose texture,
because they met with such moisture in the hands of Cypris.

14.31 (33) As when sap from a fig tree curdles and binds white milk.

(A simile for the unifying action of Love, according to Plutarch, *On
Having Many Friends* 95A–B.)

14.32 (34) Having glued barley-groats with water

(Probably an illustration of how different elements join to form compounds.)

14.33 (32) A joint binds two things (DK) [or, There is a need for two
    joints (Inwood)].

(Text and context uncertain.)

14.34 (91) <Water> has a greater affinity with wine, but with olive oil
    it is unwilling <to mix>.

(According to Alexander and Philoponus, Empedocles explained these
phenomena in terms of the compatibility of the "pores" in the three
substances.)

14.35 (93) The brightness of gleaming saffron is mixed with linen[12]

(Cited to exemplify how some things are especially suited to others.
Linen readily absorbs dye.)

14.36 (92) [On the question why mules are sterile,
    Empedocles explains that the mixture of seeds becomes thick,

12. Reading *glaukoîo krókou* and *aktís* with Wright and Inwood.

although the seed of both the horse and the ass is soft.
For the hollow parts of each fit together with
the thick parts of the other,
and as a result a hard substance comes from soft ones]
like copper mixed with tin.[13]

(Context from Aristotle, *Generation of Animals* 2.8 747a34–b7.)

14.37 (96) Pleasant earth in her well-made[14] crucibles obtained
two parts of bright Nestis out of the eight,
and four of Hephaestus, and white bones came into being,
fitted together divinely by the glues of Harmonia.

14.38 (98) Earth came together by chance in about equal quantity
to these,
Hephaestus and rain and all-shining AITHER,
anchored in the perfect harbors of Cypris,
either a bit more or a bit less of it among more of them.
From them blood came into being and other forms of flesh.   5

14.39 (85) Mildly-shining flame chanced upon a little earth.

Response to Parmenides

See also **14.19**

14.40 (11) Fools. For their thoughts are not far-reaching,
who expect that there comes to be what previously was not,
or that anything perishes and is completely destroyed.

14.41 (12) For it is impossible to come to be from what in no way is,
and it is not to be accomplished and is unheard of that what is
perishes absolutely.
For each time it will be where a person thrusts it each time.

14.42 (15) A man who is wise would not divine such things as this
with his thoughts (PHREN)—
that as long as they live what they in fact call life
they are, and have things bad and good,
but before they took on the fixed form of mortals and after they
have dissolved, they are then nothing.

13. This alloy is bronze, a metal harder than either of its ingredients.
14. Reading *eutúktois*.

14.43 (8) I will tell you another thing. There is coming to be of not a
single one of all
mortal things, nor is there any end of deadly death,
but only mixture, and separation of what is mixed,
and nature is the name given to them by humans.

(Plutarch quotes this fragment to show that Empedocles uses *PHYSIS*,
"nature," in the sense of "coming to be" [Plutarch, *Against Colotes*
1111F–1112A].)

14.44 (9) Whenever they arrive in the AITHER mixed so as to
form a man
or one of the wild beasts or bushes
or birds, that is when <people> speak of coming into being;
and whenever they are separated, that <is what they call> the
ill-starred fate of death.
They do not call it as is right, but I myself too assent to their
convention.   5

14.45 (13) None of the whole is either empty or over-full.

14.46 (14) Of the whole, nothing is empty; from where, then, could
anything come to it?

(Of dubious authenticity.)

Cosmic Cycle

See also **14.19, 14.22**

14.47 (35) But I shall return to that path of songs
which I recounted before, drawing off from one account
this account.
When Strife had reached the lowest depth
of the vortex, and Love comes to be in the middle of the whirl,
at this point all these things come together to be one single
thing,   5
not at once, but willingly banding together, different ones from
different places.
As they were mixed, myriads of tribes of mortal things poured
forth,

but many contrariwise remained unmixed while they were
    mingling—
all that Strife still held back aloft. For it had not
entirely completed its blameless retreat from them to the
    furthest limits of the circle,   10
but it remained in some of the limbs, while from others it had
    withdrawn.
But as far as it would continually run out ahead, so far
    continually would follow in pursuit
the gentle immortal onset of blameless Love.
Immediately things became mortal which formerly had learned
    to be immortal,
and things previously unmixed became mixed, interchanging
    their paths.   15
As they were mixed, myriads of tribes of mortal things
    poured forth,
fitted with all kinds of forms, a wonder to behold.

14.48 (36) When they were coming together, Strife was being
displaced to the extremity.

14.49 (26) They [i.e., the four elements] dominate in turn as the cycle
    revolves,
and they decrease into one another and grow in their turn, as
    destined.
For there are just these things, and running through one
    another
they come to be both humans and the tribes of other beasts
at one time coming together into a single KOSMOS by Love   5
and at another each being borne apart by the hatred of Strife,
until they grow together into one, the whole, and become
    subordinate.

(I omit lines 8–12 since they are virtually identical to **14.19** lines 9–13.)

14.50 (27) There neither the swift limbs of the sun are discerned,
nor the shaggy force of earth nor the sea.
Thus by the dense concealment of Harmonia is made fast
a rounded sphere, exulting in its circular [or, joyous] solitude
    [or, motionlessness].

14.51 (27a) No dissent or unseemly battle in its limbs.

14.52 (28) But equal to itself on all sides, and wholly without limit,
a rounded sphere, exulting in its circular solitude
[or, motionlessness].

14.53 (29) For two branches do not spring from its back
nor do feet or swift knees or organs of generation,
but it was a sphere and equal to itself on all sides.

14.54 (30) [Empedocles says this too about the mastery of Strife]
But when great Strife was nourished in the limbs
and leapt up to its rightful prerogatives as the time was fulfilled,
which is established for them in turn by a broad oath . . .

(Context from Simplicius, *Commentary on Aristotle's Physics* 1184.12–13)

14.55 (31) [When Strife has again begun to gain mastery, movement
again occurs in the Sphere]
All the limbs of the god trembled, each in turn.

(Context from Simplicius, *Commentary on Aristotle's Physics* 1184.2–3)

Structure of the Present World

14.56 (39) . . . if indeed the depths of earth and plentiful AITHER are
boundless,
as has vainly traversed the tongues of many, and is poured
out from
mouths of men who have seen little of the whole.

(This fragment attacks those like Xenophanes, who believed that the
earth extends downwards without limit [Aristotle, *On the Heaven* 2.13
294a21–25].)

14.57 (51) swiftly upwards

(Empedocles thus describes the movement of fire, according to
Eustathius, *Commentary on Homer's Odyssey* 1.321.)

14.58 (53, 54) [AITHER was borne upwards not by Strife, but
sometimes he speaks as if it happened by chance]
For thus in its course it sometimes chanced to meet with
<the other elements> in this way, but often otherwise.

[and sometimes he says that fire by nature is borne
  upwards, but]
AITHER sank beneath the deep-rooted earth.

(Context and fragments from Aristotle, *On Generation and Corruption*
2.6 334a1–5.) See also **14.97**.

14.59 (37) Earth increases its own form and AITHER increases AITHER.

(Cited as evidence that Empedocles viewed growth as a matter of addition [Aristotle, *On Generation and Corruption* 2.6 333a35–b1].)

14.60 (52) Many fires burn beneath the ground.

14.61 (41) <The sun> after being gathered together traverses the
  vast heaven.

(Quoted to show that Empedocles regards the sun as a big aggregation of
fire [Apollodorus, quoted in Macrobius, *Saturnalia* 1.17.46].)

14.62 (44) <The sun> shines back towards Olympus with
  fearless face.

14.63 (40) sharp-arrowed sun and mildly-shining moon

14.64 (43) Thus the <sun's> ray, having struck the broad circle of
  the moon . . .

14.65 (47) For <the moon> gazes straight at the pure circle of her
  lord [i.e., the sun].

14.66 (45) A round alien light spins round the earth. ["Alien" in the
  sense of "not its own," "belonging to something else,"
  i.e., the sun.]

14.67 (42) <The moon> keeps off its [the sun's] rays
  when it goes above and darkens a portion of the earth
  the size of the breadth of the gray-eyed moon.

14.68 (46) It spins <round the earth> like the track of a
  chariot, and around the extremity it . . . [15]

15. Following the unmetrical reading of the manuscripts, which I take to be a close
paraphrase.

(Quoted to show that Empedocles held that the moon's orbit is close to the earth [Plutarch, *On the Face in the Moon* 9 925B]. A chariot-race in a stadium is meant, in which the chariots would turn as close as possible to the turning-posts.)

14.69 (48) Earth makes night by obstructing <the sun's> rays.

14.70 (49) during the desolate blind-eyed night [the air is dark].

(Context from Plutarch, *Table Talk* 8.3.1 720E.)

14.71 (50) Iris [the rainbow] brings wind or a great storm from
the sea.

(Attributed to "Empedocles or one of the others" by Tzetzes, *Allegories of the Iliad*, book 15, l. 85.)

14.72 (55) The sea is the earth's sweat.

14.73 (56) Salt is solidified when blasted by the force of the sun.

14.74 (94) In the depths of a river, a dark color arises from
the shadow,
and is observed as well in deep caves.

(Quoted as Empedocles' explanation of the fact that the deep parts of water are dark, while the shallow parts are bright [Plutarch, *Natural Phenomena* 39].)

14.75 (104) And to the extent that they happened to fall together at
great intervals . . . [or, . . . the finest things happened to
fall together]

(Context unknown.)

Origins of Animals

14.76 (57) By her [Love] many neckless faces sprouted,
and arms were wandering naked, bereft of shoulders,
and eyes were roaming alone, in need of foreheads.

14.77 (58) [In this situation, the members were still] single-limbed
[as the result of the separation caused by Strife, and] they
wandered about [aiming at mixture with one another.]

(Context from Simplicius, *Commentary on Aristotle's On the Heaven*, 587.18–19.)

14.78 (59) But when divinity was mixed to a greater extent with divinity,
 and these things began to fall together, however they chanced to meet,
 and many others besides them arose continuously.

14.79 (61) Many came into being with faces and chests on both sides,
 man-faced ox-progeny, and some to the contrary rose up
 as ox-headed things with the form of men, compounded partly from men
 and partly from women, fitted with shadowy parts.

14.80 (60) Trailing-footed cattle with countless hands.

14.81 (62) Come now, hear these things about how, as fire was being separated,
 it raised up the nocturnal shoots of men and women, much-wailing.
 For the story is not off the point or ignorant.
 First the whole-natured forms rose up out of the earth,
 having a portion of both water and heat.   5
 These the fire sent up, desiring to come to its like,
 not yet showing forth at all the lovely shape of limbs
 or a voice or[16] the member native to men.

14.82 (128) Nor was there any god Ares among them nor Kudoimos ["uproar"]
 nor was Zeus king, or Kronos or Poseidon,
 but Cypris was queen. . . .[17]
 Her they propitiated with reverent statues
 and painted figures and unguents with varied odors,   5
 and with offerings of unmixed myrrh and fragrant frankincense,
 pouring on the ground libations of yellow honey.

16. Reading *oút' aû*.
17. This line is incomplete.

No altar was drenched with the unspeakable[18] slaughter
    of bulls,
but this was the greatest abomination among humans,
to destroy life and devour the noble limbs.   10

14.83 (130) All were tame and kindly towards humans—
    both animals and birds—and friendliness burned brightly.

See also **14.87**

Generation of Animals

14.84 (64) Indeed longing to have sexual intercourse comes upon him
    through sight.[19]

14.85 (66) Divided meadows of Aphrodite

(A "disgraceful" expression used of the female genitalia, according to
the source, an anonymous ancient commentator on Euripides, *Phoenissae*,
l. 18.)

14.86 (65) They were poured in clean <places>. Some, encountering
    cold, become women.

14.87 (67) That which has to do with males came to be in the warmer
    part of the earth,
and this is why men are dark and have stronger limbs and
    more hair.

14.88 (63) But the nature of the limbs is rent asunder, partly
    in a man's . . .

(This fragment is quoted twice by Aristotle, once with approval, to show
that Empedocles held that the seed of an animal does not come complete
from either parent [*Generation of Animals* 1.18 722b8–12] and once with
disapproval to show that he held that the body of the seed is rent asunder
[ibid. 764b15–17].)

14.89 (86) Divine Aphrodite fashioned eyes out of them [the four
    elements]

18. Reading *arrḗtoisi*.
19. Reading *tôi d' epì kaì póthos eîsi di' ópsios ammísgesthai* with R. Dyer
(*Mnemosyne* 27 [1974]: 175–76) and Inwood.

14.90 (87) Aphrodite, after furnishing them with bonds of love . . .

(Occurring "shortly after" **14.89**, according to Simplicius, *Commentary on Aristotle's On the Heaven* 529.24.)

14.91 (70) Amnion

(A word used by Empedocles of the membrane that surrounds the embryo.)

14.92 (69) Twice-bearing

(Empedocles used this word to describe women, to indicate that pregnancies last seven or nine months, never eight [Proclus, *Commentary on Plato's Republic* 2 34.26 (Kroll)].)

14.93 (68) On the tenth day of the eighth month <the blood>
          becomes white pus.

(Empedocles' account of lactation [Aristotle, *Generation of Animals* 4.8 777a7].)

Fishes, Animals, Trees, and Plants

14.94 (82) The same things become hairs and leaves and dense
          feathers of birds,
          and scales on stout limbs.

14.95 (72) How both tall trees and sea-dwelling fishes . . .

14.96 (74) . . . leading the museless tribe of fertile fishes

14.97 (76) This [i.e., fire] <occurs> in the heavy-backed shells
          of sea-dwelling creatures,
          and indeed truly of stony-skinned tritons and turtles.
          There you will see earth dwelling in the uppermost parts of
          the flesh.

(Quoted to show that for Empedocles fire does not always go up and earth down, but they are arranged appropriately and usefully [Plutarch, *The Face in the Moon* 14 927F–928A and *Table Talk* 1.2.5 618B].)

14.98 (83) But in hedgehogs
sharp-pointed hairs bristle on their backs.

14.99 (77) leaf-retaining

(Empedocles used this word for evergreens [Plutarch, *Table Talk* 3.2.2 649C].)

14.100 (78) [Empedocles declares that evergreen and continuously
fruiting trees flourish] with bounties of fruits in the spring
each year.

(Quotation and context from Theophrastus, *On Plants: The Explanations* 1.13.2.)

14.101 (79) In this way tall trees first lay eggs in the form of olives.

14.102 (80) Therefore pomegranates are late-produced and apples are
extra succulent.

14.103 For all of them that exist with closely packed roots below,
flourishing with more widely spaced shoots.

(Empedocles fr. 152 [Wright], not in DK.)

14.104 (81) Wine is water from the grapemeat [literally, "bark" or
"skin"] fermented in wood.

Physiology

14.105 (100) This is how all things inhale and exhale. In all, bloodless
tubes of flesh extend deep in the body.
At their mouths the furthest extremities of the nostrils
are pierced through with closely arranged holes, so that they
keep in
blood but a clear path for air is cut through.   5
Then, whenever the delicate blood leaps back from there
the bubbling air leaps in with a raging swell,
and when it [the blood] springs up, the animal exhales again,
as when a young girl
playing with a clepsydra of shining bronze,

when she puts the passage of the pipe against her
    pretty hand   10
and dunks it into the delicate form of silvery water,
no liquid enters the vessel, but the bulk of air,
pressing from inside on the close-set holes, keeps it out
until she uncovers the compressed stream. But then
when the air is leaving, the water duly enters.   15
In the same way when water occupies the vessel and
    the bronze
mouth and passage is blocked by mortal flesh,
the air striving eagerly to get in from without restrains
    the liquid,
commanding the approaches around the gates of the gurgling
    strainer,
until she removes her hand. At that point again, in reverse
    order,   20
as the air enters, the water duly runs out.
In the same way when delicate blood in violent motion
    through the limbs
springs backward to the inmost recesses,
immediately a stream of air raging in a swell comes in,
and when the blood leaps back, it exhales an equal amount
    back again.   25

14.106 (90) Thus sweet catches hold of sweet, bitter rushes
    towards bitter,
sour goes to sour and hot rides upon hot.

(Quoted as Empedocles' "like-to-like" theory of nutrition [Plutarch,
Table Talk 4.1.3 663A and Macrobius, *Saturnalia* 7.5.17–18].)

Perception

14.107 (109) For by earth we see earth, by water, water,
    by AITHER, divine AITHER, and by fire, destructive fire,
    yearning by yearning [Love] and strife by mournful Strife.

14.108 (89) Acknowledging that there are effluences from all things
    that come to be . . .

14.109 (84) As when someone planning for a journey in the
    wintry night

prepares a light, a gleam of blazing fire,
attaching a linen lantern against all the winds,
which scatters the blast of blowing winds,
but the light springs out, as much as it is finer,   5
and shines at the threshold with unwearying beams.
Thus at that time the original fire lay hidden
in the round pupil, enclosed in membranes and fine garments
which are pierced straight through with marvelous passages
which keep back the depth of water flowing around   10
but let the fire pass through as much as it is finer.

14.110 (88) A single sight [i.e., visual impression] comes from both
  [eyes].

14.111 (95) When they first grew together in the hands of Cypris

(Quoted as part of Empedocles' explanation of why some see better by
day and others by night [Simplicius, *Commentary on Aristotle's On the
Heaven* 529.26].)

14.112 (101) Hunting with its nostrils the fragments of
      animals' limbs
    which they were leaving behind from their feet on the soft
    grass . . .

14.113 (99) Fleshy twig

(Empedocles thus called the ear [Theophrastus, *On Sensation* 9 = DK
31A86].)

14.114 (102) So in this way all things have obtained both breathing
      and the sense of smell.

Cognition and Epistemology

14.115 (105) <The heart>, nurtured in the seas of rebounding
      blood,
    where most especially is what is called thought by humans,
    for the blood round the heart in humans is thought.

14.116 (108) Insofar as they change and become different, so far,
      it follows,
    are different thoughts always present to them.

14.117 (103) In this way by the will of chance it thinks all things
 [or, . . . all things have thought[20]].

14.118 (106) Wisdom grows in humans in relation to what is present.

(Cited to show that for Empedocles thought and perception work similarly [Aristotle, *On the Soul* 3.4 427a21–23].)

14.119 (107) For from these [the four elements] all things are joined
 and compounded
 and by these they think and feel pleasure and pain.

See also **14.4, 14.6, 14.8, 14.17**

The Fate of the DAIMONES

See **14.18, 14.82, 14.83**

14.120 (119) From such honor and how great an amount of bliss . . .

(Apparently describing life before the Fall [Plutarch, *On Exile* 17 607D].)

14.121 (124) Alas! Wretched race of mortals! Unfortunate!
 Out of such quarreling and groaning were you born.

14.122 (120) We came beneath this roofed cave.

14.123 (118) I wept and wailed upon seeing the unfamiliar place.

14.124 (121) . . . Joyless place,
 where Murder, Anger and tribes of other spirits of death
 and squalid Diseases and Rottings and works of dissolution[21]
 wander in darkness through the meadow of Disaster.

14.125 (122) There were the maidens Earth and far-seeing Sun,
 bloody Battle and serious Harmonia,
 Beauty and Ugliness, Speed and Slowness,
 lovely Truth and dark-haired Unclarity.

20. Cf. **14.6** l.10.
21. This line may not belong here.

14.126 (123) Growth and Wasting, Sleeping and Waking,
Movement and Fixity, many-crowned Greatness
and Defilement, Silence and prophetic Voice.

14.127 (126) Wrapping <it> in an alien garb of flesh.

14.128 (145) Therefore, while wandering in harsh evils,
you will never relieve your spirit from wretched distress.

14.129 (142) Neither, then, the roofed halls of aegis-bearing Zeus
nor the house of Hades [? receives] him.

14.130 (117) For I have already once become a boy and a girl
and a bush and a bird and a [mute] fish [from the sea].[22]

14.131 (127) Among beasts they come into being as lions whose lairs
are in the mountains,
their beds on the ground, and as laurels among shaggy trees.

(These the best animals and plants for a DAIMON to become [Aelian,
Natural History 12.7].)

14.132 (146) In the end they are prophets and bards and physicians
and chiefs among men on earth,
and from there they arise as gods mightiest in honors.

14.133 (147) Sharing the same hearth and table with other immortals
relieved of human distress, unwearied.

14.134 (134) For he [Apollo, or god in general] is not furnished in his
limbs with a human head.
Two branches do not spring from his back.
He has no feet, no swift limbs, no hairy genitals,
but is only mind (PHREN), holy and indescribable,
darting through the entire KOSMOS with his swift thoughts.

(This is Empedocles' criticism of those who believed in anthropomorphic gods [Ammonius, *Commentary on Aristotle's On Interpretation*
249.1–5].)

22. The words in brackets are conjectures; the text is corrupt.

Prohibition on Killing and Other Prohibitions

See **14.82**

14.135 (135) But what is lawful for all extends far
through the wide-ruling AITHER and through the
immense glare.

(This refers to the injustice of killing living things [Aristotle, *Rhetoric*
1.13 1373b6–17].)

14.136 (139) Alas that the pitiless day did not destroy me
before I thought of the wicked deeds of eating with my lips.

14.137 (137) A father lifts up his own dear son who has
changed form,
and, praying, slaughters him, committing a great folly.
And they are at a loss,
sacrificing him as he entreats them. But he, refusing
to hear the cries,
slaughters him and attends an evil feast in his halls.
Likewise a son seizes his father and children their mother
and tearing out their life devour the dear flesh.

14.138 (136) Will you not cease from harsh-sounding murder?
Do you not see
that you are devouring each other in the carelessness of
your thought?

14.139 (138) Having drawn off [i.e., severed] the soul with bronze.

14.140 (143) [It is necessary to cleanse oneself]
after cutting[23] from five springs with the long-pointed bronze.

14.141 (140) Keep completely away from laurel leaves!

14.142 (141) Wretched, wholly wretched! Keep your hands off beans!

14.143 (144) Fast from evil.

23. "Cutting" is used here metaphorically to mean "drawing off" (Aristotle, *Poetics*
21 1457b13–16 = DK 31B138), so that the fragment probably refers to an act of
killing. The context, provided by Theon of Smyrna (*Mathematics Useful for Reading
Plato* 15.9–11 = DK 31B143), then connects the fragment with the pollution
incurred by bloodshed.

Life and Character

Empedocles' approximate dates are 492–432; he is a contemporary of Zeno and Melissus, and a generation younger than Parmenides. For his relation to Anaxagoras, see pp. 201–202. He came from Acragas, an important Greek city in Sicily, and has firm intellectual connections with the western Greek lands. Shortly after the panhellenic foundation of Thurri in 444, he visited that city in southern Italy, where he may have met such men as Herodotus the historian and Protagoras the Sophist. Southern Italy was home to Pythagorean traditions and other (Orphic) religious beliefs in the afterlife that strongly influenced Empedocles. Finally, Elea, the home of Parmenides, whose philosophical importance for Empedocles was crucial, was also located in southern Italy.

In Acragas Empedocles was active in politics and, despite his wealthy and aristocratic background, helped suppress an oligarchic regime and fought ardently for democracy. He was exiled and may have died in the Peloponnese, although more spectacular stories about his death are told. Most famous is that he leapt into the crater of Mt. Etna "wishing to confirm the report about him that he had become a god."[24] He had been hailed as a god by the people of Selinus, a neighboring town of Acragas, for freeing them from a pestilence caused by their polluted river, by diverting two nearby streams at his own expense, so as to flush out the unhealthy stream. But this token of reverence hardly accounts for Empedocles' ego and flair for showmanship. In public he wore a purple robe, a gold crown, bronze shoes, and a laurel wreath. He wore his hair long, had a retinue of boys to attend him, and adopted a grave demeanor. He was known as a physician and magician (professions by no means distinct in antiquity). According to a widely known story he kept a woman alive for thirty days without breathing or pulse. In addition, he was a philosopher who articulated a complex and novel theory of the KOSMOS, and a fervent preacher of a doctrine of a fall from a state of original purity and of ultimate redemption. Not surprisingly, he is one of the most difficult Presocratics to understand, and also one of the most interesting.

Writings

His philosophical oeuvre is composed in the heroic dactylic hexameter also used by Xenophanes and Parmenides. The genuinely poetic quality of his writing, which has been admired since antiquity, constitutes an obstacle to understanding his literal message, though its figurative and emotional con-

---

24. Diogenes Laertius, *Lives of the Philosophers* 8.69 (= DK 31A1).

tent give it a vividness and urgency unmatched in philosophical writings before Plato. His style suits his purpose, which is not primarily to give an account of the KOSMOS, though it involves this too, but to exhort us to save our souls and to show us how. His surviving fragments constitute the largest bulk of material surviving from any Presocratic, but they admit of widely differing interpretations, and readers from the time of Aristotle, who presumably had access to the entire works, have found themselves perplexed. Because of the difficulties and because of the large amount of material, my discussion of Empedocles will be more selective and less comprehensive, also more dogmatic than in previous chapters.[25]

Empedocles composed tragedies, a historical poem on the Persian War, a poem to Apollo, and medical writings as well as his philosophical poetry, which will be our exclusive concern and for which two titles are recorded: *On Nature* and *Purifications*.[26] The traditional view, that these were two separate poems on different, incompatible themes, has recently come under heavy attack.[27] The alternative proposal, that there was only one poem which was known by both titles,[28] has much to recommend it. It solves a number of problems; for example, ancient authors who quote from Empedocles show no awareness of the existence of two poems, and modern attempts to allocate the fragments to the two poems have not achieved any consensus.

On the traditional view, *On Nature* was a "scientific" poem that treated the elements, Love and Strife, the nature of compounds, the origin and present structure of the KOSMOS, the origin of animal species, and topics in

---

25. Diverse accounts abound. See p. 270 n. 59 for references.

26. It is doubtful that Empedocles titled his poem either *On Nature* or *Purifications*. The former title is attributed to the writings of many of the Presocratics, but the word "nature" is unlikely to have been used in the general sense of "the whole of nature" or "the nature of things" before the time of Aristotle. (At *Phaedo* 96a, Plato seems to treat the expression "on nature" as unfamiliar and requiring explanation, whereas Aristotle and his followers use it as a standard term.) The latter title is not found for Empedocles' poem in sources earlier than the second century A.D. (Diogenes Laertius, Theon of Smyrna, Hippolytus, and Herodian) and is likely to have been attached to it because of the similarity of its theme (or one of its important themes) to other works of that title.

27. C. Osborne, "Empedocles Recycled," *Classical Quarterly* 37 (1987): 24–31; and *Rethinking Early Greek Philosophy: Hippolytus of Rome and the Presocratics* (Ithaca, N.Y., 1987), pp. 24–31, tentatively followed with minor qualifications by B. Inwood, *The Poem of Empedocles* (Toronto, 1992), pp. 8–19.

28. According to the alternative proposal, Diogenes Laertius, the source that speaks most clearly of two works, is discounted as having been misled by the occurrence of the two titles in *his* sources.

physiology, perception, cognition, and epistemology, while *Purifications* was a "religious" poem, concerned with the Fall of spirits from a godlike state into mortal creatures, their transmigration, and hope of ultimate redemption and regaining divine status through abstention from certain practices and following certain rituals. But on this account the poems not only treat different subjects, but are mutually contradictory, for the "scientific" poem maintains that the only everlasting things are the four elements (earth, water, air, and fire) and the two entities which cause them to move (Love and Strife); all other things are perishable compounds—whereas the "religious" poem requires the soul to be immortal. Moreover, the development of the KOSMOS in the "scientific" poem, in which the soul must take part, is thought incompatible with the everlasting divine bliss that is the lot of the redeemed soul.

But this interpretation can be questioned. In the first place a clear distinction between the "scientific" and the "religious" was alien to presocratic thought (Heraclitus and Parmenides provide the most striking cases of this fact), or indeed to Greek philosophy in general (though of course the philosophers' notions of the divine were in the main remote from the Olympian gods). Thus there is no a priori reason why the nature, history, and prospects of the human soul should not form part of a work on the nature, history, and prospects of the KOSMOS and of the elements and compounds within it. Further, if there really is inconsistency, it may not make much difference for our overall interpretation of Empedocles whether the incompatible features occur in different poems or in different parts of the same poem. Either way we must qualify or restrict our conclusions accordingly. And finally, there may be no inconsistency at all, if we are prepared to accept an appropriate conception of immortality—one bound up with the fate of the elements and devoid of personal identity. In what follows, I adopt a unitarian approach in which, after presenting Empedocles' "scientific" ideas, I shall offer an interpretation of his "religious" views, which so far from being inconsistent with the former material, coheres with it to form a whole.[29]

A purification is a means of removing a state of pollution in which an individual, family, or city would find itself as the result of committing a certain kind of forbidden action (manslaughter, for example), or failing to perform a required one (such as sacrifices). Pollution would be incurred whether or not the improper behavior was done intentionally. Pollution and

29. Those who remain unconvinced by the present attempt to link the two aspects of Empedocles' thought can easily enough detach them. The account of Empedocles' "scientific" views can remain unchanged, as can most of the account of the "religious" views, except for what has to do with the soul's physical nature and its participation in the cosmic processes.

purification are conceptions of Greek religion, not Greek law. Purification can be achieved through ritual means (sacrifice, pouring libations, or ritual bathing to wash away the stain), or through abstaining from certain kinds of behavior.

The title *Purifications* therefore refers to the "religious" aspect of the poem, which describes the pollution and subsequent Fall of divinities from a state of bliss, their successive incarnations in mortal creatures, and the means of purification by which they can be freed from the necessity of rebirth and can return to a condition of blessed happiness.

The Beginning of Empedocles' Poem

The poem begins[30] with an address to his friends in his native city (**14.19**) in which he describes himself as thought of as a god, greatly honored, and sought after for his knowledge of medicine, of the future, and of how to make a fortune. His superiority to other humans (**14.10**) enables him to learn directly from a divine source (**14.4** l. 2, **14.16**) an otherwise unreachable truth (**14.14, 14.8**), in particular, knowledge about the gods (**14.15, 14.13**). He speaks as a seer like Teiresias, confident of his knowledge, assured of its importance, and feeling no need to offer justification. And yet he acknowledges that there are limits to what ordinary mortals can or are willing to understand (**14.8** lines 8–9, **14.2, 14.4** l. 1).

The poem is dedicated to Pausanias, Empedocles' lover[31] (**14.3**), who is presumably the "you" the fragments frequently address. Empedocles will teach his knowledge to Pausanias to the extent that he will be able to comprehend it, and to that extent enable Pausanias to transcend the limitations of human experience (**14.8**). Empedocles makes extraordinary claims for the powers this knowledge will bring (**14.7**) and for its value as compared with the misguided concerns of most men (**14.6**). He warns Pausanias not to reveal to others what he learns (**14.2, 14.17** lines 1–3).

14.18, also from the beginning of the poem,[32] vividly tells of the origin of the pollution and the punishments it brings. Pollution arises from bloodshed and making false statements under oath.[33] Those who incur this pollution are long-lived DAIMONES (singular, DAIMON) (a looser word for divinity than THEOS, "god"). The punishment for these sins is a vast period

---

30. Diogenes Laertius, *Lives of the Philosophers* 8.62 (= DK 31A1).

31. Diogenes Laertius, *Lives of the Philosophers* 8.60 (= DK 31A1).

32. Plutarch, *On Exile* 17 607C (= DK 31B115).

33. Greek oaths were sworn "by (one or more of) the gods"; to swear falsely is a religious offense which can bring divine wrath on the individual or on his family or entire city.

of exile[34] from the blessed gods, during which the fallen divinity is born and reborn in different forms of life and is driven into exile by each of the four elements in turn. The fragment's intensely emotional tone is explained by Empedocles' own involvement: he is one of the fallen divinities now suffering this awful fate—and so are we, which gives us a powerful motive to heed his earnest message, to become aware of our divine nature, our fate, and the means of our redemption. To comprehend this teaching, we must learn as well the nature and workings of the KOSMOS and our place in it. This is the link between the "scientific" and "religious" sides of Empedocles' philosophy, as it is between the two sides of Pythagoreanism.[35] His overall message is "religious," as the fact that **14.18** occurred near the beginning of his poem shows. But it is embedded in and supported by a cosmology and a physical theory that are highly original and fascinating in their own right. The remainder of this chapter will treat these latter subjects first and afterwards will return to the theme of the divinities and their (our) prospects.

Physical Principles

14.19, which appeared "right at the start" of Empedocles' treatise,[36] introduces the chief characters and processes of the KOSMOS: four elements (fire, air, water, earth) and two sources of change (Love and Strife), which cause the reciprocal processes of unification and separation.

At the elemental level there are four basic substances (l. 18). These are eternal (l. 35) and fixed in quantity (lines 27, 32–33). They do not change into one another (l. 36), come to be, suffer destruction, or undergo change in their basic qualities (lines 31–34). They maintain their identity intact (l. 25). Each exists fully, and aside from them (and Love and Strife) there is nothing (l. 30). Empedocles calls them not "elements," but "roots" (an evocative term which suggests that they are living sources from which other things grow), which he gives the names of gods (**14.20**). The Sicilian goddess Nestis represents water, Zeus is fire, and Hera and Aidoneus (another name for Hades) probably represent air and earth, respectively.[37] Empedocles uses a range of terms for his elements. Fire is also flame, sun (Helios), "the shining one" (Elektor), and Hephaestus. Water is also called rain and two names (Pontos, Thalassa) that both translate as "sea." Air is

---

34. Thirty-thousand seasons need not be meant as a precise time span.
35. See p. 114.
36. Simplicius, *Commentary on Aristotle's Physics* 161.14 (= DK 31B17).
37. These identifications have been disputed since antiquity.

Heaven (Ouranos) and AITHER. Earth is referred to in several ways (Chthon, Gaia, Aia) that all translate as "earth."

The variation in names raises an important question—did Empedocles conceive of his elements as pure substances? Since he knew that rain is fresh water and sea is salt,[38] he should recognize that sea water is impure in comparison with rain water. This way of thinking leads to the concept of perfectly pure water, air, etc.—idealized forms of these materials which perhaps never occur in isolation in the KOSMOS around us, out of which substances we encounter (such as rain and sea water) are composed. But the use of "sea" and "rain" indifferently as names for the element water may point to the opposite view, that sea and rain (perhaps other liquids too) are each fully as much water as any of the others, so that the term "water" covers many liquids, and likewise "air" many gases, and "earth" many solids. Alternatively, if Empedocles held that the elements are, properly speaking, "pure," the variety of names by which he calls them may be a deliberate maneuver to avoid identifying any single familiar substance with a pure element. **14.20**, then, may be more than allegory, since ordinary conceptions of the gods are misguided (**14.134**; with lines 4–5 compare **14.6** 1. 10): the names "Zeus," "Hera," etc., really refer to the elements.

The four roots join to form "mortal" compounds (**14.19** lines 34–35, **14.21** lines 9 ff., **14.27**, **14.28**, **14.37**, **14.38**), which unlike the "immortal" elements (**14.47** 1. 14), come to be and suffer destruction. More properly stated, they are formed by mixture and dissolved by separation of their component elements (**14.43**).

Mixing the elements to form compounds and dissolving compounds into separate elements are functions of Love and Strife, respectively (**14.21**, **14.24**, ?**14.26**, **14.27**, **14.29**, **14.30**, **14.31**). Love attracts dissimilars to dissimilars, while Strife, in separating dissimilars, attracts like to like. Love and Strife are opposed to one another (**14.19**, **14.21**, **14.22**), and exist always (**14.23**).

How Empedocles conceived of Love and Strife is problematic. One issue is whether they are something like forces, which operate on matter but are immaterial, as we might expect from statements that compounds are made up of the four elements (not the four elements plus Love and Strife) (**14.19** lines 34–36, **14.21** lines 13–14, **14.49**). But he describes Love and Strife in terms appropriate to material entities with spatial location: "equal in all directions," "among them, equal in length and breadth," and "spinning among them" (**14.19** lines 19, 20, 25). Also, Love and Strife occupy different parts of the KOSMOS at different stages of its existence (**14.47**). Aristotle aptly complains that Empedocles makes Love and Strife principles

---

38. Cf. **14.72**. **14.73** may refer to the evaporation of seawater to produce salt.

"both as movers and as matter (for they are parts of the mixture)."[39] Love and Strife must be physically present among the elements to operate on them, and yet the elements are thought to be the only physical constituents of compounds (cf. **14.37, 14.38**).

Empedocles expresses the relation between Love and Strife and the elements by saying that the latter mix and are separated "by Love," "by the hatred of Strife" (**14.19** lines 8–9), "in Anger" and "in Love" (**14.21** lines 7–8), "through the bidding of Strife" (**14.22** l. 9), etc.[40]—language suggesting that he thought of Love and Strife as agents, not constituents. And yet the agent acts by its presence: its effects do not remain if it departs, whereas compounds continue to exist because of the continuing presence of Love, and likewise, the elements remain separate from one another because of the continued presence of Strife (**14.47** lines 7 ff.)

Another issue is whether Love and Strife are responsible for all changes in the KOSMOS. It is tempting to think of the elements as inert matter and Love and Strife as what make them move.[41] But such an interpretation runs the risk of anachronism, since earlier philosophers had supposed motion to be an inherent feature of their primary substance, not requiring an external cause. Moreover, the elements seem to have motions due to their own nature: fire and air upwards (**14.57, 14.58**)[42] and no doubt water and earth downwards,[43] and the whirling vortex motion of the KOSMOS (**14.47** l. 4) "compels" the earth to move to the center:

14.144 And so, if the earth is now at rest by compulsion, it came together, brought to the middle by the vortex motion.[44]
(Aristotle, *On the Heaven* 2.13 295a9–10 = DK 59A88)

On the basis of this evidence, I conclude that Love and Strife are directly responsible not for all motion, but specifically for the mixing and separation of the elements. For a compound to form we need both the correct amounts and proportions of its constituent elements and also Love (and, I shall

39. Aristotle, *Metaphysics* 12.12 1075b2–7 (not in DK).

40. See also **14.24** lines 2, 4, **14.22** l. 5, **14.27, 14.29, 14.30, 14.37, 14.49** lines 5–6, **14.50**.

41. Aristotle takes this line, identifying Empedocles' four elements as "material causes" and Love and Strife as "efficient causes" (*Metaphysics* 1.4 985a29–33 = DK 31A37).

42. The assertion that Empedocles recognizes chance as a cause of motion (**14.58, 14.38** l.1, **14.75**) is an Aristotelian interpretation that can be disregarded.

43. There is evidence that Empedocles did not state this fact clearly (Aristotle, *On the Heaven* 2.13 295b2–3, not in DK).

44. Empedocles is mentioned just below at 295a17 as holding this theory.

argue below, Strife) in the right amounts and proportions to unite them in the right way (**14.37, 14.38, 14.31** [if the context is given correctly], **14.27, 14.29, ?14.30**).

How, then, do Love and Strife affect the elements? They are not simply mechanical forces. Things under the influence of Love "love another," while those under Strife's power are "enemies" and "very bitter" (**14.22**). He calls Love by other names (Friendship, Aphrodite, Joy, Harmony) and declares that she is responsible for friendly thoughts and peaceful deeds (**14.19** l. 23). The cosmic unifying force is identical with the familiar force of Love that unites different humans. Love's operation in the KOSMOS is psychological as much as physical. Through her the different elements are attracted to or "yearn for" one another (**14.21** l. 8). Similarly, Strife—also called Quarrels and Hatred, and characterized as destructive, evil, and as that which operates by hatred—makes the elements bitter and causes them to hate each other. In addition, Love and Strife are moral agents. Love and her effects are good, Strife and its effects are evil. Empedocles' KOSMOS is therefore far from simply a physical environment, but has psychological and moral aspects built into it from the very foundations. This combination of different realms of reality seems odd today. It seemed equally odd to Aristotle only a century after Empedocles, but if we recall the tradition of Heraclitus and the Pythagoreans, it is not out of place in the first half of the fifth century.

The equality of Love and Strife is a striking feature of Empedocles' system, and must be understood at the moral and psychological level as well as at the mechanical level. The analysis of opposites made by his predecessors made it unthinkable for Empedocles to attempt to account for strife, hatred, and evil in the world if the only relevant principle was a principle of love, harmony, and good. Opposites are equally powerful and cannot be generated one from the other. Also, since at the mechanical level, both separation and union are seen to take place, a principle of separation or unification without a corresponding opposite principle would ultimately lead to a dead end at which all possible separation or unification had occurred. Further, if there were only a single principle, Empedocles would be vulnerable to questions Parmenides had raised: how did the cosmic process get started in the first place, and what was the original arrangement like?

Events in the KOSMOS are the effects of Love and Strife on the four elements. For cosmology, the mechanical effects of mixture and separation are most important. The two motive principles cause the four material principles to move in various ways. As they move they form temporary ("mortal") compounds that, through the effects of Love and Strife, eventually dissolve into their constituent elements or are transformed into other compounds. Compounds undergo this sort of coming to be and destruction and other changes as well. Growth, for example, is a matter of the addition of more fire, air, water and/or earth to what was already in the compound. For example, the sum total of earth in the universe remains constant, but more of this fixed amount is temporarily invested in the growing thing.

The nature of the compounds requires careful attention. The terms "elements" and "compounds" are not Empedocles' but come from modern chemistry. The four roots are in important ways comparable to such elements as oxygen and hydrogen;[45] but how far do his compounds resemble chemical compounds?

14.37 gives the ratio of elements in bone: two parts earth, two parts water, and four parts fire. Empedocles does not explain how he arrived at this formula, but the example is helpful nonetheless. It suggests that Empedocles' conception of compounds involves a law of fixed proportions, and that a compound such as bone is to be thought of along the lines of a modern chemical compound, such as water, which contains a fixed proportion of hydrogen atoms to oxygen atoms. Thus **14.37** would be the ancestor of such formulas as H_2O and CO_2.

14.38 undermines this result, though, since it talks of earth "in about equal quantity" and "a bit more or a bit less," and since it may mean that blood and other forms of flesh, which seem to be different compounds, have the same composition. But **14.38** is unclear: perhaps the slightly different proportions constitute different forms of flesh, each of which has fixed proportions, or perhaps the different proportions are meant to account for variations in the same form of flesh. In any case, there is no reason to think that Empedocles developed systematic methods for discovering the composition of compounds, or that **14.37** and **14.38** are based on anything other than sheer speculation.[46]

Second, how are the elements united in a compound—as a physical mixture, a solution, or a chemical compound? In physical mixtures like salt and pepper, the ingredients come in particles, and each particle preserves its identity in the mixture. They can be separated out of the mixture by mechanical means, since there is no chemical bonding. The different bits just sit next to one another in no determinate order, and there is no definite ratio of the mixture. Any amount of salt can be mixed with any amount of pepper. With solutions like gin and tonic, most of these same characteristics obtain, including the absence of any definite ratio in the mixture. One difference is that it is not a merely mechanical process to separate the

45. However, as far as we know, Empedocles did not analyze his "roots" into anything corresponding to subatomic particles, and unlike modern chemists he held that they cannot be created, destroyed, split, fused, or transformed into one another.

46. The view that blood is composed of all four elements may be connected with Empedocles' theories of perception and thought. See pp. 283–84.

ingredients. There may be some weak bonding effects, but no true chemical bonding. In chemical compounds there are fixed proportions of the ingredients and the ingredients lose their identity. In H_2O, we do not have two atoms of hydrogen and one of oxygen,[47] but one molecule that does not behave like hydrogen or like oxygen, but like water. To recover the constituent elements from the compound is not simply a matter of sorting.

Which if any of these three kinds of composites is the mixture of elements that constitutes an Empedoclean compound? Any answer to this question must take into account Empedocles' repeated assertion that the four elements do not perish (**14.22**, lines 10–13, **14.21** lines 13–14). They continue to exist in compounds even though they have different appearances. This is also the case in all three of the models of mixture being considered. How mixtures can come to have different properties from their ingredients is suggested by **14.36**, which tells against the salt-and-pepper model, since it shows that some properties of the compound are due to the interaction of the components. Simple juxtaposition is not enough. Apparently more helpful is fragment **14.28**, which likens the formation of compounds out of the elements to colors formed by blending primary colors. When a certain amount of red and yellow are blended to produce a certain shade of orange, neither of the original colors is any longer apparent, but they continue to exist as components of a color whose appearance is different from theirs. Since the original colors cannot be extracted from the compound by a simple mechanical process of separation, the fragment also tells against the salt-and-pepper model. But this interpretation of the fragment is not certain since **14.28** sets out to explain how a small number of basic elements (Greek painters used four basic colors) can combine to produce a vast array of mixtures, not how the pigments blend in forming a mixture. The number is under discussion, not the nature of the mixtures.

Another piece of evidence comes from **14.37** and **14.38**, which identify determinate ratios of the elements in compounds. This evidence points towards the chemical compound model rather than the gin-and-tonic one, though the uncertainties of **14.38** (discussed above) must not be disregarded.

Finally, **14.37** and **14.38** give Love a role in the compounds themselves, not just in forming them. This strongly suggests that Empedocles thought that we cannot create blood simply by pouring equal amounts of fire, air, water, and earth together and stirring, but that they must be held together in the compound in the appropriate way.[48] This is further evidence for the

---

47. In any case, hydrogen and oxygen do not normally occur in single atoms.

48. **14.13** is compatible with a theory that blood and other kinds of flesh are made of the same constituents in the same ratios, but bonded differently, thus forming what modern chemists call isomers.

view that Empedocles' compounds are more like chemical compounds than mixtures or solutions. The role of Love in extant compounds thus corresponds to the modern notion of chemical bonding.

Another question is whether there are "atoms"—smallest bits of fire, air, water, and earth. Such a view is compatible with gin-and-tonic mixtures and with the blending of pigments, as well as with the chemical-compounds interpretation, and it fits with Empedocles' belief that the four elements are preserved in compounds. Two statements of Aristotle's are illuminating:

> **14.145** [How do compounds come to be out of the elements?] For those who talk like Empedocles . . . it must be a matter of composition as a wall comes to be out of bricks and stones. Also this mixture will be composed of elements that are preserved, placed next to one another close by. In this way, then, there come to be flesh and all the rest.
> (Aristotle, *On Generation and Corruption* 2.7 334a26–31 = DK 31A43)

> **14.146** If the dissolution [of an element into smaller and smaller parts] is going to come to an end, either the end-product will be indivisible [atomic] or it will be divisible but will never in fact be divided, as Empedocles means to say.
> (Aristotle, *On the Heaven* 3.6 305a1–4 = DK 31A43a)

Although **14.145** seems to argue for atoms, **14.146** excludes them. The two passages are compatible as long as the "building blocks" in **14.145** are not atomic, but are the (still divisible) bits that form a given compound. However, it may be mistaken to pursue this issue so far. **14.145** shows that in Aristotle's opinion Empedocles is committed to minimum particles, but also that this is Aristotle's opinion; he could not find an explicit statement in Empedocles' works. And this fact suggests that Empedocles did not push the analysis of the composition of his four elements to that depth. Since the Atomists presented theories of the ultimate structure of matter, it is natural to look for one in Empedocles too, but since philosophers of previous generations had not explicitly raised such questions, they may not have occurred to him.

Another feature of Empedocles' view on mixture and combination is described in another passage of Aristotle.

> **14.147** Some believe that each thing is acted on when the last agent—the agent in the strictest sense—enters through certain pores, and they say that this is how we see and hear and use all our other senses. Moreover we see through air and water and transparent substances because they possess pores which cannot be seen on account of their smallness, but are close together and arranged in rows. Those which

are more transparent have these properties to a greater degree. Now
some, including Empedocles, declared that this theory applied to certain things—not only to things which act and are acted on, but they
also declare that those things undergo mixture whose pores are sym-
metrical with one another.   (Aristotle, *On Generation and Corruption*
                                    1.8 324b25–35 = DK 31A87)

We will return to the doctrine of pores in connection with Empedocles'
theory of perception. For present purposes, the last sentence is most important. Not all substances are equally susceptible of mixture (**14.34, 14.35,
14.36**). Mixture is facilitated when the pores of one component are the
right size for the projecting bits of the other. Empedocles also accounts for
the property of transparency by means of pores. However, the theory raises
difficult questions that Empedocles does not seem to have faced. Aristotle
makes a number of criticisms that are worth repeating.

> **14.148** Now as to all who say that processes of being acted on occur on
> account of movement in the pores, if it takes place even though the
> pores are filled, the pores are unneeded. For if the whole is acted on in
> these circumstances, it would be acted on in the same way even if it
> had no pores, but were continuous. . . . But also if these pores are
> empty (even though there must be bodies in them), the same conse-
> quence will follow. . . . In general it is odd to posit the pores. For if
> the agent does nothing by contact, it will not do it by passing through
> the pores, either. But if it does act by contact, then even if there are
> no pores, when things are naturally related in this way to one another,
> they will act and be acted on.
> (Aristotle, *On Generation and Corruption* 1.8 326b6–24, not in DK)

Despite these unclarities and shortcomings, Empedocles' views on the nature of matter are an enormous advance on his scientific predecessors. The
first clear distinctions between elements, mixtures, and compounds,[49] the
first sketch of analyses of compounds into constituent elements, and the
first recognition of the importance of bonding are found in his fragments.
The reason for these achievements is to be found in his philosophical
predecessors, for Empedocles was keenly aware of the Eleatics, in particular
Parmenides, and to a large extent constructed his physical theory with the
Eleatic challenge in mind.[50]

---

49. Empedocles' main precursor here is Parmenides, whose conception of elements in *The Way of Mortal Opinions* was noted previously (p. 176).
50. Verbal echoes of and allusions to Parmenides' poem are found frequently in
Empedocles' fragments.

Response to Parmenides

Where Parmenides had identified two wholly separate worlds—the World of Being that fully is and the World of Becoming that in no way is, Empedocles identifies two types of entity (elements and compounds[51]) both of which are real and are intimately related. He insists that reality consists of the four elements. "There are just these very things" (**14.19** l. 34, **14.21** l. 13), which "are always and continuously the same" (**14.19** l. 35), but "running through one another at different times they come to be different things" (**14.19** lines 34–35), i.e., compounds.

All the features barred from Parmenides' World of Being are found at the level of compounds: plurality, coming to be, destruction, change, motion, and the distinctions in space and time these characteristics require. Thus, the phenomenal world is saved. But it is grounded in the elements, which observe many of Parmenides' strictures on Being. Admittedly there is an irreducible plurality, but a severely limited one: just four basic substances. And of course, the elements move and can be divided and united to form smaller or larger pieces (**14.22** lines 1–3). But the total amount of each does not change, and at this level there is no coming to be or destruction, no change in qualities, and each element is qualitatively uniform. The qualitative differences among the elements contradict Parmenides' claim "For it is not lacking. If it were, it would lack everything" (**11.8** l. 33), which entails that what is has all possible attributes. Fire lacks the distinctive attributes of air and vice versa, but both are fully. The joining together of elements to form compounds and the dissolution of compounds into their component elements do not violate the permanence of the elements: they continue to exist while in compounds. The coming to be and destruction of compounds, and the changes they undergo are in this way reducible to the movement, mixture, and separation of the elements. "Coming to be" and "destruction" turn out to be misnomers (**14.44**), though when used of compounds they have a basis in reality (**14.43**). Empedocles, unlike Parmenides, does not reject or discard ordinary language,[52] nor does he set out to reform it. Instead, he has no objection to following its practice (**14.44** l. 5) once he has shown how to interpret it to avoid the impossibilities it seems to involve.

Empedocles was impressed by the force of Parmenides' arguments, especially those against generation and destruction, and it is plausible to view his physical theory as a response that takes the form not of counter-

---

51. Love and Strife can be disregarded in the present section.
52. See **11.2** lines 7–8, **11.6** lines 8–9, **11.8** lines 7–9, 16–17.

arguments but of accounting for the world of appearance in a way that violates as few as possible of Parmenides' strictures.

In fact, Empedocles wholeheartedly accepts Parmenides' thesis that nothing can be generated out of what in no way is or perish into nothing (**14.40, 14.41, 14.42**). The generation and destruction of compounds is out of and into the elements, and of *them* there is no generation or destruction, as is maintained in arguments at **14.19** lines 31–33.[53] The arguments in lines 32–33 assume that the four elements exist in their present quantities and argue that they cannot become more or less. Increase is impossible for (a) "what could increase this totality?" (i.e., there is nothing aside from the four elements, therefore nothing left over which can become any of them), and (b) "where would it come from?" (i.e., the place occupied by the four elements is all there is; there is not even any place for anything aside from the four elements). This argument is supported by **14.45**,[54] which denies that any part of the whole is "empty or over-full": there are no gaps (places not occupied by any of the elements) in the universe, nor are there any "crowds" (places occupied by more than one). The sources do not preserve any argument of Empedocles for these theses, and it would be in keeping with the present interpretation if he did not attempt to prove them but proceeded by asserting what his system required.[55]

The argument against destruction in l. 33, "How [or, where] could it perish, since nothing is empty of these," also depends on the nonexistence of gaps. It suggests that if there were gaps, perishing would be possible—presumably there would be some place other than that occupied by the elements for the pieces of elements being destroyed to go to. This thought may have a connection with **14.41**, which argues against absolute destruction by saying "each time it will be where a person thrusts it each time." Apparent destruction is really just disposal,[56] and any attempt to destroy a piece of an element is unsuccessful since it only winds up shuffling the positions of things.

Empedocles holds that the universe is a plenum, and that motion is possible. Motion is a matter of *antiperistasis*, or reciprocal replacement in which A occupies the place of B, which in turn occupies that of C . . . which occupies that of A, as when a fish swims through water and occupies

53. Compare Parmenides' arguments at 11.8 lines 6–21.

54. **14.46**, if it is authentic, may support it too, though it may be a confused recollection of **14.45** and **14.19** l. 33.

55. Empedocles' denial of void may well be based on interpreting the prohibited "what is not" as void, but the fragments do not make this clear. Melissus argues on this basis against the existence of void (**15.9** sec. 7–10). He holds that what is is full. He does not argue, however, that it is not *over*-full.

56. Well put by Inwood, op. cit. (p. 256 n. 27), p. 25.

a region formerly occupied by water, and simultaneously water (not necessarily the same bit of water) occupies the region where the fish had been.[57]

Empedocles disagrees with Parmenides' views that the senses and the opinions of mortals are unreliable (**11.1** l. 30, **11.6** lines 6–7, **11.7** lines 3–4). That is not to say he finds them wholly trustworthy. They are unable to apprehend the divine (**14.41**). The sense organs are feeble ("narrow") and impeded by our environment (**14.8** lines 1–2). We tend to generalize on the basis of insufficient experience, and this is the wrong way to go about learning the whole nature of things (**14.8** lines 7–8). Still, used properly, the senses can help us gain understanding (**14.17**). Empedocles' distinction between understanding and the senses (most clearly in **14.17** l. 8) and his admonition not to prefer any one sense over the others, but to use each appropriately (**14.17** lines 4–7), hardly amount to an epistemology, but they do grant some value to the senses, as is to be expected in a philosopher who preserves the phenomenal world.

Cosmic Cycle

Not only does Empedocles conceive a new approach to traditional questions about the basic form(s) of matter and the source(s) of movement and change, but he also postulates a new kind of system of the KOSMOS, a system governed by the interactions of Love and Strife and the four elements. I will begin this section with a summary of the principal features of the cosmic cycle, reviewing the evidence for the different phases of the cycle, and will then take up a number of related issues.

The essential principle of Empedocles' KOSMOS is an eternal pattern of alternate and reciprocal increases and decreases in the influence of Love and Strife over the four elements. At one extreme of the cycle, Love has complete dominance and Strife has none; at the other extreme, Strife dominates all, Love none. At the time of Love's complete dominance, the elements are completely and uniformly mixed and bonded into a single spherical compound comprising all the material in the universe. When Strife prevails utterly, there is no mixture at all, and the elements are completely separated from one another: all earth in one mass, and likewise for all water, air, and fire. In between these extreme states, Love and Strife are both on the field. The transition between them is a gradual process in which the one that has dominated steadily loses influence, and the other

---

57. Melissus denies that this kind of motion is possible (**15.9** sec. 9–10); Parmenides' argument against motion (**11.8** lines 26–31) depends not on the nonexistence of void, but on the absence of temporal distinctions which he had previously proved. See also Aristotle's discussion in *Physics* 4.8.

gains until it has complete control. Of the four phases of the cycle the two extremes are static, the two transition periods dynamic. The processes of increasing mixture and increasing separation that take place in the transition periods have as their limits the states achieved at the extremes, at which no further mixture (in the one case) or separation (in the other) is possible. The elements can interact only during the dynamic transition periods; only then are formed a plurality of compounds (including living creatures) that come to be, perish, move, and undergo other sorts of changes and interactions. Compounds and living things are formed in both transition periods. The most striking feature of the cycle is that it involves two separate cosmogonies—one in the period of increasing Love and one in that of increasing Strife—which proceed in reverse directions from one another, the one occurring as the four elements move from complete separation to complete unity, and the other occurring as they separate out of the state of complete unification. It likewise involves a separate destruction of the KOSMOS for each transition period.[58] The KOSMOS as we know it is not permanent, but doomed—a temporary by-product of the effects of Love and Strife on the four elements—yet other KOSMOI will arise in future transition phases, to be obliterated in turn in the periods of complete dominance of Love and Strife.[59]

The different phases of the cosmic cycle are unevenly set forth in the existing fragments. **14.47** describes the transition from the reign of Strife to the reign of Love. The fragment begins where Strife has reached the lowest depth of the whirl and has pinned Love in the center (lines 3–4). At that point, the four elements begin to unite. Ultimately they join together perfectly as a single thing (l. 5), but this does not happen instantaneously (l. 6). As they unite under the influence of Love, many temporary ("mortal") compounds are formed (l. 7), but these compounds form only in regions to which Love's power has extended. Strife retreats gradually to the

---

58. Hence the "double coming to be of mortal things" and their "double failing" mentioned most prominently in **14.19**.

59. My view of the cosmic cycle agrees in its general lines with the orthodox interpretation (Guthrie, *HGP*; O'Brien, *Empedocles' Cosmic Cycle* [Cambridge, 1969]; Barnes, *The Presocratic Philosophers*, rev. ed. [London, 1982]; Wright, *Empedocles: The Extant Fragments* [New Haven, 1981]) and recently defended by Graham ("Symmetry in the Empedoclean Cycle," *Classical Quarterly* 38 [1988]: 297–312). Revisionist readings abound. Several are set out and discussed by A. Long ("Empedocles' Cosmic Cycle in the 'Sixties," in *The Presocratics*, ed. A. Mourelatos, [Garden City, N.J., 1974], pp. 397–425) who proposes one more of his own. Also notable are KRS and Osborne, "Empedocles Recycled," *Classical Quarterly* 37 (1987): 24–50.

edge of the KOSMOS (lines 9–11, see also **14.48**), and mixture does not occur where Strife is still present (lines 8–9). Love chases Strife away (lines 12–13). In general, this phase of the cosmic cycle is marked by the mixture of immortal elements to form mortal compounds (lines 14–17).[60]

When Love triumphs completely, there is no longer any separation or any distinct compounds. All that exists of all the elements is blended into a single, featureless, motionless, unchanging sphere, held fast by the bonding force of Love.[61] This state is described in **14.50**, **14.51**, **14.52**, and **14.53**. Very little survives about the other two phases. The next transition stage begins at its appointed time with movement in the sphere (**14.54**, **14.55**) As Strife becomes more prominent, the four elements separate (**14.9**). The condition of total Strife is not described in extant fragments, but must be inferred from information in **14.19** (especially lines 8–10, 16–18). The physical process by which this separation happens is called a whirl or vortex (**14.47** lines 3–4), as in Anaxagoras' system (see above, pp. 223–24). Aristotle declares why a vortex is an appropriate mechanism for Empedocles to use.

> **14.149** And so, if the earth is now at rest by compulsion, it came together, brought to the middle by the vortex motion. For all identify this as the cause, judging by what happens in liquids and in the air. For in them the larger and heavier things are carried towards the middle of the vortex. (Aristotle, *On the Heaven* 2.13 295a9–13 = DK 59A88)

The circular motion observed in whirlwinds and whirlpools sorts things by size and weight. This mechanism accounts for why, in the present state of the KOSMOS—in which the effects of Strife are widespread and there is considerable, though not complete, separation of the elements—earth, the heaviest of the four elements, is in the center, and is surrounded successively by water, air, and fire. Further, there is evidence that the cosmic

---

60. **14.47** l. 14 need not cause problems. Fire, say, is immortal, but sometimes a bit of fire is formed into a compound and sometimes it is not. In the latter case it appears as fire, in the former it does not. And since fire (the element, though not a particular flame) is immortal and compounds are mortal, Empedocles treats himself to a mildly paradoxical expression.

61. Aristotle, followed by Philoponus, complains that the uniformity of the Sphere contradicts the permanence of the four elements and their inability to change into one another. (Aristotle, *On Generation and Corruption* 1.1 315a4–14, not in DK; Philoponus, *Commentary on Aristotle's On Generation and Corruption* 19.3–20.4 = DK 31A41). The permanence of the elements can be sustained if we suppose that their identity is preserved in the sphere as it is in "mortal" compounds where, as happens in the sphere (**14.50** l. 1), the constituent bits of the elements that form the compounds are not recognizable as such.

vortex exists: the circular movements of the heavenly bodies around the earth. When separation is complete, Strife reigns supreme, and the cycle is ready to continue once again into the transition to the reign of Love.

The cosmic cycle efficiently accounts for the workings of the KOSMOS. It requires only the four elements and two motive principles already discussed, and it does not postulate any properties of Love and Strife aside from their functions of uniting and separating. It makes clever use of the Anaximandrian concept of dynamic equilibrium of opposed principles and of the Heraclitean concept of stability through change (cf. **14.19, 14.45**). The fact that the elements are immortal and have always behaved in this cyclical pattern makes it unnecessary to account for how they came to be or started to behave that way in the first place, so that Empedocles does not fall foul of Parmenides' use of the Principle of Sufficient Reason (**11.8** lines 9–10).

The general outline of the cosmic cycle is clear, but several of its details require discussion. (1) Although his system is founded on a cyclical alternation of Love and Strife, Empedocles says little to explain why the alternation takes place. **14.54** suggests that there is a set time for Strife (and also, no doubt, for Love) to prevail, so that the cycle is regular, but it offers no physical explanation, only a reference to "a broad oath," an image reminiscent of Anaximander's "ordering of time" (**5.22**) and Heraclitus' "ever-living fire . . . kindled in measures and extinguished in measures" (**10.71**), and perhaps of Parmenides' "limits of great bonds" (**11.8** lines 26, 31). Aristotle's sour comment on this fragment

> **14.150** At the same time he says nothing about the cause of the change, except that it is naturally that way.
> (Aristotle, *Metaphysics* 3.4 1000b12–13 = DK 31A30)

is perhaps unfair, since if the alternation of Love and Strife is a basic fact of the system, it is also a brute fact, incapable of explanation within the system. From the systematic point of view, Aristotle has a point: Empedocles just asserts that that is how it is. But the reference to an oath—an unbreakable, sacred principle voluntarily agreed to by the two great equal powers—removes the claim from the level of mere assertion and grounds the system in a transcendental religious conception that can provide the needed guarantee of everlasting stability.

(2) The dual births and destructions of the KOSMOS imply that both generation and destruction are attributable to Love and also to Strife, despite Empedocles' tendency to speak of Love as causing generation and Strife as causing destruction (e.g. **14.22, 14.24, ?14.26, 14.27**). Since KOSMOI and compounds can no more exist in the Sphere of Love than in the complete

separation under total Strife, for Love to achieve domination involves the
destruction of all compounds and the KOSMOS that arose in the transition
from Strife to Love, and equally, the formation of KOSMOS and compounds
in the opposite transition phase is due to Strife's breaking up the Sphere
of Love.

(3) Although the surviving fragments do not say so, the present KOSMOS
is located in the period of increasing Strife.

> **14.151** He says that the KOSMOS is in a like state both now in the period of
> [sc. increasing] Strife and previously in the period of [sc. increasing]
> Love.
>
> (Aristotle, *On Generation and Corruption* 2.6 334a5–7 = DK 31A42)

The elements are now mostly separated, with the vast bulk of each already
separate from the others, so Strife must be far along in its advance towards
total rule. This situation may account for the prevalence of hostility and
war among humans. Since we live in a period of increasing Strife, the
present is worse than the past and the future will be worse yet—a view
supported by traditional stories about a decline from a Golden Age.

(4) The cycle is symmetric—there are similar states of the KOSMOS in
each transition phase. The strongest evidence for this important feature is
14.151. It follows that the history of the birth, growth, maturity, decline,
and death of the KOSMOS in its present phase is just the reverse of the
events that take place in the opposite phase. This fact has two major
consequences: it makes Empedocles' work easier, since some events are
easier to describe and understand as due to separation and others as due to
unification, and it effectively doubles the amount of our knowledge about
the specifics of Empedocles' dual cosmogonies.

(5) Although the KOSMOS that occurs in the period of increasing Love is
described in outline in **14.47**, Empedocles failed to provide a detailed
cosmogony for this phase.

> **14.152** It is not reasonable to produce an account of coming to be from things
> which are separated and in motion. For this reason even Empedocles
> omits an account of coming to be in the period of [sc. increasing]
> Love. For he would not be able to put together the heaven by con-
> structing it out of separate things, and making the compound through
> Love. For the KOSMOS is composed of separate elements, so that it
> must have come to be from a single united thing.
>
> (Aristotle, *On the Heaven* 3.2 301a14–20 = DK 31A42)

Such a cosmogony would proceed backwards from other Greek cosmogonies, which describe the process of differentiation of plurality out of an

original unity. Nevertheless, **14.47** indicates briefly that compounds are formed in the period of increasing Love, and some of the remarks on the origin of animals refer to this period. Conversely, a cosmogony starting from the Sphere of Love would resemble other cosmogonies and would not present any special problems.

(6) The universe is spherical in all four phases. At the time of Love's total dominance, there is a single spherical compound of all that exists of the four elements (**14.50, 14.52, 14.53**). In the present transition period (and so in the opposite one too), the KOSMOS is also spherical, as witnessed by the cosmic vortex (**14.149**, cf. **14.47** l. 4), the statement that in the transition period from total Strife to total Love, Strife was retreating "to the furthest limits of the circle" (**14.47** l. 10),[62] and by later accounts of Empedocles' cosmology (e.g., **14.154**). It is likely that when Strife has complete rule the universe is spherical too—with all the earth gathered in a sphere at the center and surrounded by spherical shells of water, air, and fire, as is largely the case now.

(7) While the transition periods are obviously times of change and movement, the extreme phases know no change. In addition, the Sphere of Love[63] is motionless, as **14.52** may say[64] and **14.55** strongly suggests. Aristotle implies that under complete Strife the sphere keeps rotating with the vortex motion, which was the mechanical means by which Strife caused the elements to separate.

14.153 This [the vortex] is the reason all who generate the heavens give for the earth's coming together at the center; but they seek the explanation for why it remains. . . . Others, like Empedocles, say that the circular motion of the heavens, which is faster than that of the earth, prevents it like water in cups and for the same reasons. For when the cup is whirled in a circle the water, whose natural movement is downward, does not fall down, even though it is often underneath the bronze. Although if the vortex did not prevent it . . . where will it move? For it moves to the middle by constraint and stays there by constraint.

        (Aristotle, *On the Heaven* 2.13 295a13–24 part = DK 31A67)

62. KUKLOS, the word translated "circle," is frequently used of the spherical vault of heaven.

63. I shall continue to refer to the KOSMOS during the period of Love's total dominance in this customary way even though the world is spherical in the other periods too.

64. The word in question, MONIĒ, can be derived from MONOS, "alone," or from MENŌ, "to remain"; hence the alternative translations.

(8) How long do the phases last? **14.151** and the principle of symmetry it suggests call for the transition periods to have the same length, which Empedocles did not specify, but which must be quite lengthy—long enough for the elements to form into a KOSMOS, and for the KOSMOS to run its course. Symmetry would also require the periods of total Love and total Strife to have the same length as each other, but not necessarily the same as the transition periods; but this is not certain. **14.47** l. 5 makes it likely that the period of total Strife is instantaneous: all things begin to come together at the very moment when Strife has achieved its maximum effect. On the other hand, the Sphere of Love is described in ways that make it seem to last more than an instant. The evidence for both extreme phases is weak, however, and it can be taken in ways consistent with the phases of maximal Love and Strife both instantaneous, with both of them lasting for an extended period, and with the phase of maximal Love extended and that of Strife instantaneous.[65] The best Empedoclean evidence on the point is **14.19** lines 12–13: "in that they never cease interchanging continually, in this way they are unchanging in the cycle." If we take "interchanging continually" seriously, there can be only instants of maximum Love and Strife—another application of Heraclitus' principle of stability through change.

(9) Where are Love and Strife located during the cosmic process? **14.47** begins at the phase where Strife reigns supreme: it has driven Love to the center and occupies the whole vortex. Then Strife gradually withdraws and Love gradually moves out from the center to occupy more and more territory. When Love triumphs completely she occupies the whole and Strife is at the extremity.

At this point Empedocles' inability to conceive of anything existing without a spatial location causes difficulties. Love and Strife are eternal, so they must always be somewhere. So even when Love is totally dominant Strife must be somewhere, and likewise Love must be somewhere when Strife rules supreme. Yet there is nowhere apart from the region occupied—and occupied without gaps—by the four elements. So even at their periods of no influence, Love and Strife still occupy *some* territory, which means that they are present in some region occupied by one or more of the elements, which means that they are causing their characteristic effects in those regions, since for them to be somewhere is for them to act there. But this implies that there are *no* times at which either is completely dominant, which conflicts with Empedocles' claims that there are. Empedocles mini-

---

65. **14.54** need not imply a period of rest under the Sphere of Love, only that Strife's period of ascent happens at the right time and takes the right length of time.

mizes this problem by confining Love to "the middle of the whirl" and Strife to "the furthest limits of the circle," but it is a problem that he cannot make vanish completely.

Another problem arises in connection with the locations of Love and Strife during the transition periods. **14.47** strongly suggests that at any moment during those phases, Love completely controls a determinate volume, a sphere with a definite radius, whose center is the center of the universe; and Strife completely controls the rest, a spherical shell extending from just where Love leaves off to the extremity. But this interpretation seems impossible to maintain, since it implies that at any given moment there is no region of the universe where the effects of both Love and Strife are felt, whereas this is plainly the case in our current situation, where "mortal" compounds are seen to be formed (through Love) and subsequently destroyed (through Strife). The geographical implications of **14.47** simply cannot be pursued so far in this direction. Empedocles must allow for regions where neither Love nor Strife is fully in control. It is therefore tempting to suppose that the geographical language of **14.47** is metaphorical and that Empedocles really means that at any moment, apart from the total domination of Love or Strife, the effects of both are felt throughout the universe. For example, near the time of Strife's complete control, Strife will be present everywhere in nearly full strength and Love will be present everywhere too, though with hardly any strength.[66] Compounds dissolve much more easily than they are formed or held together, but the small amount of Love still left is able to be concentrated sufficiently here and there to overcome Strife locally and permit compounds to be formed and to stay together at least for a time. But **14.47** lines 8–11 make it difficult to accept such a metaphorical reading as the whole truth: during the increase of Love some things (at least for awhile) are "still held back aloft": Strife's power over them is still complete. It therefore seems likely that Empedocles believed that at any moment in the transition periods there is a region where Love holds complete sway, one where Strife does, and one where the effects of both are felt. As Love increases, the first of these regions grows from the center to occupy the entire universe, the second shrinks from occupying the whole universe to occupying as small a space at the extremity as is compatible with the remarks in the previous paragraph, and the third at first grows and then shrinks back to no size at all. Whether it grows so

---

66. This is not to say that Love and Strife can occupy precisely the same spot; a given region may contain some places where Love prevails (where there are compounds) and others where Strife does (where the elements are separate). At the moment being described, there are few compounds, and these are distributed through the universe.

large as to occupy the entire universe is not clear, though this view is compatible with the fragments and is possibly the most satisfying interpretation. Thus, at the midpoint of each transition period Love and Strife have equal power everywhere—the universe is equally balanced between them: the battle is equal.

Origin and Structure of the Present KOSMOS

In **14.9** Empedocles promises to tell how the present KOSMOS developed. The following testimonia, not all of them easily reconcilable, give a general picture.

14.154 Out of the first mixture of the elements, the air was separated off and it flowed round in a circle. After the air, the fire escaped, and since it did not have anywhere else to go, it ran out upwards underneath the solid barrier around the air. There are two hemispheres moving in a circle around the earth, one entirely of fire, and the other a mixture of air and a little fire, which he believes to be night. The origin of the motion resulted from a chance collection in one region of fire which weighed heavily. In its nature the sun is not fire, but a reflection of fire like that which occurs from water. He declares that the moon was formed separately out of the air that was cut off by the fire. For this air solidified like hail. It has its light from the sun.
(pseudo-Plutarch, *Stromata*, quoted in Eusebius, *Preparation for the Gospel* 1.8.10 = DK 31A30)

14.155 The AITHER was separated apart first, fire second, next the earth, and water gushed forth from the earth when it was excessively constricted by the force of the rotation. The air was evaporated from the water and the heaven came to be out of the AITHER, and the sun from the fire, and the bodies round the earth were "felted" from the others.
(Aetius 2.6.3 = DK 31A49)[67]

The overall resemblance and the differences between this account and those of earlier Presocratics (especially Anaximander and Anaximenes) are noteworthy.[68] Empedocles is in the same tradition, but improves on his predecessors. **14.154** and **14.155** make no mention of Love or Strife, but in

67. **14.155**'s distinction between AER ("air") and AITHER does not entail a fifth element. It recalls the distinction, as old as Homer, between the bright upper air (AITHER) and the murky lower air (AER) (see p. 50). Since Empedocles calls one of his four elements AIR and AITHER indifferently, we should probably think of these as two forms of the same element.

68. See pp. 36–37, 55–56.

both the effects of the vortex are apparent: the four elements are largely separated and the gross structure of the universe is established, with earth in the center, seas on the earth's surface, atmospheric air above that, and the region of fire above that. The heavenly bodies are formed. The KOSMOS has a finite size (14.56), and in it the separation of the elements is not complete (14.57–14.60). Though some details are obscure, in general the account of the formation and state of the present KOSMOS conforms to Empedocles' physical theory and cosmic cycle. Empedocles had a considerable interest in astronomy, especially in the sun and moon (14.61–14.70). He states that the moon shines with light reflected from the sun (14.65, 14.66), gives the correct explanation of solar eclipses (14.67), and correctly holds night to be due to the earth's shadow (14.69).

Generation of Animals

14.156 The first generations of animals and plants came to be in no way complete, but split apart with parts not grown together. The second generations arose when the parts grew together, and were like images of fantasy. The third were of whole-natured beings. The fourth no longer arose from the elements, such as earth and water, but from each other from that time, in some because the nourishment grew thick and in others because the beauty of the females caused an excitement of the sexual impulse. (Aetius 5.19.5 = DK 31A72)

We possess fragments which bear on all four of the stages that this passage identifies (Stage 1: **14.76, 14.77**; Stage 2: **14.78–14.80**; Stages 3 and 4: **14.81**).

Stage 1 occurs in the period of increasing Love.[69] Since Strife is still largely dominant, compounds form with difficulty. Love has enough influence to unite elements to form body parts which "wandered about aiming at mixture" (**14.77**, cf. **14.21** lines 7–8), but not enough to unite the body parts into animals.

As Love's influence increases, greater intermixture becomes possible, and we reach Stage 2. In **14.78**, I understand the "divinities" to be the four elements and "these things" to be the isolated body parts formed in Stage 1. Previously they "wandered about" but were unable to join together. Now they are able to do so when they "chance to meet." The increased power of Love ensures that they will meet, but still it is an apparently random process, which forms monstrous combinations such as minotaurs and centaurs. The following passage is evidence that this same process led to extant types of animals as well.

69. Aristotle, *On the Heaven* 3.2 300b30 (= DK 31B57).

14.157 Empedocles says that . . . next came together these ox-headed man-progeny, i.e., made of an ox and a human. And all the parts that were fitted together in a manner which enabled them to be preserved became animals and remained because they fulfilled each other's needs—the teeth cutting and softening the food, the stomach digesting it, the liver turning it into blood. And when the head of a human came together with a human body, it caused the whole to be preserved, but it does not fit together with the body of an ox, and so it is destroyed. For whatever did not come together according to the appropriate formula perished. (Simplicius, *Commentary on Aristotle's Physics* 371.33–372.8 = DK 31B61)

The natural history of humans and other living species thus begins in Stage 2, when limbs happen to form viable combinations. In a viable species the parts "fitted together" not only in such a way that the individual can survive (the point of **14.157**), but also in a way that makes reproduction possible, so that the species can continue itself without having to be renewed by further chance combinations of limbs. The situation where animals renew their own kinds apparently represents a still further advance of Love.

The general picture so far requires a few remarks. First, the grotesque picture of body parts being formed and wandering about in isolation from one another is absurd to anyone who thinks of them as organic parts rather than simply as material components. Aristotle, the great teleologist, ridicules this notion of random combinations and says that Empedocles should have admitted "olive-headed vine-progeny" as well[70]—a suggestion we may suppose he would have accepted. Aristotle argues that the body parts are formed and put together "for an end," and therefore not by chance.[71] In terms of the examples of **14.157**, teeth come to be for the end of cutting and softening the food, and so an animal is an organic whole, made up of parts which cooperate for the survival of the individual and the species. By contrast, Empedocles, with his view that survival is due to chance rather than design and is determined by fitness to survive, is more modern than Aristotle, whose teleological approach to nature precludes randomness and chance from playing a significant role.

Second, **14.157** speaks of humans being originally formed in Stage 2, which occurs in the period of increasing Love. Since the world is now in the period of increasing Strife (**14.156**), this is important evidence for the view that the same things occur in both transition phases.

Finally, the claim in **14.157** that humans are formed in Stage 2, together with its obvious implication that from that point onwards humans would

70. Aristotle, *Physics* 2.8 199b10–13 (= DK 31B62).
71. Aristotle, *Physics* 2.8.

reproduce themselves, conflicts with **14.156**, which places sexual reproduction in Stage 4, with the "whole-natured beings" of Stage 3 in between. I shall return to this crucial point.

14.81 is devoted to Stage 3, mentioned in **14.156**, and as lines 1–2 indicate, Stage 3 arose before humans did.[72] But it says that the "whole-natured forms" arose first, not third, and that they did so "as it was being separated." Further, the last two lines strongly suggest that individual limbs had not yet come to be. The obvious place in the cosmic cycle for such a situation to occur is shortly after the breakup of the Sphere of Love, when Strife has little power and the elements are still mostly in a state of mixture, with little differentiation and fragmentation yet occurring. In contrast to the first stage, in which individual limbs wandered around, we now have beings in which no distinct limbs are evident (**14.81** lines 7–8). These odd beings made of earth joined with portions of air ("heat"), water, and fire are in some way the ancestors of humans. The word "shoot" in the sense of "sapling" (l. 2) suggests that these beings somehow mature into full human form, but it is difficult to imagine how the transformation could come about. Perhaps as the increase of Strife leads to further differentiation these creatures split apart to form familiar kinds of animals.[73] The explicit denial that the "whole-natured forms" had sexual organs (l. 8) reveals that sexual reproduction, and probably reproduction in general, was not possible in this stage, so that once again Empedocles holds that self-reproducing species occur only during what **14.156** identifies as Stage 4.

On the overall interpretation here being offered of symmetry between the two transition periods, all four stages of animal development will occur in each period. The sequence in the period of increasing Love will be 1—2—4—3, and in the period of increasing Strife it will be 3—4—2—1.[74] Since our present (fourth) stage is the only one in which animals are able to reproduce their kind, there is a sense in which we live in the highest stage of development, but this is not Empedocles' view. For the increasing domi-

---

72. Simplicius confirms this point: "Empedocles speaks these verses in the second book of the *Physics* before the articulation of male and female bodies" (*Commentary on Aristotle's Physics* 381.29–30 = DK 31B62).

73. An account along these lines, which some think to be related more or less closely to Empedocles' account, can be found in Plato, *Symposium* 189e ff.

74. Some interpreters claim that Empedocles has a single account of the origin of animals extending over both transition periods: Stages 1 and 2 occurring in the period of increasing Love and Stages 3 and 4 in the period of increasing Strife. I consider this reading wholly implausible in view of the gross discontinuity it requires between Stages 2 and 3, when everything is fused in the Sphere of Love, as well as of the evidence of **14.157** that humans arose in the period of increasing Love.

nance of Strife over Love has psychological and moral implications. In important ways the sphere of Love is the best period of existence, in some way a golden age of peace and harmony to be yearned for. And within the present condition of animal nature (Stage 4) life was happier and more harmonious earlier, when Love was more powerful, as described in **14.82** and **14.83**. The thought of an increase over the amount of Strife already present in the world is a grim prospect to be viewed with dread.

Physiology

A doctor as well as a philosopher, Empedocles was famed as the founder of the Sicilian medical tradition, which rivalled Hippocrates' school at Cos, and was called the empirical school because of its reliance on observation. His interest in humans and animals is evident in his cosmology and his discussion of the principles of his system. His examples of mixtures of the elements are usually animals or their parts, his standard word for nonpermanent compounds is "mortals," and he frequently calls the parts of the universe or the elements "limbs."

Not enough survives from his accounts of animals and plants to make any reconstruction possible, but his biological interests were unusually wide (**14.94–14.104**), he made efforts to relate biological phenomena to his physical theory (**14.97**), and he was keen to identify similarities between plants and animals (**14.94, 14.101**). He developed elaborate theories of many physiological processes, notably reproduction (**14.84–14.93**), digestion (**14.106**), perception (**14.107–14.114**), and thought (**14.115–14.119**), as well as offering speculations on the material composition of bodily parts (**14.37, 14.38**).

Fragment **14.105** contains a fascinating discussion of respiration. The phenomena to be explained are inhalation and exhalation of air. Where does air go after passing through the nose, how does it enter the body, and what pulls it in and drives it out? Empedocles explains breathing as due to the movement of blood within the body. Little hollow tubes full of blood lead into the body from the interior of the nostrils. When the blood withdraws inwardly, air rushes in to fill the gap, and is expelled again when the blood returns to occupy the tubes once more. What makes the fragment so interesting is Empedocles' comparison of this process with the action of a clepsydra, a device made of baked clay, which looked something like an old showerhead, perforated at the bottom with many small holes. It could be used to take a measure of water or wine out of a large container and transfer it to a small one—a useful device for serving drinks at parties—but it would also have made a delightful toy for children. Empedocles uses it as a simile, in fact a model, for how respiration takes place, and it quite possibly provided the inspiration for his theory. (This is typical of Empedocles' philosophical style. We have already seen him using an analogy taken from a craft—a painter mixing primary colors on a palate [**14.28**]—to account for another natural phenomenon.) The comparison works best if the air we breathe corresponds to the water taken up by the clepsydra, the blood in our bodies to the air in the clepsydra, and the mouths of the internal tubes to the small holes in the clepsydra. The essence of the comparison is that (a) as air in the clepsydra keeps water out, so the blood in our tubes keeps air out, (b) as water enters the clepsydra when the air retreats, so air rushes into the tubes when the blood retreats, and (c) as the water leaves the clepsydra when air returns, so the air is expelled from the tubes when the blood returns. The comparison therefore works at the descriptive level but does not explain the phenomenon of respiration. Empedocles does not suggest that there is anything in us corresponding to the girl or her finger, and there are elements in the clepsydra case that do not apply in the case of breathing. Nothing in respiration corresponds to the clepsydra's ability to retain liquids when the upper opening is blocked. Empedocles does not claim that the air we breathe in is trapped in us. Likewise, nothing in the clepsydra corresponds to the fact that blood does not (normally) get expelled after the air. Though both air and water can pass through the perforations of the clepsydra, something about our structure keeps the blood from flowing out through the tubes (Empedocles might have attributed this fact to blood's being thicker than air, and so unable to pass through the tubes' mouths, which are narrower than the rest of the tubes), but the comparison does not explain it.

14.105 is sometimes said to contain a report of a scientific experiment. If so, it is the earliest record of an experiment in Greek science, and one of the few from all antiquity. (In this respect Greek science differs strikingly from modern science.) But Empedocles is not describing anything like a scientific experiment as we now understand the term. First, it occurs as a simile, a literary device. Second, Empedocles does not say that he performed the operation he describes. Third, no properties of a clepsydra could possibly give experimental evidence for a theory of breathing. Fourth, the behaviors of the child and the clepsydra are familiar, whereas an experiment is a procedure whose outcome is unknown before the experiment is performed. Finally, in an experiment, the outcome confirms or refutes an hypothesis; the experiment tests the hypothesis. But belief in the theory of respiration is neither strengthened nor weakened by the comparison with the clepsydra.

Perception and Cognition

Empedocles' discussion of sense-perception relies on his theory of pores, used also to explain properties of mixtures (**14.147**). Physical objects give off effluences—constant streams of particles (**14.108**). (**14.112**, which apparently describes how dogs follow the scents of animals, illustrates how this thesis applies to the sense of smell.) We become aware of the effluences when they strike us and pass through the appropriate pores.

> **14.158** Empedocles speaks similarly about all the senses and says that perception occurs by a process of fitting into the pores of each sense. This is why they cannot distinguish each other's objects, since the pores of some happen to be too wide or too narrow for the perceived thing, since some objects pass through without coming into contact and others are altogether unable to enter.
>
> (Theophrastus, *On Sensation* 7 = DK 31A86)

Once the effluences have penetrated the proper pores, we become aware of them by virtue of the presence of the elements in the sense organ, for Empedocles made perception an instance of the principle that "like affects like" (**14.107**).

Empedocles' treatment of the senses was the most detailed up to his time,[75] and most of our information concerns his theory of sight. Two mechanisms are instrumental for vision: effluences from visible objects that strike the eye, and fire emitted by the eye itself. This phenomenon is described in **14.109**, which employs a simile.[76] This phenomenon too is due to effluences and pores. The pores in the pupil permit the fire to leave the eye while keeping in the water of the aqueous humor. How the emitted fire and the effluences from visible objects interact to enable us to see is obscure. Empedocles was also interested in other issues regarding vision—how we form a single visual image from two eyes (**14.110**) and why some see better by day and others by night (**14.111**). He also had views on why eyes are of different colors and on how mirrors work.

He had a theory of pleasure and pain closely related to his theory of perception:

> **14.159** We feel pleasure by things that are alike in their parts and mixture, and pain by opposites . . . [so that they are] certain perceptions or accompanied by perception.
>
> (Theophrastus, *On Sensation* 9, 16 = DK 31A86)

Finally, thought too works on the principle of "like by like" (**14.119, 14.118**). Thought takes place not in the brain but in the blood around the heart

---

75. A lengthy account of his doctrines on perception is found in Theophrastus, *On Sensation* 7–24 (= DK 31A86). This passage is translated by Inwood, op. cit. (p. 256 n. 27). See also Guthrie, *HGP*, vol. 2, pp. 228–43.

76. Many of the comments on the simile in **14.105** apply here too. See pp. 281–82.

(**14.115**). In fact, **14.115** identifies thought with this blood. Blood is the seat of thought because, being composed of all four elements in equal proportions (**14.38**), it is most receptive, able to be affected by all physical things. Different thoughts are due to differences in the composition of our blood from time to time **14.116**.[77] On this crude theory Empedocles cannot distinguish between thought and perception, but he does distinguish between the means of thinking and perceiving on the one hand and the perceiver or thinker on the other: by means of the earth, water, etc., in the blood, we, the percipient beings, are able to see earth, water, etc. Even so, it can be objected that we perceive not merely the four elements, but also compounds, and Empedocles owes us an account of how this happens.

> **14.160** For they suppose that we recognize like by like, as if supposing that the soul were the *things*. But these [the four elements] are not the only things, but there are also many others, or rather things composed of the elements are perhaps infinite in number. Now grant that the soul recognizes or perceives what each of these is composed of, still by what will it recognize or perceive the compound? For example, what is a god or a human or flesh or bone? And likewise for any other compound. For each of these is not simply the elements in any which way, but with some formula and composition, as even Empedocles speaks of bone [**14.37**]. So there is no benefit for the elements to be in the soul unless the proportions and composition are going to be there too. For each one will recognize what is like it, but nothing will recognize the bone or the human, unless these too will be in it. But there is no need to say that this is impossible, for who would wonder whether there is a stone or a man in the soul, and likewise for the good and the not good. And the same holds for the rest.
> (Aristotle, *On the Soul* 1.5 409b26–410a13, not in DK)

Despite the obvious shortcomings of Empedocles' theories of perception and cognition, they are worked out within the terms of his physical theory. In effect he did not consider psychology separate from physiology, which is a part of physics. The fact that Empedocles has much more to say on these subjects than his forebears may stem from his concerns to rebut Parmenides' rejection of the senses and the thoughts of mortals. By explaining how our sensations and thoughts arise from interaction between our bodies and the outside world, Empedocles takes an important step towards establishing that our perceptions and thoughts are or can be reliable (see **14.8**, **14.17**, **14.6**). **14.4**, unless it is meant to be purely figurative, may allude to a physical process involved in understanding what our senses apprehend, but it is tantalizingly obscure.

77. That there can be differences in composition of the blood is hinted at in **14.38**, l. 4, "a bit more or a bit less."

The Fate of the DAIMONES

Empedocles' "religious" teachings I take to be the point of his philosophy; the physical theory, cosmic cycle, and other topics so far discussed set the stage for the account of the DAIMONES: their initial happy state, original sin and Fall, subsequent sufferings, and ultimate prospects for regaining paradise.

14.18 introduces this subject in terms that link it closely with the physical theory: the broad oaths that render the punishment inevitable (lines 1–2) recall the broad oath that fixes the time when Strife begins to disrupt the sphere of Love (**14.54** l. 3), the outcast divinities are driven the rounds of the four elements (lines 9–11), the vortex of the heavens is mentioned (l. 11). Three other features of the fragment are noteworthy. First, Empedocles does not present this doctrine as an impersonal observer. He, too, is suffering the effects of previously incurred pollution and is anguished at his situation (lines 12–14). Second, he attributes his present miserable state to his having placed his "reliance on raving Strife" (l. 14, cf. l. 4). Strife's moral dimension as evil is foremost, as the goodness of Love is emphasized in other fragments. Third, the unhappy divinities are exiles from the gods (l. 13), having fallen from a happy state of association with the blessed ones (l. 6).

The happy state of the pure divinities is described in **14.82**: Love (Cypris) reigns supreme (l. 3), not Ares, the god of war, or Zeus with his violent thunderbolt, or Kronos who gained power by castrating his father;[78] bloodshed was unknown, and all animate nature lived harmoniously (**14.83**). This blessed state ended as Strife increased. Killing took place for the first time, and polluted divinities began to suffer the punishment described above. A number of fragments describe their Fall and unhappy state (**14.120–14.129**). As the divinities endure their long exile (**14.18** l. 7), they are born into the bodies of living things one after another. Empedocles' doctrine of reincarnation depends heavily on Pythagorean beliefs. He lists his own previous incarnations in **14.130** and describes Pythagoras in a way suggestive of this doctrine (**9.6**). Certain incarnations are better than others (**14.131**) Incarnation as a human is best, and among humans prophets, bards, physicians, and political leaders are closest to the divine (**14.132**). Empedocles himself was a prophet, bard, and physician, and played a leading role in politics at Acragas. His claim to be a god (**14.1** l. 4) (if it is that[79]) is only an anticipation of his next life, and his close connection with divine functions of prophecy, healing (the work of Apollo and Asclepius), and music (depending on direct inspiration of the Muse) also warrants his

---

78. See p. 8.
79. See p. 287 n. 82.

claim to knowledge of the divine truth (see **14.15**), which makes him and others like him, blessed (**14.13**). **14.132** presents the prospect of leaving this vale of tears and returning once again to our former happy state, described wistfully in **14.133**.

In a sense that is not made clear, a fallen DAIMON "grows to be," "comes to be," or "is" different kinds of living things (**14.18** l. 7, **14.130**–**14.132**). In speaking of his own past, Empedocles says "*I* have become . . . " (**14.130**). Thus, the fragments imply that the DAIMON preserves its identity through its incarnations, and more strongly that a living thing's own identity continues from one incarnation to the next. Thus, the DAIMON is the bearer of personal identity. The body is not. Bodies are merely "alien garbs of flesh" (**14.127**), which the DAIMON wears and discards. The DAIMON occupies the place of the soul (PSUCHE) in the Pythagorean doctrine of reincarnation. By calling it DAIMON rather than PSUCHE,[80] Empedocles stresses our transcendental and divine nature.

The critical issue in a redemptionist view of this type is what, if anything, we must do to achieve or hasten our salvation. Taken literally, **14.18** l. 6 implies a negative answer: fallen DAIMONES are sentenced to a fixed period of exile: thirty-thousand seasons. But this round figure may mean only that the exile is for a very long period, not necessarily of definite length, an interpretation that agrees with Empedocles' insistent zeal to instruct and reform. For if salvation is simply a matter of serving time, it is hard to see what is to be gained from the purifications Empedocles prescribes.

Most prominent are abstinence from killing animals and eating meat. Killing, which violates a universal law (**14.135**), is the cause of the DAIMONES' Fall (**14.18**, **14.136**) and the cause of continuing pollution. **14.137** explains why we must avoid killing: all living beings are related through reincarnation, so the pollution incurred is the same as if you kill your nearest human relatives. **14.138** draws the implications that all killing is murder, every act of eating meat is cannibalism. **14.139** and **14.140** also seem related to this subject.

Empedocles enjoins other prohibitions as well.

14.161 He teaches his listeners to be continent regarding sexual intercourse with a woman, lest they collaborate and cooperate in the works which Strife produces, always dissolving and destroying the works of Love.
(Hippolytus, *Refutation* 7.2.9., printed as a context of DK 31B115)

---

80. Claims like this are not meant to be taken dogmatically, since so much of the original work is lost. Still, the word PSUCHE occurs only once in Empedocles' fragments (**14.139**), and there it means "life."

There are also specific prohibitions against eating (or touching?) laurel leaves and beans (**14.141**, **14.142**), the former doubtless connected with **14.132** and the latter showing Empedocles' Pythagorean connections.[81] In general, **14.143** commands us to avoid evildoing. In a positive direction, Empedocles stresses the importance of knowledge about the gods (cf. **14.15,14.13**).

This is not the place to venture a thorough treatment of these different doctrines, which perhaps are more at home in a history of religion than of philosophy. But it is important to take up the question of whether Empedocles' "religious" message is compatible with his physical doctrines. The principal difficulty is how to reconcile the apparently immortal nature of the DAIMONES with the two extreme phases of the cosmic cycle, in one of which there are no compounds (including, presumably, the DAIMONES), and in the other of which—where the totality of the four elements is formed into a single compound—there seems to be no place for the gods and DAIMONES of **14.18**.

But are the DAIMONES immortal? Empedocles says only that they "possess immensely long life" (**14.18** l. 5), like the gods (**14.21** l. 12, **14.28** l. 8). In fact, only Love, Strife (**14.23**), and the four elements (e.g. **14.47** l. 14) are clearly immortal.[82] As far as the fragments go, the DAIMONES can be exceptionally long-lasting (yet still "mortal") compounds. The increase of Strife's strength and the breakup of the Sphere of Love are the conditions in which the DAIMONES are differentiated, "born," out of the total mixture of the elements. Likewise, they must perish by the time in the future when the elements become totally separated under Strife, after which they can be born again and perish again at appropriate times in Love's ascendancy.

The DAIMONES are not indifferent to their fate. At any moment in their careers as fallen divinities, DAIMONES yearn for the unity and mutual affection of their parts which occurred before the Fall and even more in the Sphere of Love. It was a gross error to "put their reliance on raving Strife" (**14.18** l. 14), and their complete dissolution into mutually hating parts (cf. **14.22** lines 5–9) under Strife's predominance, although inevitable, is not an end to be desired,[83] and fortunately will not last forever—indeed it may be only instantaneous.[84]

---

81. See pp. 88–89.

82. In **14.15** l. 1, the Muse is called immortal—a conventional epithet—and in **14.1** l. 4 Empedocles need not be calling himself an immortal god: "as it seems" (l. 5) may well mean that *others* consider him such. In the context of **14.21**, the "immortal things" of l. 4 ought to stand for the element air.

83. My view that the DAIMONS' constant aim is to resist the effects of Strife is my principal disagreement with the interpretation of Inwood, op. cit. (p. 256 n. 27), to which the present interpretation is otherwise heavily indebted.

84. See p. 275.

This program fits into Empedocles' cosmic cycle in the following way. The Sphere of Love breaks up when Strife's divisive influence is strong enough to keep the totality of all four elements from bonding together any longer in one uniform compound. It breaks up mainly into compounds in which Love strongly prevails, so that there is a firmly bonded mixture of all four elements. The "whole-natured forms" of **14.81** are found at this stage. As Strife waxes and Love wanes, such uniform compounds become more difficult to form and to maintain in existence, though not impossible. They can be found wherever Love prevails to a sufficient degree locally, as exceptions to the general conditions of increasing separation of the elements. As Strife nears its state of total dominance, they become increasingly rare until finally, at (or shortly before) the moment when Strife crushes Love completely, there is no longer enough Love anywhere for them to exist—although the possibility recurs at (or shortly after) the moment when Love's uniting effects are first felt by the elements that had been wholly separated under total Strife. The situation in the transition period leading up to the reign of Love is symmetric, with such compounds becoming increasingly easier to form and maintain until the moment when they are all unified in the Sphere of Love.

Empedocles' description of god (**14.134**) is in keeping with this picture. God strongly resembles the "whole-natured forms." The only important difference between the account of god and of the "whole-natured forms" is that god is described as "pure mind." But since thought requires the presence of all four elements (**14.115**), it is possible that the "whole-natured forms" *are* gods. For present purposes, though, it is enough that gods are the sorts of things associated with the local prevalence of Love in a strong degree. We may suppose that their life, founded on Love and unity, is happy, unweary, and free of distress (**14.133**), and we may further suppose that the bonding force of Love is so strong in these compounds as to give them "immensely long life." Even the intrusion of a certain amount of Strife need not sunder the bonds, though it would create circumstances that the deity, a thinking, conscious being, would recognize as inferior to its pristine Strife-less state and that it would be strongly motivated to remedy, to the extent possible.

In the present period of increasing Strife, although it is increasingly difficult to expel Strife and return to a state where the constituent parts are bound only by Love, it is certainly worth the effort. And even though the effort is ultimately in vain, since Strife will separate all the elements, it is in vain "ultimately" only in the limited context of the present transition phase. Strife's period of total dominance will end at the time guaranteed by the "broad oath" of **14.54**. In the following transition period, it once again becomes possible to expel Strife locally.

The Sphere of Love is the best possible condition, but it is not within the capacities of individual mortal compounds to bring it about. On the other hand, some mortal compounds have some power to affect the relative prevalence of Love or Strife within themselves, by doing or refraining from certain activities and by thinking friendly or hostile thoughts.

The position of the DAIMONES is now clear. They are long-lived divine beings compounded of all four elements, in which Love has great strength. By committing certain sins a DAIMON introduces Strife into its composition—not enough to disperse its constituents and so destroy it, but enough to disturb the unity that existed before. In punishment it is forced to become living creatures of various kinds. Its goal is to be purified of Strife and return to its state before the Fall, though this is a difficult task to accomplish, given the increase of Strife in the universe and also given the nature of animate existence, which involves Strife-increasing sexual reproduction (**14.161**) and the likelihood of committing Strife-promoting actions unwittingly (**14.138**). But it is not a hopeless task, for at present the power of Love in the KOSMOS is still quite strong, since compounds form and stay together quite well, and since Love's psychological effects are frequently powerful. Earlier on in human existence, it was even easier, to judge by **14.82** and **14.83**.[85] And even though at some point the task does become impossible, until Strife dominates totally there is some Love in the KOSMOS, and hence the possibility and desirability of increasing its local concentration. After Strife's reign, it becomes increasingly feasible to secure a local concentration of Love, which can produce the complete local fusion of elements that constitutes a blessed god. The DAIMON's identity continues when it is a god,[86] although the description of deity in **14.134** leaves little room for individuality. On the other hand, personal identity is lost when the gods are absorbed along with everything else into the Sphere of Love.

Until it becomes a god, the DAIMON will be living things—plants, animals, and humans (**14.131**).[87] Presumably every living thing has a DAIMON. Although some embodiments are better than others (**14.131, 14.132**), it is hard to see how to construct a sequence of species rank-ordered in terms

85. These fragments do not conflict with **14.18**, since **14.82** does not establish that bloodshed had not occurred, only that it was (still) considered "the greatest abomination," and **14.83** does not say that there was no Strife at all, only that Love was still more influential.

86. **14.18** and **14.133** make it clear that there is a plurality of gods, so that our DAIMON is not reabsorbed into a single divine nature at this stage.

87. Will they take on other forms as well? **14.18** describes a passage through the four elements that fallen DAIMONES must endure, and it is unclear how these episodes are related to the series of living incarnations.

of desirability, or to understand why a notorious carnivore should receive top rank among animals. But if it is correct to think that Empedocles' urgent exhortations to change our way of life are aimed at reducing Strife in us so that we can recover our divine birthright, there must be a direct link between behavior in one incarnation and what form the next incarnation takes, although the surviving information on Empedocles does not state this doctrine explicitly.

Following Empedocles' prescriptions will help achieve the nearest state possible in our present place in the cosmic cycle to the divine ideal of total fusion. Abstaining from killing and eating animals will reduce the amount of Strife in which we are involved (and therefore the amount which is involved in us) and similarly will abstaining from heterosexual intercourse (**14.161**). The general command "fast from evil" (**14.143**) amounts to a prohibition on participating in works of Strife (cf. **14.128**).

So far we have only a list of acts to avoid—almost a ritual means to purification. But salvation requires knowledge too. Empedocles' stress on knowing the nature of the gods (**14.13**, **14.15**, cf. **14.14**) is more than conventional piety. Knowledge of the gods requires learning Empedocles' whole philosophy, since the gods' nature must be understood on the one hand in terms of the cosmic system and the physical theory that underlies it, and on the other in terms of the relation between the gods and ourselves, since we have been gods and have the potential to be gods again. We can attain our godhead only through ridding ourselves of Strife, which requires us to know our own nature and that of Strife and its role in the KOSMOS.

Conclusion

Empedocles sparkles like a diamond among the Presocratics—many-faceted and appearing different from different directions. A poet and a politician, a physician and a philosopher, a scientist and a seer, a showman and a charlatan, he was a fallen divinity who proclaimed himself already a god, and a visionary who claimed to control nature. It has been well said that "the Hellenic mind has its romantic as well as its classical aspect, and both reach their climax without incongruity in the genius of this remarkable Sicilian. . . . Empedocles sums up and personifies the spirit of his age and race."[88] I have focussed mainly on his philosophical and scientific views, and only secondarily on his equally remarkable religious message, although I have attempted to defend the two sides of Empedocles' thought from the charge that they contradict one another. It would not be surprising if the same person who was clearly aware of the nature and importance of Parmenides' challenge to our understanding of the world and who developed a

88. Guthrie, *HGP*, vol. 2, p. 126.

cosmic system that met this challenge so effectively also conceived of a doctrine of the role of the individual in this KOSMOS. However, any reconstruction must fill in gaps and smooth out the rough spots caused by materials which join poorly or seem to conflict. For Empedocles leaves crucial questions hanging, and his prophetic style is sometimes too lofty to descend to mean details. Further, his poetic and oracular mode of expression may reflect his manner of thinking. Yet we must keep in mind that it is historically unreasonable to expect much in the way of a detailed, coherent, and consistent account of the KOSMOS: Empedocles' most recent forerunners as cosmologists were Anaxagoras, Parmenides (in *The Way of Mortal Opinions*), and Heraclitus, whose accounts, as far as our evidence permits us to judge, were far less complete and detailed than Empedocles'.

In any case, we must admit that along with Anaxagoras, Empedocles extended the realm of natural inquiry, at times saw the need for detailed discussions, and made noble attempts to rescue the study of the KOSMOS from the Eleatic challenge. With Anaxagoras and Empedocles, philosophy thus reached a new, higher level. This was apparent to Aristotle, who found it important to discuss the ideas of these men more frequently and extensively than those of any earlier Presocratic even though he had a low opinion of Empedocles.[89] It is not so much that their views on astronomy, physiology, etc., were better than those of their predecessors; their contribution is philosophical more than scientific. This, too, is part of Parmenides' legacy. The Eleatic challenge compelled later cosmologists to pay attention to the philosophical foundations of their systems, and the resulting theories have a plausibility lacking in earlier work.

89. *Metaphysics* 1.4 985a5 (= DK 31A39), *On Generation and Corruption* 1.1 315a3–25 (not in DK), 1.8 326b6–28 (not in DK), 2.6 (not in DK).

15

Melissus of Samos

Fragments

15.1 [Melissus proved through this common axiom that what is is ungenerated. He writes thus:[1]] Whatever was, always was[2] and always will be. For if it came to be, it is necessary that before it came to be it was nothing. Now if it was nothing, in no way could anything come to be out of nothing.   (Melissus, DK 30B1, quoted by Simplicius, *Commentary on Aristotle's Physics* 162.23–26)

15.2 Now since it did not come to be, it is and always was and always will be, and does not have a beginning or an end, but is unlimited. For if it had come to be it would have a beginning (for having come to be it would have begun at some time) and an end (for having come to be it would have ended at some time[3]). But since it neither began nor ended, it always was and always will be and does not have a beginning or end. For whatever is not entire cannot always be.

(Melissus, DK 30B2, quoted by Simplicius, *Commentary on Aristotle's Physics* 29.22–26, 109.20–25)

15.3 [Just as he says that what came to be at some time is limited in its being, he also wrote clearly that what always is is unlimited in being, saying:] But just as it always is, so also it must always be unlimited in magnitude. [But by "magnitude" he does not mean what is extended in space.]

(Melissus, DK 30B3, quoted by Simplicius, *Commentary on Aristotle's Physics* 109.29–32)

15.4 For he himself proves that what is is indivisible. For if what is is divided, it moves. But if it moved, it would not be. [But by "magnitude" he means the distance across[4] its substance.]

(Melissus, DK 30B10, quoted by Simplicius, *Commentary on Aristotle's Physics* 109.32–34) (continuation of **15.3**)

---

1. All of Melissus' extant fragments are preserved by Simplicius. I quote Simplicius' remarks, where relevant. The page and line references to Simplicius' text cover both the fragments and the quoted remarks.

2. Alternative translation: "It always was whatever it was" (KRS).

3. Although a better attested manuscript reading yields the translations "(it would have begun coming to be at some time)" and "(it would have ended coming to be at some time)," this reading makes less sense in the context.

4. Simplicius' meaning here is obscure and may reflect his Neoplatonism.

15.5 [That he intends what is to be bodiless he indicated, saying:] Now if it is, it must be one. But being one, it must not have body. But if it had thickness, it would have parts and no longer would be one.

(Melissus, DK 30B9, quoted by Simplicius, *Commentary on Aristotle's Physics* 109.34–110.2 [continuation of **15.4**], 87.6–7)

15.6 [And he put unlimited in being right next to eternity, saying:] Nothing that has both a beginning and an end is either eternal or unlimited. And so whatever does not have them is unlimited.

(Melissus, DK 30B4, quoted by Simplicius, *Commentary on Aristotle's Physics* 110.2–4) (continuation of **15.5**)

15.7 [From "unlimited" he concluded "one," from the argument:] If it is not one, it will come to a limit against something else.

(Melissus, DK 30B5, quoted by Simplicius, *Commentary on Aristotle's Physics* 110.5–6) (continuation of **15.6**)

15.8 [Although what is perceived seems clearly to be, if what is is one, there will be nothing else besides this. For Melissus says:] For if it is <unlimited>,[5] it will be one. For if there were two, they could not be unlimited, but would have limits against each other.

(Melissus, DK 30B6, quoted by Simplicius, *Commentary on Aristotle's On the Heaven* 557.14–17)

15.9 [Now Melissus speaks thus, summarizing what he has previously said and introducing the points about motion:]

1. Thus it is eternal and unlimited and one and all alike.
2. And it cannot perish, or become greater, or be rearranged, or feel pain or distress. For if it experienced any of these, it would no longer be one. For if it became different, it is necessary that what is is not alike, but what previously was perishes, and what is not comes to be. Now if it should become different by one hair in ten thousand years, it will all perish in all of time.
3. But it is not possible for it to be rearranged,[6] either. For the arrangement that previously was is not destroyed and an arrangement that is

5. I follow most editors in adding this word, which is not in the manuscripts of Simplicius.

6. "Arrangement" here translates "KOSMOS." "Rearranged" translates a verb whose root is the word "KOSMOS." This section can be taken to deny that the KOSMOS can change.

not does not come to be. But when nothing either comes to be in addition or is destroyed or becomes different, how could anything that is be rearranged? For if it became at all different, it would indeed already have been rearranged.

4. Nor does it feel pain. For it could not be all if it were feeling pain. For a thing feeling pain could not always be. Nor does it have equal power to what is healthy. Nor would it be alike if it were feeling pain. For it would feel pain either because something is being taken away or added, and it would no longer be alike.

5. Nor would what is healthy be able to feel pain. For what is healthy and what is would perish, and what is not would come to be.

6. And the same argument applies to feeling distress as to feeling pain.

7. Nor is any of it empty.[7] For what is empty is nothing, and of course what is nothing would not be. Nor does it move. For it is not able to give way anywhere, but is full. For if it were empty it would give way into the empty. But since it is not empty, it does not have anywhere to give way.

8. It cannot be dense and rare. For it is impossible for the rare to be equally full as the dense, but the rare immediately proves to be emptier than the dense.

9. And it is necessary to make this the grounds for deciding whether something is full or not full: if something moves or can move, it is not full. But if it neither moves nor can move, it is full.

10. Now it is necessary that it is full if it is not empty. Now if it is full, it does not move.   (Melissus, DK 30B7, quoted by Simplicius, *Commentary on Aristotle's Physics* 111.18–112.15)

15.10 [After saying of what is that it is one and ungenerated and motionless and interrupted by no void, but is a whole full of itself, he goes on:]

1. Now this argument is the strongest indication that it is only one. But also the following are indications.

2. For if there were many, they would have to be such as I say the one is. For if there is earth and water and air and fire and iron and gold, and one thing is alive and another is dead, and black and white, and all the other things that people say are true, if indeed these are, and we see and hear correctly, each must be such as we decided at first, and must not change or come to be different, but each thing must always be just as it is. But as the case stands, we say we see and hear and understand correctly.

3. We think that what is hot becomes cold and what is cold, hot, and

7. Alternative translation: "Nor is it at all empty."

what is hard becomes soft, and what is soft, hard, and what is alive dies and comes to be from what is not alive, and all these things become different, and anything that was and what is now are not at all alike, but iron, which is hard, is worn away by contact with the finger, and also gold and stone and anything else that seems to be strong,[8] and earth and stone come to be from water.

4. Now these things do not agree with one another. For we say that there are many things that are eternal and have forms and strength, but all of them seem to us to become different and change from what we see at each moment.

5. Now it is clear that we were not seeing correctly and that that plurality does not correctly seem to be. For they would not change if they were real, but would be as each of them seemed. For nothing is stronger than what is real.

6. But if it changes, what is is destroyed, and what is not has come to be. Thus, if there are many, they must be like the one.

(Melissus, DK 30B8, quoted by Simplicius,
Commentary on Aristotle's On the Heaven 558.19–559.12)

Life, Work and Philosophical Connections

Although a Samian, Melissus is philosophically an Eleatic. As commander of the Samian fleet, in 441 he won two victories over the Athenian fleet headed by Pericles. This date makes him probably somewhat younger than Zeno, Anaxagoras, and Empedocles. He was reportedly[9] a student of Parmenides, which is possible despite the distance between Samos in the eastern Aegean and Elea on the west coast of Italy. He follows the arch-Eleatic in the main, but innovates within the Eleatic framework. His treatise, like Parmenides', was a systematic series of arguments that deduce the attributes of what is, but he wrote in prose, not verse, made no claims to divine inspiration, and stated and argued for his theses more lucidly than Parmenides. There are indications (though no proof) that he knew of Anaxagoras and Empedocles.[10] He was approximately contemporary with Leucippus, the originator of the atomic theory, and Diogenes of Apollonia.

8. I follow Barnes in omitting the words "so that it happens that we neither see nor know the things that are," which are found in this place in the manuscripts.

9. Diogenes Laertius, *Lives of the Philosophers* 9.24 (= DK 30A1), Aetius 1.3.14 (= DK 30A9). But on such matters these sources are unreliable.

10. **15.10**, with its mention of Empedocles' four elements and of some of the opposites mentioned by Anaxagoras (**13.4**, **13.20**), may betray familiarity with the doctrines of those two philosophers.

He is said (though not reliably) to have been the teacher of Leucippus,[11] and there are traces of his influence on the Atomists.

Much of Melissus' work (which may have had a title: *On Nature*[12]) is preserved in his actual words, and we also possess several summaries of his reasoning.[13] As a result his views and methods are accurately known. He agrees with Parmenides that what is is one, uncreated, indestructible, indivisible, unchangeable, motionless, and all alike. He disagrees on two points. For Parmenides what is, is spatially limited and exists in a timeless present.[14] For Melissus it is spatially and temporally infinite.

Melissus' Arguments

Following a brief proof that anything that is did not come to be (**15.1**), which resembles one of Parmenides' arguments for the same thesis (**11.8** lines 12–13), **15.2** contains an argument for temporal eternity. The sequence of thought is: (a) if something came to be, it had a beginning. But (by **15.1**) it did not come to be, therefore it does not have a beginning. Therefore, it always has been. And (b) if something came to be, it has an end. But it did not come to be, therefore it does not have an end. Therefore it will always be.

The argument is faulty. The ideas of having a beginning and an end are not needed. Also, the first sentence of (b) is inadequately justified by the premise translated as "for having come to be it would have ended at some time," which is false and stronger than needed for the desired conclusion.[15] Further, both halves of the argument are fallacious, having the form: 'If *A* then *B*, but not-*A*, therefore not-*B*.'[16] And the role of the final clause of **15.2**, "for whatever is not entire cannot always be," is unclear.[17]

---

11. Tzetzes, *Chiliades* 2.980 (= DK 67A5).

12. Simplicius, *Commentary on Aristotle's Physics* 70.16–17 (= DK 30A4).

13. Pseudo-Aristotle, *On Melissus, Xenophanes and Gorgias*, chs. 1–2 (= DK 30A5); Simplicius, *Commentary on Aristotle's Physics* 103.13–104.20 (printed in DK, vol. 2, pp. 268–70); Philoponus, *Commentary on Aristotle's Physics* 50.30–52.11 (not in DK).

14. This is so whether we understand IT to be spherical or without spatial distinctions altogether. See pp. 172–73.

15. The argument is unimproved on a different reading: "for it would have ended coming to be."

16. Aristotle ridicules the argument for this bad reasoning (*Sophistical Refutations* 5 167b13–20 = DK 30A10).

17. Is it a second argument for 'no beginning or end'? But why do we need another argument? And Melissus does not make it clear that it is a second argument. In any

The argument amounts to the following: (a′) what is did not come to be, therefore it has always been, and (b′) what is did not come to be, therefore it will always be.[18] Given that what is, is at the present time (which Melissus obviously believes), (a′) is valid, on the interpretation of coming to be presented in **15.1**. (b′) is clearly invalid, but Melissus is here following Parmenides[19] in assuming that destruction (i.e., ceasing to be) is eliminated together with coming to be. In fact a parallel argument to **15.1** can be constructed against destruction, which would then entitle Melissus to the valid (b″) what is, is not subject to destruction (and what is, is at the present time), therefore what is will always be.

The difference between Melissus' unlimited eternal existence and Parmenides' limited, durationless existence seems more important than it is. They agree that there is no generation or destruction and that what is exists at every moment. They differ in that Melissus accepts that there are many moments, while Parmenides admits only one.

15.3 shows that Melissus believed that what is, is spatially infinite. It is unclear whether we have Melissus' argument for this important thesis. If **15.3** infers infinite extent from infinite duration, it is either grossly fallacious or depends on an unstated theory of the relation between time and space. If **15.3** does not argue the point but remarks that infinite extent follows from a parallel argument to that for infinite duration, we are invited to look back to **15.2**: indeed "beginning" and "end" have spatial as well as temporal applications, and something with spatial extent that lacks a beginning and an end in space is indeed infinitely large. But this interpretation leaves Melissus open to the charge that he equivocates on "beginning" and "end," since he needs to use them spatially, but has only justified their temporal use. **15.6** is also relevant if "unlimited" means "unlimited in size." But again, either the premise of the argument (the first sentence of **15.6**) depends on an equivocation, or else it is unsupported as regards its spatial application. Some hold that **15.2** rules out coming to be in space as well as in time on the grounds that anything that comes to be must begin to do so at a certain place and cease to do so at another. But Parmenides did not push the parallel between space and time so far, and if this was Melissus' intention, he does not make it clear, since **15.2** is phrased in terms of

---

case, it is obscure. Some have thought that it restates an argument that what is did not come to be. If so, it is out of logical sequence.

18. Contrast **11.8** lines 5, 19–20.

19. In **11.8** lines 6–13, Parmenides argues only against coming into being, but he claims (l. 14) to have disproven destruction as well.

time, not space.[20] In addition, **15.6** commits the fallacy observed in **15.2**, inferring a proposition of the form "If not-A then not-B: from one of the form "If A then B."

Parmenides and Melissus agree that what is, is unique: (**15.7**, **15.8**, cf. **11.8** l. 6). Melissus provides a clearer statement of the thesis than is found in Parmenides (indeed, he is the first to call what is by the appellation "the one," thus stressing its uniqueness), and a clear argument for it:[21] unity follows from unlimitedness (**15.8**, a fuller version of the argument in **15.7**).[22] The argument depends on the doubly unlimited nature of what is, since there is no objection to there being two unlimitedly large objects each at a different time, or two eternal objects each in a different place. Since what is has no limits in either respect, it occupies all space for all time, which could not be the case if anything else also occupied any space at any time.

15.9 begins by listing the properties treated in **15.1**, **15.2**, **15.3**, **15.6**, **15.7**, **15.8**, and an additional property, "all alike." The argument for this property goes as follows:

> **15.11** Being one it is all alike. For if it were unalike, being plural, it would no
> longer be one, but many.
>
> (pseudo-Aristotle, *On Melissus, Xenophanes and Gorgias*
> 1 974a12–14 = DK 30A5)

"Alike" is best taken to mean "qualitatively uniform," having the same qualities throughout. If what is were nonuniform, it would not have the same qualities throughout; there would be at least two regions differing from one another, at least two distinct parts. But then, each part would have a separate identity; we would no longer have one thing but a plurality.

The argument is fallacious, no reason being given why a single thing cannot have different kinds of parts (a stool has four legs and a seat, and yet is one stool). However, it invites further consideration of the nature of (true) unity and of the relation between whole and part. For the notion of unity can be strengthened to make the argument valid,[23] as can the concep-

---

20. In **15.2**, "no beginning or end" results from the fact that what is did not come to be, and the claim makes sense only if taken temporally.

21. It is difficult to find anything clear on the topic in Parmenides. See p. 169.

22. Since this argument requires what is to be unlimited, Parmenides could not have used it.

23. Cf. Barnes, *The Presocratic Philosophers*, rev. ed., (London, 1982), pp .204–10; but this strengthening makes more of the unity of what is than is warranted by the argument for unity in **15.7** and **15.8**.

tion of "whole" (along the lines that nothing is whole that can be divided into qualitatively different parts).[24]

Melissus next states more properties of what is: "it cannot perish, or become greater, or be rearranged, or feel pain or distress" (sec. 2). These points are taken up in turn: perishing in sec. 2, becoming greater and rearrangement in sec. 3, feeling pain in secs. 4–5, and feeling distress in sec. 6. Secs. 2 and 3 argue along similar lines: what is lacks these indicated features because they involve becoming different, which violates the unity and uniformity of what is. Similar reasoning can be used to rule out all kinds of change. The claim that what is feels no pain or distress comes out of the blue, with no known precedents in Eleatic thought, and with no apparent motivation. We are left wondering whether the passage is meant to prove that what is is healthy (see secs. 4–5) or that it is absurd to think that what is could be either healthy or in pain.

The final stretch of **15.9** (secs. 7–10) identifies what is with what is full, and what is not, or nothing, with what is empty, and uses the nonexistence of what is empty to deny the possibility of motion. Melissus thus introduces into Greek philosophy the conception of the void, which would shortly become one of the bases of the atomic theory.[25] He also analyzes the pair of opposites, dense and rare, in terms of full and empty, i.e., what is and what is not, to take away one of the foundations of Anaximenes' theory that the plurality of substances in the world is due to condensation and rarefaction, and also to show that Anaximenes, who had analyzed hot and cold in terms of rare and dense, could be outdone at his own reductionist game.[26]

Here too, Melissus' argument is clearer than the corresponding argument in Parmenides.[27] It achieves its clarity by conceiving what is more concretely than Parmenides did. For Parmenides, what is not is incomprehensible, and his argument against the existence of what is not depends on its unintelligibility.[28] Further, what is not can have no characteristics at all. In particular, it is not the sort of thing that could be extended in space. Void, on the other hand, *can* be conceived of, and Melissus shows that he has conceived of it adequately, even while insisting that it does not exist.

The Eleatic philosophy entails that sense perception is wholly misleading.

---

24. The argument would then require the additional premise that whatever is one is whole in this sense, which is also unwarranted by the preceding material.

25. See pp. 313–17.

26. For Anaximenes' reductionism, see p. 53.

27. **11.8** lines 26–31.

28. **11.2** lines 7–8.

Parmenides knows this and occasionally hints at it,[29] but here again it is Melissus who produces a clear argument (**15.10**). The obvious conflict between what the senses report and what Eleatic logic proves (**15.10** secs. 2–4) forces a choice upon us: do we prefer reason or the senses? Melissus prefers reason and so rejects the senses (sec. 5).

One feature of this argument merits mention. Melissus says (sec. 2) "if there were many, they would have to be such as I say the one is." In the context of **15.10**, this move introduces a needless complication into the argument. In addition, Melissus does not follow up this claim. If there are many, and each of them is like the one, then each is the only existing thing. The conflict between Eleaticism and common sense could hardly be put more sharply, and so the argument could be finished sooner and more efficiently than it is. When he uses the claim in question, Melissus does not fasten on the uniqueness or infinite spatial extent of what is, but on its uniformity, changelessness, and permanence. This restricted view of the properties of what is may have played a role in the formation of ancient atomism.[30]

15.4 and **15.5** treat the property of indivisibility. **15.4** does not explain why what is moves if it is divided. With the principle of **15.9** sec. 9 that if X moves then X is not full, **15.4** implies that if what is is divided, it is not full. Melissus may have in mind a kind of division that physically separates the parts—what then is in between? What is not, i.e., void—and then motion is possible (**15.9** sec. 7). More interestingly, he may be thinking of the limits of the parts resulting from the division. If we suppose that the parts of what is full are themselves full, and that the whole equals the sum of its parts, then since what is, is full, its parts are also full, and since what is, is all that is full, its parts amount to all that is full. Thus, the limits or boundaries of the parts of what is, being different from the parts, are not full, which (by **15.9** sec. 9) permits motion. Strict Eleatic logic also entails that the limits of the parts of what is are empty, therefore are nothing, therefore do not exist—another reason to reject divisibility. On this reading, **15.4** opens the difficult question of the ontological status of the limits or boundaries of existing things—only to close it quickly. The blunt weapon of the Eleatic dichotomy "it is or it is not" (**11.8** l. 16), which Melissus reworks as "it is full or not full," does not encourage the subtlety needed to work out different ways of being.

15.5 can be reconstructed as follows: (a) what is is one, therefore (b) what is is without parts, therefore (c) what is has no thickness, therefore (d) what is does not have body. This is an astonishing conclusion, which

---

29. **11.6** l. 7, **11.7** lines 3–4.

30. See pp. 312–13.

seems to contradict the claims that what is is infinitely extended in space (**15.3, 15.6**) and full (**15.9**, secs. 7–10, where "fullness" seems to mean the kind of solidity that applies to bodies). For (a) if what is has no thickness, how can it be infinitely extended, and (b) if what is has any extension at all, why can it not be divided into parts?

Melissus might respond to question (a) by saying that bodies have extension and also limits, so something infinitely large is not properly speaking a body. Nor does it, properly speaking, have thickness, because thickness is a measure of the distance between a body's extremities. If this was Melissus' thought, he again touched on important and difficult conceptual issues—this time concerning measure and extension—again without making an effort to clarify them.

Regarding question (b), Melissus cannot say that what is, is empty and so cannot be divided into parts because there is nothing to partition, for what is, is full, not empty.[31] Instead, he declares that what is, is bodiless and lacks thickness. This is the first statement of incorporeal existence that we have in Greek philosophy, but it is unsatisfactory as it stands, since it leaves open the question how something spatially extended and "full" can be bodiless and lack thickness.[32]

Summary

Melissus received abuse from Aristotle. "A bit crude" in comparison with Parmenides, "invalid arguments starting from false assumptions," "a tiresome argument which gives no difficulty—grant one absurdity and the rest follow," "but why should his premises be correct? Someone else might assert the exact opposite. For he has not shown that his starting point is correct."[33] Aristotle objects principally to details of Melissus' logic, and

31. Commentators are driven to desperate measures here, saying that the fragment is not genuine or that it represents an attack by Melissus on pluralists—an attack which seems to come home against Melissus himself.

32. I take it that thickness means something like bulk or mass. If it means simply possessing a third spatial dimension, Melissus would be saying that what is is two-dimensional, which still does not give any reason why it cannot be divided, and which would yield an interpretation of what is for which we are totally unprepared by the fragments and testimonia. It is worth mentioning that Parmenides' IT does not run into these troubles on the interpretation I have preferred (pp. 172–73), since IT exists without spatial distinctions.

33. Quotations from Aristotle, *Metaphysics* 1.5 986b25–27, *Physics* 1.2 185a9–12 (both = DK 30A7), and pseudo-Aristotle, *On Melissus, Xenophanes and Gorgias* 1 975a3–5 (= DK 30A5).

Melissus is indeed guilty of committing a number of blunders in his reasoning.

Melissus' writings, however, have the merit of making Eleatic philosophy more comprehensible. The clearly sequenced structure of his work and the short, sharp arguments improve on Parmenides' opaque and oracular verse. In addition, Melissus set up some of his arguments in ways which later philosophers could take advantage of, even in refuting him. The arguments touch on many important philosophical issues that had not previously been raised. Even when he does not explore them himself, he leaves them as a legacy to future philosophers and reveals features of the Eleatic position in need of further discussion.

16

Fifth-Century Atomism:
Leucippus and Democritus

The third and most ambitious response to the Eleatic challenge was the atomic theory, invented by Leucippus and developed by Democritus. Leucippus is a shadowy character[1] who we are told was from (a) Miletus, (b) Elea, and (c) Abdera[2], though these claims could simply reflect the facts that (a) his philosophy was strongly of the Ionian type, (b) he was keenly aware of the Eleatic challenge, and (c) his pupil Democritus was from Abdera. Of his dates we are equally in the dark. Democritus, born c. 460, was his student. It is likely that Leucippus proposed the atomic theory in the decade 440–430. He wrote works called *The Great World System* and *On Mind*.

Democritus' birthdate is inferred from his own statement[3] that he was young in the old age of Anaxagoras (born c. 500). Diogenes Laertius reports that Anaxagoras was forty years older than Democritus.[4] Since this makes Democritus ten years younger than Socrates, the title "Presocratic" is not quite correct. He lived to a ripe old age (perhaps over 100), therefore well into Plato's career and into the time when Aristotle had begun his philosophical work. Born on the Thracian mainland in the remote Greek city of Abdera, which also produced the Sophist Protagoras, Democritus traveled widely in non-Greek lands for study and research. He is unique among the philosophers treated in this book in the large number of his writings. We know the titles of about seventy works, on a wide variety of subjects. The main headings are ethics, natural philosophy, mathematics, "music" (in the broad Greek sense which includes language and literature[5]), technical subjects (including medical writings and works on farming, painting, and military strategy), and writings based on his travels. He

1. Virtually nothing is known about his life. Epicurus (341–271), the most famous Atomist of antiquity, is reported to have denied Leucippus' existence (Diogenes Laertius, *Lives of the Philosophers* 10.13 = DK 67A2).

2. Diogenes Laertius, *Lives of the Philosophers* 9.30 (= DK 67A1).

3. Democritus, DK 68B5.

4. Diogenes Laertius, *Lives of the Philosophers* 9.41 (= DK 68B5).

5. The term "music" was originally used of any art governed by a Muse, such as singing, playing instruments, dancing, and poetry.

was later known as the laughing philosopher, allegedly because of his reaction to human follies.

More fragments survive from Democritus than from any other presocratic philosopher, but the great majority are on ethics, and their authenticity and their exact relation to the atomic theory are in many cases doubtful. Our knowledge of atomism depends on testimonia (as opposed to actual fragments) to a greater degree than is the case for our knowledge of the theories of Empedocles and Anaxagoras; unfortunately, the Aristotelian tradition that preserves most of the information is hostile to atomism.

Attempts have been made to distinguish between Leucippus' and Democritus' contributions to the atomic theory.[6] In general, it appears that Leucippus, like Empedocles and Anaxagoras, sketched out a physical theory in response to the Eleatics, as well as a cosmogony and cosmology that treated additional problems. Democritus then did what had not been done before, and his contribution is a turning point in the history of thought. He accepted the theory essentially as stated by Leucippus, but went on to explain in detail a wide range of natural phenomena, working out elaborate (though not always very clear) accounts of how the five senses function and also how thought and other cognitive activities take place. He also saw (possibly) the need for developing a mathematical basis for his physical theory and (certainly) the need for an appropriate theory of knowledge. To a greater extent than his predecessors seem to have done with their theories, Democritus aimed to establish a thoroughgoing atomistic account of all aspects of the world and of humanity. It is a great shame that not one of his works has survived complete—the price, perhaps, of doing his work in Abdera instead of Athens, and also of championing a theory that was on the one hand apparently despised by Plato (who never mentions Democritus), Aristotle (who argues powerfully against the atomic theory), and the Stoics (who constituted the dominant philosophical movement of the Hellenistic age), and which on the other was taken over and adapted by Epicurus, whose pride and influence were such that his followers revered him as The Master and paid no attention to the sources to which he owed almost all his ideas about the natural world. In what follows, little effort will be made to distinguish the contributions of Leucippus from those of Democritus, and I shall speak in general of the Atomists.

Principles of the Atomic Theory

> 16.1 Leucippus and his associate Democritus declare the full and the empty [void] to be the elements, calling the former "what is" (TO ON) and the other "what is not" (TO ME ON). Of these the one, "what is," is full and

6. Most notably by C. Bailey, *The Greek Atomists and Epicurus* (Oxford, 1928).

solid, the other, "what is not," is empty [void] and rare. (This is why they say that what is is no more than what is not, because the void is no less than body is.) These are the material causes of existing things. . . . They declare that the differences <among these> are the causes of the rest. Moreover, they say that the differences are three: shape, arrangement, and position. For they say that what is differs only in "rhythm," "touching," and "turning"—and of these "rhythm" is shape, "touching" is arrangement, and "turning" is position. For *A* differs from *N* in shape, *AN* from *NA* in arrangement, and *Z* from *N* in position.

(Aristotle, *Metaphysics* 1.4 985b4–19 = DK 67A6)

16.2 After making the shapes, Democritus and Leucippus make alteration and coming to be out of them: coming to be and destruction by means of separation and combination, alteration by means of arrangement and position. Since they held that the truth is in the appearance, and appearances are opposite and unlimited, they made the shapes unlimited,[7] so that by reason of changes of the composite, the same thing seems opposite to different people, and it shifts position when a small amount is mixed in, and it appears completely different when one thing shifts position. For tragedy and comedy come to be out of the same letters.

(Aristotle, *On Generation and Corruption* 1.1 315b6–15 = DK 67A97)

16.3 Democritus believes that the nature of the eternal things is small substances (OUSIAI[8]) unlimited in multitude. As a place for these he hypothesizes something else, unlimited in size, and he calls the place by the names "void," "nothing" (OUDEN) and "unlimited" [or, "infinite"] and he calls each of the substances "hing" (DEN) and "compact" and "what is." He holds that the substances are so small that they escape our senses. They have all kinds of forms and shapes and differences in size. Out of these as elements he generates and combines visible and perceptible bodies. <These substances> contend with one another and move in the void on account of their dissimilarity and the other differences I have mentioned, and as they move they strike against one another and become entangled in a way that makes them be in contact and close to one another, but does not make any thing out of them that is truly one, for it is quite foolish <to think> that two or more things could ever come to be one. The grounds he gives for why the substances stay together up to a point are that the bodies fit together and hold each other fast. For some of them are rough, some are hooked, others concave and others convex, while yet others have innumerable other differences. So he thinks that

---

7. APEIRON. For the sake of consistency with earlier chapters I continue to translate this word "unlimited," but in many of the passages on the Atomists it is appropriately taken as "infinite."

8. OUSIA, "substance," is a noun derived from the verb EINAI, "to be." There is a connection in language and meaning between OUSIA and ON (**16.1**).

they cling to each other and stay together until some stronger necessity comes along from the environment and shakes them and scatters them apart. He describes the generation and its contrary, separation, not only for animals but also for plants, KOSMOI, and altogether for all perceptible bodies.   (Aristotle, *On Democritus*, quoted by Simplicius, *Commentary on Aristotle's On the Heaven* 295.1–22 = DK 68A37)

16.4 Leucippus . . . did not follow the same path as Parmenides and Xenophanes concerning things that are, but seemingly the opposite one. For while they made the universe one, immovable, ungenerated, and limited, and did not even permit the investigation of what is not, he posited the atoms as unlimited and ever moving elements, and an unlimited multitude of shapes among them on the grounds that they are no more like this than like that, since he observed that coming to be and change are unceasing in things that are. Further, he posited that what is is no more than what is not, and both are equally causes of what comes to be. For supposing the substance of the atoms to be compact and full, he said it is "being" and that it moves in the void, which he called "not-being" and which he declares is no less than what is. His associate, Democritus of Abdera, likewise posited the full and the void as principles, of which he calls the former "being" and the latter "not-being." For positing the atoms as matter for the things that are they generate the rest by means of their differences. These are three: rhythm, turning, and touching, i.e., shape, position, and arrangement. For like is by nature moved by like, and things of the same kind move towards one another, and each of the shapes produces a different composition when arranged in a different compound. Thus, since the principles are unlimited, they reasonably promised to account for all attributes and substances—how and through what cause anything comes to be. This is why they say that only those who make the elements unlimited account for everything reasonably. They say that the multitude of the shapes among the atoms is unlimited on the grounds that they are no more like this than like that. For they themselves assign this as a cause of the unlimitedness.
                    (Simplicius, *Commentary on Aristotle's Physics*
                    28.4–26 = DK 67A8 68A38)

16.5 Leucippus and Democritus have accounted for all things very systematically and in a single theory, taking the natural starting point as their own. For some of the early philosophers held that what is, is necessarily one and immovable. For the void is not, and motion is impossible without a separate void, nor can there be many things without something to keep them apart. . . . Leucippus thought he had arguments that agreed with perception in not abolishing coming to be, destruction, motion, or plurality. Agreeing on these matters with the phenomena and agreeing with those who support the one [i.e., the Eleatics] that there could be no motion without void, he asserts that void is not-being and nothing of what is is not-being, since what strictly is, is completely full. But this is not one, but they are unlimited in multitude and invisible because of the minuteness of their size. These move in the void (for there is void) and they produce coming to be by coming together, and destruction by coming apart, and they act and are acted upon wherever they happen to be in contact (for in this way they are not one), and they generate <compounds> by becoming combined and entangled. A plurality could not come to be from what is in reality one, nor one from what is really many, but this is impossible. (Aristotle, *On Generation and Corruption* 1.8 324b35–325a36 = DK 67A7)

There are two types of elements: atoms and void. Atoms are indivisible (the word ATOMOS means "uncuttable," "unsplittable") building blocks too small to be seen, which move in the void and combine to form compounds, some of which are large enough to be perceived. Atoms are called "full," "solid," "compact," "what is," "being," and "hing," while void is empty (KENON, the word translated "void" means "empty"), "rare," "unlimited" or "infinite," "what is not," "not-being," and "nothing." Among these descriptions of atoms and void, which emphasize their strongly contrasting natures, "hing" contrasts with "nothing" as "nothing" minus the negative "not." This translation reflects the Greek, in which OUDEN ("nothing") minus OU ("not") gives DEN, a word which neatly makes the Atomists' point.[9]

Atoms

Atoms are eternal (16.3), and, as the following passages show, uniform in substance, without perceptible qualities, and differing only in their spatial properties—size and shape, the latter illustrated by the letters of the alphabet (16.1).

16.6 They declare that their nature is one, as if each were a separate piece of gold. (Aristotle, *On the Heaven* 1.7 275b32–276a1 = DK 67A19)

16.7 Plato and Democritus supposed that only the intelligible things are true; Democritus <held this view> because there is by nature no perceptible substrate, whereas the atoms, which combine to form all things, have a nature deprived of every perceptible quality.
(Sextus Empiricus, *Against the Mathematicians* 8.6 = DK 68A59)

9. The Atomists did not invent this word, which was used by the sixth-century lyric poet Alcaeus (fr. 23 [Diehl]).

> **16.8** Democritus specified two <basic properties of atoms>: size and shape;
> and Epicurus added weight as a third.   (Aetius 1.3.18 = DK 68A47)

Moreover, there are an unlimited number of atoms, with an unlimited number of shapes moving in unlimited void. The Atomists offered arguments for the view that the number of shapes is unlimited. (A) Truth is in the appearance; appearances are unlimited; therefore the shapes are unlimited (**16.2, 16.4**). (B) They are no more like this than like that; therefore there is an unlimited multitude of shapes (**16.4**)—an argument that evidently depends on the Principle of Sufficient Reason, encountered previously in Anaximander and Parmenides.[10]

The unlimited number of shapes entails an unlimited number of atoms.

> **16.9** Since the bodies differ in shape, and the shapes are unlimited, they
> declare the simple bodies too to be unlimited. But they did not deter-
> mine further what is the shape of each of the elements, only assigning a
> spherical shape to fire. They distinguished air and water and the others
> by largeness and smallness.
>   (Aristotle, *On the Heaven* 3.4 303a11–15 = DK 67A15)

This property in turn, presumably, was thought to entail an unlimited amount of void for them to move in (although we do not have any record of arguments that the void is unlimited).

Parallel reasoning to (B) would conclude that there are atoms of all possible sizes ("all kinds of . . . differences in size" [**16.3**]). Indeed, one source declares that Democritus believed there can be an atom the size of the KOSMOS (**16.22**). But since there is strong evidence (**16.3, 16.5, 16.11**) that both Leucippus and Democritus held that the atoms are very small, indeed "invisible because of the minuteness of their size," it is best to hold that Democritus believed that atoms could in principle be any size (which could have led to the interpretation that he held that some atoms are in fact huge), and yet he, like Leucippus, believed that in fact they are all too small to be seen.[11] This question aside, however, it seems that size as well as shape governs the sorts of compounds in which an atom can be found (**16.9**).

All atoms are made of the same stuff. Moreover, this stuff, and consequently the atoms themselves, have no perceptible qualities. They are not hard or soft, hot or cold, wet or dry. These are properties of macroscopic perceptible compounds of atoms and depend on the atomic structure of the compounds rather than the nature of the individual component atoms.

---

10. See **5.13, 11.8** lines 9–11.
11. For further discussion of this point, see Guthrie, *HGP*, vol. 2, pp. 394–95.

It is not certain why the Atomists supposed that atoms have no perceptible qualities, but their theory lends itself to some speculations. First, with such atoms it is easier to account for a wider range of changes in quality at the macroscopic level. For example, iron, which is gray, becomes red when heated. If it were composed of gray atoms this change would be hard to explain. But if color depends on atomic structure and movement, we may suppose that heat alters the structure and movement of the atoms in the iron. Second, individual atoms cannot be perceived,[12] hence they cannot have perceptible qualities. Third, since an atom lacks such qualities it can form part of many different compounds with different qualities, as a spherical atom can in one context be a soul atom and in another a fire atom. Fourth, the atomic theory is a beautifully simple theory that rests on a small number of principles. Part of its simplicity resides in the fact that atoms have so few inherent properties.

The atoms are impassive, incapable of being affected or acted upon.

16.10 These men [Leucippus, Democritus, and Epicurus] said that the principles are unlimited in multitude, and they believed them to be atoms and indivisible and incapable of being acted upon because they are compact and have no share of void. (For they claimed that division occurs where there is void in bodies.)
(Simplicius, *Commentary on Aristotle's On the Heaven* 242.18–21 = DK 67A14)

Also, "on account of their hardness the atoms are not acted upon and do not change" (**16.34**). Since they are quality-less, they cannot change in quality. Nor can they change in quantity by becoming either more or fewer (which would involve generation or destruction) or by growing or shrinking. The only sort of change an atom could suffer would be change in its spatial properties (size and shape), which is prevented by the absence of internal void (so that it cannot bend or break). The unique statement that the atoms are also incapable of acting (**16.34**) must be understood in this context: they cannot cause changes in other atoms. The contrary claim that "they act and are acted upon whenever they happen to be in contact" (**16.5**) will refer to their behavior not as individual atoms, but as components of compounds.

The atoms' indivisible nature was the subject of a lively debate. The following passage records some of the Atomists' arguments on the point.

12. For the Atomists' account of vision, which depends on atoms being emitted from the perceived object (hence a single atom, which cannot emit other atoms, is invisible), see pp. 331–32.

16.11 Those who abandoned division to infinity on the grounds that we cannot divide to infinity and as a result cannot guarantee that the division cannot end, declared that bodies are composed of indivisible things and are divided into indivisibles. Except that Leucippus and Democritus hold that the cause of the primary bodies' indivisibility is not only their inability to be affected but also their minute size and lack of parts.   (Simplicius, *Commentary on Aristotle's Physics* 925.10–15 = DK 67A13)

The atoms are indivisible because (A) they cannot be affected, (B) they are so small, and (C) they have no parts. But all three of these considerations beg the question. For example, we cannot know that they have no parts unless we already know that they are indivisible (assuming that "parts" is meant in the only way that makes sense in the context: parts into which a thing can be divided).

The first part of **16.11**, however, puts these arguments in a different light (if the reasoning can be attributed to the Atomists). Zeno had shown (Argument 2, pp. 183–85, above) that unacceptable consequences follow on the assumption that a finite-sized object is infinitely divisible. Complete the division and either the resulting least parts have no size or they have some positive size. But either way, the parts cannot be reassembled to form the original object. If they have no size, when put together they result in something with no size. If they have a positive size, no matter how small, when an infinite number of them are put together, the result is something of infinite, not finite size. The Atomists avoided this argument.[13] In the absence of a guarantee that bodies are infinitely divisible, they simply declared that they are not: i.e., that bodies are ultimately composed of indivisibles. This amounts to hypothesizing the existence of atoms in the absence of a conclusive reason not to do so. The next step would be to describe the atoms so as to corroborate their indivisibility and also explain why we fail to perceive them directly—and the properties mentioned above contribute to this enterprise.

Another passage goes further, arguing that bodies cannot be "everywhere divisible."

16.12 Democritus would appear to have been persuaded by arguments that are relevant and appropriate to the science of nature. The point will be clear as we proceed. For there is a difficulty in supposing that there is

13. Aristotle says that "some gave in to (Zeno's arguments) by positing atomic magnitudes" (Aristotle, *Physics* 1.3 187a1–3 = DK 29A22). They "gave in" in the sense that they admitted their logical force, and avoided them by denying the hypothesis on which they depend, that what is is infinitely divisible.

some body, a magnitude, that is everywhere divisible and that this [the complete division] is possible. For what will there be that escapes the division? . . . Now since such a body is everywhere divisible, let it be divided. What, then, will be left? A magnitude? But this cannot be. For there will be something that has not been divided, whereas we supposed that it was everywhere divisible. But if there will be no body or magnitude left and yet the division will take place, either <the original body> will consist of points and its components will be without magnitude, or it will be nothing at all, so that it could come to be out of nothing and be composed of nothing, and the whole thing would then be nothing but an appearance. Likewise, if it is composed of points, it will not be a quantity. For when they were in contact and there was a single magnitude and they coincided, they made the whole thing none the larger. For when it is divided into two or more, the whole is no smaller or larger than before. And so, even if all the points are put together they will not make any magnitude. . . . These problems result from supposing that any body whatever of any size is everywhere divisible. . . . And so, since magnitudes cannot be composed of contacts or points, it is necessary for there to be indivisible bodies and magnitudes.

(Aristotle, *On Generation and Corruption*
1.2 316a13–b16 = DK 68A48b)

Now "everywhere divisible" is different from "infinitely divisible." Dividing a magnitude one meter long in half and then dividing one of these halves in half, etc., is an infinite division that leaves pieces of positive size: one piece half a meter long, one piece a quarter of a meter long, etc. Dividing the magnitude everywhere, perhaps by dividing it into two pieces half a meter long and then dividing both of these pieces into halves and continuing to subdivide each of the products of the previous division, leaves pieces of no positive size. But even though being everywhere divisible is a stronger condition than being infinitely divisible, it, rather than infinite divisibility, is the antithesis of atomism and hence a view the Atomists need to reject. Thus, **16.12**'s argument is appropriate. If the argument succeeds there is good reason to adopt some kind of atomic theory. However, the argument rests on the assumption not just that a magnitude is everywhere divisible, but that division can be carried out in such a way that the magnitude is actually divided at every place, which is quite a different claim, and one that proponents of the former need not accept.

As far as the evidence goes, then, the Atomists did not prove that there are atoms. A body can be everywhere divisible even if not actually divided everywhere. But they did succeed in avoiding the Scylla and Charybdis of Zeno's Argument 2. This is sufficient to show that physically indivisible bodies are possible, though not enough to escape all of Zeno's arguments. For physical indivisibility does not guarantee geometrical or theoretical indivisibility.[14] Atoms have sizes and shapes, and shapes involve spatial extension. For example, Democritus speaks of fire as composed of spherical atoms. A spherical atom may be a very small sphere, but in thought even if not with a knife, we can distinguish one part of the sphere from the other. And once we can do this much, others of Zeno's paradoxes take hold—the Dichotomy and the Achilles (see pp. 187–89). We cannot traverse an atom because we would first have to cross half[15] of it, then half the remainder, etc.

It is a matter of current controversy whether the fifth-century Atomists believed that atoms are geometrically or theoretically as well as physically indivisible.[16] The philosophically correct move would be to distinguish between kinds of indivisibility and hold that atoms are theoretically divisible, but not physically so. Alternatively and plausibly, the Atomists may not have explicitly distinguished among different kinds of indivisibility. (Such distinctions are more at home in Aristotle than in the fifth century.) They may have conceived of divisibility and indivisibility solely as physical properties and felt free to distinguish parts of atoms in thought, without supposing that doing so requires atoms to be divisible in any way. They would then be in a position to admit that atoms are theoretically and geometrically divisible once the relevant distinctions were made.[17] In fact, as we saw in discussing Zeno, theoretical divisibility to infinity is an illusory problem. There is no need to take any step to oppose it (let alone a philosophically unsound step) because the option Zeno offers between final parts of no size and final parts of some size is misleading: neither of these results will obtain.

The Atomists were aware of the positive Eleatic doctrines of Parmenides and Melissus as well as Zeno's attacks on plurality, and there is no doubt

---

14. As I use these terms, an atom is geometrically indivisible if we cannot distinguish (even without physical division) the sides from the corners, the center from the edges, the right half from the left half (given its position), etc. An atom is theoretically indivisible if it lacks geometrically or otherwise distinguishable parts. For a different account of kinds of divisibility, see Barnes, *The Presocratic Philosophers*, pp. 356–57.

15. Half on the Dichotomy paradox, some larger fraction on the Achilles.

16. Champions of theoretical indivisibility include Guthrie, *HGP*, vol. 2, pp. 396, 503–7, and Furley, *The Greek Cosmologists*, pp. 124–31; among the opponents are Barnes, *The Presocratic Philosophers*, pp. 352–60. Epicurus seems to have believed that atoms are theoretically divisible into theoretically indivisible parts.

17. H. Mendell argues ably for this view ("Democritus on Mathematical and Physical Shapes and the Emergence of Fifth Century Geometry," unpublished essay).

that atomism is a response to the Eleatic challenge. It preserves the world of experience with its change, coming into being, destruction, etc., by saying that these features are due to unchanging atoms that have many of the properties of Parmenides' one being. Melissus said "if there were many, they would have to be such as I say the one is" (**15.10** sec. 2), and some say that the Atomists responded by endowing each of their atoms with the attributes of the one. This is true to an extent. Like the Eleatic one, each atom is uncreated and indestructible, therefore eternal. It is continuous and indivisible. It is unchanging in quality; in fact, like the Eleatic one, it has no qualities. Moreover, relatively to itself it does not move: its logically distinguishable parts always have the same positions relative to one another. Each atom is, of course, finite in size (like Parmenides' but unlike Melissus' one).[18] Contrary to Parmenides' demand, an atom is not spatially invariant: different parts do have different locations relative to one another. But still, at the level of the individual atom, not considered in its relations to other atoms, there is temporal invariance. Since there is no change or internal motion, an atom is identical with itself throughout its eternal existence.

Void

The void fulfills two main functions. It enables the atoms to move, and it makes possible and preserves their uniqueness and identity: "motion is impossible without a separate void, nor can there be many things without something to keep them apart" (**16.5**). Regarding the latter point, they held that if there were no void to separate atoms, all there is would consist of a single infinitely large indivisible mass of matter. "Division occurs where there is void in bodies" (**16.10**). Strictly speaking, atoms are never in contact with one another.

> **16.13** When Democritus said that the atoms are in contact with each other, he did not mean contact strictly speaking . . . but the condition in which the atoms are near one another and not far apart is what he called contact. For no matter what, they are separated by the void.
> (Philoponus, *Commentary on Aristotle's On Generation and Corruption* 158.27–159.3 = DK 67A7)

Even in a compound, where they are very close to one another, they are separated by void, so that a compound is not like a jigsaw puzzle with no gaps between the pieces. Why not? Because atoms are identified only by

18. See pp. 172–73, 297.

their spatial extension, and if two atoms fit together perfectly with no gaps, so that the resulting thing is uniformly dense, compact, etc., they would no longer be two, but would have become one. And the Atomists, echoing Eleatic sentiments, insist that compounds are not true unities: "it is quite foolish <to think> that two or more things could ever come to be one" (**16.3**), "a plurality could not come to be from what is in reality one, nor one from what is really many" (**16.5**).

According to some sources, the Atomists posited that void exists (**16.3**, **16.4**, and **16.5**[19]). However, they did offer arguments. One, which is another application of the Principle of Sufficient Reason, goes as follows.

> **16.14** There is no more reason for the thing to be than the nothing.
> (Democritus, DK 68B156)

The following passage presents four of their reasons for believing in the void, all of which are inconclusive.[20]

> **16.15** People mean by void an interval in which there is no perceptible body. Since they believe that everything that is is body, they say that void is that in which there is nothing at all. . . . So it is necessary to prove[21] . . . that there is no interval different from bodies . . . which breaks up the whole body so that it is not continuous, as Democritus and Leucippus say, and many other natural philosophers, or anything outside the whole body, which is continuous. They say that (1) there would be no change in place (i.e., motion and growth), since motion would not seem to exist if there were no void, since what is full cannot admit anything. . . . (2) Some things are seen to contract and be compressed; for example, they say that the jars hold the wine along with the wineskins, since the compressed body contracts into the voids that are in it. Further (3) all believe that growth takes place through void, since the nourishment is a body and two bodies cannot be together. (4) They also use as evidence what happens with ash, which receives as much water as the empty vessel.   (Aristotle, *Physics* 4.6 213a27–b22 = DK 67A19)

Void is to be distinguished from air, whose corporeal nature had been hinted at as far back as Anaximenes and was assumed in Empedocles' clepsydra analogy (**14.105**). Nor is it the same thing as space. Consider a

---

19. **16.4** and **16.5** put the Atomists' hypothesis of the existence of void in an anti-Eleatic context.

20. Aristotle points out their shortcomings in *Physics* 4.7.

21. This passage forms part of Aristotle's treatment of void in which he presents the arguments offered in favor of the thesis that void exists, and shows why they fail.

fish in a body of water, such as the water in a fishbowl. The water and the fish both occupy space and have locations; they occupy different regions of space and have different locations. Similarly, atoms and void both occupy space and have location. Where there is void there are no atoms, and where there are atoms there is no void. The atoms move through the void in the same sense as that in which the fish swims through the water. Thus, the water and the void are both *in* space and neither is to be confused with the space in which the fish or atoms move.[22] I disagree with Aristotle's interpretation that void is the space or place in which the atoms move (**16.3**).[23]

The Atomists emphasized void's existence and nature with a paradox: Leucippus "asserts that void is not-being, and nothing of what is is not-being, since what strictly is is completely full" (**16.5**); "what is is no more than what is not, because the void is no less than body is" (**16.1**); "both [what is and what is not] are equally causes of what comes to be" (**16.4**). Further, Democritus calls the void "nothing" (**16.3**), so that nothing exists.

These assertions do more than pose riddles; they fly in the face of the Eleatic challenge. Parmenides had declared that "it is not possible for nothing to be" (**11.6** l. 2), and that what is not cannot be known or declared (**11.2** lines 7–8), and he had forbidden inquiry along that path (**11.2** lines 5–6). Moreover, he had ruled out plurality on the grounds that there are no stretches of what is not to separate bits of what is (**11.8** lines 44–49),[24] and Melissus had disproved the possibility of motion on similar grounds (**13.9** sec. 9). In this intellectual context it is simply unsatisfactory to assert baldly that "nothing" is one of the physical principles and to declare that nothing exists just as much as "hing."

Some think that calling the void "nothing" is a move to avoid Zeno's Argument 3 (pp. 185–86), which would entail an infinite number of atoms in a finite area. Zeno argued "if there are many . . . there are always others between the things that are, and again others between these, and so the

22. For further discussion of these issues in Melissus as well as the Atomists, see D. Sedley, "Two Conceptions of Vacuum," *Phronesis* 27 (1982): 175–93.

23. Aristotle declares that proponents of the existence of void conceive of it as "place in which there is no body" (*Physics* 4.7 213b33, not in DK). Since Aristotle defines the place of something as "the innermost motionless boundary of what contains it" (*Physics* 4.4 212a20–21, not in DK), or, less precisely, as "what contains the thing whose place it is, and is no part of that thing" (*Physics* 4.4 210b34–211a1, not in DK), he takes void to be, in some sense, a potential container of body.

24. On the interpretation offered in chap. 11, these lines contain Parmenides' argument for spatial invariance, while **11.8** lines 22–25 argue for temporal invariance: there are no spatial or temporal stretches of what is not separating bits of what is.

things that are are unlimited" (**12.5**). The Atomists can respond that in between the things that are (atoms) is nothing (void), so Zeno's regress fails to take hold.

However, the existence of what is not represents a major departure from Eleatic doctrine. The anti-Parmenidean declaration "what is not is" was considered previously. But further, the existence of void goes against Melissus' argument "Nor is any of it empty. For what is empty is nothing, and of course what is nothing would not be" (**15.9** sec. 7). As we have seen, the Atomists, while agreeing with the premise that what is empty is nothing, deny the last assertion of the argument, and claim that what is nothing (the void) is.

The void also runs afoul of Parmenides' more abstract reasoning. "Nor is it any more in any way . . . or any less" (**11.8** lines 23–24) and "It is right for what is to be not incomplete; for it is not lacking; if it were (lacking), it would lack everything" (**11.8** lines 32–33); "For it must be not at all greater or at all smaller here than there" (**11.8** l. 44); "Nor (is it the case that) what is is in such a way that there could be more of what is here and less there" (**11.8** lines 47–48). The Atomists' claim, that void is just as much as atoms are, is sufficient to meet some of these claims. Although in a sense there is less where there is void than where there are atoms, still, void is on a par with atoms in the relevant respect, being. But the argument at **11.8** lines 32–33, which Parmenides uses to establish that what is has all coherently conceivable and describable attributes, cannot be met in this way. Void obviously lacks most of the attributes of the atoms, and so would not be. The Atomists might counter this argument either by denying the premise on which it turns, "it must either fully be or not" (**11.8** l. 11), or by distinguishing between the existential interpretation of that principle, which they accept at the atomic level (void and atoms both exist fully), and the predicative interpretation, which they could deny (an existing thing can fail to have all possible predicates).

Still, the assertion that "nothing" exists is badly defended. The argument that there is no less reason for "nothing" than for "hing" to be would not have impressed Parmenides, who believed there to be a good reason why "nothing" could not be: it cannot be thought or spoken of. But this is a consequence of an argument of which one premise is that it is not possible for nothing to be (**11.6** lines 1–2). This premise is undefended and need not be accepted if there is no reason to. Democritus argued that in the absence of a reason to accept the premise, there is no reason not to hold that "nothing" is just as much as "hing," and he could give as a positive reason for believing in its existence the role it plays in his system.

The assertion that what is not is just as much as what is, thus may not simply be a paradox for paradox's sake. It succinctly brings out the fundamental conflict with Parmenides and invites us to consider the role "what is not" plays in the atomic theory, so that we can judge by reference to the success of the theory the merits of the claim that what is not is.

Can the void be spoken and thought of? In a sense it can, quite obviously. It can be characterized in terms of its rules of occupying space, making possible the motions of atoms, etc. But the Atomists tend to describe it negatively, by contrast with the atoms. It is "empty" as opposed to "full," and is "rare" only in an extended use of that word. Although the presence of void is needed to account for certain qualities of compounds, it is more natural to describe those compounds as consisting of atoms more or less separated, or atoms arranged in a certain way. If atoms are quality-less, so is the void, and the void per se lacks even the spatial properties of atoms. It has no shape or size of its own (aside from its infinite amount). Thus, the Atomists can hold that the void is per se virtually unthinkable and inde-scribable, and except for the various ways it can be described by contrast with and in relation to the atoms, the only feature it has of its own is infinite extension.

Atomic Motion

The infinitely many atoms are all in motion in the infinite void. As an atom moves it may meet with other atoms of the same kind or of different kinds. Such collisions can result in the atoms rebounding away from one another or in their coming together to form compounds. Before discussing compounds, it will be useful to discuss the atoms' motion.

Aristotle makes several complaints against the Atomists' accounts of atomic motion.

16.16 This is why Leucippus and Democritus, who say that the primary bodies are always moving in the void (i.e., the unlimited) must specify what motion they have and what is their natural motion.
(Aristotle, *On the Heaven* 3.2 300b8–11 = DK 67A16)

16.17 Concerning the origin and manner of motion in existing things, these men too, like the rest, lazily neglected to give an account.
(Aristotle, *Metaphysics* 1.4 985b19–20 = DK 67A6)
(continuation of **16.1**)

16.18 For they say that there is always motion. But they do not say why or what motion it is, nor, if it is of one sort or another, do they state the cause. (Aristotle, *Metaphysics* 12.6 1071b33–35 = DK 67A18)

It seems certain that they did not specify the nature or cause of the atoms' original motion. Thus, the isolated statement

16.19 They say that motion occurs on account of the void. For they too say
that nature undergoes motion in respect of place.

(Aristotle, *Physics* 8.9 265b24–25 = DK 68A58)

must mean merely that the void is a necessary condition for motion, not that
it is a cause in the sense of the source of the motion.

However, Aristotle's objections are misconceived. Since atoms and void
are eternal and eternally in motion, there was no initial state corresponding
to the period in Anaxagoras' cosmogony in which "all things were together" (**16.1**). The Atomists therefore avoid Parmenides' question "what
necessity would have stirred it up to grow later rather than earlier" (**11.8**
l. 10). There is no need to posit a cause of the beginning of motion, since
motion has always existed.

Likewise there is no need to talk of an original form of motion. An atom's
motion now is determined by its most recent history of contact with other
atoms, like the motion of billiard balls after they have collided. If we have
perfectly elastic billiard balls and a billiard table with perfectly elastic cush-
ions, and the balls roll on the table without friction or wind resistance, then
if the balls are in motion, they will never stop moving unless affected from
the outside in the future, and likewise, unless they have been affected from
outside in the past, they have always been moving. There is no initial static
condition and no first movement, but at any moment—past, present, or
future—their motion is determined by their immediately previous history.
There is good evidence that this was the Atomists' view of atomic motion.

16.20 Leucippus and Democritus said that their primary bodies, the atoms,
are always moving in the unlimited void by compulsion.

(Simplicius, *Commentary on Aristotle's On the Heaven*
583.18–20 = DK 67A16)

16.21 Democritus, saying that the atoms are naturally motionless, declares
that they move "by a blow."

(Simplicius, *Commentary on Aristotle's Physics*
42.10–11 = DK 68A47)

16.22 Democritus says that the primary bodies (these are the compact things)
do not possess weight but move by knocking against one another in the
unlimited, and there can be an atom the size of the KOSMOS.

(Aetius 1.12.6 = DK 68A47)

16.23 These men [Leucippus and Democritus] say that the atoms move by
hitting and knocking against each other, but they do not specify the
source of their natural motion. For the motion of knocking each other

> is compelled and not natural, and compelled motion is posterior to
> natural motion.   (Alexander, *Commentary on Aristotle's Metaphysics*
> 36.21–25 = DK 67A6)

These passages agree that the atoms move as the result of striking one
another. As **16.20** asserts, this is always the case: an atom is always moving,
at all times its movements are due to previous collisions, and there was no
first collision. In Aristotelian terminology, such motion is "compelled" as
opposed to "natural." Aristotle's belief in natural motion, a body's motion
toward its natural place,[25] and its priority to compelled motion affects
several of the sources. The atoms do not have an inherent tendency either
to be at rest or to move in any particular direction or towards any particular
location, and so they do not have any "natural" motion.[26]

> **16.24** They said that moving in virtue of the weight in them, <the atoms>
> move[27] in respect of place through the void, which yields and does not
> resist. For they said that they "are hurled all about." And they attribute
> this motion to the elements as not only their primary but their only
> motion, whereas things composed of the elements have the other kinds
> of motion. For they grow and decrease, change, come to be and are
> destroyed as the primary bodies combine and separate.
> (Simplicius, *Commentary on Aristotle's Physics*
> 1318.35–1319.5 = DK 68A58)

> **16.25** Democritus indicated a single type of motion, that due to vibration.
> (Aetius 1.23.3 = DK 68A47)

The words translated "are hurled all about" and "vibration"[28] are ety-
mologically related and presumably refer to the same kind of movement,
the bouncing back and forth of the atoms between collisions.

Our discussion of the atoms' original and natural motion leads directly to
the vexed question whether they have weight. The evidence is conflicting
and problematic: in addition to **16.8** there is also the following.

25. The four Aristotelian elements have natural places. For example, earth's is at
the center of the KOSMOS, and the natural motion of earth is toward the center. See
Aristotle, *On the Heaven* 1.8.

26. I take it that this fact is behind the first clause of **16.21** and the second clause
of **16.23**.

27. KINEISTHAI. For Aristotle this word covers motion in place and also other
changes, such as the "motions" listed at the end of this passage.

28. The words are PERIPALASSESTHAI and PALMOS, both derived from the root PAL-,
"to shake."

16.26 Democritus and later Epicurus said that all the atoms have the same nature and possess weight, but since some are heavier, when these settle down the lighter ones are squeezed out and move upwards, and in this way they say that some things appear light and others heavy.
(Simplicius, *Commentary on Aristotle's On the Heaven*
569.5–9 = DK 68A61)

16.27 Democritus says that each of the indivisibles is heavier according as its quantity is greater.   (Aristotle, *On Generation and Corruption*
1.8 326a9–10 = DK 68A60)

16.28 Those <who call the primary bodies> solid can rather say that the larger is heavier. But since compounds do not appear to behave in this way, but we see many that are smaller in bulk but heavier, as bronze is heavier than wood, some think and say that the cause is different—that the void enclosed within makes the bodies light and sometimes makes larger things lighter, since they contain more void. . . . But those who make these distinctions must add not only that something contains more void if it is lighter, but also that it contains less solid.
(Aristotle, *On the Heaven* 4.2 309a1–14 = DK 68A60)

Also **16.22**.

It will help to draw two distinctions. First, atoms may have weight and yet not have it as one of their primary properties (**16.8**). Since atoms are all made of the same uniform stuff, their size and shape will determine how much of that stuff is in them, which will in turn determine their weight (**16.27**). Second, weight can be understood in different ways, including (A) as a tendency to move or otherwise be affected by a certain force (for example, gravity), or alternatively (B) as a tendency to move in a certain direction (for Aristotle, this direction is towards the center of the KOSMOS; for Epicurus, it is downwards), or (C) as a tendency to move in certain ways under certain conditions, differently in different conditions, with no universal tendency to move in any particular direction. As our treatment of atomic motion has shown, the Atomists are committed to view (C). An atom's motion at any moment is determined solely by its previous collision with other atoms. No appeal need be made to any immaterial force like gravity, which has no place in ancient atomism. However, in certain contexts, such as the KOSMOS we live in, matter does have a tendency to move in a certain direction and in general to display the characteristics we associate with weight: for example, that heavier bodies sink and lighter ones rise, and that there is no necessary relation between a body's size and its weight. Some of these phenomena are explained in **16.26** and **16.28**. Others are due to the effects of the cosmogonic vortex, in which like atoms move toward like and the heavier ones toward the center (see pp. 324–26). If this account is correct, the Atomists succeed in accounting for many phenomena of gravity and weight within the confines of their materialistic and mechanistic theory.

If all events are due to the mechanical motion and interaction of atoms in the void, atomism seems to entail a rigid determinism. Perhaps surprisingly, the problems determinism raises for understanding human actions and for central concepts in ethics were not explored until later in the Greek philosophical tradition. Nevertheless, the Atomists and those who discussed their theory did recognize some of its implications for causality. The single surviving sentence of Leucippus bears on this aspect of the atomic theory.

16.29 No thing happens at random but all things as a result of a reason and
    by necessity.   (Leucippus, DK 67B2)

At first sight this appears to deny the mechanistic picture of the atomistic universe presented previously. "Nothing at random" gives the impression that all things happen for a purpose, and "all things as a result of a reason" suggests that the universe is governed by a purposeful intelligence, much like Heraclitus' rational LOGOS. But these impressions are misleading. The key to the fragment is the notion of necessity. Leucippus holds that everything that happens—all movements and interactions of atoms in the void—happens of necessity in that, given the nature of atoms and void, and given the positions and motions of the atoms, things cannot happen otherwise. This necessity is blind necessity, as opposed to conscious or unconscious plan and purpose. It follows immediately that nothing happens by chance or at random. Moreover, there is a reason why everything takes place—not because there is a governing mind, but in the sense that every event has an explanation.[29]

Democritus followed Leucippus in this view.

16.30 Democritus leaves aside purpose, but refers all things which nature
    employs to necessity.
       (Aristotle, *Generation of Animals* 5.8 789b2–4 = DK 68A66)

16.31 <Concerning necessity> Democritus <speaks of> knocking against
    <each other> and motion and "blow" of matter.
             (Aetius 1.26.2 = DK 68A66)

---

29. The word translated "reason" is LOGOS. This word need not imply the existence of a reasoning agent, only that a reason could in principle be given if one were sought.

16.32 <Democritus> seemed to employ chance in his cosmogony, but in his detailed discussions he declares that chance is the cause of nothing, and he refers to other causes.

> (Simplicius, *Commentary on Aristotle's Physics*
> 330.14–17 = DK 68A68)

All events are the necessary consequences of the interaction of atoms, so that chance and purpose form no part of a correct explanation of anything that happens.

Compounds

"They declare that the differences (among these) are the causes of the rest. Moreover, they say that the differences are three: shape, arrangement, and position. . . . For *A* differs from *N* in shape, *AN* from *NA* in arrangement, and *Z* from *N* in position" (from **16.1**). It is possible that the use of letters to illustrate properties of the atoms goes back to the Atomists themselves. This analogy is carried further in **16.2**: tragedies and comedies are written with the same letters.[30] These three kinds of differences are of different types. Whereas the first kind (*A* and *N*) illustrates differences in shapes of individual atoms, the second explicitly and the third implicitly have to do with the roles of atoms in compounds. The second shows how the same atoms can form different compounds (here think of the syllables 'an' and 'na'), and the third shows how a single atom can play different roles depending on its immediate context. Both fire and souls are composed of spherical atoms, but that is not to say that souls are fiery or that fire has the attributes of soul. A single spherical atom out of context cannot be identified as either a soul atom or a fire atom, and in fact by itself it is neither, though in the appropriate context it can be either.[31]

Compounds arise when atoms moving through the void come into contact with one another and instead of rebounding become enmeshed.

> **16.33** These atoms, which are separate from one another in the unlimited void and differ in shape and size and position, and arrangement, move in the void, and when they overtake one another they collide, and some rebound in whatever direction they may happen to, but others become

30. It is likely that the analogy in **16.2** comes from an atomist text, though it could be Aristotle's.

31. Aristotle's unsympathetic report that "Democritus declares the soul to be some kind of fire and hot, for the shapes and atoms being infinite, he says the spherical ones are fire and soul" (*On the Soul* 1.2 403b31–404a2 = DK 67A28), is therefore unfair. Moreover, for all the sources tell us, the atoms which make up souls could be spheres of different sizes from those that make up fire.

entangled in virtue of the relation of their shapes, sizes, positions, and arrangements, and stay together, and this is how compounds are produced. (Simplicius, *Commentary on Aristotle's On the Heaven* 242.21–26 = DK 67A14) (continuation of **16.10**)

16.34 What does Democritus say? That substances unlimited in multitude, atomic and not different in kind, and moreover incapable of acting or being acted upon, are in motion, scattered in the void. When they approach one another or collide or become entangled, the compounds appear as water or fire or as a plant or a human, but all things are atoms, which he calls forms; there is nothing else. For from what is not there is no coming to be, and nothing could come to be from things that are because on account of their hardness the atoms are not acted upon and do not change.
(Plutarch, *Against Colotes* 8 1110F–1111A = DK 68A57)

Compounds, though composed of eternal atoms, are not permanent. They last until struck from outside in the right place by other atoms of sufficient size and appropriate shape, moving with appropriate speed (**16.3**).

Perceptible qualities of compounds are due to the shape, size, arrangement, and position, and possibly the motions, of the quality-less atoms that compose them. Democritus attempted to apply this general principle to specific cases, as the following passages show.

16.35 Leucippus and Democritus, calling the smallest and primary bodies atoms, <say> that in virtue of differences in their shapes and position and order, some bodies come to be hot and fiery—those composed of rather sharp and minute primary bodies situated in a similar position, while others come to be cold and watery—those composed of the opposite kinds of bodies. And some come to be bright and shining while others come to be dim and dark.
(Simplicius, *Commentary on Aristotle's Physics* 36.1–7 = DK 67A14)

16.36 He makes sweet that which is round and good-sized; astringent that which is large, rough, polygonal, and not rounded; sharp tasting, as its name indicates, that which is sharp in body, and angular, bent and not rounded; pungent that which is round and small and angular and bent; salty that which is angular and good-sized and crooked and equal sided; bitter that which is round and smooth, crooked and small sized; oily that which is fine and round and small.
(Theophrastus, *Causes of Plants* 6.1.6 = DK 68A129)

The naiveté of these accounts is less important than Democritus' recognition of the need to show how the theory could be put to use to explain specific phenomena.

Void is also invoked to account for certain qualities. In heavy things the atoms are closely packed, leaving little room for void, and in light things there is more void (**16.28**). A similar account is given of hard and soft, and an attempt was made to distinguish the heavy from the hard and the light from the soft in terms of the position of the atoms.

> **16.37** Iron is harder and lead is heavier, since iron has its atoms arranged
> unevenly and has large quantities of void in many places . . . while lead
> has less void but its atoms are arranged evenly throughout. This is why
> it is heavier, but softer than iron.
>   (Theophrastus, *On Sensation* 62 = DK 68A135)

Equally important, changes in compounds are explained in terms of changes in the spatial relations of atoms: compounds are generated and grow when atoms combine in appropriate ways; they decrease and are destroyed when the atoms separate; they alter (change in quality) when the component atoms change their arrangements and relative positions (**16.2, 16.3, 16.24**). The same explanation also goes for phase changes.

> **16.38** We see that the same continuous body is sometimes liquid and some-
> times solid—not suffering this change by means of separation and
> combination or by turning and touching as Democritus says; for it did
> not become solid from liquid by being transposed or changing its nature.
> (Aristotle, *On Generation and Corruption* 1.9 327a16–20 = DK 68A38)

The Atomists' aim is clear: to account for the macroscopic phenomenal world in terms of the behavior of the microscopic atoms. They present a two-world theory in which the phenomena in one world are reduced to entities and events in the other. The two worlds are strikingly different: the complex phenomenal world with its many different kinds of things, which behave in many ways, is contrasted with the simple world of atoms which are made of but a single type of material, which differ only in size and shape, and whose only behavior is to move in place. The claim that all qualities, events, and changes in the phenomenal world can be reduced to changes in the relative positions of eternal, unchanging, quality-less atoms is remarkably ambitious even in the presocratic tradition, and Democritus' efforts to show how the theory works in detail are unique among the Presocratics.

Cosmogony

The origin of the KOSMOS is described in the following passage.

> **16.39** [Leucippus] declares the universe to be unlimited. . . . Of this, some is
> full and some is empty [void], and he declares these [full and void] to

be elements. An unlimited number of KOSMOI arise out of these and are destroyed into these. The KOSMOI come into being in the following way. Many bodies of all sorts of shapes by virtue of being cut off from the unlimited move into a great void. They collect together and form a single vortex. In it they knock against one another and move around in all different ways, and they separate apart, like moving towards like. When they are no longer able to rotate in equilibrium, the fine ones depart into the void outside as if sifted. The rest remain together, become entangled, and hurry on their way together, and form a first spherical complex. This stands apart like a membrane, enclosing all kinds of bodies in it. As these whirl around by virtue of the resistance of the center, the surrounding membrane becomes thin, since the adjacent atoms are always joining the fluid motion when they come into contact with the vortex. And the earth came into being in this way when the atoms moving to the center remained together. And again the surrounding membrane-like thing itself grows because bodies strike it from outside. Moving in a vortex it acquires whatever it comes into contact with. Some of these become intertwined and form a complex, at first damp and muddy, but when they have dried out and rotate with the vortex of the whole, they catch fire and form the nature of the stars.

(Diogenes Laertius, *Lives of the Philosophers* 9.31–32 = DK 67A1)

This passage begins by distinguishing the universe (literally, "the whole") from a KOSMOS: the former is the totality consisting of all the atoms and all the void; the latter is a world system that is limited both spatially and temporally. There are an infinite number of KOSMOI scattered randomly through the universe, and they come to be and suffer destruction at different times. Though each KOSMOS has its own unique history, since **16.39** is a general account of the origin of KOSMOI, it follows that KOSMOI significantly resemble one another.

Many details of the cosmogony are muddy, but the general picture is clear. (a) Atomic collisions and motions sometimes bring a vast number of atoms of different shapes into a region of the universe where they are relatively isolated from other atoms. (b) The motions and interactions of these atoms create a vortex in which (c) similar atoms move toward one another. The mechanical nature of this sorting is described in the following fragment, which illustrates again[32] Democritus' tendency to employ arguments by analogy—in this case, a correspondence in the behavior of animate and inanimate things.

16.40 Animals flock together with animals of the same kind—doves with doves, cranes with cranes, and likewise for the other irrational kinds. It is also thus for inanimate things, as can be seen easily in the case of

32. See **16.1**.

seeds being sifted and pebbles on the shore. For through the swirling
motion of the sieve lentils are placed separately with lentils, wheat with
wheat, and barley with barley, and through the motion of the waves,
long pebbles are cast to the same place as long ones and round ones to
the same place as round ones, as if the similarity in these had some
mutually attractive force for things.   (Democritus, DK 68B164)

To return to **16.39**, (d) the rotation of the vortex drives the smaller (therefore lighter) atoms to the periphery, and finally (e) out of the system
altogether, while (f) the remaining atoms form a spherical structure ("like a
membrane"—a spherical shell, not a solid sphere), which continues to
revolve. (g) In the continued rotation, like-to-like separation continues,
with the larger, heavier atoms coming together toward the center to form
the earth, and the outer shell becoming increasingly thinner. But then
(h) the outer shell is increased when other atoms in the vicinity are caught
up in the whirl. (i) Some of the atoms in the shell form a system that (curi-
ously) is at first moist but later (j) ignited and thus forms the visible stars.

It is worth adding that there is nothing inevitable in this sequence of
events. We may imagine that for every time a KOSMOS is formed, there are
many times when a sufficiently large number of atoms come together (stage
a) but fail to form a vortex (stage b), just hovering in the same area until
their interactions cause them to disperse.

The crucial features of this cosmogony are that it results from mechanical atomic movements without purpose or divine agency, and that our
KOSMOS is not special, only one of an infinite number of similar KOSMOI
with similar histories. That our world is not unique or located at the center
of the universe, and that we are insignificant from a cosmic point of view,
are strikingly modern ideas and drastic departures from common sense and
from what sense experience would lead us to believe. The Atomists' readiness to embrace these counterintuitive consequences of their physical system is a measure of their boldness.

A system that posits an infinite number of worlds naturally invites speculation about their nature. The small amount of information on the ancient
Atomists' views on this matter is contained in the following testimonium,
which leaves it unclear whether they described the other worlds in detail.

16.41 There are an infinite number of KOSMOI of different sizes. In some
there is no sun or moon. In some the sun and moon are larger than
ours and in others there are more. The distances between the KOSMOI
are unequal and in one region there are more, in another fewer. Some
are growing, some are at their peak, and some are declining, and here
one is coming into being, there one is ceasing to be. They are destroyed
when they collide with one another. Some KOSMOI have no animals,

plants or any moisture. . . . A KOSMOS is at its peak until it is no longer able to take anything in from outside.

(Hippolytus, *Refutation* 1.13.2–4 = DK 68A40)
(the omitted words are translated in **16.43**)

16.41 states that a KOSMOS is destroyed when it collides with another— apparently a cosmic vortex can move through the void the way whirlwinds move through the air. But the mention of KOSMOI that are declining and failing suggests that they can also be destroyed from within, as it were. The final sentence explains the circumstances in which a KOSMOS declines without explaining why those conditions occur. This theory may reflect ancient theories that the bodies of animals deteriorate in old age through loss of the ability to absorb nutrition. If so, the "death" of a KOSMOS could be understood as the final stage in such decline, where its atoms are dispersed—again, through the mechanical motions of its constituent atoms. There is no set lifespan for a KOSMOS, but the mechanical necessity of atomic interactions guarantees that KOSMOI must come to an end.

Cosmology

The Atomists paid more attention than many of their predecessors to astronomy. Their views stemmed from a variety of sources as far back as Anaximenes, and they do not seem to have made a consistent effort to explain heavenly phenomena in terms of the behavior of atoms and void. The following theories are representative.

16.42 The orbit of the sun is furthest out, that of the moon is nearest to the earth, and the others are in between these. All the stars are on fire because of the speed of their motion, but the sun is also on fire because of the stars. The moon has only a small share of fire. The sun and moon eclipse . . . [something is missing from the text] because the earth is tilted toward the south. The regions to the north are always covered with snow and very cold and frozen. The sun eclipses rarely, but the moon does so continuously because their orbits are unequal.

(Diogenes Laertius, *Lives of the Philosophers* 9.33 = DK 67A1)
(continuation of **16.39**)

16.43 In our own KOSMOS the earth came into being before the stars. The moon is lowest, then the sun, then the fixed stars. The planets themselves have different heights.

(Hippolytus, *Refutation* 1.13.4 = DK 68A40)

Leucippus placed the sun furthest from the earth (**16.42**), Democritus the stars (**16.43**). The Pythagoreans may have previously paid attention to the orbits of the planets,[33] but Democritus had a special interest in them (perhaps a result of his travels in the East where he could have gained knowledge of Babylonian astronomy) and wrote a treatise on them. Democritus also agreed with Anaxagoras on the nature of the Milky Way and of comets.[34] Both Atomists place the earth at the center of our KOSMOS, and they agree that it is supported by air beneath it.[35] For Leucippus it is flat; for Democritus, concave.[36] Democritus departs from tradition by making the earth not round but oval or oblong, with its length one and one-half times its width.[37] Leucippus, interestingly, believed that the earth, still under the influence of the vortex, "revolves about the center,"[38] but (again because of the role of the vortex) he failed to go on to make the heavenly bodies stationary and explain their apparent movements as due to the earth's rotation. Democritus explained the angle between the celestial north pole and the zenith as due to the earth's having tilted.[39]

> **16.44** Because the southerly part of the surrounding <and supporting air> is weaker, the earth, as it was growing, tilted in this direction. For the northern parts are intemperate, but the southern parts are temperate. This is why it tilted in this direction, where it is above average in fruits and growth.   (Aetius 3.12.2 = DK 68A96)

Apparently, the extra weight of vegetation tended to push the southern part down, while the air there, thinner because of the excessive heat in that region, was less able to support it.

In meteorological matters, Democritus was more consistent in offering atomistic explanations.

> **16.45** Democritus stated that thunder results from an uneven union <of atoms> compelling the cloud which surrounds it to move downwards.

33. See **9.31**, **9.32**, and discussion pp.105–107.

34. The Milky Way is the light of stars from which the earth blocks the rays of the sun (Aristotle, *Meteorologica* 1.8 345a25–31 = DK 59A80); comets are a conjunction of planets so near as to be in apparent contact (Aristotle, *Meteorologica* 1.6 342b27–29 = DK 59A81).

35. This view goes back to Anaximenes (see **6.8**).

36. Diogenes Laertius, *Lives of the Philosophers* 9.30 (= DK 67A1), Aetius 3.10.5 (= DK 68A94).

37. Democritus, DK 68B15.

38. Diogenes Laertius, *Lives of the Philosophers* 9.30 (= DK 67A1).

39. Here he disagrees with Empedocles and Anaxagoras, who held that the heavens tilted (Aetius 2.8.2 = DK 31A58 for Empedocles, Aetius 2.8.1 = DK 59A67 for Anaxagoras).

Lightning is the collision of clouds, as a result of which the atoms which give rise to fire move together through empty places with much void to the same place by means of their jostling alongside one another. A thunderbolt occurs when there is a violent motion of purer and finer fire-producing atoms which are more even and "close-fitted" (the word Democritus himself uses). A waterspout occurs when collections of fire containing much void are held back in regions with a lot of void and in wrappings of special membranes, and form bodies because of this rich mixture and make a rush toward the depth.

(Aetius 3.3.11 = DK 68A93)

The Microcosm

In a famous fragment, Democritus calls a human being "a small (MIKROS) KOSMOS".[40] The idea that humans function on the principles that govern the world is hardly new with the Atomists. Earlier Presocratics at least as far back as Anaximenes had exploited it, explaining cosmic phenomena in terms of human phenomena and vice versa. The roots of the idea extend far back into prephilosophical animistic thought. Although the conception was not new with the Atomists, it had particular force for them since they set out to account for all aspects of the KOSMOS, including animals and human beings, on atomic principles. Their task, then, was to explain how life can arise out of the movement of atoms and how all life's activities can be reduced to atomic behavior. To account for these aspects of the world was perhaps the severest challenge the Atomists faced, and it may be that "microcosm" was their battle cry.

For the origin of life, including human life, Democritus follows Anaximander and other Presocratics in saying that living beings arose from water and mud, a "moisture which gives rise to life."[41] This is all we are told. Living things differ from the inanimate by the presence of soul. For the Atomists, the soul consists of spherical atoms, because of their mobility. Change and movement are therefore seen to be the key features of living things. The fact that spherical atoms are also the constituents of fire has already been remarked. If there is any connection between these two functions of such atoms, it will be that most animals are warm while alive and cold after death. The soul is a material entity. The soul's atoms are not destroyed at death, but disperse from the dead body. They disperse gradually, an idea that makes sense in terms of the likely physical behavior of the atoms and which also accounts for the fact that some vital functions, such

---

40. Democritus, DK 68B34.
41. Aetius 5.19.6 (= DK 68A139).

as the growth of hair and fingernails, continue for a time after death.[42]
Democritus informs us that there were no certain criteria that doctors
trusted for determining the end of life.[43]

The soul atoms are scattered throughout the body. Their small size and
their shape make them most able to move among other atoms without
getting entangled into compounds. In what seems a hopelessly naive way,
the Atomists believed that the motions of an animal's body are produced by
contact of the easily moving soul atoms with other atoms in the body.
Aristotle's criticism is appropriate.

> **16.46** Some say that the soul moves the body in which it is found in the same
> way as it moves itself, Democritus, for example, whose view is similar to
> what we find in Philippos the comic poet. He says that Daedalus made
> the wooden statue of Aphrodite move by pouring quicksilver into it.
> Democritus speaks similarly, since he says that moving spherical atoms,
> whose nature is never to stay still, draw the entire body along with them
> and move it. But we will ask if these same things also produce rest.
> How they will do so is difficult or impossible to state. In general, the
> soul does not appear to move the body in this way, but through choice
> of some kind and through thought.
>   (Aristotle, *On the Soul* 1.3 406b16–25; part = DK 68A104)

Sensation and Thought

The other principal functions of soul are sensation and thought, and Democritus probably believed that the soul atoms that perform these functions
are concentrated in the head.[44] The Atomists had much to say about sensation in general and the five senses individually. Leucippus proposed a clear
but crude theory, which Democritus elaborated. Theophrastus' long and
critical discussion of Democritus' doctrines[45] provides most of our information. In general, all sensation results from the contact of atoms. Atoms
of the perceived object strike atoms in the sense organ, which transmit the
sense impressions to the soul atoms. In effect, all five senses are reduced to
the sense of touch. Thus, Democritus makes all sensory objects objects of
touch.[46] Since sensation depends on the interaction of the sensed object

42. Tertullian, *On the Soul* 51 (= DK 68A160).

43. Celsus 2.6 (= DK 68A160).

44. Aetius 4.5.1 (= DK 68A105).

45. Theophrastus, *On Sensation* 49–83 (= DK 68A135).

46. This is Aristotle's observation (Aristotle, *On Sensation* 4 442a29–b1 = DK
68A119).

and the sensing animal, the condition of the sensor affects the sensations: sensations are relative to the observer. On the other hand, they are not purely relative since they also depend on the sensed object, which exists objectively, and whose atoms have objective attributes of size, shape, and position. This tension between subjectivism and objectivism is crucial in understanding the epistemology of the Atomists.[47]

Two of the senses, touch and taste, involve direct contact of the sensed object with the body of the sensor. With the remaining three, sight, hearing, and smell, where the object does not normally touch the sense organ, the Atomists need to explain in atomic terms how the object can affect our senses at a distance.

We saw previously how Democritus associates different tastes with different atomic shapes **(16.36)** and different tactile qualities with different atomic arrangements **(16.35, 16.37)**. No more need be said here about these senses, except to point out an objection Theophrastus makes to the doctrine of taste and which he says applies to the atomist account of all five senses.[48] Atomic shape is an objective property, and if different tastes are defined in terms of different atomic shapes, taste is objective too. But this view contradicts the relativity of sensations to the sensor. The same thing may taste sweet to some and bitter to others, but an atom cannot be spherical to some and otherwise to others. (Cf. **16.50**.)

Democritus' account of sight is the most interesting account of a sense that takes place at a distance. The Atomists adapted Empedocles' doctrine that physical objects give off films or effluences which enter our body through pores.[49] For the Atomists, the effluences are thin films of atoms that form an image of the object and move through the space between the object and the eye. Leucippus offered a simple theory: these films, which have the shape of the sense object, strike the eye, where they form a reflection of the object in the pupil. In this way vision occurs.[50] Democritus modified this theory.

> **16.47** The visual impression does not come to be in the pupil right away, but the air between the eye and the object is contracted and stamped by the object and by the seeing thing. For there is a continual effluence from everything. Then this [air], which is solid and changed in color, forms an impression in the eyes which are moist.
>
> (Theophrastus, *On Sensation* 50 = DK 68A135)

47. See pp. 334–335.
48. Theophrastus, *On Sensation* 69 (= DK 68A135).
49. See p. 282–283.
50. Alexander, *Commentary on Aristotle's On Sensation* 24.14–22 (= DK 67A29).

Good vision requires the parts of the eye to be in good condition. For instance, the "veins" must be straight and dry, to conform in shape to the images or impressions and to transmit them accurately to the soul atoms in the body.[51] The mechanics of vision are hard to understand. The nature of the interaction between the film of atoms from the object and the atoms emitted by the eye is especially obscure. The account as we have it leaves many questions open. Why do physical objects not decrease in size as the result of continually losing films of atoms? When we see the Parthenon, how can a film the size of the Parthenon fit into an eye? (Is this why Democritus modified Leucippus' theory and spoke of contraction in the intervening air?) This account explains how a visual impression has the same shape as the object, but does not explain how we see colors, and although Democritus says a good deal about color, it is unclear how to fit what he says into his account of vision.

Democritus recognizes four primary colors: white, black, red, and yellow.[52] He associates each of these with certain atomic shapes and arrangements of atoms on the surface of objects. For example, in things with hard surfaces, which are bright, conspicuous, and without shadows, white is associated with smooth atoms; and in friable things with easily crushed surfaces, it is associated with round atoms set slantwise to one another and in pairs, with the entire arrangement as even as possible. The other colors arise from mixtures of the primaries, and Democritus goes into some detail about how particular blends yield particular colors.[53]

Thought resembles sensation. Both sensations and thoughts are "alterations of the body" and both "take place when images enter from outside."[54] "He makes thought dependent on bodily condition as is appropriate, since he makes the soul a body."[55] Further, thinking arises from the same sort of process as sensations do, especially sight. Apparently the films of atoms that activate thought are not in all cases the same as those that activate the sense organs, though those too affect thought after the sense organs transmit them to the soul. But since not all thinking is reflection on present sensations, some of the films entering from outside affect the soul directly, not through the mediation of the senses. The atoms in these films may be too fine to be noticed by the senses.[56] A similar account is offered of dreams.[57]

---

51. Theophrastus, *On Sensation* 50 (= DK 68A135).
52. These were the four basic colors used by Greek painters.
53. Theophrastus, *On Sensation* 73–82 (= DK 68A135).
54. Aetius 4.8.5, 4.8.10 (= DK 67A30).
55. Theophrastus, *On Sensation* 58 (= DK 68A135).
56. This interpretation follows Guthrie, *HGP*, vol. 2, pp. 452–53.
57. Plutarch, *Table Talk* 8.10 p. 735A–B (= DK 68A77).

The naiveté of these attempts to explain the phenomena of sensation and thought does not need to be stressed. They raise many questions that they seem unable to answer, and they are open to many obvious objections. From our information about these theories,[58] it appears that the Atomists failed to face three issues in particular. First, they reduce all thought and sensation to movements of the soul atoms, but do not say why some movements are perceived as sounds, others as tastes, and others as thoughts. Second, they do not clearly distinguish between mental events and the concomitant bodily states. Third, they do not account for the voluntary and apparently undetermined nature of some thought, but seem to think that our thoughts are determined by the atomic films striking us at a given moment. Cicero makes fun of this flaw: "If I begin to think of the island of Britain, will its film of atoms fly to my breast?"[59]

Although these theories are easy to criticize, we must recall that Leucippus and Democritus were the first philosophers to attempt so detailed an account of thought and perception. They performed an important service by exploring how far a purely materialist theory of cognition can go. The questions their accounts left open and the objections others made to their views stimulated further thought on the subject and pointed out to later investigators (notably their harsh critics Aristotle and Theophrastus) many important problems that needed to be tackled.

Knowledge

The philosophies of Anaxagoras, Empedocles, and the Atomists save the phenomenal world from the Eleatic challenge by postulating a more fundamental level of reality that conforms in some degree to the demands of the Eleatics and which also accounts for the sensible phenomena that the Eleatics rejected. These accounts raise important questions not only about the nature of reality but also about our knowledge of reality. For if one goal of the exercise is to rescue the senses and the sensible world, and doing so requires explaining them as mere epiphenomena of a realm of reality that is inaccessible to the senses, does it not follow that the senses and the world they reveal are unredeemed? And if another goal is the empiricists' aim to ground knowledge in the reports of sense perception, is it not fatal if the basic entities prove to be in principle imperceptible? For the system will rest upon things whose existence and behavior are not known through the principal avenue of knowledge.

These issues are more pressing for the Atomists than for Empedocles or

58. Our information depends almost entirely on the hostile Aristotelian-Theophrastean tradition and may not always be fair to the Atomists.

59. Cicero, *Letters to his Friends* 15.16.1 (= DK 68A118).

Anaxagoras, whose basic things are in some sense perceptible. Democritus paid them due attention. He wrote a work called *Canon*, or *Canons*,[60] which opposed scientific demonstration and contrasted the senses unfavorably with the mind as sources of knowledge,[61] and one called the *Confirmations* (*Kratunteria*) in which "he promised to attribute to the senses the power of conviction."[62]

It is deeply frustrating that little remains of Democritus' work on this subject. Even the descriptions of the works just mentioned seem to conflict with one another, and the situation is no better with the other material we possess. The problem is partly due to the nature of our sources. Sextus Empiricus (second century A.D.), to whom we owe much of our information, tries to make Democritus into a fellow sceptic, but does so by quoting him out of context. Immediately after the sentence quoted at the end of the previous paragraph, he goes on to say that Democritus' theory of perception does not provide a basis for certain knowledge. For perception depends on interaction between our body and atoms from the perceived object, and since the atomic composition of both our body and the object is subject to change from time to time, our perceptions are not sufficiently stable for exact understanding.

> **16.48** None the less he is found condemning them [the senses]. For he says, "We in fact understand nothing exactly [or, exact], but what changes according to the disposition both of the body and of the things that enter it and offer resistance to it."
>
> (Democritus, DK 68B9, part, and context from Sextus Empiricus, *Against the Mathematicians* 7.136 = DK 68B9)

Further, some of Democritus' epistemological discussion was cast in the form of a dialogue between mind and the senses (see below, **16.56**), which makes it extremely difficult to assess isolated excerpts.

In general, the atomic theory provides a variety of viewpoints from which to approach epistemological issues, and our severely limited sources may simply not add up to a coherent theory just because their contexts have been lost. In what follows I attempt to make sense of the extant information by fitting it into the framework of the atomic theory developed earlier in this chapter. Two principal distinctions govern the following discussion: that between the objective and subjective components of sensation (see

60. Epicurus' work on epistemology had the same title.

61. Sextus Empiricus, *Against the Mathematicians* 8.327 (= DK 68B10b), 7.138 (= DK 68B11).

62. Sextus Empiricus, *Against the Mathematicians* 7.136 (= DK 68B9).

pp. 330–31), and that between judgment of perceptible qualities, based on the senses, and judgment of atoms and the void, based on the mind.

16.49 There are two kinds of judgment, one legitimate and the other bastard. All the following belong to the bastard: sight, hearing, smell, taste, touch. The other is legitimate and is separated from this. When the bastard one is unable to see or hear or smell or taste or grasp by touch any further in the direction of smallness, but <we need to go still further> towards what is fine, <then the legitimate one enables us to carry on>.[63]   (Democritus, DK 68B11)

16.50 By convention [or, custom], sweet; by convention bitter; by convention, hot; by convention, cold; by convention, color; but in reality, atoms and void.[64]   (Democritus, DK 68B9, part)

Knowledge of atoms and void is legitimate because it is objective and based on what exists in reality. The senses yield bastard judgment because they reveal perceptible qualities, which are properties not of atoms but of compounds. Worse, these qualities are not even objective properties that compounds have in their own right, but result from interaction between the perceived object and the observer's sense organs. How an object appears differs from perceiver to perceiver and in the same perceiver from time to time, depending on the condition of the sense organ, so that there is no objective reason to attribute any particular quality to a given object. Such attributions are only "by convention." Thus, the senses fail to produce legitimate judgment for three separate reasons: they have a subjective component, their objects are compounds, not the primary entities atoms and void, and the qualities they perceive are not the basic atomic properties of shape, order, and position.

Some of Democritus' remarks so emphasize the difficulty of going beyond appearances to reality that he has seemed to some a thorough sceptic about the possibility of knowledge:[65] in addition to **16.48**, also the following.

63. This fragment trails off into corruption, but there is general agreement about the sense of what is missing.

64. The contrast between "by convention" (NOMOS) and "in reality" recalls that between NOMOS and PHYSIS which was prominent in other intellectual contexts in the late fifth century. See chap. 22.

65. Notably Barnes, *The Presocratic Philosophers*, pp. 559–64. Asmis, *Epicurus' Scientific Method*, pp. 337–50, casts him as a sceptic about humans' capacity to attain knowledge since we must employ the senses, but as possibly holding a rationalist belief in the ability of reason to attain truth without the use of sense perception. Guthrie, *HGP*, vol. 2, pp. 454–65, does a good job of posing the problems and setting out the evidence.

16.51 A person must know by this rule [KANON: measuring stick, standard]
that he is separated from reality.

(Democritus, DK 68B6)

16.52 In fact it will be clear that to know in reality what each thing is like is a
matter of perplexity [or, . . . that people are at a loss to know in reality
what each thing is like]

(Democritus, DK 68B8)

16.53 In reality we know nothing about anything, but for each person opinion
is a reshaping [of the soul atoms by the atoms entering from without].

(Democritus, DK 68B7)

16.54 Either nothing is true, or at least to us it is unclear [or, hidden].

(Aristotle, *Metaphysics* 4.5 1009b11–12 = DK 68A112)

On the other hand, there is good evidence that Democritus was far from a
sceptic, as in reports like the following.

16.55 It is because these thinkers suppose knowledge to be sensation, and this
to be a physical alteration, that they say that what appears to our senses
must be true.

(Aristotle, *Metaphysics* 4.5 1009b12–15 = DK 68A112)

(continuation of **16.54**)

Also "truth is in the appearance" (**16.2**).[66] The apparent contradiction[67]
between these claims and the previously quoted fragments makes for severe
difficulties in understanding the Atomists' epistemology. I suggest that **16.2**
and **16.55** reflect Democritus' view that sensations do have an objective
basis in reality (being caused by the atoms of the perceived object) and are
not simply arbitrary fictions of our mind. Sensations, which are the effects
of atomic interactions, really exist. "True" here may mean "based in reality" as opposed to fictional.

Democritus also recognizes a genuine form of judgment alongside the
obscure judgments due to the senses. And although atoms and void are

66. Another passage attesting this view is Aristotle, *On the Soul* 1.2 404a28–29
(= DK 68A101).

67. The fact that **16.55** occurs in Aristotle just after **16.54** has been taken to prove
that Aristotle did not think that the two statements are contradictory (Guthrie,
HGP, vol. 2, p. 460), but it is quite likely that Aristotle took them out of different
contexts in Democritus.

imperceptible, the Atomists claim to have grasped the truth. How this can happen is suggested by the report[68] that Democritus approved of Anaxagoras' assertion **(16.21)** "Appearances are a sight of the unseen." Perception of macroscopic phenomena constitutes the first step in acquiring knowledge of the microscopic truth.

In what appears to be a moment of self-awareness, Democritus portrays the senses as addressing the mind in a dialogue or legal suit, as follows.

> **16.56** Wretched mind, after taking your evidence from us do you throw us down? Throwing us down is a fall[69] for you!
>
> (Democritus, DK 68B125)

Mind's reply should be that the senses provide the necessary starting point for inquiry. Even though the resulting theory reveals the shortcomings of the senses, it could not have been reached without their help. Moreover, sensible attributes include shape, size, position, and arrangement (conspicuously absent from **16.50**), the primary qualities of the atoms. And even though we cannot perceive atoms and void, still, our sensations have an objective basis in compounds of atoms, which, although not basic entities, certainly exist. As **16.2** explains, the behavior and appearance of sensible compounds are grounds for inferences to the nature and behavior of their constituent atoms. Again, "appearances are a sight of the unseen." Thus, sensible reality constitutes the data that the atomic theory is to account for. Finally, far from simply discrediting the senses, the atomic theory explains how and why they go wrong, and how they are related to truth and reality.

We have no information on how the atomists believed it is possible to move from the level of sense experience, in which we are separated from reality and believe in qualities that have no real existence, to the level of reason, in which we possess secure, objective knowledge of the truth of things. Thought, like the senses, depends on films of atoms and on the condition of the atoms in the thinking soul. It has been suggested that the mind has direct awareness of atoms by virtue of their striking its atoms, but this does not explain how the senses provide the evidence the mind uses in grasping the truth of things. Some process of reasoning is needed to get from the one kind of grasp to the other, and it is doubtful that so crude a materialist theory as fifth-century atomism could come close to accounting for such a mental process.

---

68. Sextus Empiricus, *Against the Mathematicians* 7.140 (= DK 59B21a).

69. The word is a technical term in wrestling for a fall. It is sometimes translated here more colorlessly as "downfall."

The Gods

Since all sensation and thought result from our contact with atoms from outside us, and since we have conceptions of gods, there must be a basis in reality for these conceptions. Democritus therefore recognized the existence of gods, but the sources leave his actual views on this subject unclear. The most interesting information is the following statement.

> **16.57** Democritus says that certain images of atoms approach humans, and of them some cause good and others evil, and as a result he prayed "to meet with propitious images." These are large and immense, and difficult to destroy though not indestructible. They indicate the future in advance to people when they are seen and emit voices. As a result people of ancient times, upon perceiving the appearances of these things, supposed that they are a god, though there is no other god aside from these having an indestructible nature.
> (Sextus Empiricus, *Against the Mathematicians* 9.19 = DK 68B166)

This passage makes it seem that the images themselves are gods, but other sources[70] say that Democritus also said that the gods are things that are the source of these images in the same way that other physical objects emit films of atoms that affect our mind and senses. The ability of these images to predict the future must be a concession to ordinary superstitious belief, since it is hard to square with the atomic theory. The extremely long-lasting but not eternal nature of these gods seems to show that Democritus was willing to accommodate his theology to common belief only within limits. No atomic compound is completely indestructible.

Ethics

The vast majority of Democritus' fragments are on ethical matters, though the authenticity of many of the ethical fragments is disputable. Democritus seems to have thought that the atomic theory provided a physical basis for ethics.

> **16.58** Cheerfulness arises in people through moderation of enjoyment and due proportion in life. Deficiencies and excesses tend to change suddenly and give rise to large movements in the soul. Souls which undergo motions involving large intervals are neither steady nor cheerful. . . .
> (Democritus, DK 68B191)

This fragment must be taken in connection with the statement that

---

70. Cicero, *On the Nature of the Gods* 1.12.29 (= DK 68A74); Clement, *Stromata* 5.88 (= DK 68A79).

16.59 The goal of life is cheerfulness, which is not the same as pleasure . . . but the state in which the soul continues calmly and stably, disturbed by no fear or superstition or any other emotion. He also calls it well-being and many other names.

> (Diogenes Laertius, *Lives of the Philosophers* 9.45 = DK 68A1)

The references in **16.58** to movements in the soul and large intervals seem to refer to the atoms that constitute the soul. Not that all movement of the spherical soul atoms is bad: they remain the most mobile atoms of all, and the functioning of the soul depends on their movements.

16.58 and **16.59** identify a particular physical condition of soul as the goal of life and give us an indication (cheerfulness) by which we can recognize whether our soul is in this state. The remainder of the fragment (not quoted here) specifies certain ways of thinking and behaving (avoid envy, consider yourself fortunate in comparison with the truly wretched, etc.) that will contribute to a life aimed at this goal. The identification of the objective physical basis of cheerfulness or well-being as the goal of life accords with Democritus' distinction between cheerfulness and pleasure. Not all pleasures are to be pursued.

16.60 Accept nothing pleasant unless it is beneficial.

> (Democritus, DK 68B74)

16.61 To all humans the same thing is good and true, but different people find different things pleasant. (Democritus, DK 68B69)

What is beneficial is what helps attain or maintain a state of well-being, the one thing that is good for all. Still, pleasure is not altogether divorced from cheerfulness. Some pleasures are beneficial and we should pursue them. As for the rest, it is within our power to master them.

16.62 Brave is not only he who masters the enemy but also he who masters pleasures. Some are lords of cities but slaves of women.

> (Democritus, DK 68B214)

We even have the capacity to reform ourselves so as to take pleasure in beneficial things.

16.63 Nature and teaching are closely related. For teaching reshapes the person, and by reshaping makes <his> nature.

> (Democritus, DK 68B33)

In this fragment, METARUSMEIN, translated "reshape," must designate an alteration in the RUSMOS or "rhythm" (the Atomists' technical term for shape)[71] of the soul's atoms. When these atoms are rearranged, the soul undergoes a significant alteration: its very nature (its atomic structure) is affected. The word PHYSIOPOIEIN, translated "makes <his> nature," is found only here. Doubtless an invention of Democritus, the word boldly puts his point that we can be affected at the most fundamental level by our experiences, and contributes as well to the interpretation of this point in terms of the atomic theory. In this way what we find pleasant depends on our soul's state, and since we can affect this, we can also determine our pleasures.

> **16.64** Best for a person is to live his life being as cheerful and as little distressed as possible. This will occur if he does not make his pleasures in mortal things. (Democritus, DK 68B189)

> **16.65** All those who make their pleasures from the belly, exceeding the right time for food, drink, or sex, have short-lived pleasures—only for as long as they eat or drink—but many pains. (Democritus, DK 68B235)

We are to "make our pleasures" from the things that promote and preserve the objective, lasting state of true cheerfulness. Thus, Democritus the laughing philosopher is no simple hedonist, but the proponent of a naturalistic ethics based on his physical theory and also on both the real condition and the potentialities of human nature.

Many of the ethical fragments can be read in the light of this connection between physical theory and ethics. It is easy to relate Democritus' counsels of moderation, prudence, doing right rather than wrong, and obeying rather than disobeying the laws to this view of the goal of life. However, it is not clear that he worked out a detailed ethical system, as some have claimed.[72]

How Far Atomism?

The atomic theory is a theory about the nature of physical reality. However, it is possible to develop atomistic philosophical interpretations of other phenomena as well. Some later Greek philosophers held that time is not continuous, but composed of indivisible least instants, and likewise for spatial extension ("place") and motion.[73] I have alluded to the controversy

71. See **16.1**.

72. For an interesting attempt to construct an ethical theory out of the fragments and relate it to the atomic theory and to fifth-century medical doctrines, see G. Vlastos, "Ethics and Physics in Democritus," *Philosophical Review* 54 (1945): 578–92, and 55 (1946): 53–64; reprinted in *Studies in Presocratic Philosophy*, vol. 2, pp. 381–408.

73. Simplicius says that the Epicureans believed in atomic units of all these types

of whether the fifth-century Atomists believed that atoms are theoretically as well as physically indivisible, and it is quite possible that Epicurus was following Democritus in his atomistic view of time.

One interesting fragment survives that is relevant to the question of indivisible spatial magnitudes.

> **16.66** If a cone is cut by a plane parallel to the base, what should we think about the surfaces of the segments? Do they prove to be equal or unequal? For if they are unequal, they will make the cone uneven, but with many steplike notches and roughnesses, but if they are equal <the surfaces of> the segments will be equal, and the cone will appear to have the property of a cylinder, being composed of equal, not unequal circles, which is most absurd. (Democritus, DK 68B155)

The difficulty is that the fragment states the dilemma but does not indicate Democritus' solution. Clearly enough, an atomistic view of space would compel him to say that the apparently smooth surface of a cone is really (i.e., at the atomic level) jagged, but in that case there is no real dilemma at all. In the end it must be admitted that the fragment as it stands is compatible with spatial atomism but cannot be used as evidence that Democritus advocated that view.

It is reasonable to press on to ask what the subject matter of geometry is for Democritus. For he was a mathematician of note. He is credited with stating, though not proving, the theorems that the volume of a cone is one-third that of a cylinder with the same base and height and that the volume of a pyramid is one-third that of a prism with the same base and height.[74] Is geometry somehow related to the atomic theory or is it a separate subject, not intended to describe physical reality at all, whether compounds, atoms, or the void?[75] Given Democritus' interest in the shapes of atoms, it seems to me very likely that geometry, viewed as the analysis of magnitudes, which include shapes, was not meant to be without application in the physical world in general or to atoms in particular. That geometry applies to the atoms themselves becomes almost inescapable on the interpretation of atoms as geometrically divisible though physically divisible (see p. 312).[76]

(*Commentary on Aristotle's Physics* 934.23–30, not in DK). See discussion in A. Long and D. Sedley, *The Hellenistic Philosophers*, vol. 1, pp. 51–52.

74. Archimedes, *Method* 430.2–9 in vol. 2 of Heiberg's edition (Leipzig, 1913), printed in a note at DK, vol. 2, p. 174.

75. This latter view is held by Furley, *The Greek Cosmologists*, vol. 1, pp. 129–31. It accords with and is to some extent dependent on Furley's belief that Democritean atoms are theoretically indivisible.

76. In this interpretation I agree with H. Mendell (op. cit. [p. 312 n. 17]), who discusses the issues more fully.

The Fate of the Atomic Theory

The view that matter is composed of atoms did not, of course, die with Democritus. In fact, there is a historical link between fifth-century atomism and today's atomic theory. But it is far from true either that once discovered, the atomic theory gained universal acceptance or that twentieth-century atomic theory closely resembles the atomism of Leucippus and Democritus. In what follows I shall briefly sketch a few of the most important stages in the history of responses to and developments in the atomic theory, both in antiquity and in modern times.

PLATO. Although Plato mentions many of his philosophical predecessors and contemporaries, he never refers to Democritus by name. Nevertheless, some points of contact have been found between the Atomists' cosmogony and that given in Plato's *Timaeus*, and the "geometrical atomism" of that dialogue may owe some of its inspiration to Democritus. Still, the differences between the two thinkers are profound. Plato's idealism makes beauty, goodness, and order the foundations of a grand teleological scheme that is the antithesis of Democritus' non-moral, mechanical materialism.

THE ARISTOTELIAN TRADITION. Aristotle, his commentators, and Theophrastus knew of fifth-century atomism and frequently discussed it. Their attitude is in general hostile and their discussions mostly consist of unsympathetic criticisms based on their own system, which is incompatible with atomism.

EPICURUS (341–271). Democritus had a number of followers during his lifetime and after his death. The most important was Epicurus, who founded a school of philosophy in Athens. Like other philosophers of the Hellenistic period, Epicurus' chief interests were in ethics, but the physical theory on which his entire philosophical system rested was Leucippus' and Democritus' atomic theory with a few modifications. There are only a finite number of atomic shapes; atoms are physically but not theoretically indivisible, though they have theoretical parts which are indivisible; weight is a fundamental property of atoms; atoms had an original motion in which they were falling at equal velocities in parallel downward trajectories through the void; the initial collisions resulted from occasional uncaused "swerves." In the area of human action, the swerve, as the only kind of atomic movement not caused mechanically (and therefore, in theory, predictably) by interaction with other atoms, becomes the key to account for free will. The gods are located in the tracts of the universe between KOSMOI— remote and unconcerned with human events, and therefore wrongly considered as figures of awe and dread. As with Democritus, the soul is composed of atoms and disperses at death; Epicurus inferred from this thesis that there is no afterlife to fear. This is not the place to go further into Epicurean philosophy, but from what has been said it is clear that atomism remained a vital part of the Greek intellectual tradition long after the end of the presocratic period. In this respect it is unique among the presocratic systems.

MODERN ATOMIC THEORY. Epicurus' atomism was revived in the seventeenth century by Descartes' opponent Gassendi, and in the eighteenth century it was common ground that matter was composed of ultimate units that are hard, unchanging, and endowed with shape and weight. The classical chemical theory of the nineteenth century continued to envisage atoms as the smallest units of matter, and the distinction between atoms and molecules is a recognizable development of the ancient distinction between atoms and compounds. The idea that atoms have physically separable parts (electrons, protons, etc.) is anathema to the ancient atomic theory, but the obvious response is that what corresponds to Democritus' unsplittable atoms are what we (incorrectly) call subatomic particles. The most important differences between ancient and modern atomic theory therefore are not in the splittability of the modern (so-called) atom. Rather they are to be found in the nonmaterialistic aspects of the modern atom. Nothing in the ancient theory corresponds to the forces that bind the atom together or that bind atoms together into molecules, and the thought that in some sense matter and energy (a concept absent in the ancients) are equivalent is incomprehensible to the thought of Democritus.

In addition, the atomic theory is accepted for different reasons now. In the fifth century it was presented as one response among others to the Eleatic challenge. Those few who accepted it will have done so for philosophical reasons or because they found the theory satisfactory, or at least preferable to its rivals, as a device for explaining many aspects of the world. But the theory was supported by a priori reasoning rather than empirical evidence. In this, ancient atomic theory was no worse than other ancient theories of the ultimate nature of reality. There is no need to do more than state that, by contrast, modern atomic theory is based on empirical evidence and has gradually emerged as the hypothesis that has best withstood experimental and theoretical challenges. It is subject to further extension and modifications, and even to wholesale revision on the basis of further theoretical and experimental work. Thus, ancient and modern atomic theory, while historically related, are different not only in detail but also in approach, but here as elsewhere much of the philosophical ground covered by the modern theory was first explored and seen to be fertile by the keen-sighted ancients.

17

Diogenes of Apollonia

Fragments

17.1 (1)[1] In my opinion, a person beginning any discourse must present a starting point (or, principle) that is indisputable, and an explanation (or, style) that is simple and serious.[2]

17.2 (2) [In *On Nature*, the only one of his works that has come into my hands, he proposes to give many proofs that in the principle he posits there is much intelligence. Immediately after the introduction he writes the following.][3]

1. In my opinion, to sum it all up, all things that are, are differentiated from the same thing and are the same thing.
2. And this is manifest. For if the things that are now in this KOSMOS— earth, water, air, fire, and all the rest that are seen to exist in this KOSMOS—if any one of these were different from another, being different in its own nature, and if it were not the case that being the same thing it changed and was differentiated in many ways, they could not mix with each other in any way, nor could help or harm come to one from another, nor could a plant grow from the earth, nor an animal or anything else come to be, unless they were so constituted as to be the same thing.
3. But all these things, being differentiated out of the same thing, come to be different things at different times and return into the same thing.

17.3 (3) [In what follows he shows that in this principle there is much intelligence.]

For without intelligence it (the "same thing" of **17.2**) could not be distributed in such a way as to have the measures of all things—winter and summer, night and day, rains and winds and good weather. If anyone wants to think about the other things too, he would find that as they are arranged, they are as good as possible.

17.4 (4) [He continues as follows, saying that men and the other animals live and have soul and intelligence from this principle, which is air.]

1. The numbers in parentheses are the numbers of the fragments in DK. (1) = DK 64B1.

2. Diogenes Laertius, who quotes this fragment (*Lives of the Philosophers* 9.57 = DK 64A1), says that it was the beginning of Diogenes' book.

3. **17.2–17.5** are quoted by Simplicius (*Commentary on Aristotle's Physics* 151.28– 153.17 = DK 64B2–5), some of whose comments on them are here put in brackets.

Moreover, in addition to the preceding indications, the following too are important. Humans and animals live by means of air through breathing. And this (air) is both soul and intelligence for them, as will be displayed manifestly in this book. And if this departs, they die and their intelligence fails.

17.5 (5) [Then, a little later he continues clearly.]

1. And in my opinion, that which possesses intelligence is what people call air, and all humans are governed by it and it rules all things.
2. For in my opinion this very thing is god, and it reaches everything and arranges all things and is in everything.
3. And there is no single thing which does not share in this.
4. But no single thing shares in it in the same way as anything else, but there are many forms both of air itself and of intelligence.
5. For it is multiform—hotter and colder, drier and wetter, more stable and possessing a sharper movement, and unlimitedly many other alterations are in it, both of flavor and of color.
6. And the soul of all animals is the same thing, air hotter than the air outside in which we are located, but much colder than the air near the sun.
7. This heat is not identical in any two animals, since it is not identical even in any two humans, but it differs—not greatly, but so that they are similar.
8. Moreover, it is impossible for any of the things that are being differentiated to be exactly like one another without becoming the same thing.
9. Now since the differentiation is multiform, also the animals are multiform and many and are like one another in neither shape nor way of life nor intelligence, on account of the large number of their differentiations.
10. Nevertheless, all things live, see, and hear by means of the same thing, and all get the rest of their intelligence from the same thing.
    [And next he shows that the sperm of animals has the form of air and thoughts come into being when air occupies the whole body through the veins, together with blood. In the course of this discussion he gives an accurate anatomy of the veins. In these words he is clearly seen to say that the principle is what people call air.[4]]

17.6 (7) And this very thing is an eternal and immortal body, and by means of it some things come to be and others pass away.

17.7 (8) But this seems clear to me, that it is large and strong and eternal and immortal and knowing many things.

4. The account of the veins is preserved in Aristotle, *History of Animals* 3.2 511b30–512b11 (= DK 64B6).

Dates and Life

Practically nothing is known of Diogenes' life. He was probably active in the two decades after 440, which would place him later than Empedocles and Anaxagoras and contemporary with Melissus and Leucippus. In what follows, I follow the commonly held view that Diogenes knew the theories of these four philosophers, but not those of Democritus.[5] Though there are other cities of the same name, his birthplace was probably the Apollonia on the Black Sea, a colony of Miletus with whose foundation Anaximander was associated. Although only a few fragments survive, Diogenes was well known. His doctrines were influential and are echoed in Aristophanes and Euripides, as well as medical writers. He may have been a physician himself. His longest fragment (not given here) is a detailed account of the veins in the human body, and he may well be the Diogenes whom Galen names as the author of a treatise containing "the diseases and their causes and remedies."[6] His "simple and serious" (17.1) style places him alongside Anaxagoras in the Ionian prose tradition.

The Material Principle, Air

The hints we are given about the order of the fragments[7] suggest that Diogenes postponed identifying the material principle until he had discussed certain metaphysical issues.

Empedocles had avoided coming-to-be and destruction by saying that apparent coming-to-be and destruction are really mixture and separation of four basic kinds of "things." Anaxagoras had posited a large (perhaps infinite) number of types of basic "things," which drove coming-to-be and destruction even further away. But if the world consists of a plurality of radically different things, it is not easy to understand how they can interact and affect one another. Accordingly Diogenes argues for a monistic world system: all things (and he singles out Empedocles' four elements for specific mention) are modifications of a single basic substance (17.2).

More explicitly than Anaxagoras,[8] Diogenes makes the order in the universe the result of intelligence, and argues that since everything is arranged in the best possible way, it follows that what caused the arrangement is intelligent (17.3). This is the first occurrence of the Argument from De-

---

5. Certainty on this issue is impossible, and it has been held, for example, that Melissus' philosophy is a response to Leucippus and Diogenes.

6. Galen, *On Medical Experience* 22.3 (not in DK), tr. Walzer (Oxford, 1944).

7. See p. 344 n. 2 and the comments prefaced to 17.2 and to 17.3.

8. See pp. 222–23.

sign—a version of which was employed by Aquinas as one of his proofs of God's existence—and is the clearest indication in presocratic philosophy of a teleological view of the workings and structure of the world.

Diogenes accepts the Eleatic prohibition against coming-to-be and destruction (**17.8**), and unlike Anaxagoras and Empedocles, declares that plurality and change are due to differentiations, or alterations, of a single basic substance (**17.2** secs. 2–3), air. Most scholars think that Diogenes' arguments that the principle is air are what he refers to as "the preceding arguments" in **17.4** sec. 1, and that they are lost. I find it more likely that Simplicius, who quotes **17.2** through **17.5** in a single passage, did not omit so crucial a part of the account, and that "the preceding indications" are the arguments for a single intelligent material principle (**17.2-17.3**) that do not specify what the principle is, and "the following" establish that the principle is air. The train of thought is: all things are made of the same stuff; this stuff is intelligent; therefore, all intelligence is due to the presence of this stuff (implicit conclusion); in humans and animals, intelligence, like life, is due to the presence of air; therefore, air is the stuff of which all things are made.

Air takes on other forms "when condensed and rarefied and when it changes in its attributes."[9] The first two of these mechanisms come from Anaximenes, who, however, held that other attributes are due to these two.[10] Other attributes of air mentioned in the fragments are hot, cold, dry, wet, stability and mobility, flavor and color (**17.5** sec. 5), but the evidence does not say whether these are primary modifications of air or effects of condensation and rarefaction.

In any case, the assertion that air is modified by condensation and rarefaction is of particular interest after Parmenides' dictum "nor is it any more in any way, which would prevent it from holding together, or any less, but it is all full of what is" (**11.8** lines 23–24) and Melissus' argument that "it cannot be dense and rare" (**15.9** sec. 8) "nor is any of it empty" (**15.9** sec. 10), so that there is no void. The Atomists, as we have seen, argued for the existence of void.[11] Diogenes, too, holds that void exists (**17.8**). As noted previously, it is uncertain whether Diogenes wrote before or after Melissus or Leucippus, or who was responding to whom, but in the post-Parmenidean philosophical scene, the idea that condensation and rarefaction entail the existence of non-being, thus of void, could have occurred to anyone. I find it most plausible that Diogenes followed Leucippus in

---

9. Theophrastus, quoted by Simplicius, *Commentary on Aristotle's Physics* 25.5–6 (= DK 64A5).

10. See p. 51.

11. See p. 314.

accepting the existence of void and that one of the main functions of void in his theory was to provide a basis for the differentiation of air, so that (as for the Atomists[12]) void makes plurality and change possible. Thus, Diogenes agrees with the Eleatics (as against Anaxagoras and Empedocles) that reality is in a sense one, but the price of his material monism is admitting (as Anaxagoras and Empedocles did not need to do) the existence of void.

Anaxagoras held that Mind is unmixed with and unlike anything else, and yet it rules all things. Diogenes strongly disagreed. And where Anaxagoras did not explain how Mind effects its control, the reasoning found in **17.2** leads to the conclusion that the governing substance must be a modification of the same stuff of which everything else is composed (**17.5** secs. 1–2).

Like Anaxagoras' Mind, Diogenes' principle is intelligent (**17.5** sec. 1).[13] The word he uses (NOESIS, here translated "intelligence" and "thought") is related to Anaxagoras' word for Mind (NOUS). Even though not all things are intelligent, their ultimate material identity with thought (air) enables them to be affected by the intelligent ruler of the universe.

In keeping with the early Ionians, Diogenes asserts that the eternal, immortal (**17.6**) primary substance that governs and rules all things is divine (**17.5** sec. 2). He seems to argue from air's divinity to air's possessing intelligence and governing all things (**17.5** secs. 1–2). The attributes with which the divine air is endowed form an impressive list (**17.5** secs. 1–2, **17.6**, **17.7**), which makes explicit the implications of hints on the divine nature of the originating substance found in earlier thinkers, including Anaximander and Heraclitus.

Although air is intelligent and all things are forms of air, not all things are intelligent. Only living things can be intelligent. What makes animals and humans alive, their soul, is air, for when we stop breathing we die (**17.4**). Diogenes successfully integrates this prephilosophical conception of the breath as the soul or animating principle into his system as a rational, material basis for the distinction between inanimate and animate beings (cf. **17.5** secs. 6, 10).

The air that is soul is hot, since warmth is characteristic of the living. Further, by identifying the directive cosmic intelligence with air, Diogenes accounts for the intelligence of humans and animals through their breathing,[14] which maintains them in contact with the cosmic air. Under the heading of intelligence he includes the sense faculties (**17.5** sec. 10).

---

12. See p. 313.
13. Also, Simplicius' comments prefaced to **17.2** and **17.3**.
14. For a similar idea in Heraclitus, see **10.129**.

If all animals have souls consisting of warm air, and if warm air is the cosmic intelligence that rules all things and makes them turn out in the best possible way, why are some kinds of animals less intelligent and less well endowed in other ways than others? Diogenes sought to answer this question by talking of small differences in the forms of animating air possessed by different animals (17.5 secs. 7, 9). In fact, it is clear that there are differences in the nature of animating air not only from species to species, but even from individual to individual (17.5 sec. 7). The variation in the forms of air that animate different individuals of the same species is not great—presumably it differs less among individuals of a single species than among individuals of different species.

The place of 17.5 sec. 8, the earliest statement of the principle of the identity of indiscernibles, in Diogenes' train of thought is uncertain. It may serve as a ground for the claim that different animals have different amounts of heat.

Cosmogony and Cosmology

Diogenes concerned himself with standard topics in cosmogony and cosmology. He also had a deep interest in physiology (especially embryology) and provided physiological accounts of perception and cognition. I shall mention his most interesting ideas in these fields, though our information on them is almost entirely secondhand.

He accepted the Atomists' view that the KOSMOS is surrounded by infinite void, and although the evidence is conflicting, he probably agreed with the Atomists that in the infinite void there are an infinite number of KOSMOI that come to be and pass away.

17.8 Air is the element. There are unlimited KOSMOI and unlimited void. The air by being condensed and rarefied is generative of the KOSMOI. Nothing comes to be from or perishes into what is not. The earth is round and is supported in the center (of the KOSMOS) and has undergone its process of formation through the rotation resulting from the hot and the solidification caused by the cold.
(Diogenes Laertius, *Lives of the Philosophers* 9.57 = DK 64A1)

17.9 All things are in motion and there are infinite KOSMOI. His account of cosmogony is the following: the whole is in motion and comes to be rare in one place, dense in another. Where the dense part chanced to come together it formed the earth by revolving, and the other things in the same way. The lightest things occupied the highest location and produced the sun.
(pseudo-Plutarch, *Stromata* 12 = DK 64A6)

This information, together with **17.5** secs. 1–2, implies that a KOSMOS is formed when some of the intelligent, divine, unlimited air causes itself to differentiate, some being rarefied and the rest condensed. Most of the details of Diogenes' cosmology are borrowed from other Presocratics. In particular, the notion of a cosmogonic principle that is a self-starter harkens back to Anaximenes, rather than any of the post-Parmenidean cosmogonies. Contemporary references include the Atomist beliefs in infinite void and infinite KOSMOI (**17.8**), which are not eternal but eventually return to their precosmic state (**17.2** sec. 3), and an elaboration of Anaxagoras' idea that the heavenly bodies are stones:[15] Diogenes specifies them to be pumice,[16] a very light stone (it floats on water) that is porous, the better to contain fire and let it shine through.

Perception and Cognition

Theophrastus gives a long account of Diogenes' views on perception and cognition.

> **17.10** Diogenes attributes the senses, as well as life and thought, to air. . . . The sense of smell is due to the air around the brain. . . . Hearing occurs when the air in the ears is set in motion by the air outside and is passed on towards the brain. Sight occurs when things are reflected in the pupil, and this, being mixed with the air inside, produces sensation. Evidence of this is the fact that if the veins (in the eyes) become inflamed, it is not mixed with the air inside and we do not see, although the reflection is there just the same. Taste occurs in the tongue because of its rare and soft nature. Concerning touch he declared nothing, neither its functioning nor its objects. . . . The interior air, which is a small part of god, is what perceives. Evidence of this is that often when we have our mind on other matters we neither see nor hear.
> (Theophrastus, *On Sensation* 39–42 = DK 64A19)

This passage mostly speaks for itself. Diogenes' distinction between the external conditions needed for sensation (reflection in the pupil) and the actual occurrence of sensation is worth noting, as is his identification of the perceiving and thinking element in us with god, i.e. the cosmic air. Theophrastus goes on to report physiological accounts (in which air is prominent) of other related cognitive functions.

> **17.11** Pleasure and pain arise in the following manner: pleasure whenever a large amount of air is mixed with the blood and makes it light, being in

15. See p. 229.
16. Aetius 2.13.5 (= DK 64A12), 2.20.10 (= DK 64A13), 2.25.10 (= DK 64A14).

accordance with its nature and penetrating the whole body, and pain whenever the air is contrary to its nature and is not mixed, and the blood coagulates and becomes weaker and denser. Similarly also boldness and health and the opposites. . . . Thought, as was said, is due to air that is pure and dry. For moisture hinders the mind. For this reason thought is diminished when we are asleep, drunk, or full. . . . This is why children are foolish. . . . They are also prone to anger and in general easily roused and changeable because air, which is great in quantity, is separated by small intervals. This is also the cause of forgetfulness: when the air does not go through the entire body, people cannot comprehend.

(Theophrastus, *On Sensation* 43–45 = DK 64A19)
(continuation of **17.10**)

Although the idea that a wet soul is less efficient than a dry one goes back to Heraclitus,[17] this is the most thorough and consistent attempt before Democritus to work out a physical basis for mental phenomena. Diogenes is classified with the Atomists as holding that sensations are relative to the individual, since they are affected "by our opinion and [bodily] conditions."[18] Still, there is an objective element in them, since they also depend on external conditions, for instance, the reflection of an external object in the pupil.

Conclusion

Diogenes proposed an updated form of Ionian monism, perhaps because he was dissatisfied with the complexities of the post-Parmenidean pluralistic systems of Anaxagoras, Empedocles, and Leucippus. Though he made some important innovations, he took an essentially conservative approach, exploiting existing ideas and synthesizing them in new and more effective ways. He was aware of the Eleatic challenge and met it by skillfully deploying elements of the philosophies of Anaxagoras and the Atomists, though not following either system blindly. The resulting physical theory has strong links with his Milesian forebears, in particular, Anaximenes, as well as echoes of other Ionians: Xenophanes and Heraclitus. In the context of the second half of the fifth century, Diogenes' aim to return to the simplicity of the beginnings of the presocratic tradition is breathtaking in its ambition. It is a pity that the evidence available to us is too scanty to tell how successfully he carried out his mission. What we know of the fundamentals

17. **10.104–10.106**.
18. Aetius 4.9.8 (= DK 64A23).

of his theory leads me to think that he had the materials to construct as plausible a system as any other Presocratic.

What remains makes it clear that Diogenes embodies both the strengths and the weaknesses of the presocratic tradition. With him, in a way, we reach the end of the line. It is as if there is little work left to do but tidy up details, picking and choosing among earlier theories. The topics to discuss and the general approach to take in treating them and the overall goal of the project are settled, and the results are as we see. Democritus made an important attempt to break out of this mold by working out his theory in a far greater detail than had been done by the others and by attempting to apply it in a large number of areas. In ways he is no longer a Presocratic. But it would take the additional philosophical work of Plato and Aristotle, especially in the areas of logic, metaphysics, epistemology, and method, before significant advances in the study of nature could be expected.

18

Early Greek Moral Thought
and the Fifth-Century Sophists

The presocratic philosophers[1] are remembered mainly for their attempts to understand the physical world—how it functions, how it came to be the way it is, what it is made of. Largely because of the Eleatic attack, they were forced to take up problems of logic, metaphysics, epistemology, and philosophy of mind. Noticeably absent from this list are moral, political, and social philosophy. Indeed, the ancient tradition has it that these philosophical areas remained untouched until Socrates (469–399) began to explore them.

> **18.1** From the earliest philosophy down to the time of Socrates . . . numbers and movements were treated and the source from which all things arise and into which they return. Those philosophers diligently investigated the sizes of the stars, their distances and paths, and all heavenly matters. Socrates, however, was first to call down philosophy from the sky, establish it in the cities and even bring it into homes. He compelled it to investigate life and customs and things that are good and evil.
>
> (Cicero, *Tusculan Disputations* 5.4.10, not in DK)[2]

However, this picture is incorrect. As we have seen, many of the Presocratics expressed opinions on questions in moral, political, and social philosophy.[3] Moreover, serious treatment of such questions goes much further back—as far back as Greek literature does, to the poems of Homer and Hesiod, which date to the eighth century, some 300 years before Socrates.

---

1. The distinction between Presocratics and Sophists is not neatly drawn, since Democritus was born a decade after Socrates and since the earliest Sophists were born a generation before him. I will continue to use the term "Presocratic" for thinkers from Thales to Democritus who were mainly concerned with issues of the kinds treated already in this book, as opposed to the Sophists whose principal interests were somewhat different. Even so, there is overlap, since Democritus, for example, had serious interests in ethics and possibly even anthropology, and of the Sophists, Gorgias had interests along Eleatic lines, and Hippias did work in mathematics and cosmology.

2. Cicero expresses a similar idea at *Academica* 1.4.15 (not in DK).

3. Notably Xenophanes, Heraclitus, the Pythagoreans, Empedocles, and Democritus.

Among the issues Homer and Hesiod raised are the nature of the best kind of life for a man (and for a woman), the relation between humans and gods, what actions are virtuous, whether (and why) a person should be virtuous, the relation between the individual and society, and the best kind of ruler. (This list could be far longer.) In the Archaic Age (roughly 750–480), poets and prose writers such as Tyrtaeus, Solon, Theognis, and Pindar enshrined traditional Greek ethical thought and raised questions and offered solutions of increasing sophistication. This moral tradition was continued in the fifth century by such authors as the historians Herodotus and Thucydides and especially by the tragedians Aeschylus, Sophocles, and Euripides, whose treatments of moral issues are among the most sensitive and profound of any conceived in ancient Greece. Nevertheless, this work was something different from moral philosophy.

The first people who can properly be said to have done work in moral philosophy were the fifth-century Sophists. These thinkers engaged in seminal discussions in the areas of moral, political, and social philosophy and raised a host of issues in other philosophical areas as well, such as philosophy of language and epistemology. Some also engaged in scientific speculations familiar from the presocratic tradition, and one pursued themes associated with the Eleatic School.[4] The chief Sophists overlapped in time, in their travels, and in their interests, so as a result it is hard to identify clear cases where one Sophist is reacting to another. We get a picture of mutual influence colored by professional rivalry. It is equally hard to identify a set of doctrines held by all the Sophists. Instead of a "school" of thought, they constituted a more broadly defined "movement" whose common points include goals and methods, as well as subject matter.[5] Whether the Sophists should be called philosophers, however, is a controversial issue which I will take up at the end of this chapter.

The present chapter sets the stage by sketching some issues prominent in the prephilosophical moral thought of the Archaic Age, and then considers the nature of the sophistic movement, surveying the most important Sophists, prior to taking up some of the most significant philosophical issues they raised. The next chapter focuses on the NOMOS-PHYSIS debate, to which Sophists and others as well contributed. I begin with the sources of our knowledge about the Sophists.

---

4. Gorgias, in his work *On What is Not, or On Nature*. See pp. 382–86.

5. *The Sophistic Movement* is the title of an excellent book by G. Kerferd (Cambridge, 1982), which I strongly recommend for its ambitious effort to rehabilitate the Sophists as serious philosophers. The present treatment is more conservative, the result of my scepticism about the value of Plato's exposition of allegedly sophistic doctrines.

Sources

The controversial nature of the Sophists makes for special difficulties in the source materials. Very little survives of their writings: only two short rhetorical display pieces by Gorgias. Also, the Sophists lack the kind of doxographical tradition that the Presocratics possess, probably because of Aristotle's low opinion of them. Since he did not consider them serious philosophers, neither he nor his followers made systematic surveys of their views as they did for other early thinkers.[6] There was virtually no interest in the Sophists in the post-Aristotelian period until the so-called Second Sophistic movement of the second and third centuries A.D. From this period there is a work by Flavius Philostratus entitled *Lives of the Sophists*, which contains brief sections on most of the principal fifth-century Sophists. This work, however, reflects the interests of the Second Sophistic, which were rhetorical rather than philosophical.

The most extensive information about the Sophists and the sophistic movement comes from Plato's dialogues, several of which are either named after individual Sophists[7] or refer to the Sophists and their doctrines.[8] If Plato were reliable, we would know a great deal more about the Sophists than if we ignore him, and this very fact has led some to follow him too incautiously. But Plato, following Socrates, is hostile to the Sophists. In the dialogues where individual Sophists appear, they are always defeated by Socrates in philosophical discussion. And where they are treated as a group, they receive insults and ridicule rather than serious philosophical consideration.[9] Moreover, Plato is no serious historian of philosophy, but uses others' ideas as springboards for his own philosophical thought. In these circumstances, it is extremely dangerous to follow blindly his treatment of the philosophical ideas raised by the Sophists.

In what follows I adopt a middle course between refusing to use Plato at all and using him uncritically. When allowances are made for irony, humor, exaggeration, and bias, Plato gives us an idea of sophistic education and methods, and also portraits of many of the chief Sophists, which seem broadly accurate. On the other hand, I adopt a cautious approach in dealing with Plato's treatment of certain sophistic ideas—in particular, Protagorean relativism as found in the *Theaetetus*, and the political and social ideas presented in Protagoras' long speech early in the *Protagoras*.[10] While Plato

---

6. See pp. 5–6.
7. *Protagoras, Gorgias, Greater* and *Lesser Hippias, Euthydemus*.
8. Especially *Apology, Laches, Meno, Theaetetus*, and *Sophist*.
9. Especially in *Meno* 91a–92c (not in DK) and *Sophist* 221c ff. (part = DK 79,2)
10. The *Protagoras* passage is discussed on pp. 404–405.

may be paraphrasing Protagoras' own writings, it seems to me more likely that he is developing Protagoras' ideas for his own purposes, and is unreliable about the details of Protagoras' own thought.

Since Socrates is the chief speaker in almost all of Plato's works, a serious problem in Platonic studies is how far the words he puts into Socrates' mouth contain Socrates' own ideas and how far they contain Plato's, and to what extent Plato's ideas are developments of Socrates'. A similar problem arises for the Sophists, but with them it is more complicated since the positions Plato ascribes to them always come under devastating attack. My view is that Socrates and Plato are deeply indebted to the Sophists in matters of method and approach, for many of the philosophical issues they discuss, and for some aspects of their own ideas. Perhaps because their nearness made Plato unable to see his debt, and perhaps because he deliberately set out to distance the Sophists from Socrates, Plato never credits the Sophists for these points of agreement. On the other hand, where there is disagreement, he is only too ready to subject the Sophists' ideas—or his development of their ideas—to searching examination. This fact in itself is evidence that Plato and Socrates forged their own philosophical views through reflection on the Sophists, though this is not the place to pursue such ideas. As for the particular passages of Plato that contain his extensive treatments of philosophical theses of individual Sophists, it is best to take them up in connection with Plato himself.[11] In matters of doctrine the present treatment will tend to stick to non-Platonic materials.

Early Greek Moral Thought

Arete and Agathos

These two basic concepts of Greek morality are closely related and not straightforwardly translatable into English. As an approximation, ARETE can be rendered "excellence" or "goodness" (sometimes "virtue"), and AGATHOS as "excellent" or "good." The terms are related in that a thing or person is AGATHOS if and only if it has ARETE, and just because it has ARETE. The concepts apply to objects, conditions, and actions as well as to humans. They are connected with the concept of ERGON (plural, ERGA), which may be rendered as "function" or "characteristic activity." A good (AGATHOS) person is one who performs human ERGA well, and similarly a good knife is

---

11. The commentaries of C. Taylor on Plato's *Protagoras*, T. Irwin on the *Gorgias*, and J. McDowell on the *Theaetetus*, all published (by Oxford University Press) in the Clarendon Plato Series, are recommended for philosophical exposition of the issues raised in those dialogues; also M. Burnyeat, *The Theaetetus of Plato*, Indianapolis, 1990.

one that performs the ERGON of a knife well. The ERGON of a knife is cutting, and an AGATHOS knife is one that cuts well. Thus, the ARETE of a knife is the qualities, or characteristics, a knife must have in order to cut well. Likewise, if a human ERGON can be identified, an AGATHOS human is one who can and on appropriate occasions does perform that ERGON well, and human ARETE is the qualities, or characteristics, that enable him or her to do so. The classical discussion of these concepts occurs after our period, in Aristotle,[12] but he is only making explicit ideas that go back to Homer and which throw light on much of the prephilosophical ethical thought of the Greeks.

This connection of concepts makes it automatic, virtually an analytic truth, that the goal of a person—any person—is to be or become AGATHOS. Even if that goal is unreachable for someone, the ARETE-AGATHOS standard still stands as an ideal against which to measure one's successes and failures. However, there is room for debate over the nature of human ERGA, both whether there is a set of ERGA applicable to all humans and relevant to ARETE, and, supposing that there is such a set of ERGA, what those ERGA are. The existence of the ARETE-AGATHOS standard makes it vitally important to settle these issues, for otherwise human life is left adrift, with no standards of conduct.

Homer's Legacy

In the *Iliad*, the heroic ideal is well known and widely accepted as the standard by which a warrior is to be measured. It consists of several attributes, some of which we would consider external and some internal to the person. Some are thought to form part of a person's inherent nature, while others can be acquired. The ideal Homeric hero is male and well born (the nobler, the better; the best have a god or goddess as a parent or ancestor). He is a ruler and is wealthy, beautiful, excellent at fighting, excellent at counsel, excellent in leadership, brave, strong, generous to friends and harsh to enemies, reverent to the gods, aware of his worth and of his position in society, and anxious to maintain and improve it. The expectation is that these qualities go together, and little attempt is made to analyze this ideal to determine whether, say, anyone could be a hero without being beautiful. The circumstances in which this ideal is typically expressed are the activities of war. Fighting is normally hand-to-hand combat in which two warriors fight to the death. The competitive virtues are paramount, especially courage. On the other hand, within the army the cooperative qualities of counsel and leadership have great importance. Counsel is

12. Aristotle, *Nicomachean Ethics* 1.7.

given in circumstances where the leaders cooperate to decide on a course of action, and effective leadership requires behaving so as to merit the respect, loyalty, and obedience of those being led.

The *Iliad*, an epic of war, focuses on the warrior and ruling caste that occupies the highest male positions in Homeric society, but to a small extent in the *Iliad*, and much more in the *Odyssey*, the poet shows us other aspects of the life of that semimythical world. There are virtues and appropriate modes of behavior not only for warriors and rulers, but also for wives, children, parents, servants, bards, and the lesser nobles who are of local importance but not to be ranked with the heroes of the *Iliad*. The cooperative and passive values of affection, hospitality, loyalty, patience, and endurance receive almost as much attention as the competitive and active virtues of courage, strength, and cleverness.

The account just given picks out only a few features of the rich and varied world of the Homeric epics. The moral scene Homer presents is appropriate to the society it represents and quite alien to our own. It is the starting point for subsequent moral speculation that no one in the later Greek tradition could quite forget. The development of Greek moral thought through the Archaic and Classical periods can be seen as the gradual replacement of the competitive by the cooperative virtues as the primary virtues of conduct, and as the increasing recognition of the significance of peoples' intentions as well as their actions.[13]

Rapid change in Greek society in the Archaic and Classical periods called for new conceptions of the ideal human and the ideal human life and activities. The Archaic Age saw different kinds of rulers from the Homeric kings, and individual combat gave way to the united front of a phalanx of hoplites (heavy armed warriors). Even though the Homeric warrior-king was no longer a possible role in society, the qualities of good birth, beauty, courage, honor, and the abilities to give good counsel and to rule well remained. Nevertheless, the various strands of the Homeric heroic ideal began to unravel. In particular, good birth, wealth, and fighting ability no longer automatically went together. This sort of situation forced the issue: what are the best qualities we can possess? What constitutes human ARETE? The literary sources contain conflicting claims about the best life for a person, the best kind of person to be, and the relative merits of qualities thought to be ingredients of human happiness. In one way or another these different conceptions of human excellence have Homeric origins, though they diverge from it and from each other.

Lack of space makes it impossible to present the wealth of materials that

13. This is an important theme in A. Adkins' influential book, *Merit and Responsibility* (Oxford, 1962).

bear on this subject.[14] I will confine discussion to two representatives of the aristocratic tradition who wrote at the end of the Archaic Age. Pindar shows how the aristocratic ideal had survived and transformed, and how vital it remained as late as the early fifth century, and Theognis reveals how social, political, and economic reality was undermining that ideal.

Pindar

In the late sixth- and early fifth centuries, Pindar composed odes to celebrate victors in athletic competitions, including the Olympic games. His patrons, the victorious athletes, were wealthy, sometimes royal, and frequently aristocratic. Pindar champions an ideal these people would tend to adopt for their own, so his poetry is a valuable source for the aristocratic mentality of his time—a set of traditions and attitudes with which the democratic tendencies of the fifth century had to cope and which continued to exert pressure, if not always as an articulate voice, in the moral debates of the late fifth century.

Pindar unsurprisingly gives prominence to the athletic ideal with its emphasis on success. Victory at the games brings glory to a person for the rest of his life, also to his family, descendants, and city. Defeat is shameful, disgraceful. But the glory of victory (especially when spread abroad by the talents of a poet like Pindar) brings lasting fame and praise, two of the chief components of happiness, which is the supreme goal of life. Athletic competition was a form of divine worship and took place in such sanctuaries as Olympia and Delphi as part of religious festivals. Hence Pindar's insistence that success in the games and in other fields is a mark of the gods' favor and cannot be gained without their assistance. However, it also requires valor, effort, daring, strength, and wealth (which are also gifts of the gods). In fact, the gods control all human things and can give and take away happiness at will. Since humans are frail and their destiny is shaky, it is important to be reverent to the gods, who alone can make prosperity long-lasting. Hence, in evaluating persons, actions, and qualities, it is important to judge by what happens in the end. Despite the uncertainty of the future, Pindar is sure of the consequences of success: humans find good fortune hard to bear. It brings envy, slander, and mockery from others and tends to make the fortunate person proud, overconfident, and arrogant. The jealousy of other humans can be dealt with, but arrogance (HUBRIS) brings

14. Many of the most important passages are from poets of the Archaic Age, such as Mimnermus, Tyrtaeus, Solon, Pindar, and Theognis. I recommend the translations of R. Lattimore, *Greek Lyrics* (Chicago, 1955) and *The Odes of Pindar* (Chicago, 1947).

divine retribution. The gods bring down the proud. Therefore it is necessary to resist the impulses to go too far, and to be moderate in good fortune and know your limits as a human being.

There is no single passage that expresses all the elements of this complex system of values, but the following are representative.

18.2 Wide is the strength of wealth
    when, mixed with stainless virtue
    and granted of destiny, mortal man leads it home,
    most dear companion. . . .
    Even power granted of God
    is carried the better for wisdom. . . .
    This man is praised of the wise,
    I speak what men say.
    He ministers a mind that outruns his years;
    speech also; for daring he is the eagle
    of wide wings among birds;
    in games, strength, like a wall;
    among the Muses he goes lightfooted from birth;
    he has approved himself a subtle charioteer.
    To all spendors in his own land he has dared
    the entrance; now God, favoring, makes perfect his power,
    and hereafter, you blessed sons of Kronos,
    may you grant him in action as in deliberation
    such things to have; let no autumn storm blast
    of winds break the bloom.
    The great mind of Zeus guides
    the angel in men he loves.
                        (Pindar, *Pythians* 5, tr. Lattimore, not in DK)

18.3 The crucial strength is given of the gods to men;
    but two things only there are that minister to the brightest bloom
      of life as wealth blossoms:
    success and the good speech that a man hears of himself.
    Strive not to become Zeus; you have everything
    if destiny of such splendors befall you.
    Mortals must be content with mortality. . . .
                       (Pindar, *Isthmians* 5, tr. Lattimore, not in DK)

Pindar was far from a moral philosopher. Instead of argument he uses mythological archetypes to support the values he promotes and the advice he offers. No doubt his moral precepts do not form a tidy system—perhaps not even a consistent one. Sometimes they are banal to the point of vacuousness: "Praise the good," he says with all seriousness. But overall he recommends an aristocratic ideal of life appropriate for his time, a sophisticated, updated version of the Homeric ideal, in which noble birth, beauty, wealth, strength, daring, and success in competitive situations (athletics more than war, but Pindar often mentions military exploits) are prominent, as are excellence at counsel and government. Even such aesthetic qualities as appreciation for and support of music, festivals, and other lovely enterprises are quite at home in the Homeric ideal (one thinks of the Phaeacians). What is new is the occurrence of such "quiet," cooperative virtues as gentleness, righteousness, discretion, honesty, and modesty, as well as explicit advice to avoid excess and to be moderate. Nevertheless, in the world of Pindar's victorious aristocrats, as in Homer's elite warrior caste, the comfortable assumption is that all the desirable qualities hang together reasonably coherently and (with the gods' will) can be attained in a lasting way.

Theognis

A person reading Pindar would hardly suspect that the heyday of the aristocracy would soon be over. Already in Athens, a century earlier, Solon's political reforms (594) had severely limited traditional aristocratic rights and had given a political voice and role to a much larger segment of the community. While Pindar was writing his poetry, the Athenians adopted Cleisthenes' democratic reforms (508), designed to put an end to the concentrations of power through which aristocratic families had dominated the Athenian political scene. Moreover, in sixth-century Athens under Peisistratus and his sons, and in a multitude of other POLEIS as well, a kind of monarchy called "tyranny" (The word TURANNOS originally meant "absolute ruler" or "monarch," without any necessarily negative connotations; frequently these "tyrants" were enlightened rather than "tyrannical," as we use the word) had wrested influence from the aristocratic families and had recognized the growing wealth and importance of the commercial classes.

The increase in wealth, and the shift in its distribution that had begun by the seventh century, led to profound changes in the social and political scenes in the sixth century, and forced a wedge in among the complex of qualities that traditionally constituted aristocratic ARETE. Pindar's unified picture in which wealth, power, and noble birth tend to go together became ever less true to contemporary reality.

The aristocratic response to this changed situation receives its clearest expression in the poems attributed to Theognis and composed in the sixth and early fifth centuries. Even less than with Pindar can we find a consistent set of views advocated in these poems, but among the most frequently recurring themes are the view that money does not make the man, that many undeserving people are now rich and many deserving people (deserving because of their birth and social background) are now poor. It is noteworthy how Theognis plays on the different connotations of uses of the primary terms of value, AGATHOS and ARETE, and their opposites, KAKOS and KAKIA: morally good vs. evil, well born, noble vs. low born, and politically and socially powerful vs. powerless. Since the traditional positive attributes no longer regularly all went together, it was important to decide which are most important, indeed which are the essential ingredients of human ARETE.

18.4 We look for rams and asses and horses, Kyrnos,
         that are well bred, and a person wants to get offspring
      from good (AGATHOS) stock. But a noble man does not
         mind marrying
      a lowly (KAKOS) woman of a lowly (KAKOS) father, if her father
         gives him a lot of money.
      Nor does a woman refuse to be the wife of a lowly (KAKOS) man
      who is rich, but she prefers wealth to goodness (AGATHOS). . . .
      They honor money. And so a noble man marries into a lowly
         (KAKOS) family,
      and a lowly (KAKOS) man into a good (AGATHOS) one. Wealth has
         mixed the race.
      So do not be surprised, son of Polypais, that the race of
         the citizens
      is becoming obscure, since nobility is being mingled with the
         low (KAKOS).   (Theognis, lines 183–192, not in DK)

18.5 It is easier to beget and raise a child than to instill
      good thoughts in it. No one yet has devised a way
      to make the fool wise and a bad (KAKOS) person good
         (AGATHOS). . . .
      If intelligence could be fashioned and put into a man,
      never would a bad (KAKOS) person come from a good (AGATHOS)
         father,
      obeying wise words. But never will he make
      a bad (KAKOS) man good (AGATHOS) by teaching.
                                          (Theognis, lines 429–438, not in DK)

18.6 Kyrnos, a good (AGATHOS) man keeps his good judgment
         always fixed.
      He has courage whether he is found among the bad (KAKOS) or
         the good (AGATHOS).

But if god grants livelihood and wealth to a bad (KAKOS) man,
in his folly he is unable to hold back his bad (KAKOS) nature.
(Theognis, lines 319–322, not in DK)

The Sophists

What is a Sophist?

Strictly speaking, Sophists were itinerant educators who operated independently and charged fees. Different Sophists taught different ranges of subjects, but all taught rhetoric, the art of constructing and delivering public speeches, which was seen as the key to success in public and private life. They were professional rivals, competing for fame, wealth, and pupils. Their shared interest in rhetoric and related issues led them to develop philosophical theses, and their rivalry led them to challenge each other's views and formulate competing ones. Their contributions to philosophy are best understood in this light.

The Sophists were in the center of late fifth-century intellectual life. The issues they raised and discussed came to be prominent in the minds of all thoughtful people and widely known to the general public. Virtually every major author of the period makes reference to sophistic themes, so that it narrows the ground artificially if we consider only the testimonia and fragments of the Sophists themselves. The intellectual scene, which has been called the Sophistic Movement, included in its penumbra the tragedian Euripides, the historian Thucydides, the comic poet Aristophanes, the philosophers Socrates and Plato, and chief fifth- and fourth-century orators such as Lysias and Demosthenes, to mention only the most prominent. Nevertheless, we must turn to Protagoras and his like for the clearest idea of what a Sophist was. With a core definition in mind, we are in a position to relate others more or less closely to the heart of the movement.

The following five men were the most celebrated Sophists of the fifth century.

Protagoras

Born c. 490 in Abdera, the birthplace of Democritus, Protagoras claimed to be the first to proclaim himself a Sophist and to charge fees for the education he offered.[15] He grew wealthy from his profession. He visited Athens at least twice,[16] and probably did so frequently. He was a friend of Pericles, and doubtless through Pericles' influence, he was asked to draft a constitution for Thurii, the panhellenic city in South Italy founded in 444

15. Plato, *Protagoras* 317b, 349a (both = 80A5).
16. Plato, *Protagoras* 310e (not in DK).

under the leadership of Athens. He died c. 420 after practicing his profession over forty years.[17] There are reports that he was tried at Athens and either condemned to death or banished for his agnosticism regarding the gods, and that his books were collected and burned in public.[18]

The portrait of him in Plato's *Protagoras* is, despite the touch of vanity and pride it accords him, not unflattering. (Some have found him preferable to Socrates in that dialogue.) He wrote several works, most importantly *On Truth*, known alternatively as *The Throws*, i.e., arguments which will throw an opponent (the title is a term from wrestling), the *Antilogies* "Contrary Arguments," and *On the Gods*, which contained the apparently agnostic assertion:

> **18.7** Concerning the gods I am unable to know either that they are or that they are not, or what their appearance is like. For many are the things that hinder knowledge: the obscurity of the matter and the shortness of human life. (Protagoras, DK 80B4)

In many ways he was the intellectual leader of the sophistic movement. A highly successful teacher of rhetoric, he claimed to teach ARETE, the key to success in life. With Protagoras is most closely associated the doctrine that there are two arguments on any subject. Moreover, his assertion, "A human being is the measure of all things" (**18.20**), which was the starting point for a relativistic approach to philosophy, can serve as an emblem for the whole Sophistic Movement.[19]

Gorgias

Also born c. 490, Gorgias was from Leontini in Sicily. He is said to have lived over 100 years. Like other Sophists he travelled and gave public performances of display pieces written for such occasions. He would speak on any subject the audience proposed. He also taught students and received handsome fees. His flowery rhetorical style caught the fancy of the Athenians when he represented Leontini on a diplomatic mission in 427. Gorgias claimed to teach rhetoric, not ARETE, and for that reason it has been claimed that he was not a Sophist.[20] Gorgias held that rhetoric can be used

---

17. Plato, *Meno* 91e (= DK 80A8).

18. Plato, *Meno* 91e (= DK80A8), however, declares that he never ceased to enjoy a good reputation.

19. For Protagoras' contribution to the NOMOS-PHYSIS debate, see pp. 404–405.

20. Plato, *Meno* 95c (= DK 82A21), *Gorgias* 449a, 459d–460a, cf. 465c (none of these passages in DK). For the claim that Gorgias was not a Sophist, see Plato, *Gorgias*, ed. E. R. Dodds (Oxford, 1959), pp. 6–7.

for both good and evil, but is morally neutral in itself. It is a means, not an end, indeed a means by which its possessor can gain power and achieve whatever ends he or she adopts.[21] When the nature of the sophistic claim to teach ARETE is understood (pp. 369–72.), Gorgias' move is seen as a way to put himself above his rivals, a strategy in positioning himself in the competitive educational market. But, as has been well said, "rhetoric was in the curriculum of every sophist, [and] Gorgias must have put it more prominently in his shop window than any of the others."[22] Gorgias was associated with Empedocles, who also came from Sicily, and with certain Sicilian rhetoricians. He composed many speeches, also display pieces such as the surviving *Praise of Helen* and *Defense of Palamedes*, a technical treatise on rhetoric, and a remarkable work (discussed later, pp. 382–86) entitled *On What is Not, or On Nature*, which employs reasoning of the Eleatic type to argue for theses which outdo even those of Parmenides.

Prodicus

A generation younger than Protagoras and Gorgias, Prodicus was probably born c. 460 and was still alive when Socrates died (399). He came from Ceos, an Aegean island near Attica. He visited Athens on embassies from Ceos, travelled widely, and like Gorgias, grew wealthy from his public presentations and teaching. Plato makes Socrates say that Prodicus was his teacher,[23] in particular on the topic of the correctness of names, in which he was concerned to draw fine distinctions in the meanings of words.[24] Socrates also asserts that Prodicus was a teacher to whom he sent philosophically infertile people who could not benefit from his own teaching.[25] One of his display pieces, the *Choice of Herakles*, an exhortation to choose a life of virtue over one of vice, is summarized by Xenophon, who though a loyal admirer of Socrates also had a high regard for Prodicus.[26] Evaluations of this piece have run from the wildly enthusiastic to the opposite

21. Plato, *Gorgias* 456c–457c (not in DK).

22. Guthrie, *HGP*, vol. 3, p. 272.

23. Plato, *Protagoras* 341a, *Meno* 96d (neither passage in DK), *Cratylus* 384b (= DK 84A11).

24. See Plato, *Protagoras* 337a–c (= DK 84A13) for an example—or parody—of this art.

25. Plato, *Theaetetus* 151b (= DK 84A3a).

26. Summary in Xenophon, *Memorabilia* 2.1.21–34 (= DK 84B2). As evidence for Xenophon's interest in Prodicus, there is the story that while a prisoner in Boeotia he obtained release on bail to attend one of Prodicus' presentations (Philostratus, *Lives of the Sophists* 12 = DK 84A1a).

extreme.[27] Prodicus seems to have had views on scientific subjects. He was reputed to be an atheist and accounted for the origin of religion by saying that the ancients considered as gods things beneficial to humans, such as the sun, rivers, and wine, and that they regarded the discoverers of agriculture and other contributions to human welfare as gods. This criticism of Greek religion is in line with the anthropological interests current in the fifth century and is found also in Protagoras' long speech in Plato's *Protagoras*.[28] Prodicus might well have been one of the most impressive figures of the fifth century, but given the paucity of evidence, we can only be tantalized by the scraps of his reputation.

Hippias

Like Prodicus, Hippias was a member of the second generation of Sophists.[29] He was born in Elis, the district of the Peloponnese in which the Olympic festival took place, and he represented Elis on official missions. In an amusing passage,[30] Plato portrays him vividly as a polymath whose range of learning goes well beyond the other Sophists, extending to metalwork, jewelry, shoemaking, weaving, epic and tragic poetry, prose writing, metrics, musical theory, and orthography. To this list of subjects we may also add arithmetic, geometry, astronomy, painting, sculpture, genealogy, and history. His memory was phenomenal—he boasted that he could repeat a list of fifty names after hearing it only once—and he taught memory techniques as part of his curriculum. Like other leading Sophists he traveled widely and earned a great deal of money from his teaching and his performances. He made a name for himself by speaking at the Olympic festival on a range of prepared topics and offering to answer any question anyone might put to him. He made a significant contribution to geometry by discovering the quadratrix, a curve used to solve the problem of how to trisect any angle and which was also employed in attempts to square the circle, i.e., to construct a square equal in area to a given circle. He compiled the first list of Olympic victors, an important contribution to chronology and historiography. (According to tradition, the Olympic festival was first held in 776 and was celebrated every four years, thus providing a way of dating events that could be used throughout Greece, e.g., "the third year of the forty-seventh Olympiad.") In addition, he seems to have done important work in

27. Guthrie, *HGP*, vol. 3, pp. 277–78.
28. Plato, *Protagoras* 321c–322c (= DK 80C1).
29. We cannot be more precise about his dates, except that he was still alive when Socrates was put to death (399).
30. Plato, *Lesser Hippias* 368b–e.

the history of philosophy and science. He was probably the first to collect passages of poets and philosophers and group them under various headings, thus beginning the doxographical tradition continued by Aristotle and his followers. Among his prose discourses was one set after the fall of Troy, in which the young Neoptolemus asks the aged Nestor how a young man can acquire the best reputation, and Nestor responds with suitable advice for life. He also wrote a work entitled *The Names of Peoples*. Plato, who presents him as a vain, self-advertising fellow, seems to take him less seriously than other Sophists, but does not present him as unscrupulous or immoral. One is left with the suspicion that for all his success and erudition, he did not pose as much of a threat to Socrates and Plato as other Sophists did.

Antiphon

If, as I suppose, Antiphon the Sophist is identical with Antiphon of Rhamnous, the Athenian orator and politician,[31] he was born c. 480 and executed in 411 for taking part in the oligarchic regime known as the Four Hundred. We possess several of his speeches, including the *Tetralogies*, oratorical exercises consisting of groups of four speeches—opening and closing speeches for the prosecution and for the defense on fictitious charges of murder. These speeches are samples of the sophistic rhetorical instruction on how to make the strongest case for whichever side of a dispute you found yourself on. Antiphon is not mentioned by Plato. As an Athenian (Rhamnous is a village in Attica), Antiphon is unlike the other Sophists treated here since he could—and did—have a political career in Athens. He resembles the "presocratic" philosophers in that he had theories on astronomical, meteorological, and biological subjects and on the origin of the present state of the KOSMOS. Some of his fragments on these subjects are ascribed to a work entitled *On Truth*. This work of Antiphon's probably contained his attempt to square the circle which Aristotle criticized for being based on principles inappropriate to geometry.[32] For our purposes, Antiphon's most important fragments, also from *On Truth*, are his contribution to the NOMOS-PHYSIS debate.[33] In addition, there was a moral (or moralizing) work, *On Concord*, to which numerous fragments, some of

31. Their identity is disputed. For arguments against, see Guthrie, *HGP*, vol. 3, pp. 285–86, 292–94. For arguments for, see Kerferd, *The Sophistic Movement*, p. 49 f., with references.

32. Aristotle, *Physics* 1.2 185a14–17 (= DK 87B13), *Sophistical Refutations* 11 172a7 (not in DK).

33. See pp. 393–97.

them deeply pessimistic, are ascribed. Antiphon was interested in practical psychology; there is a story that he set up a kind of clinic in Corinth where he "advertised that he could treat the distressed by means of words (or, speeches), and inquiring the reasons (for their distress) he would address the afflicted with soothing words."[34]

Sophistic Education

Before the mid-fifth century, education in Greek city-states did not last long or go far. The normal education of a young, free Greek boy consisted of physical training, arithmetic, and "music" in the broad Greek sense of the word, which included learning how to read and write, and reading and memorizing works of the great poets, especially Homer, in addition to learning how to play musical instruments. This basic education was completed by age fourteen and was typically conducted by slaves. The Sophists were free men who offered a program of higher studies for those who had completed the normal curriculum and who could pay for it. The subjects the various Sophists offered to teach included astronomy, meteorology, and other scientific subjects, questions about being and becoming, legislation, and various arts.[35] Plato makes Protagoras say that other Sophists force their students to study arithmetic, geometry, and "music," whereas he, Protagoras, teaches just what they want to know—how to succeed in public and in private life.[36] In addition, many Sophists were interested in the Greek language and in literary criticism, and it is likely that they taught these subjects too.

The range of interests found in the Sophists is as wide as can be imagined in classical Greece. Plato mocked Hippias for his expertise as a metalworker, jeweler, and weaver. Hippias, Antiphon, and Protagoras all contributed to geometry.[37] But it is useful to distinguish between an individual Sophist's interests and the subjects he was prepared to teach. Hippias, as far as we know, did not offer weaving in his curriculum, and Protagoras' interest in geometry in no way conflicts with his boast not to teach that subject, but only what his students want to learn.

Protagoras' boast and Gorgias' claim to teach only rhetoric stem from the competitive nature of the Sophist's profession. Each aimed to market himself so as to bring the most fame and money and attract the greatest

34. Pseudo-Plutarch, *Lives of the Ten Orators*, p. 833C–D (= DK 87A6).
35. Plato, *Sophist* 232b–e (part = DK 80B8).
36. Plato, *Protagoras* 318d–e (= DK 80A5).
37. For Protagoras, see Aristotle, *Metaphysics* 3.2 997b32–998a3 (= DK 80B7). For Hippias and Antiphon, see pp. 366–67.

number of students. One of their techniques was the practice of giving public displays of their brilliance, for which they charged admission.[38] In these displays they would deliver a speech on an announced topic, or invite the audience either to choose from a list of topics on which they were prepared to speak or to propose any topic at all. These displays would naturally take place in public settings where the largest admission-paying crowds could be found, as well as the most potential students. Accordingly, Hippias was well known at the Olympic festival and Gorgias spoke at Olympia, at the Pythian festival at Delphi, and at the theater in Athens.

Paying pupils would attend smaller classes of the kind portrayed vividly (and amusingly) in Plato's *Protagoras*.[39] Fees could be high, which makes it probable that the price was not for a single class but for a whole course. The excitement aroused by the prospect of attending such a course, associating with a famous person like Protagoras, and joining the band of his students is well brought out by Plato in his depiction of the youthful Hippocrates.[40]

Rhetoric and ARETE

For our purposes, the most important subject taught by Sophists is hinted at by Protagoras in words put into his mouth by Plato.

> **18.8** My boy, if you associate with me, the result will be that on the very day you begin you will return home a better person, and the same will happen the next day too. Each day you will make constant progress towards being better. (Plato, *Protagoras* 318a = DK 80A5)

Shortly afterwards, he says more specifically what he teaches his pupils:

> **18.9** Good counsel concerning his personal affairs, so that he may best manage his own household, and also concerning the city's affairs, so that as far as the city's affairs go he may be most powerful in acting and in speaking. (Plato, *Protagoras* 318e–319a = DK 80A5)

In short, Protagoras taught his students how to succeed in public and private life. What he claimed to teach is, in a word, ARETE. That this was his boast follows from the intimate connection between AGATHOS and ARETE as well as from the fact that a person with ARETE is one who enjoys success, as

---

38. At Plato, *Greater Hippias* 286a-b (= DK 86a9), Hippias advertises such a performance. See also, e.g., Plato, *Cratylus* 384b (= DK 84A11).

39. Plato, *Protagoras* 314a–316b (not in DK).

40. Plato, *Protagoras* 310a–311a (not in DK).

measured by current standards. Anyone with the abilities Protagoras claimed to teach had the keys to a successful life in fifth-century Athens.

In fact, the key to success was rhetoric, the art of public speaking, which has a precedent in the heroic conception of ARETE, which included excellence in counsel. But the Sophists' emphasis on rhetoric must not be understood as harkening back to Homeric values. Clear reasons why success in life depended on the ability to speak well in public can be found in fifth-century politics and society.

The fifty-year period beginning with the end of the Persian War in 478 was the supreme moment of Athens. The city enjoyed military supremacy in the Aegean, and as leader of an alliance of Greek city-states that soon became an Athenian empire, Athens became wealthy, and by far the most powerful and influential Greek POLIS. The rulers of Athens controlled the destiny of most of Greece. At this time, and particularly after 458, Athens had as its form of government a radical form of democracy. State officials and jurymen were paid—an unusual practice in the ancient world—so that participation in government was possible for the poor as well as the rich. Further, most officials were not elected, but appointed by lot, and it was not permitted to hold such offices repeatedly. The result of this state of affairs, in which there was no continuity and no opportunity for anyone to gain much experience in ruling the state or to become entrenched in office, was that political power shifted away from these officials principally to the Assembly, the body of all adult male citizens, which discussed and decided issues of interest to the state. In the Assembly, any member could speak on any issue, and political power came to be a matter of speaking convincingly. We see the type of speeches made there in Thucydides' *History of the Peloponnesian War*, which contains many public addresses.[41] The decisions of the Assembly, which as Thucydides makes clear might be based on emotion or hysteria, were the final determiners of action. Pericles, the supreme political figure in Athens from 444 to 429, owed his success largely to his personality and intelligence, as manifested in his public speaking. After his death, his unworthy successors were called demagogues from

41. Since there were no transcripts of proceedings, Thucydides cannot be reporting the actual words spoken, but he gives, in general, a faithful picture of the subjects discussed and the styles of speaking actually used. Thucyidides' own statement of what he is doing in the speeches runs as follows: "As for the speeches delivered by the several statesmen before and during the war, it proved difficult for me to report the exact substance of what was said, whether I heard the speeches myself or learned of them from others. I have therefore made the speakers express primarily what in my own opinion was called for under the successive circumstances, at the same time keeping as close as possible to the general import of what was actually said." (Thucydides 1.22.1)

their ability to lead the people, typically in unwise paths, through their ability to speak effectively.

Rhetorical ability was important in the private sphere too. Athens was a litigious society and anyone might have to appear in court, as prosecutor or defendant. It is easy to see how success or failure in court can be regarded as essential to success or failure in one's personal life. Three features of the Athenian legal system are relevant. First, there were no lawyers. As plaintiff or defendant you spoke on your own behalf. Your speech could be written by a speech writer, but the delivery and cross-examination of witnesses were done by you. Second, there was no public prosecutor. Prosecutions were conducted by the private citizen who made the complaint. Finally, the size of juries tended to be large. The jury which condemned Socrates to drink hemlock was 501 strong. In these circumstances, pleading a case demanded rhetorical skills.

That is not to say that every kind of success depended on rhetoric. It could not make you successful in a craft like carpentry, and would not on its own make you a successful military commander. Nor is it plausible that every student of Protagoras could have become another Pericles. Protagoras acknowledged that natural aptitude was required over and above diligence.

18.10 Teaching requires nature and training. (from Protagoras, DK 80B3)

18.11 Learning must begin at an early age. (from Protagoras, DK 80B3)

18.12 Art (TECHNE) without practice and practice without art are nothing. (Protagoras, DK 80B10)

18.13 Education is not implanted in the soul unless one reaches a greater depth. (Protagoras, DK 80B11)

Protagoras recognized that he could not make a silk purse out of a sow's ear, but he claimed to be able to develop a (sufficiently young) person's abilities to the greatest extent possible.[42]

Pericles was an effective counselor in part because he could speak well, but also by dint of his personality, experience, and intelligence. To a large extent these last three factors cannot be taught, but rhetoric can be offered as a TECHNE, a technical art or skill that has rules of its own and which can be instilled through training and practice. In these ways rhetoric is like medicine, carpentry, and other technical arts, but it is different in its

---

42. See Plato, *Protagoras* 326e–328d (not in DK) for further development of this line of thought.

seemingly universal applicability. Debates can arise on any conceivable subject, including technical ones, and rhetorical skill can be turned to the topic
at hand whatever it may be. The story goes that Gorgias used his rhetorical
skill to convince medical patients to undergo surgery when physicians failed
to persuade them.[43] Socrates turned the tables on the Sophists, arguing that
if rhetoric has no specific subject matter, then so far from being a universal
art, it should not be considered an art at all.[44] And even if we grant that
rhetoric is an art that can be taught, it remains controversial whether ARETE
can be taught, and in what ARETE consists.

The Meaning of the Word "Sophist"

The English words "sophism," "sophistry," and "sophist," have negative
connotations. A sophism is a fallacious piece of reasoning, sophistry is the
technique of using fallacious arguments, etc. These English words come
directly from Greek equivalents with many of the same associations. Aristotle matter-of-factly defines a sophistical argument as one that appears
sound but is not, sophistry as what appears to be wisdom but is not, and
Sophists as those who specialize in such arguments and as those who make
money from what appears to be wisdom but is not.

In the Platonic dialogue named after him, Protagoras proclaims himself
a Sophist by profession, though he admits that it is risky to make such an
admission.[45] Clearly the meaning of the term altered from Protagoras' time
to Aristotle's. No one went around boasting that he dealt in specious arguments and inviting people to pay him to teach them what is not real wisdom,
and when Protagoras describes his profession he certainly does not do so in
such terms.[46] What, then, does the word SOPHISTES, "Sophist," mean?

It is based on the adjective SOPHOS, used originally to describe a person
skilled in a particular craft, and extended to mean generally knowledgeable
or wise. The ending -ISTES added to the stem produces a noun which
means "one who exercises wisdom," that is to say, a specialist in wisdom.
This word is analogous to KITHARISTES, one who plays the kithara or lyre,
an expert at the art of playing the lyre. The self-importance of anyone who
called himself a specialist in wisdom was probably not lost on the Greeks of

43. Plato, *Gorgias* 456b (= DK 82A22).

44. Plato, *Gorgias* 449c–458b (not in DK), *Protagoras* 311b–313a (not in DK),
318a–319a (part = DK 80A5).

45. Plato, *Protagoras* 316c–317c (not in DK).

46. Plato, *Protagoras* 318a–319a (not in DK), 328b (= DK 80A6), *Gorgias* 449a–b
(not in DK), 459d–460a (not in DK).

the fifth and fourth centuries, who had a keen sense of the ridiculous, but the word is older than the fifth-century Sophists, and was first applied to poets, musicians, seers, and sages—those who had special knowledge and insight, and the gift of communicating it to others (though as far as we know, no one before Protagoras called *himself* a SOPHISTES). Protagoras is not wholly off the mark when he says that "the sophistic art is ancient," going back to Homer and Hesiod,[47] although the wisdom Protagoras and his fellow Sophists claimed to teach was different from the lessons that could be learned from the earliest Greek poets.

The fifth-century figures who usurped the word, and the resistance they met from upholders of traditional morality and from philosophers of the stature of Socrates and Plato, are responsible for the negative associations of "sophist" and related words, which became so closely identified with Protagoras and his kind that their more general associations were mostly lost. They came to be associated with illegitimate reasoning, with arguments that appear to prove a point but are fallacious. The influence of Socrates and Plato, assisted by widespread hostility reflected in authors as diverse as the comic poet Aristophanes and the soldier and gentleman Xenophon (who compares them to whores for the way they sell their wares to any buyer, and amidst other salvos against them says "it is sufficient for each of them to be called a sophist, which is an insult, at least to those who have good judgment"[48]), is responsible for the change of connotations from the honorific to the disreputable.

Hostility to the Sophists

The main charges against the Sophists are of two different sorts. (A) The charge of prostituting themselves. Plato emphasizes the moneymaking aspect of the Sophist's work, which he uses as one of his chief criteria for determining that Socrates was not a Sophist. This charge contains two elements: (1) the Sophists teach ARETE for money, and (2) they teach it to anyone who pays. Both elements have aristocratic origins. Traditionally ARETE was learned from one's family and friends and came as the result of a long process of socialization beginning in infancy. Such training and background can hardly be bought. Further, according to the aristocratic mentality, most people are not of the right type, the appropriate social background, to aspire to ARETE. Pindar expresses these thoughts in the following lines.

47. Plato, *Protagoras* 316d (= DK 25,1).
48. Xenophon, *Memorabilia* 1.6.13 (= DK 87A3), *On Hunting* 6.13 (not in DK).

18.14 The wise man knows many things in his blood;
the vulgar are taught.
They will say anything.
They clatter like crows against the sacred bird of Zeus.
(Pindar, *Olympians* 2.86–88, tr. Lattimore, not in DK)

(B) The second principal charge is reflected in Aristotle's definitions of the terms "Sophist," etc., cited above. According to it, the Sophists are masters of dishonest arguments. Their stock in trade is fallacious reasoning. They have no regard for the truth, but specialize in eristic, the practice of using any and all means, fair and foul, to win a dispute. They "make the weaker argument stronger," the catchphrase for gaining victory with a case that should lose. To understand the basis for these claims we must look more closely at the rhetorical training the Sophists offered. Here the most important feature is the practice of arguing both sides of a case—pro and con.

"Antilogic"—The Method of Two Arguments

18.15 Protagoras was the first to declare that there are two mutually opposed arguments on any subject.
(Diogenes Laertius, *Lives of the Philosophers* 9.51 = DK 80A1)

In any deliberation there are conflicting considerations, and an advocate aims to present one side as convincingly as possible. This is the situation in the arenas for which the Sophists prepared their pupils to compete, the courts and the Assembly. Like us, the Athenians believed that a defendant is entitled to present a case for the defense, and a good defense will be as strong as the circumstances make possible. In matters of public policy, there are usually several options and reasons for and against each, and it is normally unclear which option will prove best. According to the ideas of Athenian democracy, presenting the strengths and weaknesses of each side in public debate is the best way to reach a good decision. The case is similar where the goal is to ascertain the truth rather than to gain victory for one's side. We are in the best position to recognize the truth when all views have been represented as well as possible.

We are familiar with attacks on defense attorneys for getting their clients off too lightly, and we are aware of politicians who use half-truths and faulty logic. These charges are no different from the stock accusation in fifth-century Athens, that the Sophists made the weaker argument stronger.[49]

49. In *The Clouds*, Aristophanes takes this charge one step further, staging a mock-sophistical debate between the Stronger, or Just Argument, and the Weaker, or Unjust Argument, which is won, as we would expect, by the latter.

18.16 Protagoras made the weaker and stronger argument and taught his students to blame and praise the same person.

(Stephanus of Byzantium, s.v. Abdera = DK 80A21)

18.17 This is making the weaker argument stronger. And people were rightly annoyed at Protagoras' promise.

(Aristotle, *Rhetoric* 2.24 1402a24–26 = DK 80A21)

The Sophists taught their pupils the art of "antilogic": arguing as strongly as possible for both sides of a case, thus (where one side was weaker than the other) "making the weaker argument stronger." The training involved debates or mock trials in which students would gain experience in public speaking, including presenting arguments for whichever side of the case they were assigned. Closely related are the "display speeches" of Gorgias, the *Praise of Helen*, which argues that Helen of Troy should not be blamed for forsaking her husband Menelaos to sail to Troy with Paris, and the *Defense of Palamedes*, which presents a speech Palamedes might have used to defend himself against the false accusation of Odysseus that he tried to betray the Greek camp to the Trojans.[50]

An example of "antilogic" is the *Twofold Arguments*, an anonymous collection of arguments that present considerations on both sides of certain issues: are Good and Bad the same or different?; likewise for Fair and Foul, Just and Unjust, True and False; do wise and sane people say and do the same things as fools and the insane?; can wisdom and virtue be taught?[51] The section on True and False exemplifies the style of arguing.

18.18 (1) Twofold arguments are also stated concerning the false and the true, of which one declares that true LOGOS (speech, statement) and false LOGOS are different from one another, and others that they are the same. (2) And I say the following. First, that true and false LOGOS are expressed in the same words. Second, when a LOGOS is spoken, if events have occurred the way the LOGOS is spoken, the LOGOS is true, but if they have not occurred, the same LOGOS is false. (3) Suppose it accuses someone of sacrilege. If the deed took place, the LOGOS is true, but if it did not take place, it is false. And the LOGOS of the defendant is the same. And the courts judge the same LOGOS to be both false and true. (4) Next, if we are seated one next to the other, and we (each) say "I am an initiate of the mysteries," we will all say the same thing, but only I will be true, since in fact I am (the only) one (who is). (5) Now it

---

50. Much of the *Praise of Helen* is translated below (**18.18**).

51. In the last sections of this work the author argues that officials should not be appointed by lot (as was done at Athens), discusses the power of the rhetor, and gives tips for developing the memory.

is obvious that the same LOGOS is false whenever falsehood is present to it and true whenever truth is, in the same way a person is the same individual as a boy and as a youth and as an adult and as an old man. (6) It is also stated that false LOGOS and true LOGOS are different from one another, differing in name just as they differ in fact. For if anyone asks those who say that the same LOGOS is both false and true whether the LOGOS that they are stating is true or false, then if it is false, clearly they (the true LOGOS and the false LOGOS) are two (and therefore not the same). But if it is true, this same LOGOS is also false. And if anyone has ever spoken or borne witness of things that are true, it follows that these same things are false. And if he knows any man to be true, also he knows the same man to be false. (7) As a result of the argument they say these things because if the thing occurred the LOGOS is true, but if it did not, then it is false. Therefore it is not their name that differs, but the fact of the matter. (8) Moreover, if anyone should ask the jurors what they are judging (since they are not present at the events), (9) these people too agree that the LOGOS with which falsehood is mixed is false, and that with which truth is mixed is true. This is the entire difference.   (*Twofold Arguments*, DK 90,4)

The Power of Persuasion

Argument is for the sake of persuasion, and persuasion is the key to success in the arenas (courts and Assembly) for which Sophists trained their pupils. Peitho ("Persuasion") was a goddess, and Gorgias' display piece *Praise of Helen* speaks of her power.

18.19 (5) I will set forth the reasons for which it was likely that Helen's voyage to Troy took place. (6) She did what she did through the will of Fate and the designs of the gods and decrees of Necessity or because she was taken by force, persuaded by words (LOGOI), or conquered by Love. . . . (8) Not even if speech (LOGOS) persuaded and deceived her soul, is it hard to make a defense against this charge and free her from blame, as follows. LOGOS is a powerful master, which by means of the smallest and most invisible body accomplishes most divine deeds. For it can put an end to fear, remove grief, instill joy, and increase pity. I will prove how this is so. (9) But it is to the opinion of my audience that I must prove it. I both consider and define all poetry to be speech (LOGOS) with meter. Those who hear it are overcome with fearful shuddering, tearful pity, and mournful yearning, and over the good fortunes and ill-farings of other people and their affairs the soul experiences a feeling of its own, through the words (LOGOI). Come now, let me shift from one argument (LOGOS) to another. (10) Inspired incantations bring on pleasure and bring away grief through words (LOGOI). For conversing with the soul's opinion the power of incantation charms, persuades, and changes it by witchcraft. Two arts of witchcraft and magic have been discovered—errors of the soul and deceptions of opinion. (11) All who have persuaded or who persuade anyone of anything do so by fashioning false LOGOS. For if on all subjects everyone had memory of the past, (a conception) of the present and foreknowledge of the future, LOGOS would not be similarly similar as it is for people who, as things are, cannot easily remember the past, consider the present or divine the future. Thus, on most matters, most people make opinion an adviser to their soul. But opinion is fallible and uncertain, and involves those who make use of it in fallible and uncertain successes. (12) What, then, keeps us from supposing that Helen too, against her will, came under the influence of LOGOI just as if she had been taken by the force of mighty men? For it was possible to see how persuasion prevails, which lacks the appearance of necessity but has the same power.[52] For LOGOS, which persuaded, compelled the soul, which it persuaded, both to believe what was said and to approve what was done. Therefore, the one who persuaded, since he compelled, is unjust, and the one who was persuaded, since she was compelled by LOGOS, is wrongly blamed. (13) As to the fact that persuasion added to LOGOS makes whatever impression it likes on the soul, one should attend first to the accounts (LOGOI) of the astronomers, who replace one opinion with another and so make things incredible and unclear seem apparent to the eyes of opinion; second, to compulsory competitions which use speeches (LOGOI), in which a single LOGOS written with art (TECHNE) but not spoken with truth delights and persuades a large crowd; and third, to contests of philosophers' accounts (LOGOI), in which is revealed how easily the swiftness of thought makes our confidence in our opinion change. (14) The power of LOGOS has the same relation (LOGOS) to the order of the soul as the order of drugs has to the nature of bodies. For as different drugs expel different humors from the body, and some put an end to sickness and others to life, so some LOGOI cause grief, others joy, some fear, others render their hearers bold, and still others drug and bewitch the soul through an evil persuasion. (15) It has been stated that if she was persuaded by LOGOS she did not do wrong but was unfortunate. . . . (21) By my account (LOGOS) I have removed ill fame from a woman. I have stayed faithful to the rule (NOMOS) I stipulated at the beginning of my LOGOS. I have attempted to put an end to the injustice of blame and ignorance of opinion. I wanted to write the LOGOS as a praise of Helen and an entertainment for myself.

(Gorgias, DK 82B11)

52. The text of this sentence is corrupt. I follow Diels' suggestions (DK, vol. 2, p. 291).

Sections 11 and 13 contain the germs of interesting philosophical theses. Section 11 begins with the tantalizing assertion that all persuasion involves falsehood. What, then, is Gorgias' view of truth? Can rhetoric never be used to convince people of the truth? It moulds people's opinion, which can be swayed because it is by nature fallible and uncertain. Gorgias implicitly contrasts opinion with knowledge, which is infallible and certain. He associates truth and falsity with the means by which we achieve knowledge and opinion. Knowledge is based on memory (in the case of things in the past), awareness (for things in the present), and foreknowledge (for things in the future). Memory, awareness, and foreknowledge must be true, whereas persuasion depends on something else, speech (LOGOS), which cannot produce in us the infallible and certain state of knowledge, and so is called false. Truth and falsity, then, are not attributes of beliefs or propositions that they have independently of how they are reached.

Section 13 identifies three types of occasions for persuasion. The second includes the public forums for which the Sophists prepared their pupils. The first and third include scientific and philosophical settings, where rhetoric is useful, for where the topic is obscure, rhetoric can persuade people this way or that. In the occasions mentioned, the truth is not clear; we have to do with opinion, not secure knowledge, and hence persuasion through rhetorical ability can prevail, bending the audience's opinions. In such cases, the power of speech is compelling. It can be used for good or evil, and those under its influence have no power to resist.

Protagorean Relativism

If, as Gorgias says, certainty is often unattainable and we are at the mercy of persuasion—if, that is to say, knowledge is for practical purposes unattainable and we are forced to rely on easily swayed opinions—what counts is what we believe, or are made to believe. This is the case in courts and in the Assembly. The jury did not witness the crime and bases its verdict on arguments brought by the prosecution and the defense. The Assembly does not have foreknowledge of the effects or the correctness of its decisions, but must decide what to do on the basis of arguments. In either case (and analogically in scientific and philosophical discussions) what matters is the decision. From the orator's pragmatic point of view the best case is the one for which there are the strongest arguments, which need not be the one based on truth. For what decides is a number of individual people, not the facts of the matter.

Protagoras encapsulated this view in the most famous dictum of the sophistic era.

18.20 A human being is the measure of all things—of things that are, that they are, and of things that are not, that they are not.

(Protagoras, DK 80B1)

The precise translation is debated. Is the subject humans as a whole or an individual human? (The most common translation is "Man is the measure.") Is he (are they) *a* measure or *the* measure? What is the scope of "things"? What sorts of judgments are involved—just whether a thing exists or does not exist, or more broadly, what is and what is not true to say about it? Certainty cannot be hoped for, and different answers lead to different philosophical interpretations. I favor the translation given, which accords with the rhetorical and educational aspects of Protagoras' profession as follows. The individual person, not the facts of the matter, is the practical standard for determining what is the case. Each member of the jury or Assembly is the target of the orator's skills. The truth may be as you say, but that is irrelevant if you cannot convince the appropriate people.

On the basis of this pragmatic advice to aspiring public speakers, an elaborate philosophy was developed.[53] If each person is the determiner of truth and falsity, then any judgment any person makes is true. If I judge the wind to be hot and you judge it to be cold, we are both correct. Moreover, in declaring that the wind is hot I am not contradicting you, but stating something that is true too. The wind is both hot and cold.

This doctrine was backed up by theories about the nature of perception and the nature of the relation between perception and judgment. Perceptions depend on features of the thing perceived and on features of the individual who does the perceiving, and so are both objective and subjective.[54] Both the condition of the sense organ and the nature of the object affect our perceptions. If honey tastes sweet to a healthy person and bitter to a sick person, it does so because of the way it reacts with their taste organs. Likewise, if it tastes bitter to me now and sweet later, the difference will be due to a change in my taste organs. Further, judgments are based on perceptions. If our judgments about the honey's taste or the warmth or

53. This section depends more on Platonic material than the rest of the chapter. Without Plato and sources familiar with Plato, we have little more than Protagoras' dicta "a human being is the measure" and "it is impossible to contradict," which are insufficient to reconstruct Protagoras' views. Whether or not Protagoras actually developed these ideas as Plato and the subsequent tradition assert he did must remain obscure, but the topic is so important that it requires treatment despite its shaky credentials.

54. This view of perception was shared by the Atomists. See pp. 330–31.

coldness of the wind differ, they do not conflict, because they are really assertions about our own private perceptions. "The wind is hot" boils down to "The wind feels hot to me, now," and this statement does not contradict your claim "The wind is cold," which boils down to "The wind feels cold to you, now."

We can go one step farther: the wind is both hot and cold. While it cannot be perceived as either hot or cold in the absence of a perceiver, it has objective features that cause it to be perceived as hot by a perceiver in the appropriate condition and as cold by a perceiver in a different condition.

Perceptions are incorrigible in the sense that each of us is the unique authority about the content of his or her own perceptions. No one else can offer considerations that will force a person to perceive things differently. Since judgments are based on perceptions, they are incorrigible too. And since reality, how things are, is manifested through perception and expressed in judgments, things are as they seem to a person and no one can be a judge of how things seem, or therefore of how they are, to anyone else. Thus, truth is relative to the individual. This is the doctrine of Protagorean relativism. It is a philosophical theory that is simultaneously epistemological and ontological, i.e., a theory about the nature and basis of our judgments, and also about the nature of reality.

Protagorean relativism is most plausible for the type of cases considered—judgments based directly on perceptions and which express the content of those perceptions. It is also plausible for ethical judgments, since it is notoriously difficult to find objective standards of good and bad, right and wrong. In fact, certain forms of ethical relativism were current in fifth-century Greece and will be taken up in the next chapter.

Perceptual and ethical judgments apart, how plausible is relativism? If I think that $2 + 2 = 5$, does that make it true? If I think I can survive a fall from the roof of the Parthenon, does that guarantee that I will? If I think Protagorean relativism is false, does that make it false? These and related issues are taken up in Plato's brilliant treatment of Protagorean relativism in the *Theaetetus*.[55] For now, I will take up just one problem the theory raises—a problem for the Sophists themselves.

If everyone's beliefs are true, how can one belief be better than another? If Protagorean relativism assures me that my opinion on a given subject is true, what could induce me to reject it in favor of another? These questions, which suggest that persuasion and education are impossible, attack the foundations of the Sophists' program.

The beginnings of an answer are given in the following passage of the *Theaetetus*.

55. Plato, *Theaetetus* 152a–172b, 177c–179c (neither passage in DK).

18.21 I do say that the truth is as I've written: each of us is the measure of the things which are and the things which are not. Nevertheless, there's an immense difference between one man and another in just this respect: the things which are and appear to one man are different from those which are and appear to another. As for wisdom or a wise man, I'm nowhere near saying there's no such thing; on the contrary, I do apply the word "wise" to precisely this sort of person: anyone who can effect a change in one of us, to whom bad things appear and are, and make good things both appear and be for him. . . . Remember the sort of thing you were saying before: to a sick man what he eats appears, and is, bitter, whereas to a healthy man it is, and appears, the opposite. Now what must be done isn't to make either of them wiser, because that isn't even possible; nor is it to accuse the sick one of being ignorant because he makes the sort of judgments he does, and call the healthy one wise because he makes judgments of a different sort. What must be done is to effect a change in one direction; because one of the two conditions is better. In education too, in the same way, a change must be effected from one of two conditions to the better one; but whereas a doctor makes the change with drugs, a Sophist does it with things he says.

It's not that anyone ever makes someone whose judgments are false come, later on, to judge what's true: after all, it isn't possible to have in one's judgments the things which are not, or anything other than what one's experiencing, which is always true. What does happen, I think, is this: when, because of a harmful condition in his mind, someone has in his judgments things which are akin to that condition, then by means of a beneficial condition one makes him have in his judgments things of that same sort—appearances which some people, because of ignorance, call true; but I call them better than the first sort, but not at all truer.

And as for the wise . . . where bodies are concerned, I say it's doctors who are the wise, and where plants are concerned, gardeners— because I claim that they, too, whenever any of their plants are sick, instill perceptions that are beneficial and healthy, and true, too, into them, instead of harmful ones. My claim is, too, that wise and good politicians make beneficial things, instead of harmful ones, seem to their states to be just. If any sort of thing seems just and admirable to any state, then it actually is just and admirable for it, as long as that state accepts it; but a wise man makes the beneficial things be and seem just and admirable to them, instead of any harmful things which used to be so for them. And according to the same principle the Sophist is wise, too, in that he can educate his pupils in that way.

(Plato, *Theaetetus* 166d–167c = DK 80A21a, tr. McDowell)

All judgments are true, but not all are equally good or beneficial. If I judge that honey tastes bitter, my judgment is true, but my sick condition in which honey tastes bitter is not as good as one in which it tastes sweet. Even in my sickness I believe it is better for me to be in a state where honey tastes sweet, so I am willing to submit to the directions of a physician who can change my condition so that honey tastes sweet to me. Likewise in public debates. Everyone has an (equally true) opinion about what is the just, good, and beneficial thing to do, but not all opinions are equally good or beneficial. A statesman can induce the citizens to abandon bad and harmful opinions and adopt good and beneficial ones in their place, and instead of using medicines he uses persuasion.[56] Education too is possible, since it consists in leading pupils to have good and beneficial judgments and in training them to persuade others to adopt such judgments in place of the ones they hold.

Language, Thought, and Reality

The sophistic program of education also led to discussion of the relations between thought, language, and reality. Before Plato, the most important document is Gorgias' *On What is Not, or On Nature*, two summaries of which survive. The title parodies the title standardly given to the works of the Presocratics, *On Nature*, and especially the title of Melissus' work *On Nature, or On That Which Is*. In a style reminiscent of the Eleatics, particularly Gorgias' contemporary Melissus, Gorgias argues for three theses: (A) nothing is, (B) even if something is humans cannot comprehend it, and (C) even if it is comprehensible it cannot be expressed or communicated to another.

This essay has aroused a great deal of controversy, first over the question whether it is meant as a serious contribution to philosophy, and second (by those who answer the first question affirmatively) over the nature of its contribution.[57] My view is that Gorgias did not believe any of the theses he argues for, and that the fallacies in some of his arguments are so blatant that he must have been aware of them. These are good reasons for thinking that Gorgias did not intend his work as a serious contribution to philosophy, but as a parody of a certain type of argument that was current.[58]

But there is more. The fact that the same sort of argument could be used to prove these obviously false propositions as was used to prove propositions that the Eleatics intended seriously casts doubt on their methods

---

56. Gorgias, *Praise of Helen*, sec. 14 (= DK82B11).

57. Kerferd (op. cit. [p. 376 n. 31], pp. 93–100) takes Gorgias seriously, Guthrie (*HGP*, vol. 3, pp. 192–200), less so.

58. The work is dated to the late 440's (Olympiodorus, *Commentary on Plato's Gorgias*, p. 112 = DK 82A10), which makes it contemporary with the likely date of Melissus' writings.

and conclusions. Parody can have devastating effects. Also, even if Gorgias' intent was not philosophical, and even if his arguments do not convince, the work nevertheless raises important philosophical issues which Plato and later philosophers took up. To this extent Gorgias' work has an important place in the history of philosophy. For this reason I present it in full.[59]

18.22 (66) He concludes as follows that nothing is: if (something) is, either what-is is or what-is-not (is), or both what-is and what-is-not are. But it is the case neither that what-is is, as he will show, nor that what-is-not is, as he will justify, nor that both what-is and what-is-not are, as he will teach this too. Therefore, it is not the case that anything is. (67) And in fact, what-is-not is not. For if what-is-not is, it will be and not be at the same time. For in that it is considered as not being, it will not be, but in that it *is* not being, on the other hand, it will be. But it is completely absurd that something to be and not be at the same time. Therefore, it is not the case that what-is-not is. And differently: if what-is-not is, what-is will not be, since they are opposites, and if being is an attribute of what-is-not, not-being will be an attribute of what-is. But it is certainly not the case that what-is is not, and so neither will what-is-not be. (68) Further, neither is it the case that what-is is. For if what-is is, it is either eternal or generated or eternal and generated at the same time. But it is neither eternal nor generated nor both, as we will show. Therefore it is not the case that what-is is. For if what-is is eternal (we must begin at this point), it does not have any beginning. (69) For everything that comes to be has some beginning, but what is eternal, being ungenerated did not have a beginning. But if it does not have a beginning, it is unlimited, and if it is unlimited it is nowhere. For if it is anywhere, that in which it is is different from it, and so what-is will no longer be unlimited, since it is enclosed in something. For what encloses is larger than what is enclosed, but nothing is larger than what is unlimited, and so what is unlimited is not anywhere. (70) Further, it is not enclosed in itself, either. For "that in which" and "that in it" will be the same, and what-is will become two, place and body (for "that in which" is place, and "that in it" is body). But this is absurd, so what-is is not in itself, either. And so, if what-is is eternal, it is unlimited, but if it is unlimited it is nowhere, and if it is nowhere it is not. So if what-is is eternal, it is not at all. (71) Further, what-is cannot be generated either. For if it has come to be it did so either from a thing that is or from a thing that is not. But it has come to be neither from what-is (for if it is a thing that is, it has not come to be, but already is), nor from

59. I give a translation of the version in Sextus Empiricus, *Against the Mathematicians* 7.65–86 (= DK 82B3). The shorter summary in pseudo-Aristotle, *On Melissus, Xenophanes and Gorgias*, chaps. 5–6 (not in DK), is preferable at some points.

what-is-not (for what-is-not cannot generate anything, since what generates anything must of necessity share in existence). Therefore, it is
not the case that what-is is generated either. (72) In the same ways, it is
not both eternal and generated at the same time. For these exclude one
another, and if what-is is eternal it has not come to be, and if it has
come to be it is not eternal. So if what-is is neither eternal nor generated nor both together, what-is would not be. (73) And differently, if it
is, it is either one or many. But it is neither one nor many, as will be
shown. Therefore it is not the case that what-is is. For if it is one, it is
either a quantity or continuous or a magnitude or a body. But whichever of these it is, it is not one, but being a quantity, it will be divided,
and if it is continuous it will be cut. Similarly if conceived as a magnitude it will not be indivisible. And if it chances to be a body, it will be
three-dimensional, for it will have length, width and depth. But it is
absurd to say that what-is is none of these. Therefore, it is not the case
that what-is is one. (74) Further, it is not many. For if it is not one, it is
not many either. For the many is a compound of individual ones, and so
since (the thesis that what-is is) one is refuted, (the thesis that what-is
is) many is refuted along with it. But it is altogether clear from this that
neither what-is nor what-is-not is. (75) It is easy to conclude that
neither is it the case that both of them are, what-is and what-is-not.
For if what-is-not is and what-is is, then what-is-not will be the same
as what-is as regards being. And for this reason neither of them is. For
it is agreed that what-is-not is not, and what-is has been shown to be
the same as this. So it too will not be. (76) However, if what-is is the
same as what-is-not, it is not possible for both to be. For if both (are),
then they are not the same, and if (they are) the same, then (it is) not
(the case that) both (are). It follows that nothing is. For if neither what-
is is nor what-is-not nor both, and nothing aside from these is conceived of, nothing is.   (Gorgias, DK 82B3)

It is instructive to compare the arguments in this part with those of the
Eleatics, especially secs. 69–70 with Melissus (**15.1**, **15.2**, **15.3**, and **15.6**),
sec. 71 with Parmenides (**11.8** lines 12–13), and secs. 73–74 with Zeno
(**12.4**). Parmenides believed that the only possible approaches were the two
alternatives that he considered: It is, and It is not, and he rejected the latter,
leaving the former. Gorgias now offers refutations of both alternatives,
leaving a wholly negative conclusion: Nothing is.

The second and third parts of Gorgias' essay break new ground.

18.23 (77) Next in order is to teach that even if something is, it is unknowable
and inconceivable by humans. For if things that are thought of, says
Gorgias, are not things-that-are, what-is is not thought of. And reasonably so. For just as if things that are thought of have the attribute of
being white, being thought of would be an attribute of white things, so
if things that are thought of have the attribute of not being things-that-

are, not to be thought of will necessarily be an attribute of things-that-are. (78) This is why the claim that if things that are thought of are not things-that-are, what-is is not thought of, is sound and preserves the sequence of argument. But things that are thought of (for we must assume this) are not things-that-are, as we will show. Therefore it is not the case that what-is is thought of. Further, it is completely clear that things that are thought of are not things-that-are. (79) For if things that are thought of are things-that-are, all things that are thought of are—indeed, however anyone thinks of them. But this is apparently false. For if someone thinks of a person flying or chariots racing in the sea, it is not the case that forthwith a person is flying or chariots racing in the sea. And so, it is not the case that things that are thought of are things-that-are. (80) In addition, if things that are thought of are things-that-are, things-that-are-not will not be thought of. For opposites have opposite attributes, and what-is-not is opposite to what-is. For this reason, if being thought of is an attribute of what-is, not being thought of will assuredly be an attribute of what-is-not. But this is absurd. For Scylla and Chimaera and many things-that-are-not are thought of. Therefore it is not the case that what-is is thought of. (81) And just as things that are seen are called visible because they are seen and things that are heard are called audible because they are heard, and we do not reject visible things because they are not heard or dismiss audible things because they are not seen (for each ought to be judged by its own sense, not by another), so also things that are thought of will be, even if they may not be seen by vision or heard by hearing, because they are grasped by their own criterion. (82) So if someone thinks that chariots race in the sea, even if he does not see them, he ought to believe that there are chariots racing in the sea. But this is absurd. Therefore it is not the case that what-is is thought of and compre-hended. (Gorgias, DK 82B3) (continuation of **18.22**)

Gorgias argues that there is no necessary correlation between thought and reality. It is possible to think of a human flying even though no human flies. It is possible to think of Scylla even though Scylla does not exist. Further, the first sentence of sec. 79 seems to establish a condition for there to be a correlation between thought and reality: if the object of thought exists, it must have the attributes with which thought invests it. If I think of a chariot racing in the sea and no chariot is racing in the sea, I am not thinking of a real chariot and attributing to it something that is not true of it. Rather, what I am thinking of, a chariot racing in the sea, does not exist. This is an interesting philosophical position, which invites serious discussion, but to discuss it seriously requires a great deal of work in the fields of philosophy of language and philosophy of mind—work that was not done by Gorgias or by anyone earlier than or contemporary with him.

The same can be said about the third and final part of Gorgias' essay.

18.24 (83) But even if it should be comprehended, it cannot be expressed to another. For if things-that-are are visible and audible and generally perceptible, and in fact are external objects, and of these the visible are comprehended by vision and the audible by hearing, and not vice versa, how can these be communicated to another? (84) For that by which we communicate is LOGOS, but LOGOS is not the objects, the things-that-are. Therefore it is not the case that we communicate things-that-are to our neighbors, but LOGOS, which is different from the objects. So just as the visible could not become audible and vice versa, thus, since what-is is an external object, it could not become our LOGOS. (85) But if it were not LOGOS, it would not have been revealed to another. In fact, LOGOS, he says, is composed from external things, i.e., perceptible things, falling upon us. For from encountering flavor there arises in us the LOGOS which is expressed with reference to this quality, and from the incidence on the senses of color arises the LOGOS with reference to color. But if so, it is not the LOGOS that makes manifest the external (object), but the external (object) that comes to be communicative of the LOGOS. (86) Further, it is not possible to say that LOGOS is an object in the way visible and audible things are, so that objects which are can be communicated by it, which is an object which is. For, he says, even if LOGOS is an object, it anyway differs from all other objects, and visible bodies differ most from LOGOS. For the visible is grasped by one organ, LOGOS by another. Therefore it is not the case that LOGOS makes manifest the great number of objects, just as they do not reveal the nature of one another.   (Gorgias, DK 82B3)(continuation of **18.23**)

Gorgias raises explicitly the questions of how the senses are related to their objects and how one sense is related to another. What can be seen, e.g., colors, cannot be heard, and vice versa. Speech is audible and therefore cannot communicate visible things. Moreover, speech is different and of a different kind from the external things it attempts to communicate—even the audible things. Therefore, it cannot communicate them. Sec. 85 presents a causal theory of language. Speech arises as the result of our being affected by external sensible objects. But then it is backwards to say that speech displays the object, rather it is the object that makes speech intelligible.

Again, we find a host of interesting and important philosophical arguments and theses, and again, there is no reason to suppose that Gorgias did any more philosophical work than we see here, no clear reason to suppose that he even thought that there was more work to be done. Not until Plato took up these and related issues in such dialogues as *Cratylus*, *Theaetetus*, and *Sophist*, or at least not until he posited his theory of Ideas in the *Phaedo*, do we find the beginnings of the philosophical labor required to untangle them and provide a satisfactory treatment.

Were the Sophists Philosophers?

I shall end this chapter with a topic many have thought important. From the fifth century the Sophists have often been considered intellectual charlatans, purveyors of faulty reasoning, and out to gain victory rather than reach the truth. In these ways they fare badly against philosophers, whose selfless search for truth transcends all other concerns. Plato, for whom the type of the philosopher was Socrates, sharply contrasts Socrates' manner and methods with those of the Sophists. Socrates claimed to know nothing, to have no positive doctrine to impart, whereas the Sophists claimed to be experts on everything and taught their knowledge to others. They grew rich from their profession, while Socrates, who did not offer formal instruction and did not charge people fees for associating with him, remained poor. Their claim to teach ARETE was suspect and based on a superficial and ill thought out conception of human good. Their methods were dishonest in emphasizing rhetorical tricks over real knowledge. Their technique of arguing both sides of an issue was no more likely to lead to a concern for the truth than was their emphasis on swaying crowds rather than convincing thoughtful individuals.[60] On this account the Sophists are the antithesis of philosophers, and the opprobrium cast by Plato remains to this day.

Looked at more broadly, however, Socrates can be seen as a Sophist, or as a product of the sophistic movement. True, he did not take fees for teaching, but this aspect of the matter, which Plato stresses heavily, has no importance for our assessment of the intellectual relations between Socrates and the Sophists. In fact, these relations are very close. Socrates as well as the Sophists dealt in LOGOI, arguments and reasoning. If Socrates reacted against certain sophistic doctrines, so did the Sophists. There is little uniformity in their views, and frequently they took up opposing positions on a single issue.[61]

Socrates challenged the Sophists on basic issues. What is ARETE? Can it be taught? What constitutes a good or successful life for a person? Do the Sophists, or any other humans for that matter, really have the knowledge and wisdom they claim to have? It is important to recognize that these questions were central ones not only in Socrates' thought but in the Sophists' as well, and that the Sophists were Socrates' most important precursors, contemporaries, and opponents on these topics. Without the Sophists, these issues would not have had the same importance for Socrates or even

60. Plato, *Gorgias* 458e–459b (not in DK).

61. Most notably in the NOMOS-PHYSIS debate, discussed in chap. 19.

the same meaning. Moreover, by using LOGOI to refute the Sophists, Socrates followed sophistic practice. He excelled in arguments, and developed his own methods of reasoning and techniques of argument (the "Socratic method"). In doing so he was outdoing the Sophists at their own game and inventing new moves in it, but he was still playing the same game.[62]

If Socrates' tools and methods, as well as the issues he addressed, fall within the range of the Sophists, perhaps he can be distinguished from them by his intentions. Socrates' goal was to improve the souls of those who conversed with him, whereas the Sophists showed people how to gain reputation, power, and wealth. Even here, though, the differences are not as great as they may appear. For Socrates, improving the soul is the most important thing anyone can do.[63] Success in this arena constitutes success in life. The Sophists for their part also held that the ends they promoted made for success in life. The difference comes down to one of criteria for success, but the overall goal, "living well" is the same.

Another possible way to separate Socrates from the Sophists is to say that Socrates aimed for the truth while the Sophists aimed for victory in argument. In that they taught rhetoric, it is true that they aimed to train effective, that is, successful, victorious speakers. The same can be said of the Sophists' own speeches. But how are we to treat the Sophists' contributions to the NOMOS-PHYSIS debate and other philosophical topics? By now it should be clear that we would be naive simply to follow Plato and declare that the Sophists were not philosophers because they taught for pay, etc. Plato's testimony is suspect because it is self-serving. Plato was out to dissociate Socrates from the Sophists, but the ways he did so fall short of proving that they were not philosophers.

Another approach to this issue starts from the position that the Sophists were primarily educators. Since they taught rhetoric, their interest in the nature of language is predictable. Since they taught how to win in debate, they might be expected to work out a pragmatic, relativistic conception of knowledge and truth. Since they were concerned with legislation and political power, it is unsurprising if they formulated views on the nature of political power and its relation to law and custom. All these are appropriate themes for display speeches. Moreover, since the Sophists were rivals, they would be quick to learn one another's views on these matters, formulate objections to them, and devise new, superior theories—the better to attract audiences and pupils. Let us suppose that their primary intention in doing

62. It has even been held that the method of questions and short answers, which is so characteristic of Socrates, was widely used by the Sophists: Kerferd, op. cit., pp. 32–34.

63. Plato, *Apology* 30a–b (not in DK).

this philosophical work was to advance their own standing as Sophists, to increase their wealth, fame, and importance. Is this sufficient reason to refuse to call them philosophers?

Before answering this question, let us take another tack. The material presented in this chapter and the next shows that the Sophists raised important issues in a number of fields of philosophy, and in some cases gave those issues philosophically interesting treatment. There are grounds, therefore, for asserting that the Sophists did some philosophy. If doing philosophy qualifies a person as a philosopher, then at least some Sophists were philosophers.

This answer may be all that is required. On the other hand, those who feel that philosophers must be aiming at the truth in the philosophical matters they take up, or at least that they must care in a certain way about the arguments and theses they construct and champion, may still have reservations about calling the Sophists philosophers. The *Praise of Helen*, which contains interesting philosophical ideas about truth and falsity, knowledge and opinion, speech and persuasion, was composed as a kind of entertainment (sec. 21). Part of the intention of the work is to demonstrate the power of LOGOS (a self-serving thesis for a teacher of rhetoric), and the philosophically interesting material may be subordinate to this end. For all we know, *On What is Not, or On Nature* was written in the same spirit. It is likewise possible that Protagoras did not really believe that a human being is the measure of all things, but simply articulated that view, and perhaps expanded it into a whole relativistic philosophy in order to dignify his profession and attract students. It is even possible that the Sophists who contributed to the NOMOS-PHYSIS debate were simply staking out positions that they could use to show off their brilliance and from which they could assault the stances adopted by their rivals. It is thus possible that the Sophists were no more concerned with the truth of the philosophical positions they adopted or the soundness of the arguments they advanced than modern public-relations firms need to be about the claims they make for the products they promote. And this consideration may give us qualms about designating the Sophists as philosophers.

But for all we know, they may have cared passionately for the views they expressed. If the fact that someone does philosophical work is not sufficient grounds for calling that person a philosopher and we need to know his or her attitudes and intentions as well, we must admit that we are not in a position to judge. In this matter, as in many others concerning the Sophists of the fifth century, opinions will continue to vary.

19

The NOMOS-PHYSIS Debate

In Greece and especially in Athens, the second half of the fifth century was a period of unmatched intellectual liveliness. A profusion of ideas were floated, discussed, and fought over by such distinguished figures as the tragic poets Sophocles and Euripides, the comic poet Aristophanes, the historians Herodotus and Thucydides, numerous orators, the later Presocratics (above all, Democritus), the Sophists, and, of course, Socrates and his associates. The fact that in most cases these ideas were presented in public settings, from the theater, Assembly, and lawcourts to the great festival of Olympia, proves that the general public was exposed to and presumably understood and entered into the debate. The surviving writings give a vivid picture of the intellectual scene—the issues, the manners of treatment, and the range of solutions that were in the air.

One topic in particular was discussed frequently and in a variety of contexts: the contrasting concepts NOMOS (plural, NOMOI), which can be translated "law," "custom," and "convention," and PHYSIS, "nature," and the ways of interpreting the contrast between them. These concepts themselves are interesting and complex in their own right, but more importantly, they were thought to be the keys to understanding a wide range of issues that stemmed from sources as varied as the presocratic philosophical tradition and the practical politics of running an empire. These issues include the following: Do gods exist in nature or only by custom? Does human society exist as a result of human nature or of convention? Is morality natural or only a product of custom? Are the optimal political arrangements for a state determined by the facts of human nature alone, or should laws be introduced to provide a control on nature? Am I better off to follow the dictates of NOMOS or those of PHYSIS?

There is a large and diverse body of source materials from fifth- and fourth-century writers on what is known as the NOMOS-PHYSIS debate, some found in the philosophical writings of the Sophists, Plato, and Aristotle, and some in dramatic, historical, and political writings of the period. The present chapter will present some of this material in order to display a number of the ways in which the terms of the debate were conceived and how certain issues were conceptualized and discussed in terms of these notions, and also to show how thoroughly the debate penetrated Greek intellectual life. Three passages from Plato are summarized and discussed but not translated since they are comparatively long and readily available. I have drawn materials from authors as late as Aristotle in order to make the selection as representative and useful as possible. This purpose conflicts with the title of this book, but excluding all fourth-century material would leave the the picture awkwardly incomplete. Constraints of space require the passages to speak for themselves more than elsewhere in this book, but since they speak loud and clear this should not prove a serious disadvantage.

NOMOS

There is no single English equivalent for NOMOS. It is related to the verb NOMIZO ("think," "believe," "practice") and originally meant what people (or a people) believe or practice—their customs, which, especially in early times, had the force of laws. Indeed, before the existence of written law codes, a distinction between custom and law would have been hard to draw. NOMOS has prescriptive force: it is not simply what is believed, but what is believed to be right, not just the ways of life a people practices, but what it practices as the right way of life. The word was extended to cover laws formally enacted and enforced by the state. In this usage it retains its prescriptive force: people are under an obligation to obey the laws.

A passage from Herodotus' *Histories* illustrates some of the ways the Greeks regarded NOMOS.

> **19.1** If all humans were told to select the best NOMOI from all that are, each people would upon consideration choose its own. . . . There is a vast amount of evidence for this fact, including the following. When Darius was king of the Persian empire, he summoned the Greeks who were at his court and asked how much money it would take for them to eat the corpses of their fathers. They responded that they would not do it for any price. Afterwards, Darius summoned some Indians called Kallatiai who do eat their parents and asked in the presence of the Greeks who understood through interpreters for what price they would agree to cremate their dead fathers. They cried out loudly and told him to keep still. That is what people's customs are, and I think Pindar was right when he wrote that NOMOS is king of all.   (Herodotus, *Histories* 3.38, not in DK)

This passage shows the prescriptive force of NOMOS as well as another feature frequently associated with NOMOS—variability. It was well known that NOMOS, in the sense of custom or customary beliefs or practices, differs among different peoples. Herodotus proves that the strange ways of foreign folk were a fascinating topic for the Greeks, since much of his popular *Histories* is given over to ethnographic accounts of Persians, Egyptians, Scythians, and other peoples. An earlier reference to this topic is found in Xenophanes' brief mention of how different peoples conceive of their gods (**7.5**). Moreover, NOMOS in the sense of the positive written law of a state was known to all Athenians to be the product of human con-trivance and capable of being created, abolished, or changed by the Assem-bly. Thus, even for a single people NOMOS was different at different times.

PHYSIS

PHYSIS, standardly translated "nature," has several philosophical usages. Some of these have been brought out in connection with the presocratic philosophers, the conventional name for whose writings was *Peri Phuseos* (*On Nature*). Of primary concern here is the sense of the basic nature of an individual or type of thing, in contrast to its acquired characteristics. In this way a thing's PHYSIS is its permanent or essential characteristics, or how it would be if it were not interfered with. A second relevant use is found in the phrase "by nature," which comes close to "in reality" or "as things really or fundamentally (perhaps despite appearances) are."

The Antithesis Between NOMOS and PHYSIS

The contrast between NOMOS as variable, impermanent, and artificial, and PHYSIS as necessary, universal, and permanent was a commonplace. In ar-guing for his thesis that "by nature all people, foreigners and Greeks alike, are naturally similar in all respects," Antiphon offers as evidence "things that are by nature (PHYSIS) necessary to all humans," such as breathing through the mouth and nostrils and eating with the hands.[1] In the same vein, Aristophanes refers to love (and adultery!) as necessities of nature.[2] Things that are "by nature" are necessary; also PHYSIS, in the sense of the nature of something, implies that some features of that thing are necessary, those it has by virtue of being the type of thing it is. For example, Socrates has some features by virtue of being a human. Being a human, he has human nature, the nature of a human being. As a result, he has charac-teristics, for example, breathing through the mouth and nostrils, that he shares with all other humans. These features are universal and perma-nent—they belong to all humans whenever and wherever they may live.

The nature of the contrast between NOMOS and PHYSIS can be construed variously. It is related to the contrast between the prescriptive (how things ought to be) and the descriptive (how things are), though it is not the same, since some attributed a prescriptive dimension to PHYSIS as well as to NOMOS (if things are such-and-such by nature, that is how they ought to be). Among other aspects of the NOMOS-PHYSIS antithesis is the contrast

1. Antiphon, DK 87B44 B.
2. Aristophanes, *Clouds* lines 1075–76 (not in DK).

between appearance (how things seem to someone) and reality (how things are in fact). Another is the opposition between the artificial, or man-made, and the natural. Yet another is that between the contingent, or accidental, and the necessary.

In addition, the interplay of NOMOS and PHYSIS was conceived in different ways. Some saw them as hostile to one another, each prescribing situations and behavior the other proscribes. Others saw them as complementing one another, PHYSIS providing a range of options and NOMOS determining which of these to adopt. Still others claimed that NOMOS is based on PHYSIS, thus employing the terms of the debate while undermining the dichotomy between them. We even find the phrase "NOMOS of PHYSIS," "law of nature," in the sense of "what nature prescribes," as opposed to the NOMOS which humans establish.[3]

Finally, different writers expressed different evaluations and preferences. Some held it best to follow NOMOS because it permits us to live in civilized society; without NOMOS we would be reduced to a state of nature where life is, in the memorable words of the seventeenth-century philosopher Thomas Hobbes, solitary, poor, nasty, brutish, and short. Others saw NOMOS as a conspiracy of the weaker to defeat the naturally stronger who have a natural right to rule and do what they wish. A superior person should follow the dictates of PHYSIS rather than those of NOMOS. Again, the view was expressed that we should follow NOMOS when others are looking, and PHYSIS when they are not. And some "realists" believed that as PHYSIS is necessary and inevitable, considerations of NOMOS are simply irrelevant. The rest of the chapter will show how the NOMOS-PHYSIS debate was explored and exploited in the fifth and fourth centuries.

Champions of PHYSIS

Antiphon

"Most of the things that are just according to the laws (NOMOI) are at war with nature." This statement, which is emblematic of much of the NOMOS-PHYSIS debate, occurs in the middle of a long fragment of Antiphon, which brings out the contrast between NOMOS and PHYSIS in several ways as he subverts the NOMOI of a state, arguing that it is most advantageous to follow the prescriptions of PHYSIS whenever we can get away with it.

> **19.2** (1) . . . Justice is a matter of not transgressing what the NOMOI prescribe in whatever city you are a citizen of. A person would make most advantage of justice for himself if he treated the NOMOI as important in the

3. Plato, *Gorgias* 483e (not in DK).

presence of witnesses, and treated the decrees of PHYSIS as important when alone and with no witnesses present. For the decrees of NOMOI are extra additions, those of PHYSIS are necessary; those of the NOMOI are the products of agreement, not of natural growth, whereas those of PHYSIS are the products of natural growth, not of agreement. (2) If those who made the agreement do not notice a person transgressing the prescriptions of NOMOI, he is free from both disgrace and penalty, but not so if they do notice him. But if, contrary to possibility, anyone violates any of the things which are innate by PHYSIS, the evil is no less if no one notices him and no greater if all observe. For he does not suffer harm as a result of opinion, but as a result of truth.

This is the entire purpose of considering these matters—that most of the things that are just according to NOMOS are established in a way which is hostile to PHYSIS. For NOMOI have been established for the eyes, as to what they must (3) see and what they must not, and for the ears, as to what they must hear and what they must not, and for the tongue, as to what it must say and what it must not, and for the hands, as to what they must do and what they must not, and for the feet, as to where they must go and where they must not, and for the mind, as to what it must desire and what it must not. Now the things from which the NOMOI deter humans are no more in accord with or suited to PHYSIS than the things which they promote.

Living and dying are matters of PHYSIS, and living results for them from what is advantageous, dying from what is not advantageous. (4) But the advantages which are established by the NOMOI are bonds on PHYSIS, and those established by PHYSIS are free.

And so, things that cause distress, at least when thought of correctly, do not help PHYSIS more than things that give joy. Therefore, it will not be painful things rather than pleasant things which are advantageous. For things that are truly advantageous must not cause harm but benefit. Now the things that are advantageous by PHYSIS are among these. . . .

<But according to NOMOS, those are correct> who defend themselves after suffering (5) and are not first to do wrong, and those who do good to parents who are bad to them, and who permit others to accuse them on oath but do not themselves accuse on oath. You will find most of these cases hostile to PHYSIS. They permit people to suffer more pain when less is possible and to have less pleasure when more is possible, and to receive injury when it is not necessary.

(Antiphon, DK 87A44 A, col. 1 l. 6–col. 5 l. 24)

Though Antiphon stops short of advocating that we all replace NOMOS with PHYSIS as a standard for behavior, he maintains from a variety of viewpoints that NOMOS and what NOMOS prescribes are opposed to PHYSIS and what is advantageous according to it, and he asserts that what is advantageous by PHYSIS is beneficial and hence truly advantageous. The decrees of NOMOS are extra additions, products of agreement, not natural growth; those of PHYSIS are necessary and products of natural growth, not agreement. Anyone who violates NOMOS will be punished only if caught, whereas anyone who violated PHYSIS (which is impossible) would suffer equally whether observed or not. NOMOS is associated with (mere) belief or opinion; PHYSIS with truth or reality. Toward the end of the passage Antiphon contrasts things that are naturally advantageous with those that are advantageous by NOMOS, and suggests that things that give pleasure and joy are naturally advantageous, and those that cause pain and grief are naturally disadvantageous, whereas what is advantageous by NOMOS is at least as likely to cause pain as pleasure.

The passage requires some interpretation. First, a word about the nature of the necessity of PHYSIS. We are told both that it is impossible to violate the decrees of PHYSIS and that if we did we would suffer harm. Then, NOMOS is said to make dictates contrary to PHYSIS. Finally, pleasure and pain seem to be criteria respectively of what is in accordance with, and what is contrary, to PHYSIS. When Antiphon asserts that the dictates of PHYSIS cannot be violated, it may seem that he is thinking of laws of nature like the law of gravity. If this were so, it is hard to see what role NOMOS could play. No society has as its custom or law that people must break the law of gravity!

If we start from the end of the passage, we get further. There are naturally advantageous things, like life, and naturally disadvantageous things, like death. PHYSIS tells us to pursue the former and avoid the latter. If we violate these decrees of PHYSIS the results will be bad for us, since we will have fewer advantageous and more disadvantageous things. Pleasure and pain are natural indicators of the advantageous and disadvantageous. Therefore, PHYSIS calls for a hedonistic approach to life. NOMOS, on the other hand, is frequently contrary to PHYSIS. It decrees that we shall not always (or even usually) pursue our own pleasure and avoid pain. Therefore, if we obey the dictates of NOMOS rather than those of PHYSIS, we are inhibited from pursuing our real advantage and will experience less pleasure and/or more pain than necessary. Violating PHYSIS therefore brings its own penalties, in the form of less pleasure or more pain. NOMOS, however, works differently. Since it is artificial, penalties for transgressing its decrees do not follow inevitably. You must be caught and convicted first. Hence the cynical remark at the beginning of the fragment. Even so, if justice according to NOMOS were rendered effectively, it might still be worth one's while to obey NOMOS. The penalties for transgressing the dictates of NOMOS are typically painful. Therefore, if NOMOS were enforced perfectly, going against it could be made to bring a greater amount of pain (or a lesser amount of pleasure) than would come from following the dictates of PHYSIS. That is, NOMOS could exploit the naturally advantageous and disadvantageous to the point where people would maximize their natural advantage and minimize their natural disadvantage by following NOMOS. Antiphon's reply to this thought is contained in the following passage from the same fragment.

> **19.3** Now if some assistance came from the NOMOI for those who submitted to these conditions and some damage to those who do not submit but resist, (6) obedience to the NOMOI would not be unhelpful. But as things are, it is obvious that the justice that stems from NOMOS is insufficient to rescue those who submit. In the first place, it permits the one who suffers to suffer and the wrongdoer to do wrong, and it was not at the time of the wrongdoing able to prevent either the sufferer from suffering or the wrongdoer from doing wrong. And when the case is brought to trial, there is no special advantage for the one who has suffered over the wrongdoer. For he must persuade the jury that he suffered and that he is able to exact the penalty. And it is open to the wrongdoer to deny it. . . . (7) However convincing the accusation is on behalf of the accuser, the defense can be just as convincing. For victory comes through speech.[4]   (Antiphon, DK 87A44 A, col. 5 l. 25–col. 7 l. 15)
>   (continuation of **19.2**)

NOMOS does not prevent harm from being done, but only comes into play after the fact. Even then it is no guarantee. When a case comes to court, the victim has no particular advantage over the wrongdoer, since what wins the case is not truth but persuasion.[5]

Antiphon is possibly the earliest advocate of hedonism in Greek philosophy.[6] He distinguishes what is advantageous according to PHYSIS from what is so according to NOMOS; says that what is truly (i.e., presumably, according to PHYSIS) advantageous is beneficial, not harmful; and seems to identify things that give joy and are pleasant with what is advantageous according to PHYSIS, and things that cause distress and are painful with what causes harm and is therefore, presumably, disadvantageous according to PHYSIS. Things that result in death are disadvantageous, and things that result in living are advantageous.

This position is not well worked out and Antiphon's remarks raise many questions and seem open to several serious objections. However, his treatment contains features that are important in the history of moral philosophy. The move to ground the concept of advantage in PHYSIS amounts to an

4. The last part of the text is uncertain.

5. At this point we almost expect an advertisement for Antiphon's skills as a speechwriter and Sophist. See pp. 367–69.

6. Unless Democritus' fragments were written earlier. See pp. 338–40.

attempt to provide a naturalistic basis for ethics, and the identification of life and death as standards for judging advantage and disadvantage has the effect of offering objective criteria for ethical judgments.

Callicles

A more satisfactory development of these ideas is found in Socrates' encounter with Callicles in Plato's *Gorgias*. In a memorable speech (482c–484c), of which the following is a summary, Callicles maintains that some are superior by PHYSIS, hence better people, and that they can and should use their superiority for their own selfish advantage.

PHYSIS and NOMOS are in most things opposed to one another. By PHYSIS, everything that is worse is more shameful, but by NOMOS this is not so. By PHYSIS it is both worse and more shameful to suffer injustice than to commit it, and both better and less shameful to commit injustice than to suffer it, whereas by NOMOS it is worse to suffer injustice but more shameful to commit it. Justice and injustice here are understood as characterizing respectively what is prescribed and what is forbidden by NOMOS. What PHYSIS prescribes and forbids is quite different. In fact, NOMOS is a conspiracy of the weak against the strong. The majority of people are weak. They realize that they would be unable to resist the strong if everyone were free to pursue his or her own advantage, since the stronger would get a larger share. Hence the weak majority establish NOMOI that declare it unjust and shameful to have a larger share. They are willing to settle for equal shares for all, for they see that in this way they will have more than they would if the strong were allowed to pursue their own advantage. What NOMOS declares to be just and unjust is to the advantage of the weak and to the disadvantage of the strong, but by PHYSIS it is just for everyone to be able to pursue his or her own advantage, and consequently for the strong to have more than the weak. This is the NOMOS of PHYSIS. A truly strong person will see through the sham of NOMOS, will succeed in pursuing his own natural advantage, and will become master.

Callicles subsequently explains his view more fully (488b–492c). If you are superior by PHYSIS, you are better, wiser, braver, and more powerful. PHYSIS calls for you to be free to pursue and enjoy your natural advantage and gratify your desires without restraint. You will not be restrained by other people or by NOMOS, and or by your desires either. The successful life, the life of ARETE and happiness, is a life spent in the unhindered satisfaction of one's desires.

Callicles' challenge to conventional NOMOS-based morality is powerful and thoroughgoing. It provoked some of Plato's most profound moral thinking (in the *Republic* as well as the *Gorgias*). For our purposes, its importance is its conception of the advantages of PHYSIS and its way of seeing NOMOS as a deliberate subversion of PHYSIS. All people are by nature egoists; all pursue their own advantage—even the weak pursue theirs in establishing NOMOS, since they believe that they will fare better under the restraints imposed by NOMOS than under the freedom permitted by PHYSIS. The primary command of PHYSIS is to pursue your own advantage by satisfying your desires. It is good to satisfy your desires, and a person who is able to satisfy them is better than one who is not. Thus, Callicles' position is not merely a descriptive account of human nature and behavior, but a normative account of the way people ought to behave.

Political power is also relevant, though as the discussion in the *Gorgias* goes, it is left unclear whether it is a means to the satisfaction of one's desires or is itself the object of desire. Nevertheless, the connection between desires and advantage is an important addition to the position of Antiphon, and one that makes hedonism more plausible (though the egoistic view sketched out above does not necessarily point towards hedonism). In fact, Callicles goes on to make this connection (495a), though under pressure from Socrates he withdraws from his doctrine of extreme hedonism (499b).

Thrasymachus

Callicles is mainly concerned with contrasting what is just by PHYSIS with what is just by NOMOS, to the advantage of the former. In the first book of Plato's *Republic*, Thrasymachus offers a position that is superficially similar: justice is the advantage of the stronger (338c). He illustrates this thesis by saying that the ruling (i.e., stronger) power in any city enacts laws to its own advantage (338d–339a). This assertion is apparently intended as a descriptive claim about how things actually are in the world, but when Socrates points out that rulers are fallible and sometimes make mistakes about their own interest, so that following the laws does not promote the ruler's advantage (339b–e), Thrasymachus says that a "true ruler" would never make such a mistake (340d–e). This implies that regardless of what the laws actually command, justice consists in promoting the advantage of the rulers.

In developing this position, Thrasymachus later asserts that justice consists in pursuing other people's good (343c) and injustice in pursuing your own advantage (344c). Injustice is more advantageous than justice (344a). And he caps his position by placing injustice under the heading of virtue and wisdom and regarding it as honorable and strong (348e–349a).

Thrasymachus turns conventional morality on its head. The ultimate standard, as with Callicles, is one's own advantage. Both maintain the normative claim that we should pursue our advantage. But Thrasymachus differs from Callicles on a crucial matter. For Callicles, pursuing your advantage is natural justice, whereas for Thrasymachus, pursuing your advantage is always unjust. So whereas Callicles recommends being just, while at the same time substituting one notion of justice for another, Thrasymachus holds that there is only one notion of justice, but also that justice is to be avoided, not pursued. Another difference between Thrasymachus and Callicles is that Thrasymachus drops Callicles' interpretation of one's advantage as the unrestrained fulfillment of one's desires. Thrasymachus' position is thus more general than Callicles' and it cannot be refuted just by attacking hedonism. It raises sharply the question of why anyone should be just rather than unjust, that is, why we should act to the advantage of others rather than to our own. More generally, it challenges us to consider why we should care about anyone else and whether we have any social responsibilities and obligations. Moreover, since it is put generally in terms of our interests or advantage, it calls for an answer to the question of what our interests and advantage really are—since like Thrasymachus' fallible rulers, we too may make mistakes in thinking that something is to our advantage. In addition, analogous questions arise in the political sphere. What are the responsibilities of rulers to subjects and vice versa, and what are the corresponding rights? Also, what are appropriate standards for the relations among different states? Is it right for the stronger to prevail, as Thrasymachus asserts actually happens (343d–344c)? Or are there other considerations as well, deriving either from the nature of the state or from the rights and advantages of the individuals who compose it? Plato takes up these questions in a serious way in the remainder of the *Republic*, and they have remained central topics ever since in social, moral, and political philosophy.

Antiphon, Callicles, and Thrasymachus mount an impressive attack against justice and against the prescriptions of NOMOS in general. The attack is based on the claim that PHYSIS calls for each of us to pursue our own interests and advantage, and where NOMOS conflicts with PHYSIS (which is usually the case) and so tells us to act against our own interests and to our disadvantage, we should follow PHYSIS rather than NOMOS—whenever we can get away without being observed (Antiphon), or if we are sufficiently clever to see through the sham of NOMOS and sufficiently strong to have our own way (Callicles), or if we are sensible and pursue ARETE and happiness (Thrasymachus).

Thucydides

This way of looking at things was not confined to philosophical discussion, but played an important part in the practical politics of the late fifth century, where it was used to justify imperialism and brutality. In two notable passages of his *History of the Peloponnesian War,* Thucydides presents debates in which considerations of strength and advantage are used to the exclusion of justice, mercy, and forgiveness. The first takes place in the Athenian Assembly. In 428, Mitylene, a city-state subject to Athens, had revolted along with most of the island of Lesbos. The Athenian army had put down the revolt, and the Assembly had passed a decree that the adult males of the defeated city should be put to death and the women and children enslaved. The next day there was a change of heart, so the Assembly was summoned to discuss the matter again. In the debate, which concluded with a decision to rescind the brutal decree of the previous day, Cleon spoke in favor of carrying out the decree.

> **19.4** You do not see that your empire is a tyranny, and that you have unwilling subjects who are continually plotting against you. They obey you not because of any good turns you might do them to your own detriment, and not because of any good will they might have, but only because you exceed them in strength. . . . In sum I say only this: if you follow my advice, you will do justice to the Mytileneans and promote your own interests at the same time. But if you see the matter differently, you will not win their favor; instead, you will be condemning yourselves: if they were right to rebel, you ought not to have been their rulers. But then suppose your empire is not justified: if you resolve to hold it anyway, then you must give these people an unreasonable punishment for the benefit of the empire, or else stop having an empire so that you can give charity without taking any risks.
>
> (Thucydides 3.37.2, 40.4, not in DK, tr. Woodruff)

In his reply, Diodotus, who spoke for the opposite side, showed no more concern for mercy and justice than Cleon, thus indicating that political advantage was indeed foremost in the Athenians' minds.

> **19.5** Our dispute, if we are sensible, will concern not their injustice to us, but our judgment as to what is best for us. Even if I proved them guilty of terrible injustice, I still would not advise the death penalty for this, unless that was to our advantage. Even if they deserved to be pardoned, I would not have you pardon them if it did not turn out to be good for the city. In my opinion, what we are discussing concerns the future more than the present. And as for this point that Cleon insists on—that the death penalty will be to our advantage in the future, by keeping the others from rebelling—I maintain exactly the opposite view. . . . But we are not at law with them, and so have no need to speak of justice. We are in council instead, and must decide how the Mytileneans can be put to the best use for us.
>
> (Thucydides 3.44.1–4, not in DK, tr. Woodruff)

The second episode occurred in 416 when the Athenians attacked the island of Melos, which although originally a Spartan colony was neutral in the war. The Athenians intended to bring it into their empire. Thucydides presents a discussion between envoys of the Athenians and the Melian leaders about the Athenian ultimatum: become a subject state or suffer destruction. The Athenians begin by saying that the basic fact of the situation is the relative strength of the two sides.

> **19.6** ATHENIANS: For our part, we will not make a long speech no one would believe, full of fine moral arguments—that our empire is justified because we defeated the Persians, or that we are coming against you for an injustice you have done to us. And we don't want you to think you can persuade us by saying that you did not fight on the side of the Lacedaemonians in the war, though you were their colony, or that you have done us no injustice. Instead, let's work out what we can do on the basis of what both sides truly accept: we both know that decisions about justice are made in human discussions only when both sides are under equal compulsion; but when one side is stronger, it gets as much as it can, and the weak must accept that. (Thucydides 5.89, not in DK, tr. Woodruff)

The Melians reply that justice is to everyone's advantage since even Athens may someday be at the mercy of others.

> **19.7** MELIANS: Well, then, since you put your interest in the place of justice, our view must be that it is in your interest not to subvert this rule that is good for all: that a plea of justice and fairness should do some good for a man who has fallen into danger, if he can win over his judges, even if he is not perfectly persuasive. And this rule concerns you no less than us: if you ever stumble, you might receive a terrible punishment and be an example to others. (Thucydides 5.90, not in DK, tr. Woodruff)

The subsequent dialogue demonstrates how remote considerations of justice had become.

> **19.8** MELIANS: So you would not accept a peaceful solution? We could be friends rather than enemies, and fight with neither side.
> ATHENIANS: No. Your enmity does not hurt us as much as your friendship would. That would be a sign of our weakness to those who are ruled by us; but your hatred would prove our power.
> MELIANS: Why? Do your subjects reason so unfairly that they put us, who never had anything to do with you, in the same category as themselves, when most of them were your colonies, or else rebels whom you defeated?

ATHENIANS: Why not? They think we have as good a justification for controlling you as we do for them; they say the independent cities survive because they are powerful, and that we do not attack them because we are afraid.   (Thucydides 5.94–97, not in DK, tr. Woodruff)

Nevertheless, the Athenians dismiss this consideration as irrelevant to the present. The Melians decide to resist the Athenians and place their hopes in the gods and the Spartans. To the first of these hopes the Athenians respond that it is a requirement and law (NOMOS) of PHYSIS, applying to gods as well as humans, that the strong shall rule.

19.9 ATHENIANS: The favor of the gods should be as much on our side as yours. Neither our principles nor our actions are contrary to what men believe about the gods, or would want for themselves. Nature always compels gods (we believe) and men (we are certain) to rule over anyone they can control. We did not make this law, and we were not the first to follow it; but we will take it as we found it and leave it to posterity forever, because we know that you would do the same if you had our power, and so would anyone else. So as far as the favor of the gods is concerned, we have no reason to fear that we will do worse than you.
                    (Thucydides 5.105.1–3, not in DK, tr. Woodruff)

As to the Spartans, the Athenians claim that not much help can be expected from them, since they more than most people act to their own advantage.

19.10 Of all the people we know, they are the ones who make it most obvious that they hold whatever pleases them to be honorable, and whatever profits them to be just.   (Thucydides 5.105.4, not in DK, tr. Woodruff)

And to the Melian assertion that it is to the Spartans' advantage to assist Melos, the Athenians—correctly, as events prove—reply that the Spartans will not think it to their advantage to undergo such a risk. The Athenians conclude by saying that fear of disgrace (a typical moral consideration) is a foolish motive for action; the best results come from assessing the strength of the parties involved and acting accordingly.

19.11 Do not be distracted by a sense of honor; this destroys people all too often, when dishonor and death stand before their eyes. Many have been so overcome by the power of this seductive word, "honor," that even when they foresee the dangers to which it carries them, they are drawn by a mere word into an action that is an irreparable disaster; and so, intentionally, they fall into a dishonor that is more shameful than mere misfortune, since it is due to their own foolishness. You must guard against this if you are to deliberate wisely, and you must not think it unseemly for you to submit to a city of such great power, which offers such reasonable conditions. . . . Remember what is usually the best course: do not give way to equals, but have the right attitude towards your superiors and use moderation towards your inferiors.

(Thucydides 5.111.3–5, not in DK, tr. Woodruff)

The political realism espoused by the Athenian envoys was put to the test when the Melians decided to fight for their liberty rather than submit to the Athenian demands, and after an easy victory, the Athenian army inflicted the terrible punishment they had threatened.

Conclusion

The champions of PHYSIS are agreed on the universality of nature or of human nature, and find in PHYSIS a standard for determining the advantage of an individual or a community. The writers so far considered, with the possible exception of Antiphon, claim a prescriptive force for the decrees of PHYSIS: we, or our community, should pursue its own natural advantage. Moreover, all humans and communities tend to be in competition with one another, so that my pursuing my advantage tends to conflict with you pursuing yours, and it is to my advantage for you not to attain yours.

If the competitive aspect of this view is set aside, the egoism which remains is in fact common ground in Greek moral thought. Even Socrates, Plato, and Aristotle held that a person's chief goal is his or her own happiness. And these three philosophers also agreed with the proponents of PHYSIS that not the unstable prescriptions of variable NOMOS but facts about human PHYSIS are the correct basis for determining what we should do and how we should live.

Defenses of NOMOS

Nevertheless, a case could be made for NOMOS as well. The following passages show some of the arguments that were used.

Critias

Critias champions NOMOS outright: without NOMOS, life would be insupportable and civilized society nonexistent; NOMOS raises human life above the beasts.

19.12 There was a time when human life was without order,
on the level of beasts, and subject to force;

> when there was no reward for the good
> or punishment for the bad.
> And then, I think, humans established
> NOMOI as punishers, so that justice would be the mighty ruler
>   (TURANNOS)
> of all equally and would have violence (HUBRIS) as its slave,
> and anyone who did wrong would be punished.
>
> (Critias, DK 88B25, lines 1–8)

Protagoras

The idea that humanity advanced from a primitive state to civilization was common in the fifth and fourth centuries, and found expression in many writers,[7] among them Plato, who puts into the mouth of Protagoras a "myth" of human progress,[8] which most scholars take to have a basis in Protagoras' own thought, and which makes NOMOS an important part of civilization while possibly also linking NOMOS with PHYSIS.

In the beginning, says Protagoras, humans received as gifts from Prometheus technical ingenuity and fire, through which they provided themselves with shelter, clothing, and food, and developed speech. They lived a scattered life, without cities, because they did not have the "political art," the skills needed for civilized life. As a result, many were killed by wild beasts and there was danger that the human race would be annihilated since they could not cooperate even for defense. To prevent their destruction, Zeus gave humans two further gifts: AIDOS (a sense of shame and respect for others) and DIKE (a sense of right and justice), which enabled them to have political order and to form bonds of friendship and union. Everyone is expected to have some share of AIDOS and DIKE. Without them a person cannot lead a civilized human life.

Moreover, Protagoras continues after concluding the myth,[9] it is to everyone's interest that all citizens develop their moral character, and so there is a continuous process of moral and social education which takes place from infancy to adulthood, with family, friends, teachers, and the institutions of the city itself all taking part. Each city establishes NOMOI to guide the lives of its citizens in paths of ARETE and through education and threat of punishment moulds and compels the citizens to rule and be ruled in accordance with them.

For Protagoras, the moral qualities AIDOS and DIKE make civilized life

7. See Guthrie, *HGP*, vol. 3, pp. 60–63, 79–84, for source material.

8. Plato, *Protagoras* 320c–323a (= DK 80C1).

9. Plato, *Protagoras* 324d–326e (not in DK).

possible for humans, and NOMOI establish patterns of civilized life, there being many possible patterns, and many different sets of NOMOI. In interpreting Protagoras' myth, most commentators distinguish between technical ingenuity on the one side and AIDOS and DIKE on the other, saying that the first is innate and part of human nature, i.e., we have it by virtue of our PHYSIS, whereas AIDOS and DIKE are not innate, but supplement PHYSIS. It is also possible that Protagoras intends AIDOS and DIKE as part of human nature and uses the device of the myth to show that if human nature lacked these moral qualities, life as we know it would not be possible. If this latter interpretation is accepted, the NOMOI of a community have some basis in human nature, i.e., in (distinctively human) PHYSIS.

The *Anonymus Iamblichi*

An even clearer defense of NOMOS by showing its basis in PHYSIS occurs in a work by an unknown author, extracts of which are preserved in the *Protrepticus* of the fourth-century A.D. author Iamblichus. This work is known as the *Anonymus Iamblichi* and is thought to date from c. 400 B.C.

> **19.13** (6.1) No one should set out to maximize his own advantage or suppose that power used for one's advantage is ARETE and obedience to NOMOI is cowardice. This is the most wicked thought and it results in everything diametrically opposed to what is good: evil and harm. For if humans were by PHYSIS unable to live singly but yielding to necessity came together to live with one another, and discovered all their life and their contrivances for living, but it is impossible for them to live with one another and to conduct their lives in the absence of NOMOI (since that way they would suffer more damage than they would by living alone)— on account of these necessities NOMOS and justice are kings among humans and in no way can they depart. For they are firmly bound into our PHYSIS. (*Anonymus Iamblichi*, fr. 6 = DK 89,6 vol. 2 402.21–30)

In his attack on NOMOS as a conspiracy of the weak to hold down the strong (pp. 397–98), Callicles implies that NOMOS does have important benefits for the weak, who constitute the vast majority of people. This line of thought is carried farther by the *Anonymus Iamblichi*, which denies that a Calliclean strong individual could ever gain dominance.

> **19.14** (6.2) If, then, someone were born who had from the beginning the following sort of PHYSIS: invulnerable in his flesh, not subject to disease, without feelings, superhuman, and hard as steel in body and soul—perhaps one might have thought that power used for personal advantage would be sufficient for such a person, since such a person

could be scot-free even if he did not subject himself to the law
(NOMOS). But this person does not think correctly. (6.3) Even if there
were such a person, though there could not be, he would survive by
being an ally of the laws (NOMOI) and of justice, strengthening them
and using his might for them and for what assists them, but otherwise
he could not last. (6.4) For it would seem that all people would become
enemies of a person with such a nature (PHUNTI, related to PHYSIS), and
through their own observance of NOMOS and their numbers they would
overcome him by craft or force and would prevail. (6.5) So it is obvious
that power itself—real power—is preserved through NOMOS and justice.
             (*Anonymus Iamblichi*, fr. 6 = DK 89,6, vol. 2 402.30–403.10)
                                                    (continuation of **19.13**)

A number of authors praise the benefits which NOMOS brings. Here too,
the *Anonymus Iamblichi* states the case powerfully, contrasting EUNOMIA
(a condition where the NOMOI are good and people abide by them) and
ANOMIA (the opposite of EUNOMIA), which he seems to conceive as a condition in which each person pursues his or her own advantage in competition
with others.

19.15 It is worthwhile to learn these facts about EUNOMIA and ANOMIA—how
       big the difference is between them, and that EUNOMIA is the best thing
       both for the community and for the individual, and ANOMIA is the worst,
       for the greatest harm arises immediately from ANOMIA. Let us begin by
       indicating first what results from EUNOMIA.
           (7.1) In the first place, trust arises from EUNOMIA, and this benefits
       all people greatly and is one of the great goods. For as a result of it,
       money becomes available and so, even if there is little it is sufficient
       since it is in circulation, but without it not even a great deal of money
       would be enough. (7.2) Fortunes and misfortunes in money and life are
       managed most suitably for people as a result of EUNOMIA. For those
       enjoying good fortune can use it in safety and without danger of plots,
       while those suffering ill fortune are aided by the fortunate through
       their mutual dealings and trust, which result from EUNOMIA. (7.3)
       Through EUNOMIA, moreover, the time people devote to PRAGMATA [a
       word which can mean "government," "public business," or "troubles"]
       is idle, but that devoted to the activities of life is productive. (7.4) In
       EUNOMIA people are free from the most unpleasant concern and engage
       in the most pleasant, since concern about PRAGMATA is most unpleasant
       and concern about one's activities is most pleasant. (7.5) Also, when
       they go to sleep, which is a rest from troubles for people, they go to it
       without fear and unworried about painful matters, and when they rise
       from it they have other similar experiences and do not suddenly become
       fearful. Nor after this very pleasant change [i.e., sleep] do they expect

the day to bring poverty, but they look forward to it without fear directing their concern without grief towards the activities of life, lightening their labors with trust and confident hopes that they will get good things as a result. For all these things EUNOMIA is responsible. (7.6) And war, which is the source of the greatest evils for people, leading as it does to destruction and slavery—this too comes more to those who practice ANOMIA, less to those practicing EUNOMIA. (7.7) There are many other goods found in EUNOMIA which assist life, and also from it comes consolation for our difficulties.

These are the evils that come from ANOMIA. (7.8) In the first place, people do not have time for their activities and are engaged in the most unpleasant thing, PRAGMATA, not activities, and because of mistrust and lack of mutual dealings they hoard money and do not make it available, so it becomes rare even if there is much. (7.9) Ill fortune and good fortune minister to the opposite results [from what occurs under EUNOMIA]: good fortune is not safe in ANOMIA, but is plotted against, and bad fortune is not driven off but is strengthened through mistrust and the absence of mutual dealings. (7.10) War from outside is more frequently brought against a land, and domestic faction comes from the same cause, and if it did not occur earlier it happens then. Also it happens that people are always involved in PRAGMATA because of plots which come from one another, which force them to live constantly on guard and to make counterplots against each other. (7.11) When they are awake their thoughts are not pleasant, and when they go to sleep their receptacle [i.e., sleep] is not pleasant but full of fear, and their awakening is fearful and frightening and leads a person to sudden memories of his troubles. These and all the previously mentioned evils result from ANOMIA.

(7.12) Also tyranny, so great and so foul an evil, arises from nothing else but ANOMIA. Some people suppose—all who do not understand correctly—that a tyrant comes from some other source and that people are deprived of their freedom without being themselves responsible, but compelled by the tyrant when he has been established. But they do not consider this correctly. (7.13) For whoever thinks that a king or a tyrant arises from anything else than ANOMIA and personal advantage is an idiot. For when everyone turns to evil, this is what happens then. For it is impossible for humans to live without NOMOI and justice. (7.14) So when these two things—NOMOS and justice—are missing from the mass of the people, that is exactly when the guardianship and protection of them passes to a single person. How else could solitary rule be transferred to a single person unless the NOMOS had been driven out which benefited the mass of the people? (7.15) For this man who is going to destroy justice and abolish NOMOS that is common and advantageous to all, must be made of steel if he intends to strip these things from the mass of the people, he being one and they many. (7.16) But if he is made of flesh and is like the rest, he will not be able to accomplish this, but on the contrary if he reestablishes what is missing, he might be solitary ruler. This is why some people fail to notice this occurring when it does.

(*Anonymus Iamblichi*, fr. 7 = DK 89.7, vol. 2 403.11–404.32)
(continuation of **19.14**)

Other Defenses of NOMOS

Some turned the tables on PHYSIS. Instead of viewing NOMOS as variable and PHYSIS as fixed, they declared that PHYSIS (here in the sense of one's natural abilities) varies with the individual, whereas NOMOS (here, typically, the positive law in force in a given community at a given time) holds uniformly for all.

19.16 (15) All the life of the people in cities both great and small is run by PHYSIS and by NOMOI. Of these, PHYSIS is without order and private to each individual, but the NOMOI are common, in order, and the same for all. Now PHYSIS, if it is wicked, often has low desires. This is why you will find people of that sort doing wrong. (16) The NOMOI, on the other hand, desire what is just and good and advantageous, and they aim for this and when it is found, this is published as a common command, equal and similar for all, and this is NOMOS. There are many reasons why all ought to obey it, especially because every law is a discovery and gift of the gods, a decision of sensible people, a correction of voluntary and involuntary wrongdoing, a common commitment of the city according to which all in the city ought to live. . . . (20) I will say nothing new or clever or odd, but what you all know as well as I do. If any of you wants to investigate what is the reason and what causes the Council to meet, the people to gather in the Assembly, the courts to be filled, the previous magistrates to yield their place willingly to the new ones, and all the things to take place through which the city is run and preserved, you will find the NOMOI and the fact that everyone obeys them, since if they were abolished and everyone were given the opportunity to do whatever he wished, not only is it goodbye to the constitution, but also our life would be no different from that of wild beasts.

(pseudo-Demosthenes 25.15–16, 20, not in DK)

19.17 Nothing is more hateful to a city than a tyrant, because then in the first place there are no common NOMOI, but a single person holds power after taking the NOMOS into his own possession. And this situation is no longer equal for all. But when NOMOI are written, both the weak and the wealthy have equal justice, and when slandered the fortunate is able to

make the same case as the weaker, and the lesser person defeats the
great man if he has justice on his side. That is freedom.

(Euripides, *Supplices* 429–438, not in DK)

Unwritten NOMOI

Even if customs and enacted laws were known to vary from place to place
and from time to time in a given place, the Greeks of the Classical Age did
not lose consciousness of the earlier tradition that laws are god-given. Early
lawgivers such as Lycurgus of Sparta and Solon of Athens received greater
reverence than was usually accorded to humans. Moreover, some NOMOI
were felt to be universal, either in the sense that all peoples at all times
actually recognize them or that they should recognize them even if they do
not. These NOMOI, sometimes called unwritten laws, were thought to have a
divine origin and to take precedence over (possibly faulty) human laws. The
most famous assertion of the existence and priority of these laws is made by
Antigone in Sophocles' play of that name (written in 441), when she defends her action of burying her brother in defiance of King Creon's decree.

19.18 For me it was not Zeus who made this proclamation, nor was it Justice
who dwells with the gods below who established these NOMOI among
humans. And I did not suppose that your proclamations had power
enough that you, a mortal, could prevail over the gods' unwritten and
secure practices (NOMIMA, derived from NOMOS). For they live not just
now and yesterday, but always forever. No one knows when they appeared. I did not out of fear of the will of any man intend to pay a
penalty before the gods for transgressing them.

(Sophocles, *Antigone* 450–460, not in DK)

The concept of unwritten laws is developed and defended in a dialogue
between Socrates and Hippias, as reported by Xenophon.

19.19 SOCRATES: Do you know of any unwritten laws, Hippias?
HIPPIAS: Yes, the ones uniformly observed in every country.
SOC.: Could you say that humans made them?
HIP.: How could they, since they could not all have come together and
they do not speak the same language?
SOC.: Then who do you suppose are the ones who made these laws?
HIP.: I think that the gods made these laws for men. For among all men
the first law is to revere the gods.
SOC. Is it not also the law everywhere to honor parents?
HIP.: Yes, that is too.

SOC.: And also that parents shall not have sexual intercourse with their children nor children with their parents?

HIP.: This does not seem to me to be a law of God.

SOC.: Why so?

HIP.: Because I notice that some transgress it.

SOC.: Yes, and they do many other things against the laws. But surely those who transgress the laws established by the gods pay a penalty which in no way can a person escape, as some, when they transgress the laws established by humans, escape punishment, either through not being noticed or by violence.

HIP.: And what penalty, Socrates, are parents and children who have intercourse with one another unable to avoid?

SOC.: The greatest, by Zeus! For what greater penalty could people incur in producing children than producing them badly?

HIP.: How, then, do these people produce children badly, since the fathers and mothers may both be good people?

SOC.: Because, by Zeus, the parents must not only be good; they must also be at their physical peak. Or do you think that those who are at their peak have seed similar to that of people who have not yet reached that condition or have passed it?

HIP.: By Zeus, it is unlikely that it is similar.

SOC.: Which is better then?

HIP.: Clearly, the seed of people at their peak.

SOC.: Therefore, the seed of those not at their peak are not sound?

HIP.: It is unlikely, by Zeus.

SOC.: In these conditions, then, they should not produce children?

HIP.: Certainly not.

SOC.: Therefore those who produce children in such circumstances produce them as they should not.

HIP.: I think so.

SOC.: What other people, then, will produce children badly if not they?

HIP.: I share your opinion on this,too.

SOC.: Again, is it not everywhere customary to repay good deeds with good deeds?

HIP.: It is customary, but this custom too is transgressed.

SOC.: Don't those who transgress it pay a penalty in being bereft of good friends and being compelled to pursue people who hate them? Or is it not true that, whereas those who benefit the people they have dealings with are good friends, those who do not do such people good deeds in return are hated for their unkindness, while they pursue such people most of all because of the great benefits of having dealings with them?

HIP.: By Zeus, Socrates, all this smacks of the gods. For I accept that laws which themselves contain punishment for those who break them, a better law-giver than man.

(Xenophon, *Memorabilia* 4.4.19–25, not in DK)

Xenophon's idea of unwritten laws is not altogether clear. First, they are said to be observed in every country. Next, when it is admitted that they are not actually observed everywhere, they are said to be universally valid, i.e., they ought to be observed everywhere even if they are not. With this change, we can no longer determine what laws are unwritten laws simply by finding customs that are followed by all people without exception. Socrates suggests a different criterion (reminiscent of Antiphon's assertion about the inevitability of paying a penalty for violating the dictates of nature, cf. **19.2**), that although punishment for breaking man-made NOMOI can sometimes be avoided, transgressions of unwritten laws are always punished. His discussion of incest and ingratitude points toward the idea that violating unwritten laws brings retribution inevitably, as a natural and automatic consequence. But it is hard to see how this analysis could be extended to cover some of Xenophon's other examples (such as honoring one's parents), let alone the Sophoclean case of burying a dead brother.

Aristotle recognizes two sorts of unwritten laws: the universal NOMOI so far discussed, as opposed to the NOMOI of particular states, and also the beliefs of a particular state, based on its customs and traditions, which supplement its written laws.

> **19.20** NOMOS is (A) particular and (B) common. I call (A) particular the written NOMOS in accordance with which a city is administered, and (B) common all the unwritten principles which appear to be agreed upon among all peoples.   (Aristotle, *Rhetoric* 1.10 1368b7–9, not in DK)

> **19.21** I call NOMOS (A) particular, (B) common. (A) Particular NOMOS is that which each people establishes as applying to themselves, and this is (a) unwritten and (b) written, whereas (B) common NOMOS is that in accordance with PHYSIS.   (Aristotle, *Rhetoric* 1.13 1373b4–6, not in DK)

In the latter case Aristotle is working with two different aspects of NOMOS: NOMOS as law (written legislation) and NOMOS as custom. Moreover, in the latter passage he equates universal laws with natural laws and in what follows cites Antigone's case as an example of a natural law. Now Sophocles did not make Antigone describe the unwritten laws as "natural," but in the context of the NOMOS-PHYSIS debate, the association of the universal with the natural was easy and automatic.

So far, the unwritten law is superior to and nobler than written law. It is frequently called divine and is sometimes said to have been authored by the gods as opposed to mutable, fallible, and perhaps self-interested human law. However, the window it opens for arguing in court against the legal prescriptions of the state did not go unnoticed by Sophists and other rhetoricians. By Aristotle's time it was possible to see the contrast as the source of simply one more debating move.

> 19.22 The broadest rhetorical commonplace for forcing people to utter paradoxes is that derived from what is according to PHYSIS and according to NOMOS, as Callicles is described as saying in the *Gorgias* and all the men of old believed that it happened. For they held that PHYSIS and NOMOS are opposites, and justice is fine and noble according to NOMOS but not fine and noble according to PHYSIS. Therefore a person speaking according to PHYSIS should be answered according to NOMOS, and a person speaking according to NOMOS should be brought to (considerations of) PHYSIS. Both ways it results that they utter paradoxes. They considered what is according to PHYSIS to be true and what is according to NOMOS to be what the many believe.
> (Aristotle, *Sophistical Refutations* 12 173a7–16, not in DK)

Moreover, people could invoke "unwritten laws" whenever it suited their advantage. By the end of the fifth century, appeal to the concept of unwritten law, which began as a way of invoking a higher authority when human laws were evil, had fallen to a tool that might be used to defend any illegal action. That it was actually employed in that way is suggested by an Athenian decree passed at the end of the fifth century:

> 19.23 The magistrates must not make use of unwritten law, even in a single case . . . No law can be established for an individual person unless the same law applies to all Athenians.
> (quoted in Andocides, *On the Mysteries* 87, not in DK)

Moreover, at this time the Athenians were engaged in revising their laws and inscribing them on stone tablets and setting them up in public so that anyone could consult them who wished.[10]

It hardly needs saying that the unwritten "law of nature," that the strong should rule the weak, put forward by Callicles and expressed elsewhere too, was an ideology that would support tyranny and subvert organized life as known to the Greeks.

Conclusion

The NOMOS-PHYSIS debate had no winners or losers. The notions of NOMOS and PHYSIS were sufficiently broad and loose to leave room for many positions to be staked out, most of them with something to recommend

10. The decree is quoted in Andocides, *On the Mysteries* 83–84. See references and discussion in Andocides, *On the Mysteries*, ed. D. MacDowell (Oxford, 1962), pp. 194–99.

them. In this fertile field of discussion the seeds of many philosophical problems, views and approaches were sown. But the NOMOS-PHYSIS debate was the common property of classical Greece, not the private field of the philosophers. As we have seen, the contributors to the debate included playwrights, historians, and orators, and the ideas involved played an important role in practical politics and in the courts.

The debate also has a considerable philosophical legacy. The wide range of answers given to the questions it raised and the variety of approaches taken invite reflection on how to proceed with complex and interwoven issues like these. Socrates made crucial contributions in recognizing the importance of accurate and agreed upon definitions of key terms and discovering that such definitions are difficult to find and require a great deal of work in their own right.

The debate also had an important effect on Plato. Plato is our most important single source for the debate, not because he had an antiquarian interest in it, but because he believed the issues needed further treatment. He disagreed with many of the views that had been expressed, but was in agreement with others. It is probably not too great an exaggeration to say that one of the most important bases for his ethical work in dialogues up to and including the *Republic* was his (and Socrates') reflections on issues raised by or implicit in the NOMOS-PHYSIS debate.

The legacy extends much further. Many of the issues raised for the first time in the context of the debate have remained important both for philosophers and for reflective people in general. Why should I be just? Is morality artificial or natural? What is human nature? What is the origin of society? What are the bonds of society? What is the relation between obeying the law and being good? What is the nature of our obligation to obey the law, and what limits does it have? Many current theories on these topics have their earliest ancestors in the fifth- and fourth-century context of the NOMOS-PHYSIS debate.

Books for Further Reading

General Works on Presocratic Philosophy

Barnes, J., *The Presocratic Philosophers*, revised ed., London, 1982.
Barnes, J., *Early Greek Philosophy*, Harmondsworth, 1987.
Burnet, J., *Early Greek Philosophy*, 4th ed., London, 1930.
Burnet, J., *Greek Philosophy: Thales to Plato*, London, 1932.
Cleve, F. M., *The Giants of Pre-Sophistic Greek Philosophy*, The Hague, 1965.
Cornford, F. M., *Before and After Socrates*, Cambridge, 1932.
Fränkel, H., *Early Greek Poetry and Philosophy*, trans. by M. Hadas and J. Willis, Oxford, 1973 and New York, 1975.
Freeman, K., *Ancilla to the Pre-Socratic Philosophers. A Complete Translation of the Fragments in Diels'* Fragmente der Vorsokratiker, Oxford, 1948.
Freeman, K., *Companion to the Pre-Socratic Philosophers*, Oxford, 1946.
Gomperz, T., *Greek Thinkers*, 4 vols., London, 1901–1912.
Guthrie, W. K. C., *A History of Greek Philosophy*, vols. 1–3, Cambridge, 1962, 1965, 1969.
Hussey, E., *The Presocratics*, London, 1972.
Jaeger, W. W., *Paideia: The Ideals of Greek Culture*, 3 vols., 2nd ed., Oxford, 1939–1945.
Kirk, G. S., and Raven, J. E., *The Presocratic Philosophers*, Cambridge, 1957.
Kirk, G. S., Raven, J. E., and Schofield, M., *The Presocratic Philosophers*, 2nd ed., Cambridge, 1982.

Collections of Essays

Anton, J. P., and Kustas, G. L., eds., *Essays in Ancient Greek Philosophy*, Albany, N.Y., 1971.
Anton, J. P., and Preus, A., eds., *Essays in Ancient Greek Philosophy, Volume Two*, Albany, N.Y., 1983.
Boudouris, K. J., ed., *Ionian Philosophy*, Studies in Greek Philosophy 1, Athens, 1989. Papers presented at a conference in 1988.
Furley, D. J., *Cosmic Problems. Essays on Greek and Roman Philosophy of Nature*, Cambridge, 1989. A collection of papers previously published by Furley.
Furley, D. J., and Allen, R. E., eds., *Studies in Presocratic Philosophy*, 2 vols., London, 1970, 1975.
Lloyd, G. E. R., *Methods and Problems of Greek Science*, Cambridge, 1991. A collection of papers previously published by Lloyd.
Mourelatos, A. P. D., ed., *The Presocratics*, Princeton, 1993. Reprint of 1974 ed. with updated bibliography.

Robb, K., ed., *Language and Thought in Early Greek Philosophy*, La Salle, Ill., 1983.

Shiner, R. A., and King-Farlow, J., eds., *New Essays on Plato and the Pre-socratics, Canadian Journal of Philosophy*, Suppl. 2, Guelph, 1976.

Studies of Particular Figures

Hesiod

West, M. L., *Hesiod, Theogony*, Oxford, 1966.

Anaximander

Kahn, C. H., *Anaximander and the Origins of Greek Cosmology*, New York, 1960.

Xenophanes

Lesher, J. H., "Xenophanes of Colophon: Fragments, A Text and Translation with a Commentary," *Phoenix* Suppl. Vol. 30 (Toronto, 1992).

Pythagoras and the Pythagoreans

Boudouris, K. J., ed., *Pythagorean Philosophy*, Studies in Greek Philosophy 1, Athens, 1992. Papers presented at a conference in 1991.

Burkert, W., *Lore and Science in Ancient Pythagoreanism*, trans. by E. L. Minar, Jr., Cambridge, Mass., 1972.

Huffman, C. A., *Philolaus of Croton, Pythagorean and Presocratic*, Cambridge, 1993.

O'Meara, D. J., *Pythagoras Revived. Mathematics and Philosophy in Late Antiquity*, Oxford, 1989.

Philip, J. A., *Pythagoras and Early Pythagoreanism*, Toronto, 1966.

Raven, J. E., *Pythagoreans and Eleatics*, Cambridge, 1948.

de Vogel, C. J., *Pythagoras and Early Pythagoreanism*, Assen, 1966.

Heraclitus

Hospers J., and Robb, K., eds., *The Monist* 74 (1991) no.4. Special issue on Heraclitus.

Kahn, C. H., *The Art and Thought of Heraclitus*, Cambridge, 1979.

Kirk, G. S., *Heraclitus: The Cosmic Fragments*, 2nd ed., Cambridge, 1962.

Marcovich, M., *Heraclitus*, Merida, 1967.

Robinson, T. M., "Heraclitus: Fragments, A Text and Translation with a Commentary," *Phoenix* Suppl. Vol. 22 (Toronto, 1987).

The Eleatics

Loenen, J. H. M. M., *Parmenides, Melissus, Gorgias: A Reinterpretation of Eleatic Philosophy*, Assen, 1959.
Raven, J. E., *Pythagoreans and Eleatics*, Cambridge, 1948.

Parmenides

Austin, S., *Parmenides: Being, Bounds and Logic*, New Haven, Conn., 1986.
Cornford, F. M., *Plato and Parmenides*, London, 1939.
Coxon, A. H., "The Fragments of Parmenides," *Phronesis* Suppl. Vol. 3 (Assen and Maastricht, 1986).
Gallop, D., "Parmenides of Elea. Fragments. A Text, with an Introduction," *Phoenix* Suppl. Vol. 18 (Toronto, 1984).
Mourelatos, A. P. D., *The Route of Parmenides: A Study in Word, Image and Argument in the Fragments*, New Haven, Conn., 1970.
Owens, J. ed., "Parmenides Studies Today," *The Monist* 69 (1979) no.1. Special issue.
Tarán, L., *Parmenides: A Text with Translation, Commentary and Critical Essays*, Princeton, 1965.

Zeno

Grünbaum, A., *Modern Science and Zeno's Paradoxes*, London, 1968.
Lee, H. D. P., *Zeno of Elea*, Cambridge, 1936.
Salmon, W. C., ed., *Zeno's Paradoxes*, Indianapolis, 1970.

Anaxagoras

Schofield, M., *An Essay on Anaxagoras*, Cambridge, 1980.
Sider, D., *The Fragments of Anaxagoras*, Beiträge zur klassischen Philologie 118, Meisenheim am Glan, 1981.

Empedocles

Inwood, B., "The Poem of Empedocles: A Text and Translation with an Introduction," *Phoenix* Suppl. Vol. 29 (Toronto, 1992).
O'Brien, D., *Empedocles' Cosmic Cycle*, Cambridge, 1969.
Wright, M. R., *Empedocles, The Extant Fragments*, New Haven, Conn., 1981.

The Atomists

Bailey, C., *The Greek Atomists and Epicurus*, Oxford, 1928.

Benakis, L., ed., *Proceedings of the First International Congress on Democritus*, 2 vols., Xanthi, Greece, 1984. Papers presented at a conference in 1983.

Cole, T., *Democritus and the Sources of Greek Anthropology*, Cleveland, 1967.

Furley, D. J., *Two Studies in the Greek Atomists*, Princeton, 1967.

O'Brien, D., "Theories of Weight in the Ancient World: Four Essays on Democritus, Plato and Aristotle. A Study in the Development of Ideas." Vol. 1, Democritus, Weight and Size. An Exercise in the Reconstruction of Early Greek Philosophy. *Philosophia Antiqua* 37 (Leiden, 1981).

The Sophistic Movement

Grote, G., *A History of Greece*, London, 1888.

He Archaia Sophistike (The Sophistic Movement), Athens, 1984. Papers presented at a conference in 1982.

Kerferd, G. B., *The Sophistic Movement*, Cambridge, 1981.

Kerferd, G. B., ed., *The Sophists and their Legacy*, Wiesbaden, 1981.

Robinson, T. M., *Contrasting Arguments, an Edition of the* Dissoi Logoi, New York, 1979.

de Romilly, J., *The Great Sophists in Periclean Athens*, Oxford, 1992.

Sprague, R. K., *The Older Sophists*, Columbia, S. C., 1972.

Studies of Particular Sophists

Protagoras

Cornford, F. M., *Plato's Theory of Knowledge: The Theaetetus and Sophist of Plato translated with a running commentary*, London, 1935.

McDowell, J., *Plato, Theaetetus*, Oxford, 1973.

Taylor, C. C. W., *Plato, Protagoras*, Oxford, 1976.

Gorgias

Dodds, E. R., *Plato's Gorgias*, Oxford, 1959.

Irwin, T., *Plato, Gorgias*, Oxford, 1979.

Predecessors and Origins

Cornford, F. M., *From Religion to Philosophy*, London, 1912.

Cornford, F. M., *Principium Sapientiae: The Origins of Greek Philosophical Thought*, Cambridge, 1952.

Frankfort, H., and others, *Before Philosophy*, Harmondsworth, 1949.
Onians, R. B., *The Origins of European Thought*, 2nd ed., Cambridge, 1954.
Pritchard, J. B., *Ancient Near Eastern Texts Relating to the Old Testament*, 2nd ed., Princeton, 1955.
Vernant, J.-P., *Myth and Thought among the Greeks*, London, 1983.
Vernant, J.-P., *The Origins of Greek Thought*, Ithaca, N.Y., 1982.
Vernant, J.-P., *Myth and Society in Ancient Greece*, trans. by J. Lloyd, Atlantic Heights, N.J., 1980.
West, M. L., *Early Greek Philosophy and the Orient*, Oxford, 1971.

Science and Mathematics

Dicks, D. R., *Early Greek Astronomy to Aristotle*, London, 1970.
Furley, D. J., *The Greek Cosmologists*, vol. 1, Cambridge, 1987.
Heath, T. L., *The Thirteen Books of Euclid's Elements*, 3 vols., 2nd ed., Cambridge, 1926.
Heath, T. L., *A History of Greek Mathematics*, 2 vols., Oxford, 1921.
Heath, T. L., *Aristarchus of Samos, the Ancient Copernicus: A History of Greek Astronomy to Aristarchus, together with Aristarchus' Treatise on the Sizes and Distances of the Sun and Moon*, Oxford, 1913.
Heidel, W. A., *The Heroic Age of Science: The Conception, Ideals and Methods of Science among the Ancient Greeks*, Baltimore, 1933.
Knorr, W. R., *The Evolution of the Euclidean Elements: A Study of the Theory of Incommensurable Magnitudes and its Significance for Early Greek Geometry*, Dordrecht, 1975.
Lloyd, G. E. R., *Early Greek Science: Thales to Aristotle*, London, 1970.
Lloyd, G. E. R., *Magic, Reason and Experience: Studies in the Origin and Development of Greek Science*, Cambridge, 1979.
Lloyd, G. E. R., *The Revolutions of Wisdom*, Berkeley, 1987.
Neugebauer, O., *The Exact Sciences in Antiquity*, 2nd ed., Providence, R. I., 1957.
Sambursky, S., *The Physical World of the Greeks*, London, 1956.
Szabó, A., *The Beginnings of Greek Mathematics*, Dordrecht and Boston, 1978.
Thomas, I., *Greek Mathematical Works*, vol. 1, Loeb Classical Library, Cambridge, Mass. and London, 1951.
vander Waerden, B. L., *Science Awakening*, trans. by A. Dresden, New York, 1961.
Waterfield, R., *Before Eureka: The Presocratics and their Science*, New York, 1989.

Medicine

Heidel, W. A., *Hippocratic Medicine: Its Spirit and Method*, New York, 1941.
Hippocrates, *Selected Works*, 6 vols., Loeb Classical Library, Cambridge, Mass. and London, 1922–1988.
Jones, W. H. S., *Philosophy and Medicine in Ancient Greece*, Baltimore, 1946.
Lloyd, G. E. R., ed., *Hippocratic Writings*, Harmondsworth, 1978.

Source Materials

Aristotle, *The Works of Aristotle Translated into English*, ed. by W. D. Ross, 12 vols., Oxford, 1928–1952.
Aristotle, *The Complete Works of Aristotle: The Revised Oxford Translation*, ed. by J. Barnes, Princeton, 1984.
Cherniss, H. F., *Aristotle's Criticism of Presocratic Philosophy*, Baltimore, 1935.
Hicks, R. D., *Aristotle, De Anima*, Cambridge, 1905.
Mansfeld, J., "Heresiography in Context: Hippolytus' Elenchos as a Source for Greek Philosophy," *Philosophia Antiqua* 56 (Leiden, 1992).
Osborne, C., *Rethinking Early Greek Philosophy*, London, 1987.
Ross, W. D., *Aristotle, Metaphysics*, 2 vols., Oxford, 1936.
Ross, W. D., *Aristotle, Physics*, Oxford, 1924.

Political Theory

Farrar, C., *The Origins of Democratic Thinking: The Invention of Politics in Classical Athens*, Cambridge, 1988.
Ostwald, M., *Nomos and the Beginnings of the Athenian Democracy*, Oxford, 1969.
Sinclair, T. A., *A History of Greek Political Thought*, London, 1951.

Moral Thought

Adkins, A. W. H., *Merit and Responsibility*, Oxford, 1962.
Dover, K. J., *Greek Popular Morality in the Time of Plato and Aristotle*, Oxford, 1974.
Havelock, E., *The Greek Concept of Justice, From Its Shadow in Homer to Its Substance in Plato*, Cambridge, Mass., 1978.
Lloyd-Jones, H., *The Justice of Zeus*, Berkeley, 1971.

Other Topics

Beare, J. I., *Greek Theories of Elementary Cognition*, Oxford, 1906.

Dodds, E. R., *The Greeks and the Irrational*, Berkeley, 1951.

Guthrie, W. K. C., *In the Beginning: Some Greek Views on the Origins of Life and the Early State of Man*, London, 1957.

Jaeger, W. W., *The Theology of the Early Greek Philosophers*, Oxford, 1947.

Kahn, C. H., *The Verb 'Be' in Ancient Greek*, Dordrecht, 1973.

Lloyd, G. E. R., *Demystifying Mentalities*, Cambridge, 1990.

Lloyd, G. E. R., *Polarity and Analogy: Two Types of Argumentation in Early Greek Thought*, Cambridge, 1966.

Snell, B., *The Discovery of Mind: Greek Origins of European Thought*, trans. by T. G. Rosenmeyer, Oxford, 1953.

Solmsen, F., *Intellectual Experiments of the Greek Enlightenment*, Princeton, 1975.

Stokes, M. C., *One and Many in Presocratic Philosophy*, Washington, D.C., 1971.

Stratton, G. M., *Theophrastus and the Greek Physiological Psychology before Aristotle*, London, 1917.

Urmson, J. O., *The Greek Philosophical Vocabulary*, London, 1990.

Bibliography

L'Année Philologique, The Philosopher's Index, Répertoire bibliographique de la Philosophie, and *Bibliographie de la philosophie* are important bibliographical resources for work on early Greek philosophy. Most of the work in this field appears in journal articles, and these publications cover the most important journals in the fields of classics and philosophy. In most cases they provide summaries of articles and information on book reviews as well as bibliographical information.

In addition the following bibliographies cover the period treated in this book.

Bell, G. G., Jr., and Allis, J. B., *Resources in Ancient Philosophy: An Annotated Bibliography of Scholarship in English, 1965–1989*, Metuchen, N.J., 1991.

Classen, C. J., "Bibliographie zur Sophistik," *Elenchos* 6 (1985), 75–140.

Navia, L. E., *Pythagoras: An Annotated Bibliography*, New York, 1990.

Paquet, L., Roussel, M., and Lafrance, Y., *Les Présocratiques: Bibliographie analytique (1879–1980)*, 2 vols., Montreal, 1988–89.

Extensive bibliographies are also contained in: Guthrie, W. K. C., *History of Greek Philosophy* (at the end of each volume); Barnes, J., *The Presocratic Philosophers*; Mourelatos, A. P. D., ed., *The Presocratics*; and Classen, C. J., ed., *Sophistik*, Wege der Forschung 187, Darmstadt, 1976.

Concordance with Diels-Kranz

DK	This Volume	DK	This Volume	DK	This Volume
11A2	4.5	14,8	9.13	22B16	10.112
11A5	4.3	14,8a	9.10	22B17	10.3
11A9	4.1	14,10	9.7	22B18	10.39
11A10	4.2	18,2	9.14	22B19	10.20
11A12	4.6	21A12	7.7	22B20	10.90
11A12	4.8	21A30	7.13	22B21	10.27
11A14	4.7	21A32	7.8	22B22	10.40
11A22	4.9	21A33	7.18	22B23	10.72
12A1	5.1	21A39	7.15	22B24	10.108
12A9	5.3	21B1	7.2	22B25	10.109
12A9	5.19	21B7	9.1	22B26	10.25
12A10	5.3	21B8	7.1	22B27	10.110
12A10	5.6	21B11	7.3	22B28	10.17
12A10	5.11	21B14	7.4	22B29	10.4
12A10	5.17	21B15	7.6	22B30	10.77
12A11	5.3	21B16	7.5	22B31	10.75
12A11	5.8	21B18	7.21	22B32	10.30
12A11	5.12	21B23	7.10	22B33	10.87
12A11	5.14	21B24	7.11	22B34	10.22
12A15	5.5	21B25	7.12	22B35	10.34
12A16	5.4	21B26	7.9	22B36	10.74
12A18	5.10	21B29	7.16	22B37	10.57
12A21	5.9	21B30	7.17	22B39	10.18
12A23	5.15	21B32	7.14	22B40	9.2
12A26	5.13	21B34	7.19	22B41	10.44
12A27	5.7	21B35	7.20	22B42	10.16
12A30	5.16	21B38	7.21	22B43	10.121
12A30	5.18	22A1	10.128	22B44	10.120
12B1	5.19	22A6	10.126	22B45	10.114
13A5	6.1	22A16	10.129	22B46	10.19
13A6	6.7	22B1	10.1	22B47	10.45
13A7	6.2	22B2	10.2	22B48	10.68
13A7	6.9	22B3	10.93	22B49	10.118
13A7	6.10	22B4	10.56	22B49a	10.66
13A7	6.11	22B5	10.97	22B50	10.47
13A10	6.5	22B6	10.92	22B51	10.49
13A14	6.12	22B7	10.37	22B52	10.119
13A17	6.13	22B8	10.52	22B53	10.82
13A20	6.8	22B9	10.55	22B54	10.50
13A21	6.14	22B10	10.48	22B55	10.35
13B1	6.3	22B11	10.15	22B56	10.5
13B2	6.6	22B12	10.64	22B57	10.71
14,1	9.8	22B13	10.54	22B58	10.61
14,1	9.12	22B14	10.99	22B59	10.62
14,2	9.5	22B15	10.98	22B60	10.63

DK	This Volume	DK	This Volume	DK	This Volume
22B61	10.53	22B112	10.46	29B3	12.5
22B62	10.89	22B113	10.31	29B5	12.15
22B63	10.111	22B114	10.51	30A5	15.11
22B64	10.81	22B115	10.115	30B1	15.1
22B65	10.85	22B116	10.32	30B2	15.2
22B66	10.84	22B117	10.106	30B3	15.3
22B67	10.86	22B118	10.105	30B4	15.6
22B67a	10.103	22B119	10.122	30B5	15.7
22B68	10.102	22B120	10.96	30B6	15.8
22B69	10.100	22B121	10.116	30B7	15.9
22B70	10.6	22B123	10.42	30B8	15.10
22B71	10.9	22B124	10.60	30B9	15.5
22B72	10.8	22B125	10.79	30B10	15.4
22B73	10.23	22B125a	10.117	31A30	14.154
22B74	10.7	22B126	10.69	31A30	14.150
22B75	10.26	22B129	9.3	31A42	14.151
22B76	10.76	22B136	10.107	31A42	14.152
22B77	10.104	28A46	11.20	31A43	14.145
22B78	10.28	28B1	11.1	31A43a	14.146
22B79	10.29	28B2	11.2	31A49	14.155
22B80	10.83	28B3	11.3	31A67	14.153
22B82	10.58	28B4	11.4	31A72	14.156
22B83	10.59	28B5	11.5	31A86	14.158
22B84a	10.78	28B6	11.6	31A86	14.159
22B84b	10.41	28B7	11.7	31A87	14.147
22B85	10.125	28B8	11.8	31B1	14.3
22B86	10.10	28B9	11.9	31B2	14.8
22B87	10.11	28B10	11.10	31B3a	14.16
22B88	10.70	28B11	11.11	31B3b	14.17
22B89	10.24	28B12	11.12	31B4	14.4
22B90	10.80	28B13	11.13	31B5	14.5
22B91	10.65	28B14	11.14	31B6	14.20
22B92	10.101	28B15	11.15	31B8	14.43
22B93	10.43	28B16	11.16	31B9	14.44
22B94	10.91	28B17	11.17	31B11	14.40
22B95	10.124	28B19	11.18	31B12	14.41
22B96	10.113	29A2	12.1	31B13	14.45
22B97	10.12	29A11	12.1	31B14	14.46
22B98	10.38	29A16	12.2	31B15	14.42
22B99	10.94	29A24	12.15	31B16	14.23
22B100	10.95	29A25	12.6	31B17	14.19
22B101	10.33	29A25	12.7	31B20	14.24
22B101a	10.36	29A25	12.10	31B21	14.21
22B102	10.88	29A26	12.9	31B22	14.22
22B103	10.67	29A27	12.12	31B23	14.28
22B104	10.13	29A27	12.13	31B24	14.11
22B107	10.21	29A28	12.14	31B25	14.12
22B108	10.14	29A29	12.16	31B26	14.49
22B110	10.123	29B1	12.4	31B27	14.50
22B111	10.73	29B2	12.3	31B27a	14.51

DK	This Volume	DK	This Volume	DK	This Volume
31B28	14.52	31B77	14.99	31B127	14.131
31B29	14.53	31B78	14.100	31B128	14.82
31B30	14.54	31B79	14.101	31B129	9.6
31B31	14.55	31B80	14.102	31B130	14.83
31B32	14.33	31B81	14.104	31B131	14.15
31B33	14.31	31B82	14.94	31B132	14.13
31B34	14.32	31B83	14.98	31B133	14.14
31B35	14.47	31B84	14.109	31B134	14.134
31B36	14.48	31B85	14.39	31B135	14.135
31B37	14.59	31B86	14.89	31B136	14.138
31B38	14.9	31B87	14.90	31B137	14.137
31B39	14.56	31B88	14.110	31B138	14.139
31B40	14.63	31B89	14.108	31B139	14.136
31B41	14.61	31B90	14.106	31B140	14.141
31B42	14.67	31B91	14.34	31B141	14.142
31B43	14.64	31B92	14.36	31B142	14.129
31B44	14.62	31B93	14.35	31B143	14.140
31B45	14.66	31B94	14.74	31B144	14.143
31B46	14.68	31B95	14.111	31B145	14.128
31B47	14.65	31B96	14.37	31B146	14.132
31B48	14.69	31B98	14.38	31B147	14.133
31B49	14.70	31B99	14.113	36B4	9.4
31B50	14.71	31B100	14.105	44A13	9.23
31B51	14.57	31B101	14.112	44A15	9.25
31B52	14.60	31B102	14.114	44A16	9.31
31B53	14.58	31B103	14.117	45,3	9.39
31B54	14.58	31B104	14.75	45,3	9.40
31B55	14.72	31B105	14.115	58B1a	9.24
31B56	14.73	31B106	14.118	58B4	9.19
31B57	14.76	31B107	14.119	58B4	9.32
31B58	14.77	31B108	14.116	58B4	9.36
31B59	14.78	31B109	14.107	58B4	9.43
31B60	14.80	31B110	14.6	58B5	9.20
31B61	14.79	31B111	14.7	58B5	9.35
31B61	14.157	31B112	14.1	58B8	9.21
31B62	14.81	31B113	14.10	58B8	9.38
31B63	14.88	31B114	14.2	58B9	9.45
31B64	14.84	31B115	14.18	58B10	9.46
31B65	14.86	31B115	14.161	58B22	9.29
31B66	14.85	31B116	14.25	58B26	9.26
31B67	14.87	31B117	14.130	58B27	9.44
31B68	14.93	31B118	14.123	58B28	9.22
31B69	14.92	31B119	14.120	58B30	9.27
31B70	14.91	31B120	14.122	58B30	9.28
31B71	14.27	31B121	14.124	58B35	9.34
31B72	14.95	31B122	14.125	58B36	9.30
31B73	14.29	31B123	14.126	58B40	9.11
31B74	14.96	31B124	14.121	58C3	9.16
31B75	14.30	31B125	14.26	58C4	9.14
31B76	14.97	31B126	14.127	58C4	9.15

DK	This Volume	DK	This Volume	DK	This Volume
58C6	9.17	64B7	17.6	68A104	16.46
59A12	13.31	64B8	17.7	68A112	16.54
59A16	13.24	67A1	16.39	68A112	16.55
59A42	13.32	67A1	16.42	68A129	16.36
59A43	13.25	67A6	16.1	68A135	16.37
59A45	13.27	67A6	16.17	68A135	16.47
59A47	13.28	67A6	16.23	68B6	16.51
59A47	13.30	67A7	16.5	68B7	16.53
59A58	13.29	67A7	16.13	68B8	16.52
59A88	14.144	67A8	16.4	68B9	16.48
59A88	14.149	67A13	16.11	68B9	16.50
59B1	13.1	67A14	16.10	68B11	16.49
59B2	13.2	67A14	16.33	68B33	16.63
59B3	13.3	67A14	16.35	68B69	16.61
59B4	13.4	67A15	16.9	68B74	16.60
59B5	13.5	67A16	16.16	68B125	16.56
59B6	13.6	67A16	16.20	68B155	16.66
59B7	13.7	67A18	16.18	68B156	16.14
59B8	13.8	67A19	16.6	68B164	16.40
59B9	13.9	67A19	16.15	68B166	16.57
59B10	13.10	67A97	16.2	68B189	16.64
59B10	13.26	67B2	16.29	68B191	16.58
59B11	13.11	68A1	16.59	68B214	16.62
59B12	13.12	68A37	16.3	68B235	16.65
59B13	13.13	68A38	16.4	80A1	18.15
59B14	13.14	68A38	16.38	80A21	18.16
59B15	13.15	68A40	16.41	80A21	18.17
59B16	13.16	68A40	16.43	80A21a	18.21
59B17	13.17	68A47	16.8	80B1	18.20
59B18	13.18	68A47	16.21	80B3	18.10
59B19	13.19	68A47	16.22	80B3	18.11
59B21	13.20	68A47	16.25	80B4	18.7
59B21	13.33	68A48b	16.12	80B10	18.12
59B21a	13.21	68A57	16.34	80B11	18.13
59B21b	13.22	68A58	16.19	82B3	18.22
59B22	13.23	68A58	16.24	82B3	18.23
64A1	17.8	68A59	16.7	82B3	18.24
64A6	17.9	68A60	16.27	82B11	18.19
64A19	17.10	68A60	16.28	87A4	19.2
64A19	17.11	68A61	16.26	87A4	19.3
64B1	17.1	68A66	16.30	88B25	19.12
64B2	17.2	68A66	16.31	89,6	19.13
64B3	17.3	68A68	16.32	89,6	19.14
64B4	17.4	68A93	16.45	89,7	19.15
64B5	17.5	68A96	16.44	90,4	18.18

Index of Passages Translated

Index